Latin American and La

MW00815286

Latin American and Latinx Philosophy: A Collaborative Introduction is a beginner's guide to canonical texts in Latin American and Latinx philosophy, providing the non-specialist with necessary historical and philosophical context, and demonstrating their contemporary relevance. It is written in jargon-free prose for students and professors who are interested in the subject, but who don't know where to begin. Each of the twelve chapters, written by a leading scholar in the field, examines influential texts that are readily available in English and introduces the reader to a period, topic, movement, or school that taken together provide a broad overview of the history, nature, scope, and value of Latin American and Latinx philosophy. Although this volume is primarily intended for the reader without a background in the Latin American and Latinx tradition, specialists will also benefit from its many novelties, including an introduction to Aztec ethics; a critique of "the Latino threat" narrative; the legacy of Latin American philosophy in the Chicano movement; an overview of Mexican existentialism, Liberation philosophy, and Latin American and Latinx feminisms; a philosophical critique of indigenism; a study of Latinx contributions to the philosophy of immigration; and an examination of the intersection of race and gender in Latinx identity.

Robert Eli Sanchez, Jr. is Assistant Professor of Philosophy at Mount Saint Mary's University, Los Angeles. He specializes in Mexican/Latin American/Latinx philosophy and is co-editor of *Mexican Philosophy in the 20th Century: Essential Readings* (Oxford University Press, 2017).

"A great new resource for present and future teachers and students about an exciting and important emerging field in philosophy."

— *Gregory Fernando Pappas, Editor-in-Chief of the* Inter-American Journal of Philosophy (IJP), *Texas A&M University, USA*

"*Latin American and Latinx Philosophy* fills a huge hole in our existing English language resources. The detail of the essays, the expansive coverage of topics, the superb philosophical analysis and the excellent introductory overviews will make this volume vital for everyone with an interest in this area. Bravo!"

— *Linda Martín Alcoff, Hunter College, USA*

"This is an appealing place for the interested reader to get started with some of the rich and fascinating episodes in the history of philosophy in Latin America, as well as some of the exciting recent work on Latinx philosophy in the U.S. The contributions map out an impressive cross-section of philosophical questions, historical periods, geographical regions, and methodological approaches. Throughout, the volume engages in an insightful discussion of the role of history, politics, and identity in the formation of philosophical traditions. It also advances the metaphilosophical debate concerning the self-conception of this emerging field."

— *Clinton Tolley and Manuel Vargas, The Mexican Philosophy Lab at UC San Diego, USA*

Latin American and Latinx Philosophy

A Collaborative Introduction

Edited by
Robert Eli Sanchez, Jr.

Routledge
Taylor & Francis Group

NEW YORK AND LONDON

First published 2020
by Routledge
52 Vanderbilt Avenue, New York, NY 10017

and by Routledge
2 Park Square, Milton Park, Abingdon, Oxon OX14 4RN

Routledge is an imprint of the Taylor & Francis Group, an informa business

Library of Congress Cataloging-in-Publication Data
Names: Sanchez, Robert Eli, Jr., editor.
Title: Latin American and Latinx philosophy : a collaborative
introduction / edited by Robert Eli Sanchez, Jr.
Description: 1 [edition]. | New York : Taylor & Francis, 2019. |
Includes bibliographical references and index.
Identifiers: LCCN 2019017918 | ISBN 9781138295858 (hardback)
Subjects: LCSH: Philosophy, Latin American.
Classification: LCC B1003 .L38 2019 | DDC 199/.8--dc23
LC record available at https://lccn.loc.gov/2019017918

ISBN: 978-1-138-29585-8 (hbk)
ISBN: 978-1-138-29586-5 (pbk)
ISBN: 978-1-315-10040-1 (ebk)

Typeset in Sabon
by Taylor & Francis Books

For Sofía Belén and Angela

Contents

Contributors

Alejandro Santana is Associate Professor of Philosophy and E. John Rumpakis Professor of Hellenic Studies at the University of Portland. His research interests include Ancient Greek philosophy, Indigenous Mesoamerican philosophy, and Latin American socio-political issues related to colonialism and imperialism. His publications appear in *Ancient Philosophy, Philosophical Inquiry*, the *Inter-American Journal of Philosophy*, and the *American Philosophical Association Newsletter on Hispanic/Latino Issues in Philosophy*.

Alexander V. Stehn is Associate Professor of Philosophy, Associate Director of the Center for Bilingual Studies, and Faculty Affiliate in Mexican American Studies at the University of Texas Rio Grande Valley. He specializes in U.S.-American and Latin American philosophies, but he is more proud of being an unrepentant generalist and recipient of the University of Texas Regents' Outstanding Teaching Award. His publications include the entry "Latin American Philosophy" in *The Internet Encyclopedia of Philosophy*.

Andrea Pitts is Assistant Professor of Philosophy at the University of North Carolina, Charlotte. Their research interests include Latin American and U.S. Latinx philosophy, critical philosophy of race, feminist theory, and critical prison studies. Their publications appear in *IJFAB: International Journal of Feminist Approaches to Bioethics, Hypatia, Radical Philosophy Review*, and *Inter-American Journal of Philosophy*. Andrea is also co-editor of *Beyond Bergson: Examining Race and Colonialism through the Writings of Henri Bergson* (SUNY Press, 2019).

Carlos Alberto Sánchez is Professor of Philosophy at San José State University. He is the author of *The Suspension of Seriousness: On the Phenomenology of Jorge Portilla* (SUNY Press, 2012) and *Contingency and Commitment: Mexican Existentialism and the Place of Philosophy* (SUNY Press, 2015). He is also the Editor of the American Philosophical Association's *Newsletter on Hispanic/Latino Issues in Philosophy*.

Francisco Gallegos is Assistant Professor of Philosophy at Wake Forest University. His research focuses on phenomenology, Latin American and Latinx philosophy, and the philosophy of emotions. With Carlos Sánchez, he is co-author of *The Disintegration of Community: On Jorge Portilla's Social and Political Philosophy* (SUNY Press, 2020).

Grant J. Silva is Associate Professor of Philosophy at Marquette University. His research takes place at the intersection of Latin American philosophy, social and political philosophy, and the philosophy of race/racism. His publications appear in the *Southern Journal of Philosophy, Radical Philosophy Review, Public Affairs Quarterly, The Pluralist, Expositions: Interdisciplinary Studies in the Humanities*, and *The APA Newsletter on Hispanic/Latino Issues in Philosophy*. He is currently preparing a manuscript titled *Racism as Self-Love*.

James Maffie teaches in the American Studies Department, University of Maryland, College Park. He is the author of *Aztec Philosophy: Understanding a World in Motion* (University Press of Colorado, 2014) and is currently working on a second book devoted to Aztec ethics entitled *Aztec Ethics: Balancing a World in Motion*.

Jose-Antonio Orosco is Professor of Philosophy at Oregon State University in Corvallis, Oregon. His area of specialization is social and political philosophy, focusing on theories of democracy, race, and social movements. He regularly teaches on themes within North/Latin American, Latinx, and Chicanx thought. He is one of the founding members of the Society for Mexican American Philosophy and serves on the editorial board of the *Inter American Journal of Philosophy, Transactions of the Charles Pierce Society*, and is associate editor for *Acorn: Philosophical Studies in Pacifism and Nonviolence*. His books include *Cesar Chavez and the Common Sense of Nonviolence* (University of Mexico Press, 2008) and *Toppling the Melting Pot: Immigration and Multiculturalism in American Pragmatism* (Indiana University Press, 2018).

José Jorge Mendoza is Assistant Professor of Philosophy at the University of Massachusetts, Lowell, and co-editor of *Radical Philosophy Review*. His primary areas of research are in moral and political philosophy, philosophy of race, and Latin American philosophy. His publications appear in the *Journal of Speculative Philosophy, Public Affairs Quarterly, Critical Philosophy of Race*, and *Philosophy in the Contemporary World*. He is also the author of *The Moral and Political Philosophy of Immigration: Liberty, Security, and Equality* (Lexington Press, 2017).

Kim Díaz is a philosophy instructor at El Paso Community College. She also works for the United States Department of Justice (U.S. Probation) teaching philosophy and mindfulness in two Federal re-entry and diversion programs where she has the honor of working with returning citizens. She is a founding member of the Society for Mexican-American Philosophy, the managing editor of the *Inter-American Journal of Philosophy* and, together with Mat Foust, she is the co-editor of *Philosophy of the Americas Reader* (Bloomsbury, forthcoming).

Lori Gallegos de Castillo is Assistant Professor of Philosophy at Texas State University. Her research interests include moral psychology, Latin American and U.S. Latinx philosophy, and critical philosophy of race. Her publications appear in *Inter-American Journal of Philosophy, Critical Philosophy of Race, Journal of Speculative Philosophy*, and *Topoi: An International Journal on Philosophy*. She is currently co-editor of the *APA Newsletter on Hispanic/Latino Issues in Philosophy*.

Stephanie Rivera Berruz, Dr., is Assistant Professor at Marquette University. She is the recipient of the Woodrow Wilson Career Enhancement Fellowship (2017–2018) for her work on Latinx feminisms and Latin American philosophy. Her main research interests lie in Latin American philosophy and Latina feminism as well philosophy of race, gender, and sexuality. She approaches these topics at their intersections as she is committed to the importance of diverse approaches to philosophical praxis. She recently published a co-edited anthology: *Comparative Studies in Asian and Latin American Philosophies* (Bloomsbury, 2018), and her work has been published in *The Stanford Encyclopedia of Philosophy* (2018), *Essays on Philosophy* (2018), *Hypatia* (2016), and *Inter-American Journal of Philosophy* (2014).

Acknowledgments

When I originally envisioned an introductory textbook on Latin American and Latinx philosophy, I knew I couldn't write it on my own. There is simply too much ground to cover and I don't have the expertise to do each one of the topics justice. Equally important, I knew that, whatever the final product, we would inevitably be taking a stance on the definition and value of Latin American and Latinx philosophy, something I believed we ought to do collaboratively as a community of teachers and scholars who have committed their careers to the field. However, producing a multi-authored volume that develops themes across chapters and is uniform in language and style (as opposed to an edited collection) is demanding. Each chapter underwent multiple drafts, some major and painstaking, and to make sure that we covered our bases and produced our best work, the contributors were willing to work in small groups based on overlapping themes, periods, or topics. So, first I'd like to thank the contributors for having patience with me and with the process and for allowing me to apply a heavy editorial hand. I wrote the introduction to this text in the first-person plural because this is *our* contribution in every sense of the word.

I also want to thank Neal Tognazzini, whom I considered my ideal reader. Neal is an analytic philosopher without a background in the area, but who is genuinely interested in learning about and teaching from different philosophical traditions, even if—I like to think especially if—they challenge him to think differently about his own tradition. The idea for this volume emerged from a conversation I had with Neal when he invited me to Western Washington University to introduce the philosophy department to Latin American philosophy, and it evolved as a result of our ongoing conversation. I also want to thank Neal for reading drafts of the introduction to this volume.

Finally, I would like to thank our editor at Routledge, Andrew Beck, for finding value in this project and in diversifying the canon more generally. Andrew has been thoughtful, patient, and encouraging from the beginning, and is the kind of editor needed as academic philosophy matures.

Introduction

Robert Eli Sanchez, Jr.

This volume is meant to serve as a beginner's guide to canonical texts in Latin American and Latinx philosophy, providing the non-specialist with necessary historical and philosophical context. As much as possible, it is written in jargon-free prose for students and professors who are interested in the subject, but who don't know where to begin.

The volume originated as a response to our colleagues, especially those at Hispanic Serving Institutions (HSIs), who tell us that they would like to teach (or have been asked to teach) Latin American philosophy, but who worry that they don't have the skills or expertise to do the class justice. In particular:

- They don't read Spanish.
- They are not well versed in the history of Latin American thought and culture.
- They might inadvertently construct a haphazard or uninteresting narrative of Latin American and Latinx philosophy.
- They are not specialists in comparative philosophy or the history of philosophy.
- They do not identify as Latinx and would feel like they are presuming an authority they do not have or that can only come from life experiences other than their own.

This volume, then, is primarily a response to these concerns. Each chapter introduces the reader to a handful of influential texts that are available in English,[1] and situates them in their historical context as well as contemporary philosophical discussions. Collectively, they provide a broad introduction to Latin American and Latinx philosophy, though the definition of both remains a matter of dispute.[2]

To be clear: this is not a comprehensive survey of Latin American and Latinx philosophy. Especially combined, there is simply too much to cover. What we have tried to capture here is *a* version of Latin American philosophy, as it has been defined through the development of Latinx philosophy in the United States. For many Latinx philosophers, "Latin American philosophy" is not synonymous with "the philosophy produced in Latin America." "Latin American," in other words, is not only a geographic qualifier used by historians of philosophy to classify authors and texts to distinguish them, say, from the philosophy produced in the United States or in Germany. Instead, it represents a distinctive and unified philosophical tradition that, along with the growing popularity of other non-European philosophical traditions (e.g., Africana, Jewish, Indian, Chinese, and Native American), represents an alternative to what is typically referred to, albeit vaguely and unhelpfully, as "Western philosophy" or just "philosophy."[3]

Rather than try to articulate the essence of the Latin American and Latinx philosophical tradition—as if that could be done with anything as large and unwieldy as a "tradition"—we will simply describe a number of unifying themes that drive the chapters to follow.

Four Defining Themes

One unifying theme is what Miranda Fricker calls *epistemic injustice* or a disregard of ways of knowing and intellectual contributions that don't fit the paradigm of a dominant group.[4] In chapter 2 of this volume, Alejandro Santana examines in close detail how European settlers tried to justify exterminating, subjugating, and enslaving American Indians ("Amerindians," as he refers to them) by demonstrating that they were "natural slaves," according to Aristotle's *Politics*.[5] In short, they argued that the Amerindians were not fully human *because they were not fully rational*. Although this "justification" may strike the reader today as patently false and offensive, chapters 1, 8, and 9 claim or suggest that both women and Native Americans continue to be systematically excluded from histories of philosophy because, however rich and wonderful their intellectual achievements might be, historians view them as falling short of the norms and standards of philosophical engagement. Further, as chapter 12 points out, colonial European views about rationality, philosophy, and humanity arguably explain why Latin American philosophy remains relatively invisible in academic philosophy today.[6]

Another theme that characterizes the majority of chapters is an emphasis on the importance of lived experience, historical location, one's political and social reality, privilege or lack thereof, and the relevance of these to philosophical truth, a view we might broadly refer to as *historicism* (for an elaboration of this term, see below and chapters 5 and 12). Whether discussing the need to tailor political ideals to local circumstances (chapter 3), the influence of historicism in Latin America (chapter 5), Mexican existentialism (chapter 6), Latin American and Latinx feminisms (chapter 8), the role of personal experience in the ethics of immigration (chapter 10), Latinx identity (chapter 11), or the identity of Latin American philosophy (chapter 12), there is a profound sense throughout that a defining feature of Latin American and Latinx philosophy is the general view that the standards for truth and justification are situated in history, are context-dependent, and represent distinguishing features of one's social and cultural identity.

To claim that philosophy is grounded in or represents one's historical location is not necessarily to deny the existence of universal truth. Historicism is not the same as relativism. Instead, the historicist need only insist on a few claims. The first claim, to paraphrase the Spanish historicist José Ortega y Gasset, is that in addition to being *true*, a view, belief, or system must also *be understood*, and understanding is always historically situated. On Ortega's account, Newton would not have understood the general theory of relativity, even if it were true and even if God had dropped it on his desk at the end of the 17th century.[7] The second claim is that philosophy need not be concerned only with abstract and universal objects. On the contrary, "For the person for whom small things do not exist, the great is not great."[8] The third claim, related to the theme of epistemic injustice, is that efforts to de-historicize philosophy are self-forgetful, as when the painter believes she depicts the world *as it is*, uninfluenced by her own perspective and technique, or they are chauvinistic, as when one discounts the contributions of non-European philosophers on account that they do not neatly fit into a familiar standard or model of philosophy.

A third way of characterizing Latin American and Latinx philosophy is to point out that they are especially practical and engaged. This characterization is not new. In an early effort to introduce Latin American philosophy to an English-speaking audience (1953), A. MacC Armstrong wrote:

> [Latin American] philosophy is an outdoor one, unlike European philosophy in its prevailing tendency from Descartes to Kant and the post-Kantian schools who have learnt little or nothing from Hegel. The European sage stays indoors alone in his study, meditating on the reality of himself, his chair, and his fire. ... The Latin-American, on the other hand, finds himself out in the streets, among men who meet to deal with each other and make holiday. The idea of a society without a common good strikes him as ridiculous, and he considers moral action from the angles of education, law and criminology. His favorite instances of language are idiomatic conversations, even thieves' argot, and recognizes straight away that his mental armory is not all his own work and that far from being common to every rational being it is a historical development.[9]

Put differently, the term "applied philosophy" doesn't refer to a branch of philosophy alongside metaphysics, epistemology, or the philosophy of language. Instead, it is a way of defining Latin American and Latinx philosophy.

Again, the chapters here bear this characterization out. There is a sense in which every chapter is either about an applied issue or about the way in which philosophy is applied. There is also a sense in which the volume as a whole might be considered an instance of what we might call "applied metaphilosophy."[10] Here a few specific examples to give the reader a sense of what we mean.

- In chapter 4, Alexander Stehn argues that "a central aim of Mexican philosophy was to build the Mexican nation or recreate the Mexican people by means of education." So understood, the story of Mexican philosophy continues to play out in Chicano Studies in the effort to reshape Chicanx identity.
- In chapter 6, Carlos Alberto Sánchez concludes that in Mexico "existentialism was a move toward an engaged existence, not toward a radical isolation in the loneliness of existence *à la* Camus." For the Mexican, philosophy is not only situated in "a determinate geographic *habitat*," but is also "transformative," "committed," and task-oriented.
- In chapter 9, Kim Díaz revisits "the Indian problem" introduced in chapter 2 and suggests that the effort to celebrate, defend, and advocate for indigenous peoples and cultures in Latin America (i.e., Indigenism) is misguided because it misdiagnoses the problem. The so-called Indian problem is not one of class, education, or individual freedom, but one of race and racism, and it persists because Indigenism is a movement by white people for white people. Rather than be asked or forced to assimilate, the Indian should be free to speak for herself and the non-Indian ought not pretend to know what's best for the other.
- In chapter 10, José Jorge Mendoza suggests that the ethics of immigration is a defining issue for Latinx philosophy, even though the contributions of Latinx philosophers are widely underappreciated by Anglo-American philosophers. As a corrective, Mendoza introduces the reader to the "open-border debate" and demonstrates how it might be enriched and critiqued by considering the contributions of Latinx philosophers, especially those who are personally affected by immigration policy.

Finally, one of the central themes that stands out is a preoccupation with *metaphilosophical* questions concerning the possibility, existence, identity, originality, authenticity, and value of Latin American and Latinx philosophy. This is the explicit theme of our closing chapter, as well as of chapter 5, but it crops up throughout the chapters. Here are two examples.

- In chapter 1, James Maffie argues that Aztec philosophy is fundamentally different from European philosophy. Whereas the former is path-oriented, concerned primarily with right practice or orthopraxy, European philosophy is oriented toward truth and concerned with right belief or orthodoxy. Here, then, the reader is confronted with the possibility of radical differences within "world philosophy."
- In chapter 8, Stephanie Rivera Berruz argues that Latin American and Latinx feminist ideas are worthy of close attention, but are excluded

from histories of philosophy because they fall outside a traditional conception of philosophy. What is needed, then, on her account, is a broader, more inclusive conception of philosophy.

In some cases, though a chapter may not address metaphilosophical issues directly, it may elaborate on a metaphilosophical view articulated in a different chapter. For example, in chapter 12, Lori Gallegos de Castillo and Francisco Gallegos distinguish between "the skeptics" and "the defenders" of Latin American philosophy, that is, between those who doubt and those who defend the claim that there is something unifying and distinctive about Latin American philosophy. According to one well-known defender, Ofelia Schutte, Latin American philosophy is characterized by a concern for freedom from oppression, particularly from colonial and post-colonial domination.[11] To help understand what Schutte means, or decide whether she's right, the reader will benefit from the various discussions of colonialism and liberation throughout the text. Here again are just two examples.

- In chapter 3, Jose-Antonio Orosco compares founding documents of U.S. and Latin American democracies to critique "the Latinx Threat Narrative" which "maintains that Latinx immigrants are harmful because they bring with them ideals and practices ... that could undermine the foundations of U.S. American democracies." For Orosco, this attitude toward Latinx immigrants simply ignores the fact that Latin American liberation movements were driven by the same "hemispheric-wide wave of liberal democratic fervor" that drove the U.S. Revolution of 1776.
- In chapter 7, Grant Silva examines the work of three philosophers of liberation and decolonial philosophy in order to explain what it means to do philosophy *for the sake of freedom* (as opposed to *from a position of freedom*, as is enjoyed by European and Anglo-American philosophers). Silva's chapter also serves as an indirect defense of the claim that seeking freedom from oppression is a defining feature of Latin American philosophy and part of the effort to bring about epistemic justice in light of the oppressive dimensions of colonialism.[12]

Perhaps the theme that unifies or best characterizes the foregoing themes is *identity*. As Andrea Pitts says in chapter 11, "Latinx identities are neither stable nor uncontested sites of philosophical investigation. Because they strike at the core of our lived experiences, often serving as the places from which we speak, think, write, and act, identities are a crucial site of Latinx and Latin American philosophy." Once again, this characterization is not new. In "Identity: A Latin American Philosophical Problem," the Mexican philosopher Leopoldo Zea argues that philosophy always represents and responds to one's social identity, projects, and historical circumstance—who one is, broadly construed—even when it pretends not to. He argues further that to philosophize about one's local reality, or to conceive of philosophy as a form of committing oneself, or to philosophize about one's social identity and the identity of one's philosophy, does not delegitimize an author, text, or tradition as somehow less-than-philosophical. Instead, the concern with identity that Zea believes characterizes Latin American philosophy recommends that we be transparent about the nature and value of philosophy, and he believes that it recommends a new philosophy of history and model of philosophical universality, one that has the potential to cultivate a "horizontal relation of solidarity of peers among peers and not the vertical one of dependency which had originated the unique problem of philosophy in Latin America."[13]

Note to Instructors

This volume was designed for the student and professor without any background in Latin American or Latinx philosophy. Because it includes substantive excerpts of canonical texts, it might serve as the sole textbook for an introductory course on Latin American and/or Latinx philosophy. Given that the first seven chapters proceed more or less chronologically, student and professor can work through the text from beginning to end. If the text is adopted for this purpose, we recommend reading it alongside John Charles Chasteen's *Born in Blood and Fire: A Concise History of Latin America* and/or Eduardo Galeano's *Open Veins of Latin America: Five Centuries of the Pillage of a Continent*. The professor might have her students work through both since, while *Born in Blood and Fire* is concise and reader-friendly, *Open Veins of Latin America* represents the decolonial critiques mentioned above, as the full title suggests. Both will help to enrich the historical context underwriting the philosophy presented here.

However, like Julio Cortázar's novel *Hopscotch*, this volume might be read in multiple directions, depending on one's purpose.

- In an advanced or graduate course on Latin American philosophy, the instructor might mine the text for discussions of certain themes, such as the influence of historicism and existentialism in Latin America, or variations on the theme of epistemic injustice, decolonial thought, or "the Indian problem." There are also many novelties throughout the text, such as Maffie's emphasis on Aztec *ethics*,[14] Stehn's critique of the term "*anti*-positivism," Orosco's and Mendoza's examination of Chicanx philosophers, and Díaz's moving the discussion beyond indigenism in Mexico.
- In a mid-level course, one might use this text as a kind of syllabus and teach it alongside one or more of the anthologies available in order to dive deeper into the texts excerpted here.[15]
- One might adopt this text in a standard introduction to philosophy. Here are two suggestions for how to do so.

a   If one is teaching an introduction to the history of Western philosophy, one might include this volume as an alternative narrative
and explore the differences between Western and "non-Western"
philosophy, as well as the legacy of Western philosophy outside of
Europe. One might also contrast, for example, Mexican and European existentialism, or French and Latin American positivism.

b   If the course is thematic in nature, one can include topics that are
especially relevant to Latinx students, such as immigration (chapter
10), liberation (chapter 7), or racial and ethnic identity (chapters 2
and 12). Or one can discuss an alternative view of ethics (chapter
1), the application of Aristotle's theory of natural slavery (chapter
2), metaphilosophy (chapters 5 and 12), "the problem of truth"
(chapter 5), or indigenous rights (chapters 1, 2, and 9).

• If one would like to teach a course specifically on Mexican or Mexican-
American philosophy, one might use the first six chapters to provide
historical context for, and an analysis of, many of the texts that are
found in Sánchez and Sanchez's *Mexican Philosophy in the 20th Century: Essential Readings*.

a   Relatedly, one might use this text in a course in Latin American
Studies, Chicanx Studies, Mexican Studies, or Ethnic Studies, as it
provides a *philosophical* introduction to canonical texts, such as
José Vasconcelos's *The Cosmic Race*, Samuel Ramos's *The Profile
of Man and Culture in Mexico*, and José Carlos Mariátegui's *Seven
Interpretive Essays on Peruvian Reality*.

These, of course, are only a few suggestions to inspire creative ways of
crafting one's syllabus or dreaming up new courses. Part of our goal is to provide a resource that enables the instructor to think outside the curricular box.[16]

"Latinx"

The title of this volume is perhaps a bit misleading, since it is not an introduction to Latin American philosophy and, separately, Latinx philosophy.
Instead, the conjunction ("and") is meant to suggest that our introduction
occupies a transitional space in which Latin American and Latinx philosophy,
both emerging fields in their own right, are considered together. However one
ends up defining either Latin American or Latinx philosophy, we can agree
that they are both related and distinct, and that it is now difficult to draw a
non-arbitrary line between them. Since we have focused here on a version of
the history of Latin American philosophy that has been appropriated by
Latinx philosophers who find in it valuable resources to make sense of their
own experiences as a political and academic minority in the U.S., as immigrants, and as racially and ethnically hybrid, we might regard this volume as
an introduction only to Latinx philosophy or as a Latinx introduction to

Latin American philosophy. Perhaps, since it represents a way of defining Latin American philosophy that has been appropriated by Latinx philosophers (i.e., something distinct from the philosophy produced in Latin America), it ought to be regarded as an introduction to Latin American philosophy. Or perhaps, at least for now, it is best not to draw too fine a line between the two. Only time will tell.

In the same spirit, we decided to adopt the term "Latinx" (as opposed to "Latino/a" or "Latino"), even though none of the contributors is fully satisfied with the term. Some of us are worried that it will prove to be a fad; others, that it is an Anglicization of the Spanish language imposed on Spanish-speakers, largely by academics. Others still are bothered by its inelegance and awkward pronunciation, especially in its plural form.[17] In the end, however, we came to the consensus that despite our reservations, and until something better comes along, "Latinx" best represents our desire to raise awareness about hierarchies and other forms of exclusion that are concealed by language, often in the name of tradition. In the contest between linguistic conservatism and being more inclusive, we chose the latter. (For a fuller discussion of this debate, see the end of chapter 11.)

We also hope that this volume helps to diminish the reservations of instructors who don't identify as Latinx. To be sure, there is always a real danger of misappropriation, especially if one decides to teach or specialize in non-European philosophy for the sake of ambition or professional success. However, there is no danger in coming off as an imposter if one is genuinely committed to developing an expertise in the area *and* is honest about their motivation, their privilege, and the fact that they do not speak from a position of authority on lived experiences they don't share. This is one of the great lessons of Latinx feminism and critiques of indigenism, and it is worth remembering that the same lesson weighs down on those of us who identify as Latinx but who are ever aware of our own lack of authority on much of the philosophy we teach, especially the contributions of women and native peoples. As with the use of "Latinx," however, there is too much at stake not to work through our hesitation.

Notes

1 There are a few exceptions to our English-only rule. For example, chapters 4, 5, and 9 include some original translations. We have allowed ourselves to include them, however, since we expect that the full translations will be available in the near future.

2 For a clear discussion of different ways of defining Latinx philosophy and its relation to Latin American philosophy, see Vargas's entry on Latinx philosophy in the *Stanford Encyclopedia of Philosophy*.

3 We don't mean to suggest that the question concerning the possibility and existence of Latin American philosophy as a *distinctive* and *unified* tradition originated in the United States. As several chapters demonstrate here, it is a question that exercised Latin American philosophers throughout the 19th and 20th centuries. Instead, we only want to acknowledge that our selection of themes and

texts, to whatever extent they define Latin American philosophy as a challenge to Western philosophy, is *highly* selective and represents an effort to introduce and promote Latin American philosophy in the English-speaking world, an effort largely undertaken by Latinx philosophers. In this regard, the following texts have been particularly influential: Schutte, *Cultural Identity and Social Liberation in Latin American Thought*; Frondizi, "Is There an Ibero-American Philosophy?"; Nuccetelli, "Is 'Latin American Thought' Philosophy?"; León-Portilla, *Aztec Thought and Culture,* especially chapter 1; Hurtado, "Two Models of Latin American Philosophy."

4 Fricker, *Epistemic Injustice.*

5 Throughout the text, we use the term "American" to refer to anyone from the Americas—South, Central, and North—in the same way Spanish-speakers use the term *americano.* To use the term to describe someone from the United States, we believe, is the result of a kind of provincialism, as Edgar Sheffield Brightman points out: "Provincialism! How difficult it is for us North Americans to eradicate it from our own attitudes. Our country is 'God's country.' We arrogate to ourselves the very name of 'American,' which by right belongs to every citizen of North, Central, and South America. We call our country '*The* United States,' in sublime disregard of the Mexican United States as well as the United States of Venezuela. Americans of the United States of America should be reminded that we are not the only Americans, and that our country is not the only United States. Nor is our culture the only American culture." In Romanell, *Making of the Mexican Mind,* 5.

6 For an overview of the so-called invisibility problem, see Pereda, "Latin American Philosophy"; Monahan, "On the Question of Latin American Philosophy"; Ruíz-Aho, "Latin American Philosophy at a Crossroads."

7 Ortega, *The Modern Theme,* 11.

8 Ortega, *Meditations on Quixote,* 45.

9 Armstrong, "Contemporary Latin-American Philosophy." Similar portraits can be found in Berndston, "Teaching Latin-American Philosophy"; Cannabrava, "Present Tendencies in Latin American Philosophy"; Munk, "The Spirit of Latin American Philosophy"; and Hurtado, "Two Models of Latin American Philosophy."

10 The phrase "applied metaphilosophy" refers to various discussions that consider the ethical, political, and existential consequences of defining philosophy. Someone might reject the notion from the outset, arguing that while the history of ideas, the history of philosophy, or the sociology of knowledge consider how definitions of philosophy have harmed some and benefited others, this is not strictly speaking a philosophical or metaphilosophical issue. For more on this topic, see Sanchez, "The Process of Defining Latino/a Philosophy" and "Strengthening the Case for Latin American Philosophy"; Gallegos de Castillo, "Skillful Coping and the Routine of Surviving"; and Mendieta, "Latin American Philosophy as Metaphilosophy."

11 Schutte, "Toward an Understanding of Latin American Philosophy."

12 See also Silva, "Struggle against Coloniality."

13 Zea, "Identity," 379.

14 In *Aztec Philosophy,* Maffie focuses on Aztec metaphysics and only offers a brief sketch at the very end of what Aztec ethics might look like. His chapter included here, then, is an extension of his previous book and provides a richer account of the normative and existential dimensions of Aztec metaphysics.

15 See Gracia and Millán-Zaibert, *Latin American Philosophy for the 21st Century*; Mendieta, *Latin American Philosophy*; Nuccetelli and Seay, *Latin American Philosophy.*

16 For other suggestions on how to incorporate the themes and texts discussed in this volume, see the *APA Newsletter on Hispanic/Latino Issues in Philosophy,*

particularly Volume 7, No. 1 (Fall 2007). In general, the *APA Newsletter* remains the best single source for the development of Latin American and Latinx philosophy in the US.

17 Though awkward pronunciation is sometimes cited as a reason not to adopt the term, we don't think that it needs to be that difficult. "Latinx" is pronounced LAH-tin-eks, and while the plural is sometimes spelled "Latinxs," suggesting a different, clumsier pronunciation ("LAH-tin-exes"), we recommend spelling and pronouncing the plural the same as the singular, not unlike how we have begun to employ the singular "they/them/themselves."

Bibliography

Armstrong, A. MacC. "Contemporary Latin-American Philosophy." *The Philosophical Quarterly* 3, no. 11 (Apr., 1953): 167–174.

Berndston, Arthur. "Teaching Latin-American Philosophy." *The Americas* 9, no. 3 (Jan., 1953): 263–271.

Cannabrava, Euyalo. "Present Tendencies in Latin American Philosophy." *The Journal of Philosophy* 46, no. 5 (Mar. 3, 1949): 113–119.

Cerutti-Guldberg, Horacio. "Actual Situation and Perspectives of Latin American Philosophy for Liberation." *Philosophical Forum* 20, no. 1 (1988): 43–61.

Chasteen, John Charles. *Born in Blood & Fire: A Concise History of Latin America.* 4th edn. New York: W. W. Norton & Company, 2016.

Cortázar, Julio. *Hopscotch.* New York: Random House, 1966.

Frondizi, Risieri. "Is There an Ibero-American Philosophy?" *Philosophy and Phenomenological Research* 9, no. 3 (1949): 345–355.

Fricker, Miranda. *Epistemic Injustice: Power and the Ethics of Knowing.* New York: Oxford University Press, 2009.

Galeano, Eduardo. *Open Veins of Latin America: Five Centuries of the Pillage of a Continent.* New York: Monthly Review Press, 1997.

Gallegos de Castillo, Lori. "Skillful Coping and the Routine of Surviving: Isasi-Díaz on the Importance of Identity to Everyday Knowledge." *APA Newsletter on Hispanic/Latino Issues in Philosophy* 15, no. 2 (Spring 2016), 7–11.

Gracia, Jorge J. E. and Elizabeth Millán-Zaibert, eds. *Latin American Philosophy for the 21st Century: The Human Condition, Values, and the Search for Identity.* Amherst, NY: Prometheus Books, 2004.

Hurtado, Guillermo. "Two Models of Latin American Philosophy." *Journal of Speculative Philosophy* 20, no. 3 (2006): 204–213.

León-Portilla, Miguel. *Aztec Thought and Culture: A Study of the Ancient Nahuatl Mind.* Translated by Jack Emory Davis. Norman: University of Oklahoma Press, 1963.

Maffie, James. *Aztec Philosophy: Understanding a World in Motion.* Boulder: University Press of Colorado, 2014.

Mariátegui, José Carlos. *Seven Interpretive Essays on Peruvian Reality.* Austin: University of Texas Press, 1971.

Mendieta, Eduardo, ed. *Latin American Philosophy: Currents, Issues, Debates.* Bloomington: Indiana University Press, 2003.

Mendieta, Eduardo. "Latin American Philosophy as Metaphilosophy." *The New Centennial Review* 7, no. 3 (2007): 31–50.

Monahan, Michael. "On the Question of Latin American Philosophy." *APA Newsletter on Hispanic/Latino Issues in Philosophy* 5, no. 1 (Fall 2005): 15–17.

Munk, Arthur W. "The Spirit of Latin American Philosophy." *Ethics* 72, no. 3 (Apr., 1962): 197–201.

Nuccetelli, Susana. *Latin American Thought: Philosophical Problems and Arguments*. Cambridge, MA: Westview Press, 2002.

Nuccetelli, Susana. "Is 'Latin American Thought' Philosophy?" *Metaphilosophy* 34, no. 4 (July 2003): 524–536.

Nuccetelli, Susana and Gary Seay, eds. *Latin American Philosophy: An Introduction with Readings*. Upper Saddle River, NJ: Pearson Prentice Hall, 2004.

Nuccetelli, Susana, Ofelia Schutte, and Otávio Bueno, eds. *A Companion to Latin American Philosophy*. Malden, MA: Wiley-Blackwell, 2010.

Ortega y Gasset, José. *Meditations on Quixote*. Translated by Evelyn Rugg and Diego Marín. New York: W. W. Norton & Company, 1961.

Ortega y Gasset, José. *The Modern Theme*. Translated by James Cleugh. New York: Harper & Row, 1961.

Pereda, Carlos. "Latin American Philosophy: Some Vices." *Journal of Speculative Philosophy* 20, no. 3 (2006): 192–203.

Ramos, Samuel. *Profile of Man and Culture in Mexico*. Translated by Peter G. Earle. Austin: University of Texas Press, 1962.

Romanell, Patrick. *Making of the Mexican Mind: A Study in Recent Mexican Thought*. Notre Dame: University of Notre Dame Press, 1952.

Ruíz-Aho, Elena. "Latin American Philosophy at a Crossroads. Review of *A Companion to Latin American Philosophy*, by Susana Nuccetelli, Ofelia Schutte, and Otávio Bueno, eds." *Human Studies* 34, no. 3 (Fall 2011): 309–331.

Sánchez, Carlos Alberto and Robert EliSanchez, Jr., eds. *Mexican Philosophy in the 20th Century: Essential Readings*. New York: Oxford University Press, 2017.

Sanchez, Jr., Robert Eli. "The Process of Defining Latino/a Philosophy." *APA Newsletter on Hispanic/Latino Issues in Philosophy* 13, no. 1 (Fall 2013): 1–4.

Sanchez, Jr., Robert Eli. "Strengthening the Case for Latin American Philosophy: Beyond Cultural Resources." *APA Newsletter on Hispanic/Latino Issues in Philosophy* 13, no. 2 (Spring 2014): 2–9.

Schutte, Ofelia. "Toward an Understanding of Latin American Philosophy." *Philosophy Today*, 31, no. 1 (1987): 21–34.

Schutte, Ofelia. *Cultural Identity and Social Liberation in Latin American Thought*. Albany: State University of New York Press, 1993.

Silva, Grant J. "Why the Struggle Against Coloniality is Paramount to Latin American Philosophy." *APA Newsletter on Hispanic/Latino Issues* 15, no. 1 (Fall 2015): 8–12.

Silva, Grant J. "On the Difficulties of Writing Philosophy from a Racialized Subjectivity." *APA Newsletters on Hispanic/Latino Issues in Philosophy* 18, no. 1 (Fall 2018): 2–6.

Stabb, Martin S. *In Quest of Identity: Patterns in the Spanish American Essay of Ideas, 1890–1960*. Chapel Hill: The University of North Carolina Press, 1967.

Vallega, Alejandro A. *Latin American Philosophy from Identity to Radical Exteriority*. Bloomington: Indiana University Press, 2014.

Vargas, Manuel. "Latinx Philosophy." In *The Stanford Encyclopedia of Philosophy*. Edited by Edward N. Zalta. Winter 2018. https://plato.stanford.edu/archives/win2018/entries/latinx/

Vasconcelos, José. *The Cosmic Race: A Bilingual Edition*. Translated by Didier Tisdel Jaén. Baltimore, MD: Johns Hopkins University Press, 1997.

Zea, Leopoldo. "Identity: A Latin American Philosophical Problem." In *Latin American Philosophy for the 21st Century: The Human Condition, Values, and the Search for Identity*, edited by Jorge J. E. Gracia and Elizabeth Millán-Zaibert, 369–379. Amherst, NY: Prometheus Books, 2004.

1 Philosophy without Europe

James Maffie

Mesoamerica at Contact

The Aztecs—or, as they called themselves, the "Mexica"—were the last in a series of sophisticated, urban dwelling peoples who occupied an ecologically diverse area spanning from north-central Mexico to the Yucatán Peninsula, Guatemala, Belize, El Salvador, Honduras, and Pacific Coast Nicaragua and Costa Rica. Mexica civilization was preceded most notably by Olmec, Classic Maya, Teotihuacan, Zapotec, Toltec Maya, and Toltec civilizations, and existed contemporaneously with Tarascan and Mixtec civilizations. As a distinct cultural region, Mesoamerica dates back some 3,500 years. The development of Aztec civilization was cut short (some 200 years after its founding) by the combined Spanish-indigenous forces led by Hernán Cortés in 1521, the official date of the fall of the Mexica's island capital, Tenochtitlan. Historians estimate the population of Tenochtitlan at no less than 200,000, surpassing the contemporary populations of London and Madrid, equaling those of Paris and Constantinople. The Mexica and their immediate neighbors in the Valley of Mexico spoke Nahuatl. Scholars commonly refer to this cultural group as *Nahuas*. Despite over 500 years of European and later *crioll@* and *mestizo@* hegemony, Mesoamerican peoples continue to maintain their own languages, lifeways, values, and beliefs. The Nahuatl-speaking descendants of the Mexica are no exception. Nahuatl-speakers currently comprise the largest indigenous language group in Mexico.

Did the Mexica engage in philosophical reflection, or was Emmanuel Levinas correct when declaring that "the Greeks and the Bible are all that is serious in humanity. Everything else is dancing"?[1] This chapter starts from the proposition that Mexica thinkers did indeed do philosophy, as has been cogently demonstrated by Alejandro Santana.[2] The Mexica called these thinkers *tlamatinimeh* (pl.; singl. *tlamatini*), "philosophers," "wise ones," or "sages."[3] Although Mexica philosophers talked about invisible beings and powers, doing so is no more incompatible with their having done philosophy than are Plato's talk of a demiurge, Aristotle's talk of a prime mover, or Rene Descartes's and Baruch Spinoza's talk of a Judeo-Christian god.

But even so, why bother studying Mexica philosophy? After all, didn't Plato say everything there is worth saying, and isn't the rest of philosophy merely "a series of footnotes to Plato"?[4] This chapter argues that Mexica *tlamatinimeh* pursued what scholars call a "way-" or "path-seeking" philosophy, and that this approach differs fundamentally from what scholars call a "truth-seeking" philosophy, the approach that has dominated the Western philosophical tradition since Plato. Studying Mexica philosophy enables us to examine a genuinely *alternative* way of conceiving and doing philosophy.[5]

The difference between truth-seeking and path-seeking approaches cuts broadly and deeply as the two involve two parallel constellations of alternatively conceived conceptions of wisdom, knowledge, the self, language, morality, and the good life. Truth-oriented philosophies define these notions in terms of truth (e.g., apprehending, representing, believing, and grounding one's actions and norms upon truth). Philosophy is first and foremost a theoretical endeavor aimed at apprehending truth. By contrast, path-oriented philosophies understand these notions in terms of finding, following, and extending a path. Wisdom, language, morality, and so on are about path-*making*. Knowing consists first and foremost in knowing *how* to do things, *how* to creatively extend the Mexica lifeway and by implication the entire lifeway of the cosmos into the future. Philosophy, like life itself, is first and foremost creative and practical. Philosophy is *normatively* oriented towards realizing the goals of human and cosmic balance and well-being. And so we must accordingly approach Mexica philosophers *neither* as feather-wearing Greeks *nor* as toga-wearing "Indians" but rather as people who thought about the cosmos, human existence, and the proper way for humans to live in a *uniquely indigenous Mexica* way. In short, Mexica philosophers pursued—as their present-day descendants continue to pursue—*philosophy without Europe*.

This chapter focuses upon Mexica philosophy *not* because Mexica philosophers were more philosophically advanced or sophisticated than Maya, Moche, Inka, Mapuche, or Zapotec philosophers, but rather due to the wholly contingent historical fact that we have the best contact-era written sources about the Mexica thanks to the tireless efforts of the Spanish Franciscan, Bernardino de Sahagún, and his indigenous assistants in documenting Mexica thought and practices (albeit towards the objectionable end of extirpating them). Finally, this chapter also lays the groundwork for one of the interesting questions raised by this collection of essays: to what extent, if any, have the indigenous philosophies of what is now called "Latin America" influenced subsequent *mestizo@* and *crioll@* philosophers?

Mexica vs. Franciscan Understandings of Philosophy-cum-Religion, Human Lifeways, and Ways of Being a Human in the World

In 1524 a group of Mexica philosophers from Tenochtitlan and its sister city, Tlatelolco, met the first twelve Spanish Franciscans to reach what the

Mexica called *Cemanahuac* ("place surrounded by water"), the place the Spanish invaders would soon rename "New Spain." The Franciscans attempted to engage the Mexica in dialogue with the twin aims of convincing them of the truth of Christian doctrine and of converting them to Christianity. A reconstruction of this dialogue appears in the *Colloquios y doctrina cristiana*, co-authored in 1564 by Bernardino de Sahagún and his Christianized, indigenous Nahuatl-speaking assistants, Antonio Vegeriano, Alonso Vegerano, Martín Jacobita, and Andrés Leonardo.[6] The *Colloquois* offers us an invaluable window into the philosophical-cum-religious differences dividing the two peoples. Like most, if not all, indigenous peoples in the "New World," the Mexica conceived philosophy and what *we* call "religion" or "spirituality"—together with their entire lifeway—as a single, seamless endeavor.

The Franciscans in the *Colloquois* speak first and foremost of God, a perfect, sacred, permanent, and immutable reality that transcends the imperfect, profane, and transient affairs and concerns of earthly creatures. This transcendent reality serves as the one and only foundation upon which humans must build the house of their well-being (Matthew 7: 24–27). It is a "rock of ages" to which one anchors one's life and by reference to which one navigates life's vicissitudes.

Second, the Franciscans speak of truth. They proclaim the singularity, objectivity, completeness, absoluteness, and universality of Biblical truth. There is only one truth for all peoples: that written in the Bible. They also speak of the true written and spoken word. The theological-cum-philosophical principles, admonitions, and claims of Christianity are universally true and universally applicable. Christianity is the one and only religion for all peoples. Christian religion is thus *utopian* or "of no-place" in the sense of not being tied to any one given place. One may live an upright Christian life anywhere in the world.

Third, the Franciscans speak in terms of belief, creed, doctrine, conversion, and the certainty of belief. What concerns them is that one comes to believe Biblical truth. They are concerned with *orthodoxy*, i.e. that people hold the right beliefs. Generally speaking, right living and behavior follow from right beliefs. Fourth, the Franciscans speak of Evil, original sin, and Christianity's concern for the salvation of human souls. Christianity is Manichean: the forces of unmitigated Goodness struggle with the forces of unmitigated Evil. It is also salvific: it aims for the salvation of the human soul.

The Franciscans speak surprisingly little of Christianity as a way of life. They aim for the Mexica to follow the path of Jesus but only logically posterior to believing the truth of the word of Jesus. The Christian way of life is founded on the truth of Christian doctrine. They construe Christianity specifically, and religion generally—along with its attendant philosophical-theological views—in terms of correct belief. Religion and philosophy are matters of belief; they seek and are meant to be founded upon true belief.

The Mexica respond to the Franciscans as follows:

> But we, whatever will we say to you now? Even though we are lords, we are people's mothers, we are people's fathers, perhaps then we here before you, shall we destroy the ancient [lifeway]? Those which our grandfathers, our grandmothers, considered great? Those which the lords, the rulers condoned, admired? And this, oh our lords: there are still those who guide us, who carry us, who bear us upon their backs, because of their service to our [creator beings], of whom we are penitents, tails, wings. It is said that they are wise in words. And they attend their duties by night, by day ... They observe, they attend to the journey, the steady movement of the sky, the way night divides in the middle. And they look at, they read, they lay out the books, the black ink, the red ink. They are in charge of the writings. They are in charge of us. They lead us, they tell us the way [road, path]. They arrange in order how a year falls, how the day count follows its path. ... These words that you say are new. And thus we are confused, thus we are astonished. For our engenderers, who came to be, who came to live on the earth, they did not go speaking in this way. They gave us their [lifeway]. They steadfastly followed, they served, they venerated the [creator beings]. They taught us all the ways to serve them, of serving, to honor them, thus before them we eat earth, thus we bleed ourselves, thus we make recompense [discharge our debts], thus we cast incense, and thus we kill things. ... And perhaps we will now go and destroy the ancient [lifeway]? The Chichimec [lifeway]? The Toltec [lifeway]? The Colhua [lifeway]? The Tepanec [lifeway]? ... The poor old men, the poor old women, how will they forget, how will they destroy, that which was their education, their upbringing? ... We cannot be satisfied, and we do not yet go along, we do not yet make acceptable for ourselves [what you say] ...[7]

The Mexica characterize their lifeway as having been handed down to them by their ancestors, not by a god or gods. They speak of the authenticity, genuineness, and practicability of their lifeway, and they locate these qualities in its history, not in its foundation in true divine statements or proclamations. They speak of *following a path*: the path set out for them and honed by their ancestors. They speak not of what they *believe* and so not of the objective *truth* of what they believe. Talk of belief is absent from their response. While the Mexica speak of having books, they speak of their books not as containing true descriptions of the world but as guiding them and showing them the proper way to live, i.e. as road maps for living. Similarly, while they speak of the authenticity, genuineness, and practicability of their path, they do not understand these qualities in terms of their path's being metaphysically derived from divine truth. Rather, their path is well rooted in their own history, i.e. in their ancestors' sayings, judgments, migrations, and ways of living. What's more, the Mexica speak of the existence of—and indeed, *on behalf of* the existence of—a plurality of alternative paths or lifeways: the Mexica, Chichimec, Toltec, and Tepanec. They embrace a philosophical-cum-religious *pluralism*. The Mexica do not claim that their lifeway is the single, correct lifeway for all peoples. Each people has its own lifeway. The Mexica lifeway is one among many paths or lifeways, where no one is truer than the next.

The Mexica philosophers make no mention of sin, salvation, or evil. Mexica philosophy-cum-religion is wholly this-worldly because *in and of* this world (whereas Christianity typically sees humans as being *in* the world but *not of* the world). The Mexica do not view life as oriented towards some other-worldly destination such as heaven or hell. Similarly, the Manichean notions that the universe contains Goodness and Evil per se and that the history of the universe consists of a life-and-death struggle between Good and Evil is entirely absent. They do not distinguish between sacred and profane aspects of reality. All of reality is sacred. And finally, although not explicitly mentioned in the *Colloquois*, the Mexica conceive their lifeway as *topian*, i.e. rooted in a specific place, *Anahuac*, the Valley of Mexico. One is able to live a proper Mexica life *only* in Anahuac.

The Existential Condition of Humankind and Defining Problematic of Mexica Philosophy

Mexica *huehuetlatolli* ("words of the ancients") played an important role in Mexica society in cultivating and promoting proper conduct. Among those recorded by Sahagún is one delivered by a mother to her coming-of-age daughter:

> Behold the road thou art to follow. In such a manner thou art to live. Thy lords, our lords, the noble women, the old women, the white-haired ones … they gave one, they left … their words. "Take heed. On earth it is a time for care, it is a place of caution. Behold the word; heed and guard it, and with it take your way of life, your works. We travel, we live along a mountain peak. Over here there is an abyss, over there is an abyss. If you goest over here, or if thou goes over there, thou wilt fall. Only *in the middle* doth one go, doth one live."[8]

The mother goes on to instruct her daughter regarding the proper way to live. She must endeavor to "middle" her activities, herself, and all around her by pursuing moderation (avoiding extremes) in all aspects of her life: walking, speaking, eating, cooking, weaving, dressing, bathing, sexual relations with her husband, and all her interactions with others (both human and non-human). The mother's instruction would undoubtedly have included the Mexica proverb, "*Tlaalahui, tlapetzcahui in tlalticpac*" ("The earth is slippery"), explaining that people say this of someone who had lived an upright, well-middled, and well-balanced life only to slip into excess and moral wrongdoing, as though in slick mud.[9] Losing one's balance is far too easy here on the surface of the earth. The consequences of slipping include disease, imbalancedness, disequilibrium, and disorder. The Mexica conceived these latter notions in terms of mind and body (since they drew no sharp metaphysical distinction between the two) *and* also in terms of the individual agent, her family, community, and, ultimately, the entire world. Such a person disorders herself, her family members and neighbors, and ultimately her world.

In another *huehuetlatolli*, a mother admonishes her daughter concerning the nature of human existence:

> There is no rejoicing, there is no contentment; there is torment, there is pain, there is fatigue, there is want; torment, pain dominate. Difficult is the world, a place where one is caused to weep, a place where one is caused pain. Affliction is known. ... And it is a place of thirst. This is the way things are.
>
> Hear well, O my daughter, O my child, the earth is not a good place. It is not a place of joy, it is not a place of contentment. It is merely said it is a place of joy with fatigue, of joy with pain on earth ...[10]

The foregoing passages highlight the Mexica's understanding of the human existential condition. Life on earth is *by definition* one of inescapable transience, instability, suffering, pain, disease, hunger, and death. At best, the earth is a place of "joy *with* fatigue," of "joy *with* pain" (emphasis mine). It is not a place of unmixed contentment or happiness. Furthermore, there is no firm anchorage, no fixed, transcendent "rock of ages" upon which humans may build the house of their well-being. There is no Archimedean or Cartesian-style standpoint from which to engage in theoretical reflection about the nature of things. There are only narrow, jagged mountain paths that humans must continuously navigate while walking upon a treacherously slippery earth. There is no stopping. There is no escaping. There is only continual becoming.

These passages also express the problem that human existence posed to Mexica philosophy-cum-religion: How can humans walk in balance on the slippery earth? What is the right path, the appropriate lifeway, for humans to follow? What enables humans to walk well upon this path and moreover *creatively extend* this path—and in so doing *creatively extend* their lifeway—into the future; and what *disables* them from doing so? How can humans balance their lives so as to minimize the suffering and maximize the pleasures of earthly existence?

Mexica conceived philosophy as charged with the tasks of: (a) serving as a guide for people by artfully leading them down the treacherous and slippery path of life, and (b) instructing people how to attain a middle footing so as to walk in balance upon that path. The Mexica thus regarded the pressing problem to be addressed by philosophers as quintessentially *practical*:

"What is the path (*ohtli*)?" What concerns Mexica philosophers first and foremost is *knowing how* to act, i.e. the practical understanding involved in knowing how to maintain one's balance on the slippery earth. *Theoretical* reflection about the ultimate nature of things concerns them only secondarily, if at all. Indeed, it appears they regarded such reflection as both fruitless and, more importantly, not essential to the practical task of living well. In short, Mexica philosophers embrace a *path-oriented* philosophy. They want to know *how* to act, not what to believe. They focus on orthopraxy or correct action.

Consider the following characterization of the Mexica philosopher recorded by Sahagún (with the aid of his Christianized, Nahuatl-speaking assistants, Antonio Vegeriano, Alonso Vegerano, Martín Jacobita, and Pedro de San Buenaventura) in his *Historia general de las cosas de la Nueva España* (*General History of the Things of New Spain* or *Florentine Codex* for short):

> The wise man (*tlamatini*) [is] exemplary. He possesses writings; he owns books. [He is] the tradition, the road; a leader of men, a rower, a companion, a bearer of responsibility, a guide. ... a physician, a person of trust ... an advisor, a counselor, a good example; a teacher of prudence, of discretion; a light, a guide who lays out one's path, who goes accompanying one. ... he bears responsibility, shows the way, makes arrangements, establishes order. He lights the world for one ... he reassures, calms, helps ... he makes one whole.[11]

Here, as in the *Colloquois* and in the *huehuetlatolli* above, the Mexica see their philosophers as people who are responsible for both preserving and extending into the future the life of the community; as those who know how to create a future path for the community as well as guide the community down that path; and as those who know how to maintain the community's balance as well as know how to teach others how to maintain their balance upon the slippery path of life.

The *Colloquois*, as we've seen, suggests that the Franciscans pursue a *truth-oriented* philosophy that is concerned with answering such questions as "What is the truth?" and "What is real?" What concerns truth-seekers first and foremost is apprehending the truth, since they see knowledge of the truth as the requisite logical foundation for knowing how to act. Truth-seekers focus on *orthodoxy* or correct belief, this being a precondition of Christian faith and salvation. They worry about *heterodoxy* or incorrect belief, this leading to incorrect behavior that precludes salvation.

But mustn't the Mexica likewise *believe that it is true* that this or that path is the right one, that this or that path works, and if so, aren't they therefore truth-seekers in the end? Not necessarily; the Mexica need only *adopt* a path and need only *accept* that this path works. Adopting and accepting, unlike believing, do not require having a "pro" cognitive attitude regarding the truth of what one adopts/accepts. For example, one may accept an hypothesis for the sake of argument without believing it to be true. The closest Nahuatl word, "*neltoca*," is plausibly glossed as "to accept" rather than as "to believe."[12]

In sum, Mexica philosophy thus differs from Franciscan (and the lion's share of Western) philosophy-cum-religion in the following respects:

1   Pluralism vs. universalism: is philosophy-cum religion culturally specific or universal? Is there just one for all human beings or are there many? The Franciscans are universalists: they maintain that there is only one correct philosophy-cum-religion, and that it is universal and true for all peoples. The Mexica are pluralists: they maintain that there are many culturally specific philosophies-cum-religions, indeed, as many as there are ways of being human in the world.

2   Mexica philosophy-cum-religion is thoroughly *in and of the world*; it is completely this-worldly. It aims to help humans maintain their balance during their lifetime here on earth—not in some afterlife. It is non-salvific. One's motivations for living a well-balanced life, for following the right path, do not concern one's personal fate after death.

3   Mexica philosophy-cum-religion is neither monotheistic nor polytheistic. There is a plurality of powerful creator beings who are neither divine nor "gods" in the Western sense. Creator beings are persons who simply happen to be more powerful than human beings. They are neither omnipotent, omniscient, perfect, nor benevolent. They are no more sacred than humans, insects, maize, and houses. They do not stand apart from the world but are co-extensive with the world. They are not divine legislators who issue commandments to humans or who enter into covenants with humans. Most crucially, Mexica creator beings are wholly dependent upon human beings for their continuing existence (more below).

The Five Ages and Creation of Human Beings

Mexica *tlamachiliztlatolzazanilli* ("wisdom tellings") offer additional insight into Mexica philosophy. Let's briefly examine some of these. The conquest-era document, the *Annals of Cuauhtitlan*, relates:

> Thus it is told, it is said: there have already been four manifestations and this one is the fifth age.
>
> So the old ones knew this, that in the year 1-Rabbit heaven and earth were founded.
>
> And they knew this, that when heaven and earth were founded there had already been four kinds of men, four kinds of manifestations. Also they knew that each of these had existed in a Sun, an age.[13]
>
> [...]

4 Movement is the day sign of the fifth sun, called Movement Sun, because it moves along and follows its course. And from what the old people say, there will be earthquakes in its time, there will be famine, and because of this we will be destroyed.[14]

The Mexica understood the cosmos to have undergone a cycle of four creations (Suns or Ages) and four destructions leading up to the present creation, the 5th Sun. The history of the cosmos has also witnessed the creation and destruction of four kinds of proto-humans. This Sun and this generation of humans are also destined to end. Human existence in the 5th Sun occurs in the ever-threatening shadow of inevitable cosmic destruction. We thus need to refine the above formulation of the defining problematic of Mexica philosophy as follows: How can we humans balance on the slippery earth *and* at the same time work to forestall the total demise of the 5th Age and human existence? Note that since humans are *in* and *of* the world, they cannot take refuge or comfort in the fact that they belong ultimately to some other-worldly existence, and so they cannot therefore ignore their environment. Balancing on the slippery earth requires not only that humans balance their own lives but equally importantly, that they *actively balance their environment* as well as live in balance *with* their environment (more below).[15]

According to the wisdom tellings recorded in the conquest-era document, the *Legend of the Suns*, in the process of creating the 5th Sun, the creator beings created the sky and earth. Then they:

> called an assembly; they said, "Who will be seated there, now that the heavens have been established and the Earth Lord [Tlaltecuhtli] has been established? [Creator beings], who will be seated [who will live on earth]? ..."
>
> And then Quetzalcoatl went off to Mictlan, the Region of the Dead, where he came before the Lord and the Lady of Mictlan [Mictlante-cuhtli and Mictlancihuatl]. Then he said to him, truly thus to him, "I come to take away the jade [i.e. precious] bones [of 4th Age humans] which you so honorably guard." And so then the Lord of Mictlan said to him, "What is it you will do, O Quetzalcoatl?" And again he said, truly thus to him, "The [creator beings] are anxious to know who will be settled [who will live] on the earth."

In order to retrieve the bones of 4th Age humans, Quetzalcoatl must successfully overcome a number of hardships that Mictlantecuhtli places before him. In this way Quetzalcoatl comes to "merit" or "deserve" the precious bones (more below).

> Then [Quetzalcoatl] gathered up the bones and made a bundle and carried them at once to Tamoanchan. And as soon as he brought them

> the [creator being] named Quilaztli, who is also Cihuacoatl, ground them in her jade bowl.
>
> And then Quetzalcoatl bled his penis over it. Then all the aforementioned [creator beings] performed penance … And then they said, "The [creator beings] have given birth to men, to common people [*macehualtin*], for certainly they performed penance on our behalf."[16]

The *Legend of the Suns* thus reiterates the claim made in the *Colloquois*: "They said that it is by the [creator beings] that all live. They did penance for us." We will explore further this idea below. Both documents claim creator beings are responsible for finding and providing human sustenance. The *Colloquois* states,

> And they said that it is they who give us our dinner, our breakfast, all that is potable, that is edible, the crops, maize, beans, amaranth, chia. It is they who we solicit for water, for rain, so that things grow upon the earth.

The *Legend of the Suns* tells us Quetzalcoatl retrieved maize, chia, beans, amaranth, and other human foodstuffs from *tonacatepetl* ("sustenance mountain"). Humans thus owe both their initial creation and continuing existence to creator beings.

After fashioning Sky, Earth, and Sun of the 5th Age, the creator beings are enervated, hungry, and desperately in need of nourishment.[17] In order to remedy their condition, they fashion 5th Age humans from a mixture of the ground bones of 4th Age proto-humans *and* the life-giving energies of their own blood. They do so with the aim of humans' feeding, nourishing, respecting, worshipping, and honoring them (where respecting, worshipping, and honoring are conceived as nourishment by means of words, attitudes, and actions). Fifth Age creator beings are completely dependent upon human feeding and nourishing for their continuing existence. Without it, they will perish.

The creator beings' continuing support and recreation of the 5th Age (along with its human inhabitants) also continually exhausts them, and their continuing existence thus requires continuing nourishment from humans. Humans nourish (feed) creator beings with the vital energies contained in properly spoken words ("prayers"), song, dance, instrumental music, copal incense, maize tamales, amaranth dough figures, animals (e.g., dogs, quail), butterflies, and, most essentially, their own human hearts and blood. The crucial point to remember here is that the creator beings depend *essentially* upon human nourishment; they cannot survive without it. Creator beings are therefore just as dependent upon humans as humans are dependent upon them. Each *consumes* and so *partakes of* the vital, life-sustaining energies of the other—on pain of death. The continuing reproduction and existence of 5th Age humans also depend upon human beings continually being nourished and fed by creator beings with the vital energies of creator beings contained sunlight (*tonalli*), maize, amaranth, chia, beans, squash, and water. In short, humans and creator beings are *mutually* dependent or *symbiotic*: they depend essentially upon consuming one another's life-energies. As contemporary Nahuatl-speakers of San Miguel, Sierra del Pueblo, Mexico, sing: "We eat of the earth and then the earth eats us."[18] We humans eat the flesh of Earth Mother, *Tlaltecuhtli*, in the form of maize, amaranth, chia seed, etc.; and Earth Mother eats our flesh upon our burial in the earth. It is a mutual exchange. We eat the creator beings, and the creator beings eat us,[19] and we feed ourselves to the creator beings and the creator beings feed themselves to us. Creator beings are thus said to be "mothers and fathers" to humans, and humans are thus said to be "mothers and fathers" to the creator beings.

Reproducing the 5th Age is thus an irreducibly *social* process involving the cooperative contribution of both humans and creator beings. Their mutual interdependence is not gainsaid by the fact that creator beings are more powerful than humans. Each depends upon the other for its continuing existence. We also see that humans and creator beings *co-participate* in the ongoing reproduction and existence of the 5th Age. In short, the 5th Age is the *joint* product of their inter-personal relationship of reciprocal feeding and eating. As a consequence of their reciprocal feeding of themselves *to* and reciprocal eating *of* each another, humans and creator beings "*participate in each other*."[20] Humans become "divine" and creator beings become "human" humans become "supernatural" and creator beings become "natural." In other words, there is no in principle ontological distinction between human and "divine" or between natural and supernatural. Creator beings and humans consist of the same stuff: life-energy or life-power. The foregoing distinctions, so deeply entrenched in most Western religious and secular thought, are thus wholly alien to Mexica thinking (and to that of other indigenous peoples of the "New World," for that matter). Humans and creator beings are mutually interdependent and mutually arising, eating-feeding partners who alternate their roles as feeder~being fed and eater~being eaten. This obviously represents a profoundly different understanding of the relationship between humans and creator beings than, say, one finds in Christianity, Judaism, and Islam. The ongoing reproduction of the 5th Age is not only *a product of* human~creator beings' reciprocal consuming and feeding, it is also *constituted by* their reciprocal consuming and feeding. Indeed, the entire 5th Age consists of a single, vast, dynamic social web of reciprocal, life-energy gifting and exchanging between creator beings, humans (both living and deceased), animals, plants, rivers, mountains, cooking pots, fishing nets, agricultural tools, maize and bean fields, and so on. In short, reciprocity functions "like a pump at the heart of the life" in the 5th Age.[21]

The foregoing puts to rest the stubbornly longstanding *misconception* of Mexica religion which construes the Mexica's "gods" as monstrously insatiable consumers of human hearts and blood and the Mexica themselves as groveling sycophants terrorized into murdering hundreds of thousands of innocents to feed them. This misconception is rooted in the conquistadors' and later colonialists' deliberate efforts to portray the Mexica (and other indigenous peoples) as savages engaged in human sacrifice (as well as cannibalism and sodomy) with the aim of morally and legally justifying their unprovoked war of aggression and conquest as well as genocide and enslavement of indigenous peoples (see chapter 2). Today, this misconception continues to be perpetuated by apologists for genocide, racism, settler colonialism, and imperialism, and by sensationalist popular historians and Hollywood film producers along with profit-hungry cable television history channels.[22]

Creator beings bring into existence 5th Sun human beings via a process the Mexica called *macehua*, "to merit, deserve, be worthy of, or acquire that which is deserved," and *tlamacehua*, "to deserve or merit something."[23] Kelly McDonough glosses *macehua* as "obtaining that which is desired through merit, of giving as part of the action of receiving."[24] *Macehua* designates a *process* initiated by an agent who aims to bring about some desired outcome (event or state of affairs). It is an *activity* involving effort, work, hardship, gifting, or offering on the part of the initiating person. It is by virtue of the initiate's personal expenditure of energy that she deserves or becomes worthy of the desired outcome.

Macehua is commonly *mis*translated as "to do penance" (as in the passage above). But *macehua* refers to the activity of deserving or meriting. Unlike the Christian notion of penance, *macehua* has nothing to do with: expressing repentance for sin or wrongdoing; self-punishment; self-infliction; or expiating one's sins. Similarly, the conquest-era sources often mistranslate this notion as "to sacrifice." But the very concept of sacrifice is wholly alien to Mexica thought, contrary to popular and unfortunately some scholarly opinion. The Mexica did not perform *sacrifice*. Sacrifice entails the notion of "making sacred" (from the Latin, *sacer*, "holy or sacred"; *facere*, "to make"). But since the Mexica regarded *all things as sacred*, they simply had no reason to make anything sacred. Rather, on certain occasions they sought to deserve or merit certain outcomes from creator beings by means of presenting gifts, and on other occasions, they sought to reciprocate gifts received from creator beings with what they called *nextloalli* ("debt payments" or "obligation repayments"). Having said this, there is compelling evidence that the Mexica's reciprocal gifts or "obligation repayments" did in fact include human blood and hearts.[25]

Macehua is an *interpersonal* process that initiates an *interpersonal* relationship between two (or more) persons. One attempts to initiate this relationship and merit the desired outcome through personal effort, work, and hardship or by means of gifting or offering, both of which involve the transmission of vital energy from donor to recipient. Through gifting, etc., one person tries to *bring about movement, transformation,* or *change* in another person; to get them to *act*, to *do* something, to *change* in some way.

Creator beings and humans, for example, endeavor to bring about desired outcomes from one another by means of meriting and so obligating the other to act in a specific way. *Macehua* generates a normative *tertium quid*: a dynamic, mutually interweaving relationship of reciprocal obligatedness or indebtedness; one that is not reducible to either individual person in isolation. It binds, unites, and weaves together persons into a woven social fabric. For example, reciprocal feeding and eating *middles*, weaves together, and transforms feeder and fed into *social beings* who become creative participants in a new *interpersonal* relationship characterized by dual unity and unified duality. It binds them together in a normative interrelationship of meriting-being merited, gifting-receiving, indebting-being indebted, or obligation-creating-obligation-incurring.

Macehua—and hence living in balance in the 5th Age—involves *social "know-how"* or *knowing how to get along with other persons in a social world*—social because populated by a variety of different kinds of persons (human and other-than-human, visible and invisible, who are characterized by different interrelationships and degrees of power)—in order both to remain on good terms with them and to induce them into cooperating by doing as one wishes. Social "know-how" crucially involves knowing with whom, how, when, where, and with what to conduct vital *macehua*-generating, reciprocal gift-exchanges. Such activity also standardly requires humans adopting an appropriate attitude of humility, honor, love, or respect towards the intended person(s). Finally, knowing how to get along with other persons in this manner is *not* the same as knowing how to causally manipulate, exploit, or coerce others into doing as one wishes.[26]

Macehua is a fundamentally *normative* process—*not* a descriptive, causal process in the sense of Newtonian science-style, mechanical push-and-pull, cause-and-effect. Generally speaking, normativity concerns that which is action-guiding, attitude-molding, conduct-related; it concerns how one *ought* to act, how one is *obliged* to behave or conduct oneself; what is *appropriate* or *fitting* for one to do, etc. Talk of being obligated or indebted is central to *macehua*. Normative facts, statements, and relationships possess an *"oughtiness"* that descriptions lack. Acts of *macehua* create *normative* interrelationships that bind, unite, and weave together persons. *Macehua* is a process by which one person tries to induce another person(s) into entering into a *normative relationship* that *binds, indebts, or obligates* the targeted person into performing some action, etc. This "creates a bond between the two and sets up a flow of power between donor and recipient."[27] In this way persons seek to "bind" the future actions of other persons within a normatively ordered fabric.[28]

One of the principal ways of doing this is *by means of gifting* and *meriting*. It appears to be a brute fact of Mexica metaphysics that a donor's appropriate gifting and meriting, and a recipient's subsequent reception generates *a normative relationship that binds together donor and recipient; one of mutual and alternating obligation and attendant "ought's."* By accepting the donor's gift, the recipient normatively *binds* herself to the donor and *becomes* obligated to gift back. At the same time, the donor's original gifting commits him to a normative relationship of mutual gifting with the recipient, since the recipient's obligatory reciprocal gift, in turn, obligates the donor to gifting-back to the recipient, and so on, through countless cyclical iterations of reciprocal gift-exchanging. So, for example, humans' settling of their debt *vis-a-vis* creator beings and creator beings' accepting of humans' repayment obligates creator beings, in turn, to repay humans, and so on. In sum, the mutual feeding and eating of humans and creator beings is both a descriptive and normative process. It involves a normative obligation to reciprocate. This mutual consumption weaves together the inhabitants of the 5th Age into cyclical *normative* inter-relationships. In the *social* world of the 5th Age, one *makes things happen* by entering into *macehua*-defined normative relationships with other persons and hence through the cooperation and co-participation of other persons. By keeping these reciprocal relationships going, humans not only keep humankind going but also keep the entire 5th Age going. By keeping these going, humans re-create themselves as well as re-create the entire world.

And yet we must take care not to overemphasize the normative-interpersonal to the exclusion of the descriptive-causal-impersonal, since the latter also plays an indispensable role in making things happen in the world. For example, one successfully plants a fertile, maize-yielding *milpa* (agricultural plot) *only if* one elicits the cooperation of other-than-human persons such as *Tlaltecuhtli* (earth mother), one's digging stick, and maize seeds—*but also only if* one applies one's own physical effort (muscular energy) and one's know-how in carrying out such agricultural tasks as locating fertile soil, clearing, sowing, weeding, irrigating, and harvesting.

Normativity appears to be essentially *relational* and *interpersonal* (like parenthood, for example). It is a fundamental metaphysical fact about *how the things work* in the 5th Age. Normative processes contribute *essentially* to the continuing regeneration (weaving, becoming) of the 5th Age. The Mexica cosmos is thus characterized by both normative and descriptive processes, relationships, and facts. Normative and descriptive sit side by side. What's more, the normativity of the 5th Age is *non-anthropocentric*, i.e. it is ontologically and conceptually independent of human choices, interests, actions, conventions, and even human existence. Humans are born both as individuals and as a species into a world *already* interwoven with normative relationships. Normativity is consequent upon what persons *do*, that is, upon their *macehua-generating actions*. Creator beings import normativity into the 5th Age in the very process of fashioning the 5th Age—not via commandments, covenants, or edicts. Human and other-than-human persons subsequently weave and order the fabric of the 5th Age by initiating, responding to, and maintaining well-balanced normative relationships with other persons. As a consequence, both the weaving of the 5th Age and the 5th Age as a product of this weaving are normatively ordered.

According to Mexica wisdom tellings, human beings are ex hypothesi born into a pre-existing fabric of *normative relationships* with creator beings that entails normative obligations to creator beings. Humans are by definition "those made worthy of existence" by the creator beings' hardship, effort, and gifts, and "those born indebted because merited into existence by the [creator beings]."[29] Creator beings weave humans into this preexisting, normative cosmic fabric in the very process of bringing human beings—both ontogenetically and phylogenetically—into existence. Creator beings and humans (along with all other 5th Age other-than-human persons) are members of a *single fabric or community of normative relationships*.

The originary 5th Age activity of creator beings' *macehua* serves as the objective, non-anthropocentric *roots* of Mexica ethics, ethical obligation, and ethically appropriate behavior. Mexica ethics does not rest upon human choice, will, desire, or convention. Creator beings introduce ethics into 5th Age through *macehua*-defined activities—not by commandments, edicts, or covenants. Broadly speaking, Mexica ethics is concerned with the proper/appropriate way to treat *persons* (who may or may not be human), and with the way one ought or is obliged to treat one's relatives (who may or may not be human). Creator beings and humans—along with all other 5th Age other-than-human persons—are relatives within a *single moral community* consisting of a vast woven fabric of reciprocal life-energy exchange relationships. Reciprocity functions both descriptively and normatively at the heart of this community. Mexica ethics concerns the well-balancedness of the entire 5th Age community.

The *aim* of Mexica ethics is thus straightforwardly non-anthropocentric seeing as it focuses upon maintaining well-balanced, interpersonal relationships within the 5th Age, and therefore upon the well-balancedness and ultimately the recreation and continuation of the 5th Age. It does *not* focus upon human well-being to the exclusion of or at the expense of the well-being of non-humans. Having said this, it is important to add that human well-being is an essential component of a well-balanced 5th Age. Mexica philosophy also offers a radically different understanding of the relationship between humans and their "environment" from the understanding that currently dominates Western religions, science, and popular thinking. Of all the persons inhabiting the 5th Age, humans are uniquely equipped and uniquely responsible for nurturing, caring for, nourishing, and ultimately reproducing the 5th Age and its inhabitants. The continuing existence of the 5th Age is a load or burden that rests on humans' shoulders alone.

Yet this fact does *not* mean that humans are morally entitled to *disrespect* other-than-human persons by treating them as mere objects (rather than as subjects), by treating them as mere means to human ends, or by consuming them without their permission or without constraint. (According to Mexica ethics, treating other-than-human persons [such as maize, deer, and fish] respectfully does *not* preclude eating them. Life, after all, depends upon death and thus upon killing and consuming fellow members of the 5th Age moral community. Mexica ethics does demand, however, that such killing and consuming be done respectfully, i.e. with the victim's and relevant creator being's permission and in moderation.) *Nor* does this fact mean that humans are uniquely privileged in terms of their being God's chosen people, their being morally superior to non-humans, or their being entitled to treat the world as their rubbish bin.[30] Mexica ethics, once again, is radically non-anthropocentric. Membership in the moral community to which humankind belongs is not confined to humans: it includes other-than-human persons such as creator beings, lakes, springs, mountains, trees, plants, animals, butterflies, architectural structures, statues, and tools.

The foregoing offers us a glimpse into Mexica ontology.[31] The Mexica inhabit an energized, *living world* that is populated by a variety of *animated entities*. All entities (both living and deceased) are vivified, energized, and powerful. What's more, they are *agentive*, i.e. they have the power to act and to effect changes in other things. Animate beings differ from one another in terms of their power, not their substance. One and all consist of energy-in-motion. More crucially, the Mexica live in a *social world* populated by a variety of *persons*, where persons are conceived as agents: who have intentions, will, aims, needs, and wants; who deserve respect; and who participate in social relationships defined by normative reciprocity. The 5th Age contains a variety of persons: human and other-than-human (e.g., maize, fish, birds, and creator beings); living and dead (e.g. human ancestors); some more powerful (e.g. creator beings), some less powerful (e.g. cooking pots, and digging sticks) than humans; and some corporeal and visible (e.g. humans and animals), some incorporeal and invisible (e.g. ancestors and creator beings).

While animacy is a function of one's agency and innate body-mind powers, *personhood* is a function of one's participation in social relationships of reciprocity. Personhood admits of degrees, and it is a function of one's participation in normatively defined, reciprocal relationships with other persons. It is a matter of how one behaves. Humans must develop and achieve personhood through their actions. Humans are not born persons; personhood is not a given. By contrast, however, it appears that it is only humans who must work to cultivate their personhood. Other-than-humans such as sun, wind, hills, animals, cooking pots, and trees act as persons—i.e., engage in reciprocal relationships with other persons—naturally or without effort. Finally, not all humans succeed in becoming persons. The Mexica characterized the human who fails to participate in reciprocal relationships as a partial or non-person: an *atlacatl* ("not-human, inhumane"), *atlacaneci* ("bestial human"),[32] and *tlacamimilli* ("lump of flesh with two eyes," resembling a swollen lump of maize dough or painful swollen abscess).[33] The 5th Age consists of a community of reciprocally inter-related persons, i.e. of animate beings who become and behave as persons by virtue of participating in reciprocal relationships with one another. Non-persons do not participate in this community and are consequently a source of domestic, societal, and cosmic disorder, disease, and imbalance. The 5th Age continues moving in balance to the extent it is defined by thriving, reciprocity-based, interpersonal relationships.

In conclusion, Mexica wisdom tellings function both descriptively *and* prescriptively. They tell the Mexica: (a) *how* they came to be, viz., they were *merited* by creator beings; (b) *who* they are, viz., they are those deserved into existence by creator beings and hence indebted to creator beings; (c) *how* they *ought to behave* towards creator beings, viz., they are obligated to reciprocate by respectfully repaying their debt to creator beings; (d) *how* they *ought* to go about getting things done in a social world, viz. by initiating and maintaining relationships of reciprocity with other persons; (e) *how* they must act in order to become *persons*, viz., they must participate in social relationships of reciprocal exchange with others; (f) *how* they must act in order to balance, reproduce and promote well-being in their lives and the world, viz., by initiating and maintaining reciprocity with others; and (g) *that* they neglect these normative relationships with and obligations to other persons on pain of human as well as 5th Age imbalance, disorder, and destruction. The creator beings' originary acts of *macehua* serve as *prescriptive models* for human behavior, *examples* to be emulated by humans in balancing their lives and the world at large. Mexica ethics, then, is concerned with maintaining a well-balanced and hence thriving cosmos that consists of a moral community of human and other-than-human persons. Succinctly put, Mexica ethics is an *ethics of reciprocity aimed at maintaining cosmic balance.*

Some Comparisons

Pre-conquest and contemporary indigenous philosophies across what is now called "Latin America" tend to share many of the foregoing themes. These philosophies include (among others) those of: Maya, Nahua, Wixárika (Huichol), Rarámuri (Tarahumara), Mixtec, and Otomî peoples in Mexico and Central America; pre-conquest Incas and contemporary Aymara and Quechua speaking peoples of the Andes; native Amazonia peoples; and Mapuche of the Southern Cone. In brief:

1 A cyclical succession of world creations and destructions leading to the current age and current generation of humans.
2 Reality as processive, fluid, dynamic, and defined by becoming and change rather than stasis and permanence.
3 Holism: the cosmos as a single, all-encompassing whole, the components of which are essentially interrelated and interwoven with one another as a fabric, network, or web.
4 Animism: all things are animated, powerful, charged with force (or energy), and agentive. Humans are one among many animates in the world.
5 Personalism: animate beings who participate in reciprocal interrelationships with other animates transform themselves into persons. Personhood

comes in degrees; it is an achievement, not a given, and it is not confined to humans. Not all persons are humans; not all humans are persons.

6 A moral cosmos: one that consists of a moral *community* of persons defined by interpersonal relationships of reciprocal gifting or mutual exchange.

7 Earth, sun, water, wind, mountains, springs, rivers, lakes, etc. are powerful, other-than-human persons to whom human persons owe their existence and to whom humans have *moral* obligations.

8 The health and well-being of the cosmos (along with that its inhabitants) *consists of* and *is consequent upon* the unobstructed, well-balanced circulation of life-energy throughout the cosmos—just as humans' health depends upon the unobstructed, well-balanced circulation of life-energy throughout their body-minds.

9 The cosmos consists of a vast network of reciprocal life-energy gifting. It is continually regenerated and recreated by means of such dynamic reciprocity relationships. These relationships normatively bind together all things, humans and other-than-human. Reciprocity functions like a pump at the heart of indigenous metaphysics.

10 Human beings are created in order actively contribute to the balance and hence renewal of the cosmos. Their participation is a necessary condition of the continuing becoming (existence) of the cosmos.

11 Human beings have a moral responsibility to keep the cosmos going via responding to already existing as well as creating new balance-creating acts of reciprocity.

12 Moral objectivism: morality is neither conventional, relative, nor subjective.

13 A non-anthropocentric "environmental" ethics according to which: (a) the moral rightness/wrongness of actions is defined in terms of their consequences for overall cosmic balance and all persons, not just human welfare; and (b) moral consideration is extended to all persons, not just humans.

Enacting Contemporary Indigenous Philosophy

The preceding philosophical themes find concrete expression in contemporary indigenous people's continuing life-and-death struggles throughout Latin America against the insatiable and rapacious forces of neoliberal globalization. The assault upon native peoples' lives and lifeways is carried out by both transnational corporations and by *crioll@* and *mestizo@* national elites. What is presently at stake is precisely what has been at stake in the Western Hemisphere ever since Columbus: land. Indigenous peoples are simply *in the way* of European, North American, and now also Chinese capitalist economic expansion.[34] Indigenous peoples struggle against:

a Biological genocide, construed both narrowly in terms of their own individual and group biological survival and much more broadly in terms of the lives of their other-than-human relatives—what non-indigenous thought refers to as "the environment" or "nature." This includes: (i) the ongoing struggles by Lenca peoples of Honduras led by the late Berta Cáceres (co-founder of the Council of Popular and Indigenous Organizations of Honduras [COPINH] and assassinated for her efforts) against mining, logging, and dam construction projects in Lenca lands; (ii) the ongoing struggles by Nahua and Totonac peoples in Mexico against "Hydroelectric Project Puebla #1" in the Northern Sierra Mountain Range of Puebla, Mexico;[35] and (iii) the ongoing struggles of Amazonian peoples (e.g. the Huaornis and Kichwa of Ecuador, Achaur of Peru, and Kayapos of Brazil) against big agriculture, beef, mining, and oil.

b   Cultural genocide construed in terms of preserving, maintaining, and restoring the autonomy of indigenous lifeways, languages, cultures, histories, religions, and knowledges. This includes: (i) the preservation of indigenous languages through indigenous language schooling (e.g. alternative indigenous universities such as Universidad Intercultural de las Nacionalidades y Pueblos Indígenas *Amawtay Wasi* [Inter-Cultural *Amawtay Wasi* University], Ecuador, 2004–2013); through indigenous language radio broadcasting (e.g. Mapuche language radio broadcasting, "*Wixage anai!*" in Chile, and Kachikel language broadcasting on Radio Ixchel in Guatemala); and (ii) the preservation of indigenous histories by projects such as the *Taller de Historia Oral Andina* (Andean Oral History Workshop, Bolivia).[36]

Indigenous peoples seek what Aymara activist and scholar Marcelo Fernández Osco calls "pluriversality" and "plurinationalism": a decentralized world that respects and fosters a plurality of diverse peoples ("nations"), worldviews, languages, cultures, epistemologies, religions, and lifeways; one which does not strip native peoples of their identities by forcibly trying to assimilate them into the dominant monocultural paradigm of Western capitalist consumerism, scientism, and multicultural liberalism; a world that promotes what Aymara activist and President of Bolivia (2006–), Juan Evo Morales Ayma, calls *vivir bien* ("living well, living appropriately, so that others may also live") as opposed to *vivir mejor* ("living better," which consists of consuming more at the expense of the lives of others).[37] Striking a remarkably similar tone, Subcomandante Marcos, speaking for the Zapatista Army of Liberation Movement (EZLN) in Mexico, declares: "In the world of the powerful there is no space for anyone but themselves and their servants. In the world we want everyone fits. In the world we want many worlds fit."[38]

Notes

1 Quoted in Bernasconi, "African Philosophy's Challenge to Continental Philosophy," 185.
2 Santana, "Did the Aztecs Do Philosophy?"
3 Being a philosopher was not a distinct occupation for the Mexica as it is currently in Europe and North America. Mexica philosophers were also priests, rulers, warriors, poets, and medical practitioners. Nezahualcoyotl of Texcoco (an

altepetl [city-state] closely allied with Tenochtitlan), for example, was simultaneously a philosopher, poet, engineer, ruler, and warrior. As such he more closely resembles Leonardo Da Vinci than a modern-day academic such as Bertrand
Russell.

4   I borrow this from Alfred North Whitehead who made the remark in regards to
European philosophy *only*: "The safest generalization about the European philo-
sophical tradition is that it consists of series of footnotes to Plato" (*Process and
Reality*, 39). Nevertheless, I believe it succinctly captures the sentiment of most
European and North American academic philosophers regarding all philosophy.

5   The difference between truth-oriented and path-oriented philosophies is a matter
of emphasis, degree, and defining orientation. It should not be construed as a
mutually exclusive or mutually exhaustive binary. For more, see Maffie, "*In
Huehue Tlamanitiliztli* and *la Verdad*." The conception of Mexica ethics presented here is developed in Maffie, *Aztec Ethics*.

6   Nahuatl is the language spoken by the Mexica. Outsiders typically refer to native
Nahuatl-speakers as "Nahua" or "Nahuas." There are currently 1.5 million
Nahuatl-speakers in Mexico today.

7   Burkhart, *Colloquois y doctrina christiana, English Translation of Nahuatl
Paleography*, unpublished manuscript, 1982, lines 758–1042.

8   Sahagún, *Florentine Codex,* Book VI: 101; see also p.53 (emphasis by author).

9   Sahagún, *Florentine Codex,* Book VI: 228.

10   Sahagún, *Florentine Codex,* Book VI: 93.

11   Sahagún, *Florentine Codex,* Book X:29.

12   See Cohen, "Belief and Acceptance," and Goodman and Elgin, *Reconceptions in
Philosophy and Other Arts and Sciences.*

13   *Annals of Cuauhtitlan*, in *Pre-Columbian Literatures of Mexico*, 35.

14   *Annals of Cuauhtitlan*, in *History and Mythology of the Aztecs*, 26.

15   There is no Nahuatl word *for* and no Nahua concept *of* "the environment" as
understood by Western thinkers. Rather, there is simply the 5th Sun and all its
inhabitants, some of whom are human, most of whom are not.

16   Manuscript of 1558, also known as *Legend of the Suns*, fols. 75–76, translation
by Gingerich, "*Tlamachiliztlatolçaçanilli*: A Performance Translation of the
Nahuatl 'Wisdom-Discourse Fables' from the Manuscript of 1558," unpublished
manuscript, pp. 10–11 (brackets by author). Both the *Legend of the Suns* and
Annals of Cuauhtitlan are compiled in a book called the *Codex Chimalpopoca*.

17   I borrow the notion of *other-than-human person* from Hallowell, "Ojibwa
Ontology, Behavior, and World View." This discussion draws from *Legend of
the Suns* and *Histoyre du mechique*. The Maya creation story recorded in the
Popol Vuh likewise claims that creator beings created humans in order worship
them, and that they destroyed the proto-human beings of the first four ages
because they did not know how to worship properly the creator beings.

18   Quoted in Carrasco, *City of Sacrifice*, 170.

19   See Carrasco, *City of Sacrifice*, 164.

20   Tambiah, *Magic, Science, Religion, and the Scope of Rationality*, 108. Emphasis
mine.

21   I borrow this from Catherine Allen's characterization of contemporary indigenous Andean (Quechua) metaphysics in *The Hold Life Has*, 73.

22   One of the most racist portrayals of pre-Columbian peoples is found in Mel
Gibson's 2006 film "Apocalypto."

23   Such statements are made in *Legend of the Suns* and *Colloquois de los doce*. For
translation of *macehua*, see Molina, *Vocabulario en lengua castellana y mexicana
y mexicana y castellana*.

24   McDonough, "Plotting Indigenous Stories, Land and People," 21.

25 See López Austin and López Luján, "Aztec Human Sacrifice"; and Carrasco, *City of Sacrifice*.

26 For related discussion of contemporary Nahua philosophy, see: Taggart, *Remembering Victoria*; Good, *Work and Exchange in Nahuatl Society*; Sandstrom, "Anthropology Gets Religion"; and Sandstrom and Sandstrom, *Following the Straight Path*.

27 See Lipp, *The Mixe of Oaxaca*, 83; Good, *Work and Exchange in Nahuatl Society*.

28 I borrow here from Hanks, *Referential Practice*, 364.

29 León-Portilla, "Those Made Worthy by Divine Sacrifice," 41–64. Brackets by author.

30 For related discussion, see Deloria, *God Is Red: A Native View of Religion*, and Kidwell, Noley, and Tinker, *A Native American Theology*.

31 For a thorough examination of Mexica ontology, see Maffie, *Aztec Philosophy*.

32 Molina, *Vocabulario en lengua castellana y mexicana y mexicana y castellana*, Bk II: 8r.

33 *Florentine Codex*, Book IX, 95; Book X, 11.

34 For further discussion, see Postero and Zamosc, *The Struggle for Indigenous Rights in Latin America*. Its communist lip service notwithstanding, the People's Republic of China has embraced capitalism since the early 1980s.

35 See http://voicesinmovement.org/the-aggression-continues-in-the-totonac-comm unities-by-the-hydroelectric-project-puebla-1/. Thanks to Kelly McDonough for bringing this struggle to my attention.

36 Here again a web search finds countless indigenous radio projects throughout Latin America.

37 Morales, speech.

38 EZLN, Fourth Declaration of the Lancandon Jungle, January 1996.

Bibliography

Allen, Catherine. *The Hold Life Has: Coca and Cultural Identity in an Andean Community*, 2nd ed. Washington: Smithsonian Books, 2002.

Annals of Cuauhtitlan. In *Pre-Columbian Literatures of Mexico*. Edited by Miguel León-Portilla. Translated by Miguel León-Portilla and Grace Lobanov. Norman: University of Oklahoma Press, 1969.

Annals of Cuauhtitlan. In *History and Mythology of the Aztecs: The Codex Chimalpopoca*. Translated by John Bierhorst. Tucson: University of Arizona Press, 1992.

Bernasconi, Robert. "African Philosophy's Challenge to Continental Philosophy." In *Postcolonial African Philosophy: A Critical Reader*, edited by Emmanuel Chukwadi Eze, 83–93. Oxford: Blackwell, 1997.

Burkhart, Louise. *The Slippery Earth: Nahua Christian Dialogues in Sixteenth-Century Mexico*. Tucson: University of Arizona Press, 1989.

Colloquois y doctrina christiana, English Translation of Nahuatl Paleography. Unpublished manuscript, 1982.

Carrasco, Davíd. *City of Sacrifice*. Boston: Beacon Press, 1999.

Cohen, Jonathan. "Belief and Acceptance," *Mind* 98, no. 391 (July 1989): 367–389.

Deloria, Jr., Vine. *God Is Red: A Native View of Religion*, Golden, CO: Fulcrum Publishing, 1994.

Gingerich, Willard. *Tlamachiliztlatolçaçanilli: A Performance Translation of the Nahuatl "Wisdom-Discourse Fables" from the Manuscript of 1558*. Unpublished manuscript.

Good, Catherine. *Work and Exchange in Nahuatl Society: Local Values and the Dynamics of an Indigenous Economy*. ProQuest Dissertations and Theses, 1993.

Goodman, Nelson and Catherine Z. Elgin. *Reconceptions in Philosophy and other Arts and Sciences*. Indianapolis: Hackett, 1988.

Hallowell, A. Irving. "Ojibwa Ontology, Behavior, and World View." In *Contributions to Anthropology: Selected Papers of A. Irving Hallowell*, 357–390. Chicago: University of Chicago Press, 1979.

Hanks, William F. *Referential Practice*. Chicago: University of Chicago Press, 1990.

Historia de los mexicanos por sus pinturas and Histoyre du mechique. In *Teogonía e historia de los mexicanos: Tres opúsculos del siglo XVI*. Edited by Angel María Garibay Kintana. México: Editorial Porrúa, 1965.

Kidwell, Clara Sue, Homer Noley, and George E. Tinker. *A Native American Theology*. Maryknoll, NY: Orbis Books, 2002.

Legend of the Suns. In *History and Mythology of the Aztecs: The Codex Chimalpopoca*. Translated by John Bierhorst. Tucson: University of Arizona Press, 1992.

León-Portilla, Miguel. "Those Made Worthy by Divine Sacrifice: The Faith of Ancient Mexico." In *South and Mesoamerican Spirituality: From the Cult of the Feathered Serpent to the Theology of Liberation*, edited by Miguel León-Portilla and Gary Gossen, 41–64. New York: Crossroads, 1993.

Lipp, Frank. *The Mixe of Oaxaca*. Austin: University of Texas, 1991.

López Austin, Alfredo, and Leonardo López Luján, "Aztec Human Sacrifice." In *The Aztec World*, edited by Elizabeth M. Brumfield and Gary Feinman, 137–148. New York: Abrams, 2008.

Maffie, James. "In Huehue Tlamanitiliztli and la Verdad: Nahua and European Philosophies in Fray Bernardino de Sahagún's Colloquios y doctrina Cristiana." *Inter-America Journal of Philosophy* 3(2012):1–33.

Maffie, James. *Aztec Philosophy: Understanding a World in Motion*. Boulder: University Press of Colorado, 2014.

Maffie, James. *Aztec Ethics: Balancing a World in Motion*. Forthcoming

Marcos, Subcomandante. *Fourth Declaration of the Lancandon Jungle*. January1996. https://en.wikisource.org/wiki/Fourth_Declaration_of_the_Lancandon_Jungle

McDonough, Kelly. "Plotting Indigenous Stories, Land and People: Primordial Titles and Narrative Mapping in Colonial Mexico." *Journal of Early Modern Cultural Studies* 17, no. 1(2017): 1–30.

Molina, Alonso de. *Vocabulario en lengua castellana y mexicana y mexicana y castellana*, 4th ed. Facsimile of 1571 edition. Mexico City: Porrúa, 2001.

Morales Ayma, Juan Evo. http://www.worldfuturefund.org/Reports/G77/moralessp eech.html.

Popol Vuh: The Sacred Book of the Maya. Translated by Allen J. Christiansen. Norman: University of Oklahoma Press, 2007.

Postero, Nancy Grey, and Léon Zamosc. *The Struggle for Indigenous Rights in Latin America*. Brighton: Sussex Academic Press, 2004.

Sahagún, Bernardino de. *Florentine Codex: General History of the Things of New Spain*. Translated and edited by Arthur J.O. Anderson and Charles Dibble. Santa Fe: School of American Research; Salt Lake City: University of Utah Press, 1953–1982.

Sahagún, Bernardino de. *Coloquois y doctrina cristiana. Edición facsmilar, introducción, paleografíía, version del Náhuatl y notas de Miguel León-Portilla*. Ciudad Universitaria: Universidad Nacional Autónoma del México, 1985.

Sandstrom, Alan R. "Anthropology Gets Religion: Cultural Ecology, Pantheism, and Paper Dolls among the Nahua People of Mexico." *Paradigms for Anthropology: An Ethnographic Reader*, 57–74. Edited by E. Paul Durrenberger and Suzan Erem. Boulder: Paradigm Press, 2010.

Sandstrom, Alan R. and Pamela E. Sandstrom. *Following the Straight Path: Pilgrimage in Contemporary Nahua Religion*. Forthcoming.

Santana, Alejandro. "Did the Aztecs Do Philosophy?" *APA Newsletter on Hispanics/ Latino Issues in Philosophy* 8, no. 1(2008): 2–9.

Taggart, James M. *Remembering Victoria*. Austin: University of Texas Press, 2007.

Tambiah, Stanley Jeyaraja. *Magic, Science, Religion, and the Scope of Rationality*. Cambridge: Cambridge University Press, 1990.

Whitehead, Alfred North. *Process and Reality*. New York: Free Press, 1979.

2 "The Indian Problem"

Conquest and the Valladolid Debate

Alejandro Santana

Introduction

"The Indian Problem" generally refers to a complex set of related questions that Europeans, mostly Spaniards, raised about their treatment of the indigenous peoples of the Americas (whom I will refer to as Amerindians). Understanding how this set of questions first emerged in Latin America requires some historical context, as does the Spanish controversy about them. This controversy was on full display during 1550–1551, when a debate was held in Valladolid, Spain. There, Juan Ginés de Sepúlveda and Bartolomé de las Casas debated how best to address this "problem." In this chapter, I will briefly sketch the historical context that gave rise to the main questions of "The Indian Problem." I will then outline how some problematic answers to these questions have their roots in Aristotelian philosophy. Next, I will outline the positions advanced by Sepúlveda and Las Casas at Valladolid, and then briefly sketch the contemporary relevance of both "The Indian Problem" and the context from which it emerged.

The Emergence of "The Indian Problem" during the Spanish Conquest

Beginning in 1492, Amerindians of the Western hemisphere were confronted by European explorers, mostly Spaniards, arriving on the coasts of their home lands. These explorers were ostensibly looking for new oceanic trade routes to India, but they were also looking for glory, fortune, or both. The Spanish, for their part, encountered diverse peoples and cultures inhabiting a land abundant with material wealth and natural resources.

These initial encounters were soon followed by acts of extreme violence, cruelty, and exploitation, with the Amerindians suffering at the hands of Spanish conquistadors. Dominican friar Bartolomé de las Casas tells of numerous atrocities, many of which he witnessed first-hand. He tells of Spaniards hacking innocent Amerindians to pieces:

slicing open their bellies with their swords as though they were so many sheep herded into a pen. They even laid wagers on whether they could manage to slice a man in two at a stroke, or cut an individual's head from his body, or disembowel him with a single blow of their axes. They grabbed suckling infants by the feet and, ripping them from their mothers' breasts, dashed them headlong against the rocks. Others, laughing and joking all the while, threw them over their shoulders into a river ... They slaughtered anyone and everyone in their path, on occasion running through a mother and her baby with a single thrust of their swords.[1]

Las Casas also tells of Spaniards hacking off Amerindian ears, noses, and hands simply for the fun of it, engaging in live baby-throwing contests, and feeding their dogs with the limbs of dismembered children.[2]

After subjugating Amerindian communities, the Spanish imposed an oppressive *encomienda* system, in which land and a quantity of Amerindians were entrusted to a Spanish grantee, or *encomendero*, for the profit of the grantee.[3] The Amerindians were not legally slaves and were regarded as free persons, but they were not allowed the choice to leave.[4] They were also very much treated as slaves, with numerous accounts of horrible abuses by *encomenderos*.[5]

Against this backdrop of violence and oppression, the Pope and the Spanish Crown made official pronouncements in an attempt to regulate and bring order to European—at this time, mainly Spanish and Portuguese—colonial expansion. Some pronouncements regulated the distribution of land, while others attempted to regulate the treatment of Amerindians.[6] Regarding the latter, a formal declaration known as the *Requerimiento* was adopted in an attempt to justify the conquest of Amerindian peoples, especially those who would not submit to Spanish rule. It required the Amerindians to whom it was read to acknowledge the authority of both the Pope and the Spanish Crown as their superiors and lords. It also issued an ultimatum threatening extreme violence to those who refused to acknowledge this authority.[7] The *Requerimiento* was to be read, in Spanish and in the presence of a notary, to Amerindian groups prior to the commencement of any hostilities.[8] In practice, however, it was often read without interpreters and when the Amerindians to whom it was directed were asleep or out of earshot.[9] The Amerindians were thus expected to comply—and be punished for failure to comply—with demands that they often didn't understand.

In contrast, both the Pope and the Spanish Crown later made *other* pronouncements stipulating that the Amerindians were free, rational, and not to be stripped of their possessions.[10] Amidst these official pronouncements, opinions varied about the nature and character of Amerindian peoples. They varied between what has been described as two opposing views: the "Dirty Dog" view and the "Noble Savage" view.[11] Those who held the "Dirty Dog" view described the Amerindians in various ways, but they were ultimately thought to be uncultured, uncivilized idolaters who were vicious, obscene, unintelligent, and lazy. One early proponent of this view was John Major: "Those people live like beasts on either side of the equator and between the poles live men like wild beasts."[12] John Major was the first conquest-era scholar to argue that the Amerindians were natural slaves, in the Aristotelian sense.[13] Another proponent was Domingo de Betzanos, who claimed that the Amerindians were "beasts and that God had condemned the whole race to perish for the horrible sins that they had committed in their paganism."[14] Perhaps the most strident of all was royal officer and historian Gonzalo Fernández de Oviedo:

> [The Amerindians are] naturally lazy and vicious, melancholic, cowardly, and in general a lying, shiftless, people. Their marriages are not a sacrament but a sacrilege. They are idolatrous, libidinous, and commit sodomy. Their chief desire is to eat, drink, worship heathen idols, and commit bestial obscenities.[15]

Oviedo was also in charge of the iron used to brand Amerindians like cattle, and he collected fees for its use in doing so.[16]

According to the "Noble Savage" view, the Amerindians were full human beings capable of civilization, education, and understanding the Christian faith. Antonio de Montesinos was among the earliest proponent of this view, and he expressed this in a famous and controversial sermon (1511) during which he announced to his astounded parishioners, "I am a lone voice crying in the wilderness," and asked "Are these Indians not men? Do they not have rational souls? Are you not obliged to love them as you love yourselves?"[17] Most notable was the view of perhaps the most eminent theologian of his day, Francisco de Vitoria:

> The Indian aborigines ... are not of unsound mind ... but have according to their own kind, the use of reason. This is clear because there is a certain method in their affairs; they have polities which are carefully arranged and they have definite marriage and magistrates, overlords, laws, and workshops, and a system of exchange, all of which call for the use of reason; they also have a kind of religion.[18]

Amidst all of these confusing tensions, the Holy Roman Emperor Charles V called a halt to any further conquest and commissioned a council to hear arguments on whether these conquests and treatment of the Amerindians were just.[19] The council met during 1550–1551 in Valladolid, Spain. Juan Ginéz de Sepúlveda advanced his case for the "Dirty Dog" view and was followed by Franciscan priest Bartolomé de las Casas, who presented perhaps the most ardent defense of the "Noble Savage" view. The debate was to focus on one question: "Is it lawful for the King of Spain to make war on the Amerindians before preaching the faith to them, in order to subject them to his rule, so that afterward they may be more easily instructed in the faith?"[20] *This* is central question of "The Indian Problem" during the conquest.

As mentioned above, this "problem" refers to a complex set of related questions that emerged in the aftermath of the Amerindian-European encounter. For the Spanish, these questions emerged from a fundamental tension: On the one hand, they had an insatiable desire for wealth and imperial expansion into new lands; on the other hand, they had to contend with the basic fact that people already possessed the wealth they coveted and lived on the land into which they wished to expand. This tension was complicated by the fact that the Pope granted Amerindian lands to Spain, but also charged the Spanish Crown with spreading Christianity among its inhabitants.[21] Spanish desire for conquest was thus inextricably linked to a duty to spread the faith.

These tensions led to questions regarding the nature and limits of royal authority over Amerindian peoples. By what right were the Spanish entitled to rule over the Amerindians, and what was the extent of this rule?[22] Since much of royal authority was related to the authority of the Pope, correlate questions were raised about the nature and limits of papal authority over the Amerindians regarding religious matters. What authority did the Pope have over people who were not Christian and generally had no interest in becoming Christian?

Things were further complicated by determined Amerindian resistance to this imperial and religious expansion, and the brutal tactics the Spanish used to bring them into submission. All of this vexed some who were called upon to carry out these imperial incursions, especially some in the clergy, who were tasked to carry out the conversion of peoples who were victims of extraordinary levels of violence, oppression, and property dispossession.[23] This raised additional questions about whether it was justifiable to use force to convert the Amerindians to Christianity.

Added to this were questions about whether the Amerindians could be converted to Christianity in the first place: more specifically, whether the Amerindians had the rational capacity to understand the Christian faith. And this controversy gave rise to yet another question over whether it was worth the effort to educate the Amerindians, religiously or otherwise. Perhaps most fundamentally, the brute imposition of both royal and papal authority raised questions about what rights Amerindians had both as human beings and as independently existing peoples.[24]

Answers to these questions ultimately turned on the issue of Amerindian rational capacity, and views among the Spanish on this question divided roughly along the "Dirty Dog" or "Noble Savage" lines mentioned above. More specifically, some thought that the Amerindians were not fully rational and thereby not fully human. They were "natural slaves," that is, they were made by nature to be slaves.[25] On this view, Amerindian subjugation was entirely appropriate, because it befit their naturally limited rationality and thereby their place in nature. Amerindians who resisted subjugation were clearly in the wrong, because they were resisting the legitimate authority of people who were their natural superiors. The question of whether to Christianize them would depend on whether the Amerindians had enough rational capacity, though limited, to understand the faith.

Others affirmed the view that the Amerindians were fully rational and therefore fully human. The Amerindians were thus free by nature, not natural slaves, and their wholesale subjugation was entirely unjustified. The Spanish crown could not justifiably dispossess Amerindians of their property and reduce them to servitude for the same reason it could not forcibly convert them to Christianity. If so, then the *encomienda* system—with all the natural resource appropriation, labor exploitation, and wealth extraction it involved—was also unjustified. The Amerindians were also fully capable of Christianization and, more importantly, fully capable of *peaceful* conversion. Forcible conversion was therefore inappropriate and unjustified.

In sum, the question of whether the Spanish could lawfully make war on the Amerindians prior to their religious conversion ultimately raised questions about the rational capacities of the Amerindians themselves. The answer to this question would potentially shape both imperial and papal policy regarding their subjugation, as well as on how best to convert them. Although there were diverse views on Amerindian rationality, they ultimately fell into a dichotomy: either they were to be considered fully rational or not. And this would determine whether or not they were fully human, endowed with all the rights possessed by any other human being. And if they weren't, the main explanatory concept on hand was natural slavery. The philosophical view that nature made whole groups of people fit for slavery has a long history that goes back to Aristotle, to whom I will now turn.

Aristotle's Theory of Natural Slavery

Aristotle offers the most extensive philosophical treatment and defense of natural slavery that we get from the Ancient Greek world, and his view provides the philosophical basis for Sepúlveda's position. Aristotle's view on natural slavery is explicitly elaborated in his *Politics* (book I, chaps 3–6), and his treatment unfolds in several phases.[26]

To begin with, he outlines several relationships that make up a Greek household, which was the most basic social unit of a Greek city-state (1253b1–13). A household consisted of a marital relationship between husband and wife, a procreative relationship between father and children, and a masterly relationship between master and slave. All three relations were necessary for the proper functioning of a Greek household.

For Aristotle, the master-slave relation was necessary, because a household manager needed assistants to run the household (1253b22–1254a12). As within any specialized craft, an assistant is a tool, which is a piece of property that belongs entirely to its owner. However, some tools are inanimate while others are animate. For Aristotle, slaves are animate tools; the best that can come from them is what they can do with their bodies. In this sense, slaves are more like oxen—the master uses the slave's body to perform labor that the master commands. Since slaves are tools of their masters, and tools are property, and since property belongs entirely to its owner, then slaves belong entirely to their masters.[27] With this, Aristotle gives his first definition of a natural slave (*phusei doulos*):

> For anyone who, despite being human, is by nature not his own but someone else's is a natural slave. And he is someone else's when, despite being human, he is a piece of property; and a piece of property is a tool for action that is separate from its owner. (1254a13–17)

According to Aristotle, natural slaves existed due to what he thought were some important features of how nature works (1254a16–34). He begins with claims about the nature of ruling and being ruled. Ruling and being ruled are both necessary and beneficial in life. But some are naturally suited to rule while others are naturally suited to be ruled.

Aristotle then applies these general premises to the rule between constitutive parts *within* animals (1254a34–1254b9). Soul and body are the basic constituents of an animal, and the soul is the natural ruler, while the body is the natural subject. The soul rules the body with the rule of a master, because the soul orders the body to do what it wishes. This is seen in the contrast between virtuous and depraved people: in the former, the soul is the ruler; in the latter, the body is. Since a virtuous person is a good person, the order observed in this person represents both the most natural and best state in which a person could be.

Next, Aristotle extends these considerations to the rule *between* animals (1254b10–15). Domestic animals are naturally superior to wild ones; humans are naturally superior to non-human animals; males are naturally superior to females; and rulers are naturally superior to the ruled. Indeed, the same holds for *all* human beings: it is better for the naturally superior to rule the naturally inferior. Across each category, the capacity for reason is the decisive factor for each type of rule.

For Aristotle, natural slaves completely lacked the capacity for rational deliberation and thereby were incapable of full rationality (1252a31–33; 1260a12). They had a share in reason insofar as they could understand the reasoning of their master, but they did not have it themselves (1254b22–24). This limited rational capacity meant that for Aristotle, natural slaves were *defective* forms of the human species.[28] It made them simply incapable of full virtue and thereby incapable of being fully good human beings, and this ultimately explained why they were naturally inferior to those who were their natural superiors.

Aristotle then draws his grand conclusion regarding the existence of natural slaves and whether it is beneficial to enslave them:

Therefore those people who are as different from others as body is from soul or beast from human, and people whose task, that is to say, the best thing to come from them, is to use their bodies are in this condition—those people are natural slaves. And it is better for them to be subject to this rule, since it is also better for the other things we mentioned. For he who can belong to someone else (and that is why he actually does belong to someone else), and he who shares in reason to the extent of understanding it, but does not have it himself (for the other animals obey not reason but feelings), is a natural slave. The difference in the use made of [slaves and domestic animals] is small, since both slaves and domestic animals help provide the necessities with their bodies. (1254b16–25)[29]

Given that there are such natural slaves, it would be entirely appropriate to enslave them; put simply, nature made them for it.[30] And if such people were *not* enslaved—that is, if they happened to be free—then it would be *better* to enslave them, just as it would be better for an ox to be under the care of an oxherd rather than roam free.

Here, it is important to emphasize that Aristotle did not present a novel view on slavery; instead, he developed a philosophical explanation that generally adhered to the conventional beliefs of his time.[31] As with the rest of the Ancient Mediterranean world, the Ancient Greeks widely considered slavery to be a basic fact of life, and the slave population was quite large. Although he agreed that some enslaved people were not natural slaves, he explicitly endorsed the view that some people were (1255b2–9). Aristotle thus codified and granted philosophical legitimacy to this view, the influence of which would be felt later in European history.[32] In the Western, Global North philosophical tradition, the influence of Aristotle's view is explicit in the work of the medieval philosopher and theologian, St. Thomas Aquinas, who argued for a modified version of Aristotle's view on slavery and whose view of natural law was adopted by both Sepúlveda and Las Casas.[33] It is to Sepúlveda's view that I will now turn.

Sepúlveda: *Democrates Segundo*

The basis for the position Sepúlveda took at Valladolid is detailed in his work *Democrates Segundo*.[34] There, he begins by arguing that just war is permissible under natural law. He then outlines the importance of following natural law and gives the conditions under which war is justified (*DS*, 14–26). Here, as mentioned above, Sepúlveda draws on Aquinas, who defined natural law as the "participation in the eternal law by rational creatures."[35] Natural law is underwritten by God's eternal law and is accessible to natural reason.[36] It constitutes basic moral principles built into nature to which all rational creatures are inherently inclined and, upon the proper use of reason, would find are for the common good.[37] Natural law therefore has universal jurisdiction and provides the fundamental basis for law within nations, between nations, and the just treatment of all human beings.[38] At the Valladolid debate, natural law provided one of the main bases (along with scripture and the writing of church authorities) that both Sepúlveda and Las Casas used to evaluate the justice and legality of the Spanish treatment of the Amerindians, including making war on them.

According to Sepúlveda, war against the Amerindians is just, and he gives four arguments to support his claim. First, he argues that the Amerindians are natural slaves (*siervos por naturaleza*) by invoking Aristotle's argument that the better should rule the worse:

> being barbarians by nature, uneducated and inhumane, [the Amerindians] refuse to admit the domination of those who are more prudent, powerful and perfect than they are; domination that would bring them great utilities, being also a just thing, by natural right, that matter obeys to form, body to soul, appetite to reason, brutes to man, woman to husband, children to father, imperfect to perfect, worst to best, for the universal good of all things. This is the natural order that the divine and eternal law commands to observe always. (*DS*, 58, translation my own)

And he considers it obvious that the Spanish are superior to the Amerindians (*DS*, 35–38). The Spanish are superior in theology, philosophy, astronomy, strength, humanity, justice, religion, bravery, temperance, frugality, and sobriety. The Amerindians are accomplished in none of these endeavors, nor do they have a habit of temperance or gentleness.

Although the Amerindians show some degree of ingenuity, this does not prove that they are equals to the Spanish. Birds and spiders make things that humans can't imitate. And the fact that Amerindians build houses, engage in trade, and have some rational way of living only proves that "they are not bears or monkeys" and not totally without reason; however, this does not prove that they are equals to the Spanish (*DS*, 38–39). Moreover, they practice human sacrifice and cannibalism (*DS*, 40). Given all of this, there is no doubt in Sepúlveda's mind that the Amerindians have been justly conquered by better people.[39]

Second, Amerindians practice human sacrifice and cannibalism, which are sins against natural law that Christians have a duty to stop. Scripture proves that God hates these sins: Old Testament stories detail how God exterminated people for sins like sexual immorality and idolatry (*DS*, 40–41). And natural law applies to everyone, not just those who are subject to Christian rule (*DS*, 44). Given this, such crimes should be stopped and punished.

The fact that the Amerindians are pagans who have had no previous exposure to Christianity is irrelevant. War is not appropriate for the simple fact that they are pagans; however, it is appropriate, because the Amerindians commit crimes that are hateful to God. We can even make just war on entire Amerindian nations, as these crimes are endorsed in their public institutions, thereby implicating entire nations as violators of natural law and rendering them liable to overthrow (DS, 45–46). Indeed, the Pope might not have the power or authority (*la potestad*) to oblige the Amerindians to accept Christian laws, but he does have the power to stop them from wrongdoing, and only then can they be brought to better customs and to Christianity (DS, 46).

Third, there is a duty to protect innocent people from becoming victims to the Amerindian practice of human sacrifice and cannibalism (DS, 47–51). It is important to punish offenses to God, for all upright humane people are obliged to punish offenses to friends and neighbors, including innocent Amerindians. This is especially true if punishing these offensive practices saves the lives of innocent people who would otherwise be sacrificed; failure to do so is an act of omission as serious as the crimes themselves.

Fourth, Christians have a duty to spread the faith, and this cannot be done without first subjugating those who resist. This doesn't mean that the Amerindians must be forced to *believe* Christianity, for belief can't be forced against one's will, nor should they be baptized by force (DS, 51). However, the same right that justifies their subjugation also grants the right to compel them, by force if necessary, to *listen* to gospel teaching (DS, 52).

Indeed, the Amerindians can be invited to Christianity, but they can also be forced to it (DS, 53–54). Jesus forced Paul to the ground and to the faith, and he whipped people from the temple. The gospel parable of the "Great Feast" (Luke 14:15–25) also permits one to "compel them to enter" (DS, 54). In this parable, Jesus tells the story of a man who hosts a banquet for his invited guests, who then cancel on the day of the banquet. So the man orders his servants to compel people off the streets to attend his banquet, so that his house would be full of guests. For Sepúlveda, this parable is evidence for the permissibility of compelling unbelievers to the faith, by force if necessary.[40]

Lastly, it is permissible to have preachers protected by armed soldiers. It is important for preachers to proceed with caution, as some were killed when they had wandered into Amerindian lands alone or when protective Spanish garrisons had been removed (DS, 55).

Las Casas: *In Defense of the Indians*

Las Casas' *Defense* is a large volume that aims to refute each of Sepúlveda's four arguments. To do so, he gives a relentless barrage of argumentation delivered with extraordinarily deep conviction and intense passion. It is beyond the scope of this section to cover each argument in meticulous detail; rather, I will outline Las Casas' broad argumentative maneuvers, supplying detail as necessary to convey the general point of his arguments.

Refutation of Sepúlveda's first argument

Las Casas begins by arguing that the Amerindians are *not* natural slaves. He does this by first drawing distinctions between four types of barbarians. The first kind of barbarian is "any cruel, inhuman, wild, and merciless man acting against human reason out of anger or native disposition" (D, 28–29). The second kind are "those who do not have a written language that corresponds to the spoken one" or those with a language different from ours (D, 30–31). Third are those in the strict sense, who "because of their evil and wicked character or the barrenness of the region in which they live, are cruel, savage, sottish, stupid, and strangers to reason" (D, 32). The fourth are simply all non-Christians (D, 49).

For Las Casas, the Amerindians are not barbarians of the first type; indeed, if any group of people have proven themselves to be such barbarians, it is the Spanish conquistadors: "in the absolutely inhuman things [the Spanish] have done to those nations they have surpassed all other barbarians" (D, 29). Indeed, Amerindians are barbarians of the second type; however, this type is understood in a restricted sense (D, 31). Such people are called barbarians because their language isn't understood by others; however, they can be virtuous and lead a settled life. Hence, this is not the kind of barbarian to which Aristotle was referring when he discussed natural slaves that cannot govern themselves.

What Aristotle had in mind were barbarians of the third type, which are understood in the absolute sense, as they are wild, unsociable people who do not engage in any form of civilized life (D, 32–33). However, such people are freaks of nature and must be very rare (D, 35). If this type included many people, then the design in God's creation would ultimately be ineffective and reduce the perfection of the entire universe, because it would consistently create masses of wild people who would be incapable of a proper relationship with God (D, 36). Hence, there is no good reason to believe that the entire population of Amerindians is of this type.

The Amerindians, however, are barbarians of the fourth type, but so are all other non-Christians, and this doesn't justify making war on them. Ultimately, Sepúlveda's argument fails to recognize these distinctions between different types of barbarian and thereby conflates them. He therefore commits the fallacy of equivocation, which renders his argument defective (D, 52–53).[41]

Refutation of Sepúlveda's second argument

Next, Las Casas argues that the church *cannot* make just war to punish bad Amerindian practices. The church can punish another's sins only if it has jurisdiction, or rightful authority, over them. There are four ways in which unbelievers can be subject to rightful Church authority, and *none* of these ways applies to the Amerindians; hence, the Church has no jurisdiction over them.[42]

This is because Christ has *potential* but not *actual* jurisdiction over unbelievers (D, 55–56).

God has granted Christ, and therefore the church, power over all nations, believing or unbelieving. Unbelievers who have accepted Christ and willingly received baptism are rendered actually subject to Christ and the Church. Those who have not done these things are not actually subject to Christ, but are potentially so:

> unbelievers are subject to Christ only potentially, not actually, and thus do not belong to his authority or jurisdiction, insofar as it is potential, until they be converted or die or until the end of the world, when Christ will exercise his full power over all persons by condemning the evil and rewarding the good. And then all things will be actually subject to him. (*D*, 58–59)

Given this, the Church has merely *potential* but not *actual* jurisdiction over unbelievers. Since Christ is the head of the Church, the jurisdiction of the Church cannot be greater than the jurisdiction of Christ.[43] And since Christ has potential jurisdiction over unbelievers, then so does the Church.

For Las Casas, the lack of actual jurisdiction implies that the Church and their members, including Christian rulers, cannot punish unbelievers. Las Casas establishes this with eleven sub-arguments (*D*, 71–103), which can be condensed into the following points. First, it is not the Church's business to either judge or punish unbelievers, and this is supported by numerous Church authorities, including Jerome, Ambrose, Augustine, Aquinas, Peter, Paul, and the words of Christ himself. Second, whoever is unable to punish unbelief is unable to punish idolatry. Idolatry is a sub-category of superstition, which presupposes paganism, which itself presupposes unbelief (*D*, 76). However, since the Amerindians are outside the jurisdiction of the Church, it cannot punish unbelief and therefore cannot punish idolatry. Third, for those who have neither heard nor resisted the preaching of the faith, it is simply inappropriate and out of order to begin preaching with punishment; instead, preaching should begin peacefully by freely offering the faith, the forgiveness of sins, and the exhortation to penance (*D*, 87–91). Therefore, the Amerindians are not actually subject to Christ, the Church, or any Christian; hence, there is no basis for making war on them or punishing them. As Las Casas summarizes it,

> no pagan can be punished by the Church—much less by Christian rulers—for a superstition, no matter how abominable, or a crime, no matter how serious, as long as he commits it precisely within the borders of the territory of his own masters and his own unbelief. (*D*, 97)

Refutation of Sepúlveda's third argument

Next, Las Casas argues that where the Church has jurisdiction to save the innocent, this jurisdiction (a) should not always be exercised and (b) is *no* reason to make war, especially since (c) there are viable and peaceful alternatives. There are six cases in which the Church can exercise jurisdiction over unbelievers (*D*, 118, 119, 165, 168, 183–184, and 185–186). The first is when unbelievers unjustly possess Christian lands. The second is when they practice idolatry in lands formerly under Christian jurisdiction. The third is when unbelievers are knowingly blasphemous toward the Christian religion. The fourth is when they deliberately hinder the spread of Christianity or persecute those who accept it. The fifth is when unbelievers attack Christian territories. The sixth is when they practice cannibalism or human sacrifice (Sepúlveda's third argument).

Las Casas responds to these cases with another barrage of argumentation. The first case does not apply, because the Amerindians do not unjustly hold Christian lands, and it is absurd to expect them to recognize the dominion of a far-off church that they have never before encountered (*D*, 119). The second case doesn't apply either, because the Amerindians do not practice idolatry in former Christian lands, and it is absurd to think that Christians should punish idolatry everywhere in the world, even in non-Christian lands.

Here, Old Testament stories of God punishing idolatry in far-off lands do not apply, as not all of God's actions are intended to be examples for us to imitate. In some cases, God intended his actions to be "admired rather than imitated" (*D*, 121). If God intended these actions to be imitated, then many absurdities would follow, as it would imply the destruction of many cities in pagan lands and the slaughter of many pagan people. Instead, God severely punished idolatry at first "so that by this severe example he would frighten men from committing similar sins" (*D*, 121–122). It is therefore unlawful for humans to punish unbelievers simply for being idolaters (*D*, 140).

Additionally, if believers are invincibly ignorant, then they cannot be punished simply for being idolaters.[44] Whoever is invincibly ignorant is excused from the guilt associated with acting in accordance with their ignorance.

> He is invincibly ignorant and so excused from guilt who cannot dispel that ignorance by himself or by asking others. Now unbelievers of this type cannot ferret out matters of faith by their own efforts since these matters are beyond every faculty of nature, nor is there anyone whom they can question or consult or by whom they may be taught in the ordinary course of nature. Therefore they are invincibly ignorant in their worship of idols. (*D*, 128)

In sum, the bearer of such ignorance is excused due to the extraordinary difficulty of dispelling it: One is surrounded by people with the same ignorance, and it is publicly endorsed by everyone, including people in positions of authority.

Regarding the third case, Amerindian unbelievers cannot be blamed for speaking blasphemously about Christianity, since they are not referring to the Christian religion but to Christians who have mistreated them (*D*, 165). The fourth case does not apply because the Amerindians do not know what is preached to them and thus can be excused of their malice towards Christians, including preachers. The Amerindians have suffered extreme cruelty and countless injuries at the hands of the Spanish (D, 171). Consequently, they have killed preachers, not because the preachers are Christian; they have killed preachers because the preachers are *Spanish* (D, 172). In fact, they would be justified killing many preachers—even St. Paul himself—if he had conducted himself the way the Spanish have (D, 172). At any rate, the Amerindians are entirely justified in ignoring preachers who are accompanied by armed soldiers:

> I shall speak boldly and do not flinch to state openly that if preachers are accompanied by the clatter of arms when they go forth to announce the gospel to any people, by that very fact they are unworthy to have their words believed. For what does the gospel have to do with fire-arms? What does the herald of the gospel have to do with armed thieves? Instead, those who would believe such preachers would be very inconstant and foolish rather than clever, and those who spurn their words could, to some extent, be excused in God's sight. Nor would they be obliged to believe the apostles or even Christ himself, our redeemer, if they preached the gospel in this way. (D, 173–174)

Christians are obligated to spread Christianity, but Christians are not obligated to force people to hear or accept the gospel (D, 175–176). Hence, war must not be waged to force the Amerindians to the gospel, even if they kill preachers.

The fifth case obviously doesn't apply because Amerindians have not attacked or harassed any Christian lands. The sixth case *does* apply; however, such jurisdiction should not always be exercised and is *no* reason to make war, especially if there are viable and peaceful alternatives.

Las Casas offers several reasons for his conclusion about the sixth case, which can be summarized in the following points: First, "If one cannot avoid both of two evils, he must choose the lesser evil, according to the dictates of right reason" (D, 256). For Las Casas, the death of a few innocent people due to human sacrifice and cannibalistic practices is a *lesser* evil than the eternal damnation of countless numbers of innocent people killed in the fury of war. In the fog of war, "the innocent cannot be distinguished from the guilty" (D, 256). Consequently, "more innocent persons would perish than would be rescued, and we are forbidden by a very strict negative precept [in the Ten Commandments] to kill an innocent person" (D, 256). Avoiding war also avoids the overthrow of whole nations, with all its accompanying death and destruction. Ultimately, using war to prevent cannibalism and human sacrifice is neither just nor virtuous: One mustn't punish a crime if the punishment makes things worse; hence, one mustn't punish to *prevent* a crime when many more would be killed in order to do so (D, 213). Second, God's word is more effective than war, and experience has shown that Christianity is best spread only through preaching the gospel (D, 249–250). Hence, there is a peaceful and effective alternative to war. Third and most importantly, "God and his holy Church, by means of which he wants men to be saved and to come to the knowledge of the truth, would be frustrated" (D, 257).

In the course of giving these reasons, Las Casas presents far-reaching arguments regarding cannibalism and human sacrifice that are worth summarizing. To being with, Las Casas affirms that Amerindians who practice cannibalism and human sacrifice are in grave error due to invincible ignorance. However, he argues that some instances of cannibalism are not contrary to natural law and thereby not sinful, for example, when people are starving and overcome by hunger (D, 219). Las Casas argues, however, that even if these conditions are not met, cannibalistic practices are no excuse for the Spanish to wage war on, or even punish, Amerindian peoples (D, 220).

Las Casas also argues that human sacrifice—though a grave error—is somewhat understandable:

> Just as men naturally know God exists and think that there is nothing better or greater than he, since whatever we own, are, or are capable of is given to us by his boundless goodness, we do not adequately repay him even if we offer him all that is ours, even our life. ... However, since we cannot give adequate thanks for so many favors, we are obliged to present what seems to be the greatest and most valuable good, that is, human life, and especially when the offering is made for the welfare of the state. For the pagans thought that through sacrifices of this type they could divert evils from their state and gain the good will and prosperity for their kingdoms. Therefore, whoever sacrifices to God can be drawn to this action by natural reason, especially if it lacks Christian faith and instruction. (D, 233–234)

In sum, only one of the abovementioned six cases of lawful jurisdiction applies to the Amerindians, and even in that case, waging war is unjustified.

Refutation of Sepúlveda's fourth argument

Lastly, Las Casas argues that the Church *cannot* wage war to spread Christianity. According to Las Casas, Sepúlveda errs in three major ways. To begin with, he misinterprets the parable of the "Great Feast." "Compel them to enter" does not permit using force or war; instead, it refers to various peaceful and intellectual ways in which unbelievers can be attracted to Christ (D, 271–272). None of these ways involve using violence or war to compel people to the faith. Next, Sepúlveda fails to distinguish between different types of unbelievers (D, 268).[45] The Amerindians are only one of these types—unbelievers who live in remote lands—and that type is outside the jurisdiction of the Church. Lastly, Sepúlveda again conflates these types and mistakenly grants the Church jurisdiction where it has none. These mistakes, and many others, lead Las Casas to sum up his refutation as follows:

> I think that Sepúlveda wrote that little book [*Democrates segundo*] hastily and without sufficiently weighing the materials and circumstances. ... Sepúlveda says that he does not want the Indians to be baptized unwillingly or to be forced to the faith. But what greater compulsion can there be than that which is carried out by an armed phalanx, shooting rifles and cannon, so that, even if no other effect should follow, at least their flashes of light and terrible thunder could dishearten any strong person, especially one not accustomed to them and ignorant of how they work? ... I should like the reader to answer this question: What will the Indians think about our religion, which those wicked tyrants claim they are teaching by subjugating the Indians through massacres and the force of war before the gospel is preached to them? When I speak of the force of war, I am speaking of the greatest of all evils. (D, 297–298)

Contemporary Relevance

The council that heard the arguments at Valladolid did not declare a winner, but this does not mean the debate and the controversy that gave rise to it had no constructive outcomes. Las Casas can be credited with shaping, in his lifetime, the improvement of imperial policy regarding the treatment of Amerindians.[46] He also helped lay the theoretical and legal groundwork for the development of international law and human rights.[47]

As was outlined at the end of the previous chapter, however, indigenous peoples of the Western hemisphere continue to face genocidal challenges to preserving their respective biospheres, languages, and ways of life. Although much of this can be attributed to the ravages of neoliberal globalization and transnational corporate power, close attention must also be paid to their close relationship to the presence of imperial power in Latin America.

The relevant imperial power in our time is not Spain; rather, it is the United States of America. According to one scholar, U.S. foreign policy in Latin America has been dominated by three overriding interests: "the need to protect U.S. security interests, the desire to accommodate the demands of U.S. domestic politics, and the drive to promote U.S. economic development."[48] All of these interests, however, have been undergirded by a deeper underlying belief held by U.S. officials: "that Latin Americans are an inferior people."[49] This perhaps explains why John Adams would describe plans to establish democracies in South America "as absurd as similar plans would be to establish democracies among birds, beasts, and fishes;"[50] or why Theodore Roosevelt would say that the U.S. acquisition of Mexican territory, "was inevitable, as well as in the highest degree desirable for the good of humanity at large;"[51] or why George H.W. Bush would refer to Nicaraguan President Daniel Ortega as "that unwanted animal at a garden party."[52]

Consistent with these interests and mindset, the U.S. has established a generally harsh foreign policy record in Latin America—one that has negatively impacted the general population and has often been particularly harmful to indigenous communities. Here, I will only mention some of the more striking cases, in hopes of sparking the reader's interest in conducting further research. The U.S.:

- instigated a war with Mexico (1846), in the hopes of acquiring a substantial portion of Mexican territory.[53]
- sent gunboats to Latin American ports 5,980 times between 1869 and 1897.[54]
- invaded Caribbean countries some thirty-four times by the mid-20th century.[55]
- occupied several Latin American countries for varying lengths of time, including Mexico, Guatemala, Costa Rica, Haiti, Cuba, Nicaragua, Panama, and the Dominican Republic.[56]
- was complicit in the overthrow and 1913 assassination of President Francisco Madero, a hero of the Mexican revolution, and his Vice President Pino Suaréz.[57]
- sponsored human STD experimentation in Guatemala (1946–1948), including experiments that intentionally exposed adults and children to STDs.[58]
- supported the overthrow of democratically elected presidents in Guatemala (1954), Brazil (1964), and Chile (1973).[59]
- supported repressive governments, including brutal military juntas and dictatorships, in Guatemala, El Salvador, Nicaragua, Chile, Brazil, Argentina, and the Dominican Republic.[60]
- supported Salvadoran General Maximiliano Hernández, who carried out the 1932 massacre of between 10,000 and 30,000 campesino men, women, and children, many of whom were Pipil Indians.[61]
- supported brutal Chilean dictator Augusto Pinochet, who was responsible for large scale repression of both the country's general population and its Mapuche people.[62]
- Supported death squads that engaged in both the torture and massacre of innocent civilians, including genocidal activities perpetrated on Maya communities during Guatemala's civil war (1962–1996).[63]

One historian's description of the events in Guatemala is hauntingly similar to the horror stories related by Las Casas:

Between 1981 and 1983 ... the army executed roughly 100,000 Mayan peasants unlucky enough to live in a region identified as the seedbed of a leftist insurgency. In some towns, troops murdered children by beating them on rocks or throwing them into rivers as their parents watched. "*Adiós niño*"—good-bye child—said one soldier, before pitching an infant to drown. They gutted living victims, amputated genitalia, arms, legs, committed mass rapes, and burned victims alive. According to a surviving witness of one massacre, soldiers "grabbed pregnant women, cut open their stomachs, and pulled the fetus out."[64]

In 1980s, the U.S. funded the Nicaraguan Contras with money from weapons sales to Iran, which the U.S. regarded as a state sponsor of terrorism.[65] The Contras engaged in terrorist activities, conducting raids on towns and killing those viewed as sympathetic to the Sandinista government, many of them innocent civilians.[66] On top of this, U.S. officials in charge of funding the Contras were aware that the Contras, or Contra associates, were running drugs into the U.S.[67] In the El Salvador civil war (1979–1992), the U.S. continued to support the Salvadoran armed forces despite their being involved in the assassination of Bishop Oscar Romero and other murders, including the rape and murder of four U.S. churchwomen.[68]

The U.S. also trained and supported El Salvador's Atlacatl battalion, which was responsible for the 1981 massacre at El Mozote and neighboring villages, during which over 700 people were murdered, most of them women, children, and elderly.[69] A boy who escaped the carnage offers testimony that could very well have been uttered by Las Casas himself:

> They slit some of the kids' throats, and many they hanged from the tree. All of us were crying now, but we were their prisoners—there was nothing we could do. The soldiers kept telling us, "You are guerrillas and this is justice. This is justice." Finally, there were only three of us left. I watched them hang my brother. He was two years old.[70]

U.S. support for these ghastly acts of terror shows that, in many ways, the cruel imposition of imperial power is still with us, as are its harmful effects to the population, especially to indigenous communities. It also points back to an historical context that is crucially relevant to several issues in Latin American philosophy. It is obviously relevant to Latin American and indigenous thinkers who offered both their own analyses of "The Indian Problem" and their responses to it. This history is also important in the philosophies of liberation, race, and identity. It is particularly crucial to understanding immigration issues in the Americas, as the U.S. itself bears significant responsibility for the brutal conditions that compel Latin American peoples, most notably those in Mexico and Central America, to leave their home countries.

Despite these persistent imperial dynamics, there have been signs of hope, even in the face of ruthless opposition. Several perpetrators of U.S. supported human rights abuses have been indicted, including former Chilean dictator Augusto Pinochet, former Guatemalan President Efrain Rios Montt, and former Argentine dictator Jorge Rafael Videla. Pinochet and Montt managed to avoid conviction, but Videla was convicted and sentenced to life in prison. And, as mentioned in the previous chapter, many popular and indigenous movements continue to resist state-sponsored oppression and corruption. Thus, the conquest continues but so does the fight for justice and liberation.

Notes

1 Las Casas, *A Short Account of the Destruction of the Indies*, 15.
2 Ibid., 74, 112–113, 125.
3 Pagden, Introduction to *A Short Account of the Destruction of the Indies*, xx.
4 Pagden, *The Fall of Natural Man*, 36.
5 Las Casas, *Short Account*, 24–25.
6 For example, see *Inter Caetera* (1493) and the Laws of Burgos (1512); Hussey, "Text of the Laws of Burgos (1512–1513) Concerning the Treatment of the Indians," 304–305. See also Hanke, *Aristotle and the American Indians*, 8–9; and Hanke, *All Mankind is One*, 7.
7 Hanke, *All Mankind is One*, 36.
8 Ibid., 35.
9 Pagden, Introduction, *Short Account*, xxv.
10 For example, see *Sublimis Deus* (1537), the New Laws (1542), and Hanke, *All Mankind is One*, 11. During this time, Spanish authorities often consulted with leading Spanish and Portuguese scholars, many of whom were from two groups, the School of Salamanca and "the Conimbricenses" (Cantens, "Rights of the American Indians," 23–24). According to Cantens, Las Casas and fellow Dominican Friar Francisco de Vitoria were among the first to articulate a philosophical and legal framework to address the main questions of "The Indian Problem," and this work had far-reaching implications: "Their efforts to resolve these international, sociopolitical, and legal issues constitute the basis for attributing to the School of Salamanca its important role in the history and development of modern International Law and human rights." (Cantens, "Rights of American Indians," 24).
11 Hanke, *All Mankind is One*, 9.
12 Las Casas, *In Defense of the Indians*, 339. Cited in text using abbreviation *D*.
13 Hanke, *Aristotle and American Indians*, 14.
14 Stannard, *American Holocaust*, 218.
15 Ibid., 211.
16 Hanke, *All Mankind is One*, 37.
17 Hanke, *Aristotle and American Indians*, 15.
18 Ibid., 22–23.
19 Hanke, *All Mankind is One*, 67.
20 Ibid., 67.
21 For example, see *Inter Caetera*, May 4, 1493; Hanke, *Aristotle and American Indians*, 8–9.
22 Cantens, "Rights of American Indians," 24.
23 Pagden, *Fall of Natural Man*, 36.
24 Cantens, "Rights of American Indians," 24.
25 Hanke, *All Mankind is One*, 11.
26 Aristotle, *Politics*. Cited in text using page numbers.
27 Aristotle will add that slaves are in a sense proper parts of their masters, in that slaves belong entirely to their masters; indeed, he even suggests slaves are part of the master's body (*Pol.* 1 4, 1254a8–12; *Pol.* 1 6, 1255b9–12).

28 Taylor, "Politics," 257.

29 For Aristotle, this conclusion is confirmed by the tendency of nature to make bodies of slaves and free men differently (*Pol.* 1 5, 1254b26–1255a1). The bodies of slaves are built strong enough for the work necessary for life. The bodies of free men, on the other hand, are built upright and useless for the sort of work a slave does, but they are made with all the other qualities needed for political life. Although Aristotle is aware that nature doesn't always follow this pattern, he nonetheless supports the basic idea that people with excellent bodies deserve to be masters over those with substandard bodies.

30ʼ It is also worth mentioning that Aristotle thought that different climates gave rise to certain types of people (*Pol.* 7 7, 1327b20–37). People born in northern regions were highly spirited but lacking in intelligence and craft knowledge; people in Asia have intelligence and craft knowledge, but do not have much spirit. "The Greek race, however, occupies an intermediate position geographically, and so shares in both sets of characteristics. For it is both spirited and intelligent. That is precisely why it remains free, governed in the best way, and capable, if it chances upon a single constitution, of ruling all the others" (*Pol.* 7 7, 1327b28–32).

31 Schlaifer, "Greek Theories of Slavery from Homer to Aristotle," 165–204. It is also worth mentioning that Aristotle took himself to be addressing a controversy about the legitimacy of slavery as an institution, as some of his contemporaries thought there are no relevant differences between humans to justify slavery, while others did (*Pol.* 1 3, 1253b15–22; *Pol.* 1 6.).

32 Aristotle, however, seemed to be somewhat uncertain about his own view, for he advocated freedom for slaves as a reward for good service (*Pol.* 7 10, 1330a32–33), and he willed that his own slaves be freed (Diogenes Laertius, *Lives of Eminent Philosophers*, Vol. 1, V 11–16; Nicholas D. Smith, "Aristotle's Theory of Natural Slavery," 111).

33 Aquinas thought that servitude is not grounded in natural law but on the practical utility of one man submitting to the rule of someone who is wiser (*Summa Contra Gentiles*, III, 81). Aquinas therefore proposed natural servitude as an "addition" (*Summa Theologica*, Ia IIae. 94. 5) to natural law based on "some resultant utility" mutually derived from the master-slave relationship (*Summa Theologica*, IIaIIae. 57. 3). Aquinas, however, proposed that limits should be put on master's rights on slaves, so that slaves could live in a kind of dignity befitting a full human being (Sigmund, "Law and Politics," 222).

34 Sepúlveda, *Democrates segundo: o De las justas causas de la guerra contra los indios*. Cited in text using abbreviation *DS* and page number.

35 Aquinas, *Summa Theologica* IaIIae 91.2. See also Sigmund, "Law and Politics," 223.

36 Sigmund, "Law and Politics," 222–223.

37 Sigmund, "Law and Politics," 223; Cantens, "Rights of American Indians," 24–25.

38 Sigmund, "Law and Politics," 223; Cantens, "Rights of American Indians," 24–25.

39 Here it is worth mentioning that Sepúlveda never visited the new world and relied on the testimony of others, most notably Oviedo (Hanke, *Aristotle and American Indians*, 48; Hanke, *All Mankind is One*, 105–107).

40 Sepúlveda offers other important qualifications: First, the Spanish are justified in taking both Amerindian freedom and property, because to the just victors go the just spoils, including civil slavery and property acquisition (*DS*, 61). However, the damage caused to the enemy should be in strict proportion to the damages received. Second, just victors must treat justly those who surrender and treat humanely those who are defeated (*DS*, 65–66). Third, two kinds of rule are relevant here. Royal rule, which is the rule of free men. Rule of this type is parental and fatherly, and those subject to it are like the ruler's family. The other type is masterly (*herile*) rule, which is appropriate for barbarians and therefore

the Amerindians. Rule of this type is both parental and masterly, and those subject to it are like ministers or servants to the ruler (*DS*, 66–67).

41 I owe this insight to Cantens, "Rights of American Indians," 31.

42 The first is when unbelievers live among Christians. The second is when they, or a relative, are under litigation. The third is when they have declared an oath of loyalty to a legitimate Christian authority. The fourth is when they have committed crimes somewhere in a jurisdiction of a legitimate Christian authority (*D*, 54).

43 I owe this point to Cantens, "Rights of American Indians," 31.

44 Las Casas uses "invincible" ignorance interchangeably with "probable" ignorance (*D*, 127).

45 First, there are unbelieving Jews and Moors who live in Christian lands. Second, there are apostates and heretics, namely, people who accepted the Christian faith but then renounced it. According to Las Casas, heretics can be rightfully punished for their heresy and forced to honor their solemn vow to follow the Christian faith. Third, there are Turks and Moors who persecute Christians by war. Fourth, there are idolatrous unbelievers who live in remote provinces (*D*, 268).

46 Pagden, Introduction to *Short Account*, xxvii–xxviii.

47 Cantens, "Rights of American Indians," 24.

48 Schoultz, *Beneath America*, 367.

49 Ibid., 374.

50 Ibid., 5.

51 Ibid., 375–376.

52 Ibid., xi.

53 Ibid., 26–29.

54 Grandin, *Empire's Workshop*, 20.

55 Ibid., 20.

56 Ibid., 20.

57 Schoultz, *Beneath America*, 240.

58 Presidential Commission for the Study of Bioethical Issues, "Ethically Impossible: STD Research in Guatemala 1946–1948," September 2011, 41–42.

59 Much of the information provided hereafter, with supporting declassified government documents, can be found at the National Security Archive (https://nsarchive.gwu.edu). See also Bill Moyers' documentary, *The Secret Government: The Constitution in Crisis, A Special Report*.

60 Grandin, *Empire's Workshop*, 41, 88–89; Schoultz, *Beneath America*, 349; Gonzalez, *Harvest of Empire*, 72–73, 75–76; Kornbluh, *The Pinochet File*, 209–273. Chomsky, *Turning the Tide*, 21, 148–149; Nieto, *Masters of War*, 163–164, 295–305.

61 Gonzalez, *Harvest of Empire*, 133; Nieto, *Masters of War*, 116–117.

62 Churchill, *A Little Matter of Genocide*, 112–113.

63 Often members of these death squads were U.S. trained (Nieto, *Masters of War*, 71–72, 401; Danner, *The Massacre at El Mozote*, 49–50). Many were trained at the U.S. Army School of the Americas, now called the Western Hemisphere Institute for Security Cooperation.

64 Grandin, *Empire's Workshop*, 90.

65 Kornbluh and Byrne eds., *The Iran-Contra Scandal*, 319–323; Moyers, *The Secret Government*.

66 Gonzalez, *Harvest of Empire*, 132; Nieto, *Masters of War*, 358–359; Grandin, *Empire's Workshop*, 112–117; LeoGrande, *Our Own Backyard*, 490–492; *Human Rights Watch World Report 1989*.

67 LeoGrande, *Our Own Backyard*, 391–392, 463–464; "*The Contras, Cocaine, and Covert Operations*"; Schou, "The Truth in 'Dark Alliance'.".

68 LeoGrande, *Our Own Backyard*, 60–64; UN Security Council, Annex, *From Madness to Hope*, 8, 20, 21–22.

69 Danner, *Massacre at El Mozote*, 279–280; LeoGrande, *Our Own Backyard*, 152–158; UN Security Council, *From Madness to Hope*, 105–113.
70 Danner, *Massacre at El Mozote*, 77.

Bibliography

Aquinas, St. Thomas. *Summa Theologica*. Translated by Fathers of the English Dominican Province. New York: Benziger Brothers, Inc., 1947.

Aquinas, St. Thomas. *On the Truth of the Catholic Faith: Summa Contra Gentiles*. Translated by Vernon J. Bourke. Garden City, NY: Image Books, 1956.

Aristotle. *Politics*. Translated by C.D.C. Reeve. Indianapolis: Hackett Publishing Company, 1998.

Bell, Aubrey F.G. *Juan Ginés de Sepúlveda*. London: Oxford University Press, Humphrey Milford, 1925.

Cantens, Bernardo J. "The Rights of the American Indians." In *A Companion to Latin American Philosophy*. Edited by Susana Nuccetelli, Ofelia Schutte, and Otávio Bueno. Malden, MA: Blackwell Publishing Ltd., 2010.

Chomsky, Noam. *Turning the Tide: U.S. Intervention in Central America and the Struggle for Peace*. Boston: South End Press, 1985.

Churchill, Ward. *A Little Matter of Genocide: Holocaust and Denial in the Americas 1492 to the Present*. San Francisco: City Lights Books, 1997.

Danner, Mark. *The Massacre at El Mozote: A Parable of the Cold War*. New York: Vintage Books, 1993.

Gonzalez, Juan. *Harvest of Empire: A History of Latinos in America*. Revised edition. New York: Penguin Books, 2011.

Grandin, Greg. *Empire's Workshop: Latin America, the United States, and the Rise of the New Imperialism*. New York: Holt Paperbacks, 2006.

Hanke, Lewis. *Aristotle and the American Indians: A Study in Race and Prejudice in the Modern World*. Chicago: Henry Regnery Company, 1959.

Hanke, Lewis. *All Mankind is One: A Study of the Disputation between Bartolomé de Las Casas and Juan Gines de Sepulveda on the Religious and Intellectual Capacity of the American Indians*. DeKalb, IL: Northern Illinois Press, 1974.

Human Rights Watch World Report1989. Accessed November 24, 2018. https://www.hrw.org/legacy/reports/1989/WR89/Nicaragu.htm.

Hussey, Ronald D. "Text of the Laws of Burgos (1512–1513) Concerning the Treatment of the Indians." *The Hispanic American Historical Review* 12, no. 3(1932): 301–326.

Kornbluh, Peter. *The Pinochet File: A Declassified Dossier on Atrocity and Accountability*. Updated. New York: The New Press, 2013.

Kornbluh, Peter and Malcom Byrne, eds. *The Iran-Contra Scandal: The Declassified History*. New York: The New Press, 1993.

Laertius, Diogenes. *Lives of Eminent Philosophers*. Translated by R.D. Hicks. 2 vols. Cambridge, MA: Harvard University Press, 1972.

Las Casas, Bartolomé de. *A Short Account of the Destruction of the Indies*. Edited and translated by Nigel Griffin. London: Penguin, 1992.

Las Casas, Bartolomé de. *In Defense of the Indians*. Translated by Stafford Poole. DeKalb, IL: Northern Illinois University Press, 1992.

LeoGrande, William M. *Our Own Backyard: The United States in Central America, 1977–1992*. Chapel Hill: University of North Carolina Press, 1998.

Moyers, Bill D. *The Secret Government: The Constitution in Crisis, A Special Report.* New York: Public Affairs Television, 1987. Documentary Film.

National Security Archive. https://nsarchive.gwu.edu.

Nieto, Clara. *Masters of War: Latin America and U.S. Aggression.* New York: Seven Stories Press, 2003.

Pagden, Anthony. *The Fall of Natural Man: The American Indian and the Origins of Comparative Ethnology.* New York: Cambridge University Press, 1982.

Pagden, Anthony. "Introduction." In Bartolomé de Las Casas, *A Short Account of the Destruction of the Indies.* Edited and translated by Nigel Griffin. London: Penguin, 1992.

Presidential Commission for the Study of Bioethical Issues. "Ethically Impossible: STD Research in Guatemala 1946–1948." September2011.

Schlaifer, Robert. "Greek Theories of Slavery from Homer to Aristotle." *Harvard Studies in Classical Philology* 47(1936): 165–204.

Schou, Nick. "The Truth in 'Dark Alliance'." *Los Angeles Times,* August 18, 2006.

Schoultz, Lars. *Beneath America: A History of U.S. Policy toward Latin America.* Cambridge, MA: Harvard University Press, 1998.

Sepúlveda, Juan Ginés de. *Democrates segundo: o De las justas causas de la guerra contra los indios.* Translated by Marcelino Menéndez Pelayo. Madrid: Boletín de la Real Academia de la Historia, 1892.

Sigmund, Paul E. "Law and Politics." In *The Cambridge Companion to Aquinas.* Edited by Norman Kretzmann and Eleonore Stump. New York: Cambridge University Press, 1993.

Smith, Nicholas D. "Aristotle's Theory of Natural Slavery." *Phoenix* 37, no. 2(1983): 109–122.

Stannard, Alexander E. *American Holocaust: The Conquest of the New World.* New York: Oxford University Press, 1992.

Taylor, C.C.W. "Politics." In *The Cambridge Companion to Aristotle,* edited by Johnathan Barnes. New York: Cambridge University Press, 1995.

"The Contras, Cocaine, and Covert Operations." *National Security Archive Electronic Briefing Book* No. 2. Accessed November 24, 2018. http://www2.gwu.edu/~nsarchiv/NSAEBB/NSAEBB2/nsaebb2.htm#1

UN Security Council, *Annex, From Madness to Hope: the 12-year war in El Salvador: Report of the Commission on the Truth for El Salvador* (S/25500, 1993).

3   The Continental Struggle for Democracy

The American Wars of Independence as Experiments in Justice

Jose-Antonio Orosco

In *The Latino Threat Narrative: Constructing Immigrants, Citizens, and the Nation*, Leo Chavez explores the myths and media spectacles woven together over decades that tell a story about the way in which Latinxs pose unique dangers to the well-being of the United States. One popular version of Latinx Threat Narrative holds that Latinx immigrants endanger the U.S. by destabilizing the economy with cheap labor, or by flooding the country with violent criminals, gang members, and drug dealers. This thread gained national prominence during the 2016 presidential election when Republican candidate Donald Trump kicked off his campaign by proposing to build an extensive wall between the U.S. and Mexico to staunch the flow of Mexican immigrants who were, in his opinion, drug dealers, criminals, and rapists.[1]

However, another, more subtle, strain of the Latinx Threat Narrative maintains that Latinx immigrants are harmful because they bring with them ideals and practices from Latin American political culture that could undermine the foundations of U.S. American democracy.[2] For instance, historian Victor Davis Hanson argues that many Mexican undocumented immigrants bring with them with traditions of militancy and political violence that threaten a commitment to law and order. Hanson's view builds on even earlier account by political scientist Samuel Huntington who makes the case that U.S. American democracy is built on a very specific political culture, namely one rooted in the liberalism of its Anglo-Protestant settlers. To the extent that Latinx immigrants come and live in the United States without assimilating, U.S. American democracy is imperiled, since these immigrants do not come from cultures that uphold our liberal democratic traditions and ideals. In the first section of this chapter, I explore more carefully the question of whether U.S. American democracy depends on particular cultural values.

Mexican American philosopher Francisco H. Vazquez challenges the Hanson/Huntington version of the Latinx Threat Narrative by invoking what he calls the "continental quest for democracy and social justice." Vazquez's view is that the nations of North and Latin America actually share a common philosophical beginning, a common yearning to establish new societies with similar ideals. The countries of the Americas originated ιn a revolutionary ideology that sought to overthrow authoritarian monarchical and ecclesiastical powers and to replace them with liberal democratic systems dedicated to the protection of the natural and civil rights of citizens. By studying the philosophical justifications behind all of the American wars of independence, Vazquez suggests, we can better appreciate how misguided the Latinx Threat Narrative is for maintaining that: 1) Latin America shares no political values with the United States and 2) that the cultural values of the United States uniquely support liberal democracy.

In the second section of this chapter, I seek to ground Vazquez's viewpoint by comparing some of the founding documents of U.S. and Latin American democratic societies, including the U.S. *Declaration of Independence* written by Thomas Jefferson, the letters and *Constitution of 1801* of Haitian revolutionary leader Toussaint L'Overture, the Mexican *Sentiments of the Nation* by Jose Maria Morelos, and the *Jamaica Letter* and *Angostura Address* by Simon Bolivar. Studying these documents side by side, we find evidence of a hemispheric-wide wave of liberal democratic fervor that was indeed sparked by the U.S. American Revolution in 1776, but was by no means limited to North America.[3] Yet, while we see that the North and Latin American independence movements shared a dedication to liberal democratic principles and values of the European Enlightenment, we will also notice that Latin American political thinkers demonstrated a concern for racial, economic, and social justice in ways that evaded the North American experience of nation building.

In the final section, I demonstrate how the U.S. American reaction to the Latin American wars of independence forced the United States into a national identity crisis that contributed to the tensions leading to the Civil War. The work of L'Overture, Morelos, and Bolivar, in other words, compelled the United States to decide whether it would commit itself to the ideal of all people being equal, or whether it would reject this interpretation of its original values and consciously shape itself as a white supremacist slave society. Thus, thinking about the American wars of independence through the lens of the continental quest for democracy and social justice not only helps us to dispel the myth of the threatening Latinx immigrant, but it also reframes our understanding about the meaning and potential of U.S. democracy.

The Latinx Threat Narrative and the Continental Struggle for Democracy

Victor Davis Hanson's book *Mexifornia* argues that U.S. national priorities over immigration have changed in the latter half of the 20th century, leading to social instability and cultural degradation. Hanson thinks that liberal politicians and Chicanx activists have shifted the national dialogue about immigration away from assimilation and towards a kind of multiculturalism, which permits immigrants to retain their culture and language while living in the United States. The result, according to Hanson, is a society that is increasingly fractured, with less trust and community, and more toleration for crime and social breakdown. Five years later, Hanson revisited his analysis and concluded that immigration problems in the United States had only worsened and the political divisions over these issues had become more contentious.

Hanson maintains that the debate over immigration has become more polarized because frustration over undocumented immigration has increased, particularly among working class Americans. Many undocumented workers tend to congregate in industries that put them into direct competition with working class citizens. But more importantly, according to Hanson, the continued presence of undocumented people in the U.S. affronts a basic American value: fairness. The failure of the U.S. government to control immigration flows, or to deport undocumented immigrants en masse, sends a message to working class Americans, and to other legal immigrants, that their livelihood is not its prime concern, and that basic law and order is not a priority:

> Fairness about who is allowed into the United States is another issue that reflects class divides—especially when almost 70 perfect of all immigrants, legal and illegal, arrive from Mexico alone. Asians, for example, are puzzled as to why their relatives wait years for official approval to enter the United States, while Mexican nationals come across the border illegally, counting on serial amnesties to obtain citizenship.[4]

Yet, more threatening to Hanson are the cultural attitudes that Latin American immigrants bring that could alter the political process of the United States. He references the immigrant justice demonstrations that began on May 1, 2006, when millions of undocumented immigrants and their allies marched in dozens of cities across the country in favor of immigration reform: "The largest demonstrations ... only confirmed to most Americans that illegal immigration was out of control and beginning to become politicized along the lines of Latin American radicalism."[5] The most dangerous immigrants in this regard are the Mexicans, according to Hanson. Many of them are fleeing turbulent and political circumstances in places such as Oaxaca, and have learned to respond to political institutions with violent reactions: "All this feeds the growing perception that illegal aliens increasingly are not arriving merely as economic refugees but as political dissidents who don't hesitate to take to the streets here to demand social justice, as they did back home."[6]

Samuel Huntington's *Who Are We: The Challenges to America's National Identity* warns that the political differences between Latin Americans and U.S. Americans run deeper than attitudes toward immigration reform legislation. Building on his earlier work on the clash of civilizations, Huntington argues that the United States and Latin America are founded on very different cultural traditions.[7] The United States and its political institutions are established on cultural values brought over by the original Anglo-Saxon settlers. These include notions of liberal democracy, individual rights, the Protestant work ethic, and the English language.[8] Latin America, on the other hand, is committed to maintaining Spanish, nostalgia for the past, a mistrust of people outside the family, making a virtue out of poverty, and the sense that matters can be attended to later, or the *mañana* attitude.[9] For Huntington, this means that if Latin American immigrants insist on maintaining their values in the U.S. and do not assimilate, they will spread these traditions and ways of life throughout U.S. American society and undermine the basis for our economic and political stability:

> The continuation of high levels of Mexican and Hispanic immigration plus the low rates of assimilation of these immigrants into American society and culture could eventually change America into a country of two languages, two cultures, and two peoples ... There is no Americano dream. There is only the American dream created by Anglo-Protestant society. Mexican Americans will share in that dream and in that society only if they dream in English.[10]

Against these kinds of positions, Francisco H. Vazquez counters that the American dream is more properly understood as a "continental *Americano* Dream, not the exclusive dream of the Anglo Saxon Protestant."[11] That is, rather than assume that Latin American immigrants are threats to the United States because they could potentially introduce foreign political ideals that may undermine the integrity of our major institutions, we ought to understand that the people of the Americas, North and South, share a common political heritage. U.S. and Latin Americans, in Vazquez's view, should acknowledge a common continental identity that is based on a shared historical struggle for political democracy and social justice. While it was indeed the case that colonists in North America initiated this revolutionary struggle in 1776, the banner for democracy and social justice was quickly picked up by the Haitians, and then spread throughout Spanish America in the 19th century through various wars of independence. For Vazquez, the recent undocumented immigrants who perturb Hanson and Huntington should be seen not as hazardous militants and rabble-rousers, but instead, as "modern day patriots and *insurgentes*" who seek to further entrench the political values of the continental quest for democracy that is the heritage of this entire hemisphere (*LT*, 35).

The key to understanding the importance and complexity of this continental quest, according to Vazquez, is to note the similarities in nation-building in the Americas. North and Latin American nations arose in the 18th century as reactions against the power of monarchs and the churches. They rooted their protest in the ideas of the Enlightenment, namely the concepts of individual natural rights and an understanding of legitimate government as rooted in the consent of the governed. With this ideological backing, people in the Americas altered their self-understanding from colonial European *subjects* to sovereign *citizens* of their own republics:

> The belief in natural law led to concepts such as the rights of man and all men are created equal (these are the self-evident truths and unalienable rights in the U.S. Declaration of Independence). It also led to the idea of freedom: of political institutions, religion, and trade, the belief in which was then known as liberalism. These concepts were developed over hundreds of years to oppose the notion that God had given the kings or queens the Divine Right to rule over their subjects and do with them (or to them) as they desired. (*LT*, 35–36)

Of course, not all members of these new societies were equally enfranchised as citizens. For Vazquez, it is equally important to understand the different ways in which the continental quest evolved in the distinct regions of the Americas as a struggle for social justice. These differences led to contrasts in how liberal political philosophy was interpreted. In North America, colonial society was more or less culturally homogenous, but divided along racial, gender, and class divides. Women and unpropertied men were not included in the processes of self-government. While it did rely on the labor of enslaved peoples, North America did not attempt to incorporate elements of African culture into its own. Indigenous peoples were similarly excluded, often through genocide. These realities revealed "the contradictions between the ideal that all men are created equal and the reality of women and men who are left with only the quest for equality and justice, that is, for democracy" (*LT*, 37). On the other hand, Latin American societies, by tolerating mixed marriages and syncretistic religious practices, had evolved into multicultural and multiracial cultures. Women, again, were not formally included as autonomous citizens, but the different make-up of these Latin American societies meant that the struggle for nationhood included explicit appeals to equality and social justice for marginalized groups unlike the North American independence movement: "Unlike the U.S. Revolutionary War, this initial period of the War of Independence included goals that would benefit *all* the of the people, including Indians, Blacks, and mixed race people" (*LT*, 43).

In the next section, I chart the development of the continental quest by examining how the Enlightenment themes of liberal democracy and natural rights spread across the globe, starting with the U.S. American war of independence, and then slowly incorporated more social justice themes in order to respond to the multicultural and multiracial realities of the Caribbean and Latin America.

Declarations of Independence in the Americas

The United States Declaration of Independence was adopted formally on July 4, 1776 by the Second Continental Congress, the representative body of the thirteen British colonies in North America. By that point, the colonies had already been at war with England for a year, and felt that the struggle required ideological coherence. Thomas Jefferson (1743–1826) was commissioned by the Congress to write the first draft in mid-June 1776. A committee that included Benjamin Franklin and John Adams revised it shortly afterward. While not a work of political philosophy itself, the *U.S. Declaration* is a succinct summation of the Enlightenment ideals undergirding what would become the struggle for democracy and social justice in the Americas.

After an introduction that grounds the grievances of the United States in natural law, the *U.S. Declaration* begins its most oft-quoted Preamble:

> We hold these truths to be self-evident, that all men are created equal, that they are endowed by their Creator with certain inalienable Rights, that among these are Life, Liberty and the Pursuit of Happiness ... That to secure these rights, Governments are instituted among Men, deriving their just powers from the consent of the governed, That whenever any Form of Government becomes destructive of these ends, it is the Right of the People to alter or abolish it, and to institute New Government, laying its foundation on such principles and organizing its powers in such form, as to them shall seem most likely to effect their Safety and Happiness.

At the outset, what is most notable about the *U.S. Declaration* is its affirmation of universal natural equality among all human beings as the starting point for the struggle of independence in North America. Of course, African slavery and indentured servitude were widespread practices in the colonies at the time of the adoption of the *U.S. Declaration*, so even equality before the law for residents was not a reality. Yet, this passage, with its rejection of a natural hierarchy among human beings, is startling for its willingness to overturn moral assumptions in Western political thought going back at least to ancient Greek political thought. Whereas Plato, in *The Republic*, and Aristotle, in his *Politics*, begin political reflection with the natural inequality among human beings (see chapter 2)—and justify political power for the top elites of society based on the need to provide order and stability for other members of society—the *U.S. Declaration* calls on legitimate government to recognize new moral truths revealed by reason: that the natural order of humanity is horizontal, not vertical, and no person is born to rule over others.

Equally revolutionary is the explicit rejection of the doctrine of the divine right of kings. Even though the origins of this viewpoint are ancient, one of the most comprehensive modern versions of it is by the French theologian Jacques-Benigne Bossuet. In his work *Politics Derived from the Very Words of Holy Scripture* (1709), Bossuet argued that all monarchs derive their authority from God and they deserve complete obedience and protection from their subjects: "It appears from all this that the person of the king is sacred, and that to attack him in any way is sacrilege … One must protect kings as sacred things, and whoever neglects to guard them is worthy of death."[12] The U.S. *Declaration* explicitly rejects this doctrine, holding that legitimate government is not a covenant between a Divine Being and political authorities, but a social contract among morally equal human beings for the sake of security and mutual cooperation. Government ought not be seen as a seat of power held by a paternal figure over *subjects* who sees his office as extending God's empire on Earth, but as the name for those institutions authorized by *citizens* to guard their natural rights and promote their common welfare. Failure to abide by this social contract means that political leaders forfeit their claim to the levers of power. This is typically what is meant by the idea of "consent by the governed"; government is only legitimate to the extent to which it conforms to the boundaries on power established by the society of citizens. Violent insurrection by citizens, then, becomes not an affront to God, but a legitimate tool to set the balance of natural rights and reason on firm footing once again when tyrannical political forces destabilize them.

The ideals of the U.S. *Declaration*, fortified by a successful war of independence against England, and then institutionalized into the U.S. Constitution of 1789, quickly inspired revolutionaries in Europe and the Americas. In France, insurgents began to overthrow the monarchy in the summer of 1789. The Marquis de Lafayette (1757–1834), an ally of the U.S. American revolutionary leaders, drafted, with assistance from Thomas Jefferson, the French *Declaration of Rights of Man and Citizen*. It emphasized many of the ideas of the U.S. *Declaration*, such as equality, freedom, natural rights, and the consent of the governed. It also included civil protections, such as freedom of the press (Article 11), freedom of religious belief (Article 10), and freedom from unreasonable arrest (Article 7), that would not become part of the U.S. American government until 1791, with the ratification of the Bill of Rights. Moreover, the *Declaration of Rights of Man and Citizen* did not seek to enfranchise women or to eliminate slavery. Nevertheless, these ideals brought hope to many people in France and French colonial Saint-Domingue, sparking the successful slave uprising there in 1791, and the establishment of the sovereign nation of Haiti in 1804.

While the history of the Haitian Revolution is too complicated to outline here, it is important to acknowledge the political and intellectual leadership of Toussaint L'Overture (1743–1803). Freed from slavery before the revolt, L'Overture quickly distinguished himself as a military commander during the initial months of the Revolution, and went on to guide its political development nearing independence. His defense of the Revolution, and his vision for the kind of society it sought to establish, were deeply rooted in the Enlightenment ideals first articulated in the U.S. *Declaration* and the *Declaration of Right of Man and Citizen*, and they represent the first expansion of the continental quest for democracy and social justice within the Americas.

Writing in 1797, L'Overture addressed the French Directory—the head of state at that period in the French Revolution—and warned them against plans by the French authorities in Haiti to reinstitute slavery, which had been abolished in France and its territories in 1794. He framed the issue in terms of natural rights and cautioned that the experience of freedom by enslaved Africans would drive them to scorch the earth if slavery was reintroduced:

> My attachment to France, my knowledge of the blacks, make it my duty not to leave you unaware ... either of the crimes which they contemplate or the oath that we renew, to bury ourselves under the ruins of a country revived by liberty rather than suffer the return of slavery ... Those who call for a return to slavery on this island are blind! They cannot see how [their] detestable conduct ... can become the signal of new disasters and irreparable misfortunes, and far from making them regain what in their eyes liberty for all has made them lose, they expose themselves to a total ruin and the colony to its inevitable destruction. Do they think that men who have been unable to enjoy the blessing of liberty will calmly see it snatched away? They supported their chains only so long as they did not know any condition of life more happy than that of slavery. But today when they have left it, if they had a thousand lives they would sacrifice them all rather than be forced into slavery again ...[13]

L'Overture maintained order over Haiti for the French until 1801 when he issued a *Constitution* for an autonomous colony and the perpetual eradication of slavery. He positioned himself as governor for life, while also calling for respect of some of natural rights of all residents of the island, including rights to property (Article 13), freedom from unreasonable searches and arrests (Articles 12, 63, 64), freedom to petition authorities (Article 66). Unlike the *U.S. Declaration* and *Declaration of Rights of Man and Citizen*, L'Overture's *Constitution* did not emphasize sovereign control of government institutions by citizens. Nor did it confront ecclesiastical power, since it officially recognized the Catholic Church as the only state religion (Article 6). However, this call for limited autonomy was enough to provoke the French government, which sent forces in 1802 to retake Haiti and restore a slave society. The response was just as L'Overture had warned: Haitian forces burned cities to the ground rather than turn them over to the French. This resistance compelled many of the French soldiers to pause and consider why they were fighting against armies that proclaimed the same values of liberty and equality as their own government.[14]

The success of the Haitian Revolution sent reverberations throughout the Americas, creating what Anthony Maingot calls a "terrified consciousness" among whites that forever altered political attitudes toward slavery in the hemisphere.[15] As a result of the enormous costs of trying to retake the island, France sold the rights to its properties in North America to the United States in what became known as the Louisiana Purchase of 1803. This sale opened up the possibility of continental control of North America for the United States. However, then President Thomas Jefferson was cautious of this good fortune. Despite being the author of the *U.S. Declaration* that inspired the continental quest for democracy social justice, Jefferson was first and foremost a slaveholder. He could not tolerate an autonomous nation of free blacks because of the example that it would present to the slaves within the United States. Jefferson refused diplomatic recognition of Haiti and, in fact, imposed an economic embargo on the republic in hopes that it would be economically crushed.[16] On the other hand, the sale of Louisiana strengthened and enabled Napoleon to fund his military endeavors in Europe, which included the invasion and occupation of Spain in 1808. The political disarray that followed this campaign emboldened revolutionaries in Latin America to fight for their own independence from European colonial rule.

One of the first countries to revolt was Mexico. The political instability in Spain inspired the American-born Spanish, or *criollos* as they were known, to seek answers as to who had legitimate authority over the Spanish colonies in the Americas. As Mexican philosopher Luis Villoro notes, the *criollos* were disgruntled with the colonial system, since it treated them as second-class citizens with fewer privileges than any Iberian-born Spanish residents of Mexico.[17] The *criollo* intelligentsia thus sought possibilities in traditional Spanish legal traditions for limited self-rule. But it was not until other social groups, including indigenous peasants and mixed race, or *mestizo*, workers, joined the *criollo* leadership that a popular revolution, based in democratic ideals and social justice, began. In September 1810, a *criollo* priest, Miguel del Hidalgo (1753–1811), rallied a multiracial coalition that sought to do more than elevate the *criollos* to positions of power in reformed colonial governments; it sought to eliminate racial and class distinctions, and introduce agrarian reform that would reinstate indigenous claims to land ownership.

Perhaps the best embodiment of the unique revolutionary temper of the Mexican war for independence was Jose Maria Morelos (1765–1815). Another Catholic priest, Morelos took over leadership of the revolutionary forces when Hidalgo was executed in 1811. He was a keen military and political strategist, but was also someone who could articulate the many different demands of the revolutionary movement. In 1813, he called for a congress in Chipalcingo, Guerrero to draft a constitution for a sovereign nation of Mexico. His outline for this constitution, written in consultation with Hidalgo before his execution, became known as *The Sentiments of the Nation*.

Sentiments echoes the U.S. and French Declarations in tone and substance: "The Fatherland will not be fully free and our own as long as the government is not reformed by fighting tyranny, [and] establishing liberalism in its place …" (Morelos, 184). It calls for independence from Spain, and roots sovereignty in the people, understood as all the American-born, not Iberian-born, citizens of Mexico. For Morelos, government should rule by consent of the governed, and he recommended that the Mexican federal state be divided into three branches, following the U.S. model (Article 5). Individual rights to property and privacy in the home were to be respected, but not religious expression (Article 17). As in Haiti, Catholicism was to be the one state religion allowed (Article 2).

However, the effects of the Haitian experience, and the need for social and economic justice, were obviously felt by Morelos more so than by his North American or European counterparts. He insisted on the eradication of slavery, and all official recognition of social and racial castes, in language that underscored a commitment to universal human equality: "That Slavery and the distinction of castes are both abolished forever, and everyone shall be equal, and that only vice and virtue will distinguish one American from another."[18] There was also to be abolishment of torture as a form of punishment (Article 18). Morelos maintained that laws must be promulgated that would "moderate opulence and indigence, and in these ways, improve the income of the poor, better their customs, and dispel ignorance, rapine and robbery."[19] Such measure would include eliminating most taxation except for a five percent flat tax on all individuals (Article 22), and a limit on the salaries of political representatives (Article 8). Villoro points out that notes left behind by Morelos's aides in Cuautla detail even more radical plans to confiscate the properties and natural resources owned by Spanish citizens, nobles, rich *criollos*, and then to redistribute the land and wealth to sustain the livelihoods of smaller *mestizo* and indigenous rural farmers (*IC*, 203).

Perhaps the most significant Mexican departure from the Enlightenment liberal rhetoric is the way Morelos envisioned the war of independence as a kind of "reconquest" or restoration of legitimate indigenous authority. In *Sentiments*, Morelos argued that national liberation requires expulsion of the "Spanish enemy," but drafts prepared for a speech at the Congress of Chilpancingo go even farther. There, Morelos invokes the names of Aztec emperors as the political ancestors of the Mexican revolutionaries:

> Genius of Moctezuma, Cacahma, Cuauhtémoc, Xicotencatl, and Calzontzin, celebrate your ritual about this august assembly as you celebrated the war dance in which you were attacked by the perfidious sword of Alvarado, the solemn moment in which your illustrious sons have congregated to revenge the insults and outrages which you have suffered. (Quoted in *IC*, 206)

Neither the official *Solemn Act of the Declaration of Independence of Northern America* issued by the Congress in November 1813, nor the insurgent *Constitution of Apatzingan* released a year later in 1814, relied on this appeal to indigenous traditions. However, it is clear that a major current among the Mexican revolutionaries was an attempt to fashion a kind of political liberalism grounded not only in European natural rights theory, but with a strong sense of historical and multicultural awareness as well. In this way, the Mexican war of independence opened up new and original ideological dimensions of social justice in the continental quest.

Perhaps the most iconic figure from the history of the Latin American wars of independence is Simon Bolivar (1783–1830). His military and political leadership led to the liberation of most of South America from Spanish colonialism. Yet, his legacy in the continental quest for democracy and social justice is a complicated one. Bolivar was undoubtedly a product of Enlightenment ideals, and promoted them for the development of Latin America. However, his preference was for a strain of views tied more to the French experience, such as Montesquieu, Voltaire, and Rousseau, than to the Anglo Enlightenment figures, such as John Locke, that influenced Jefferson (although Locke was an author with which he claimed to be familiar).[20] Indeed, in his *Jamaica Letter* of 1815, Bolivar follows Montesquieu, arguing that the design of political institutions for newly formed republics should not only be informed by the requirements of philosophy, but by local history, geography, and culture. This led him to the kind of historically informed republicanism that drew on accounts of the Roman and the Italian Renaissance republics for his vision for the New World.

Bolivar was undoubtedly devoted to key themes of liberal democratic thought, such as the moral equality of human beings. In his *Angostura Address*, delivered at the Congress of Angostura during the liberation of Colombia and Venezuela in 1819, Bolivar announced:

> The citizens of Venezuela, governed by a constitution that serves to interpret Nature, all enjoy perfect equality. While such equality not have been a feature of Athens, France, or North America, it is important for us to consecrate it in order to correct the differences that are so apparent here. As I see, it legislators, the fundamental principle of our system demands that equality be immediately and exclusively established and put into practice in Venezuela. That all men are born with an equal right to the benefits of society is a truth sanctioned by the most wise men, as is the following: All men are born equally capable of aspiring to the highest attainments. (*EL*, 39)

Moreover, in his address to the congress establishing the Constitution of Bolivia in 1826, Bolivar praised the draft for guaranteeing equality and the civil rights of individuals. He also followed the Haitian and Mexican examples in recommending the eradication of African slavery, a position he held since at least 1816:

> *Civil liberty* is the only true freedom; the others are nominal or of little importance insofar as they affect the citizens. The *security of the individual* has been guaranteed, this being the purpose of society and the

source of all other guarantees. As for *property rights*, these will depend on the civil codes that in your wisdom you will compose with all dispatch for the happiness of your fellow citizens. I have left intact the law of all laws—*equality*. Without this, all guarantees, all rights perish. To ensure equality, we must make every sacrifice, beginning with infamous slavery, which I have laid at her feet, covered with shame. (*EL*, 61)

Even though Bolivar advocated for political equality among citizens, he believed that circumstances in Latin America called for innovations in the state not necessarily found so prominently in other liberal democratic experiments within the continental quest. For example, Bolivar held that centuries of Spanish colonial rule had denied the *criollo* elites any extensive experience in self-rule:

> From the beginning we were plagued by a practice that in addition to depriving us of the rights to which we were entitled left us in a kind of permanent infancy with respect to public affairs. If we had even been allowed to manage the domestic aspects of our internal administration, we would understand the processes and mechanisms of public affairs … (*EL*, 19)

Moreover, the multiracial and multicultural make-up of the population of the Americas presented unique features not found in other burgeoning republican societies, such as the United State or France:

> Let us bear in mind that our people are not European, nor North American, but are closer to a blend of African and American than an emanation from Europe, for even Spain herself lacks European identity because of her African blood, her institutions, and her character. It is impossible to say with certainty to which human family we belong. Most of the indigenous people have been annihilated. The European has mixed with the American and the African, and the African has mixed with the Indian, and with the European. (*EL*, 38–39)

Here, Bolivar was not so much celebrating the *mestizaje* of Latin America, as he was recognizing it as a reality that posed the possibility of creating social and political discord. He worried that groups identifying around racial lines could undermine civic solidarity and create the violent tensions that manifest themselves during the Haitian revolt (Bolivar, 170). To address these unique challenges in Latin America, Bolivar proposed two distinct features for his constitutional system in Bolivia. The first was lifetime tenure for the President. The idea would be that the President would provide a diverse society with a "fixed point," a point of gravitas "at the center of the universe, radiating life" (*EL*, 57). The President would also be allowed to appoint the Vice President, who would be the hereditary successor for another life term. Second, the legislature would consist of three chambers named after offices in the Roman Republic, including the Senators, Tribunes, and Censors. The duty of the Censors would be to act as special prosecutors against official government corruption in the other legislative chambers and, with wide authority, to enforce public morals among the citizenry:

> It is the censors who protect morality, the sciences, the arts, education, and the press ... It is to these priests of law that I have entrusted the preservation of our sacred commandments, because it is they who must cry out against those who profane them. (*EL*, 56)

These proposals, then, were intended to provide an impression of institutional solidity and moral disciplining for a racially and culturally diverse society with limited sources of civic unity in a new republic.

Unlike Hidalgo and Morelos in Mexico, who insisted on universal equality among all citizens, Bolivar did not always adhere to it in building a broad multiracial coalition for independence. In the *Jamaica Letter*, Bolivar very clearly identifies the independence movements with the work of *criollo* elites exercising authority against the indigenous populations:

> [We] are moreover neither Indians nor Europeans, but a race halfway between the legitimate owners of the land and the Spanish usurpers—in short, being Americans by birth and endowed with rights from Europe—find ourselves forced to defend these rights against the natives while maintaining our position in the land against the intrusion of the invaders. (*EL*, 18)

Indeed, at the point in which he declared himself dictator of Colombia in 1828, Bolivar issued new decrees that reinstated some colonial era treatment of indigenous people, including special taxes on them, and new classes of officials intended to serve as "protectors" and "guardians" of indigenous citizens (*EL*, 191–196). Thus, while Bolivar shared a broad anti-monarchal stance with other independence leaders in the Americas, he was not averse to a kind of benevolent authoritarianism from the state in dealing with the diversity of ethnic, racial, and cultural backgrounds of the people of South America (cf. chapter 9).

Bolivar's willingness to embrace anti-liberal and anti-egalitarian policies put him at odds with some of the other Latin American insurgents, as well as with other republican nations, particularly the United States. As historian Caitlin Fitz points out there was widespread support for the South American independence movements within U.S. American society, and a kind of hero worship of Bolivar—in the 1820s there was a boom of U.S. American children named after the liberator of Latin America.[21] However, this adulation was not shared by the U.S. government, which generally refused to assist Bolivar in his military campaigns and political projects, leading him to quip, in frustration, in a letter to a British diplomat that the "United States ... seems destined by Providence to plague America with miseries in the name of Freedom" (*EL*, 173). Bolivar was quite ready to return the favor to the United States. His most ambitious political experiment was an attempt to create an inter-American federation of nations. Invitations were sent to most of the new American republics to attend a summit in Panama City to discuss this hemispheric partnership. There were two noticeable exceptions: Haiti and the United States. Bolivar explained in a letter to his Vice President, Francisco Santander, that these two nations were far too culturally different than the rest of Spanish America to fit in: "Therefore, I will never agree to invite them to take part in our American system" (*EL*, 167). However, Santander disagreed with the decision to exclude the U.S. and secretly requested for a delegation to attend. The political firestorm that the invitation created in Washington, D.C. illuminated some of the deep contradictions in the continental struggle for democracy and social justice between the idealism of radical Enlightenment egalitarianism and the stumbling block of white supremacist racism among the insurgent elites of North America.

The Congress of Panama and the Contradictions of U.S. American Democracy

President John Quincy Adams thought the presence of U.S. representatives at Bolivar's Congress of Panama would be an excellent avenue through which his government could advocate for republican government, religious liberty, and trade within Latin America. He did not anticipate that Southern senators would mount a coordinated response to the proposal to send a mission. This resistance, led in part by Missouri Senator Thomas Hart Benton, worked in the first few months of 1826 to derail and delay U.S. involvement in the talks. Benton held forth on the Senate floor in March in a speech that outlined the case against going to Latin America; it was so popular that it was printed as a best-selling booklet.

Benton argued that it was not clear that Adams had the power to send delegates to attend this meeting. Additionally, he was concerned that the participation of U.S. diplomats could somehow entangle the country in legal obligations to the inter-American federation. But what seemed to bother him in particular was the issue of Haiti and the possibility of agreements concerning slavery in the Americas. The Colombian Minister wrote previously to the U.S. government, explaining that the treatment of Africans in the Americas would be a topic of the Panama talks and "if possible, a uniform rule of conduct adopted in regard to it."[22] Benton reminded the Senate that the U.S. did not officially recognize the independence of Haiti, even though it maintained some trade with the island. He was very clear that it was in the best interest of the United States not to extend any diplomatic recognition of Haiti:

We purchase coffee from her and pay her for it; but we interchange no Consuls or Ministers. We receive no mulatto Consuls, or Black Ambassadors from her. And why? Because the peace of eleven states in this Union will not permit the fruits of a successful Negro insurrection to be exhibited among them. It will not permit Consuls and Ambassadors to establish themselves in our cities, and to parade through our country, and give their fellow black in the United States, proof in hand of the honors which await them, for a like successful effort on their part. It will not permit the fact to be seen, and told, that for the murder of their masters and mistresses, they are to find friends among the white people of these United States.[23]

The Congress would be made up of nations that not only recognized Haiti, but that had also abolished slavery and granted equality to Black citizens:

Five nations who have already put the black man upon an equality with the white, not only in their constitutions but in real life; five nations who have at this moment (at least some of them) black generals in their armies and mulatto Senators in their Congresses![24]

Worst of all for Benton, one of the delegates suggested by Adams, John Sargeant, was an abolitionist who opposed the extension of slavery in the territories of the United States. There was simply no way, in Benton's mind, that the rights of Southern slave holders in the U.S. would be fairly represented, and the laws of the nation respected by the member nations of the Congress:

They say they only go to consult! I say, there are questions not debatable ... I would not debate whether my slave is my property; and I would not go to Panama to "determine the rights of Hayti and of Africans" in the United States. Mr. President, I do repeat, that this is a question which ought not to be agitated by us, neither at home nor abroad. [25]

Benton left it to his colleague, Senator John Rudolph of Virginia, to invoke the contradiction between slavery and the founding ideals of the United States in a speech that went on to be reprinted in the newspapers of over fourteen states.[26] Like Benton, Rudolph opened with a caustic remark, expressing his obvious disgust at the very idea of the Congress. Rudolph said that he hoped the U.S. representatives would be open to taking "their seat in Congress at Panama, beside the native African, their American descendants, the mixed breeds, the Indians, and the half breeds, without any offence or scandal at so motley a mixture" (2 Register of Debates, 112). He then responded to a fellow Senator's claim that the political ideals of the South American republics were the same as those of the U.S. *Declaration of Independence* by calling those ideals a "pernicious falsehood":

Sir, my only objection is, that these principles, pushed to their extreme consequences—that all men are born free and equal—I can never ascent to, for the best of all reasons, because it is not true ... even though I find it in the Declaration of Independence. (2 Register of Debates, 125)

Randolph went on the criticize his fellow Virginian, Thomas Jefferson, for indulging in philosophical abstraction on the issue of equality: "I have long thought that I could discern, even in that paper [Declaration of Independence] rather more of a professor of a university than the language of an old statesmen" (2 Register of Debates, 127). Randolph warned his colleagues to be wary of Jefferson's "metaphysical madness" and realize it would be more prudent to listen to the conservative teachings of Edmund Burke. It was Burke who believed that unless political ideals are compromised and adapted to fit local circumstances the result is political terror as reformers try to force society to abide by the ideals. Randolph noted that Burke was thinking of the French Revolution, but he himself believed that Haiti should also be added to the list of examples where the ideal of equality was taken too far, with disastrous consequences. He ended his diatribe by arguing that slavery in the United States was popular and prosperous—if the Southern states had wanted to abandon slavery they had the mechanism to do so in the U.S. Constitution. They had not done so, Randolph maintained, and that should be the reality by which to measure our political ideals, not the musings of "Mathematicians and star-gazers" (2 Register of Debates, 128).

In the end, a U.S. delegation was sent to the Congress of Panama. However, it did not participate in the proceedings. One of the delegates died on the way, and by the time the other arrived, the Congress had already concluded. The Congress did not achieve Bolivar's goal of creating a united federation of American states either. It did, however, force the United States to confront the contradictions in its own self-understanding. The United States stood as both the originator of the continental struggle for democracy and social justice in the Americas and as a slave owning society devoted to white supremacy. These tensions paved the way for the conflicts that erupted into the Civil War. As Caitlin Fitz writes:

Congress's debates about Spanish America pierced to the heart of how lawmakers understood democracy, equality, and America itself, exposing sentiments that had long festered but that had seldom been uttered so publicly, so willingly, so consistently, and on such high authority ... The Panama debates both reflected and furthered a new era in American history, a movement away from the nation's founding universalist language and a toward a bold new vision of U.S. greatness. In opposition southerners' estimate, the United State became an entity separate and superior within the hemisphere; uniquely moderate, uniquely successful, and uniquely white.[27]

Conclusion

In this chapter, I have examined how the continental quest for democracy and social justice, as Francisco Vazquez outlines its history and philosophical assumptions, challenges the Latinx Threat Narrative, particularly the idea that Latinx immigrants are dangerous to the well-being of the United States. Victor Davis Hanson and Samuel Huntington both argue that Latinxs migrate from societies with very different cultural foundations than the U.S. and may transmit inherently foreign and toxic concepts into U.S. political culture, with a destabilizing effect. As I have demonstrated here, Latin American independence leaders did often proceed to build constitutions that embodied ideals responding to their own unique cultural circumstances, values, and history. However, Vazquez's account encourages us to acknowledge the fundamental similarities: the Americas were a vibrant region with multiple experiments in interpreting and implementing the Enlightenment ideals of liberal democracy and justice. Latin American founders often grappled with racial and economic caste systems in the building of multiracial democratic nations by envisioning and designing novel political institutions to embody the same political values—such as liberty, equality, and the pursuit of happiness—that drove the North Americans. Indeed, by reviewing some of these attempts to refashion liberal democracy through the lens of social justice, such as in Mexico, we see how the U.S. not only lagged behind for many decades in finding solutions to various forms of inequality, but actively resisted the attempts to live up to the universal ideals of liberty and equality it so boldly inaugurated in the modern world. Such attempts to deny the ideals of liberty, equality, and justice ultimately proved disastrous for the United States, leading to one of the most destructive wars in U.S. history. Today, we might strengthen our effort to build socially and economically just societies by studying this hemispheric history and realizing that our common past is a resource for imagining futures that do not necessarily end in a clash of civilizations.

Notes

1 Reilly, "All the Times Donald Trump Insulted Mexico."
2 I use the term "US American" instead of "American" to refer to people and institutions of the United States, recognizing that many Latin Americans have historically considered the Americas as their home and embraced "American" as their hemispherical identity.
3 Rodriguez, *The Independence of Spanish America*, 1–6.
4 Hanson, "Mexifornia."
5 Ibid.
6 Ibid.
7 Huntington, *The Clash of Civilizations*.
8 Huntington, *Who Are We*, 59–80.
9 Ibid., 253–256.
10 Ibid., 256.

11 Vasquez, *Latino/a Thought*, 3. Cited in text using abbreviation *LT* and page number.
12 Bossuet, *Politics Drawn*, 58–59.
13 Quoted in James, *The Black Jacobins*, 195–197.
14 Perry, *Arrogant Armies*, 82.
15 Maingot, "Terrified Consciousness of the Caribbean," 53–80.
16 Dubois, *The Avengers of the New World*, 303.
17 Villoro, "Ideological Currents," 188. Cited in text using abbreviation *IC* and page number.
18 Morelos, "Sentiments of the Nation," 186.
19 Ibid., 186.
20 Bolivar, *El Libertador*, xxx. Cited in text using abbreviation *EL* and page number.
21 Fitz, *Our Sister Republics*, 116–155.
22 Benton, *Speech of Mr. Benton*, 34.
23 Ibid., 35.
24 Ibid., 35.
25 Ibid., 36.
26 Fitz., *Our Sister Republics*, 208.
27 Ibid., 212–213.

Bibliography

Benton, Thomas Hart. *Speech of Mr. Benton of Missouri, Delivered in the Senate of the United States, on the Mission to Panama*. Washington, DC: Columbia Star, 1826.

Bolivar, Simon. *El Libertador: Writings of Simon Bolivar*. Edited by David Bushnell. New York: Oxford University Press, 2003.

Bossuet, Jacques-Benigne. *Politics Drawn from the Very Words of Holy Scripture*. Translated and edited by Patrick Riley. Cambridge: Cambridge University Press, 1990.

Dubois, Laurent. *The Avengers of the New World: The Story of the Haitian Revolution*. Cambridge: Belknap Press, 2005.

Fitz, Caitlin. *Our Sister Republics: The United States in an Age of American Revolutions*. New York: W.W. Norton, 2016.

Hanson, Victor Davis. *Mexifornia: A State of Becoming*. 2nd edition. New York: Encounter Books, 2007.

Hanson, Victor Davis. "Mexifornia, Five Years Later." *City Journal*. Winter2007. https://www.city-journal.org/html/mexifornia-five-years-later-12987.html

Huntington, Samuel P. *The Clash of Civilizations and the Remaking of World Order*. New York: Simon & Schuster, 1996.

Huntington, Samuel P. *Who Are We? The Challenges to America's National Identity*. New York: Simon & Schuster, 2004.

James, C.L.R. *The Black Jacobins*. 2nd Edition. New York: Vintage, 1989.

L'Overture, Toussaint. *Haitian Constitution of 1801*. https://thelouvertureproject. org/index.php?title=Haitian_Constitution_of_1801_(English)

Maingot, Anthony P. "Haiti and the Terrified Consciousness of the Caribbean." In *Ethnicity in the Caribbean: Essays in Honor of Harry Hoetnik*, 53–80. London: Macmillan, 1996.

Marquis de Lafayette. *Declaration of Rights of Man and Citizen*. http://www.historyguide.org/intellect/declaration.html

Morelos, Jose Maria. "Sentiments of the Nation." In *Mexican History*, by Nora Jaffary, Edward Osowski, and Susie Porter. Philadelphia: Westview Press. 2010.

Perry, James M. *Arrogant Armies: Great Military Disasters and the Generals Behind Them*. New York: Castle Books, 2005.

Reilly, Katie. "Here Are All the Times Donald Trump Insulted Mexico." *Time Magazine*, August 31, 2016. http://time.com/4473972/donald-trump-mexico-meeting-insult/

Rodriguez, Jaime E. *The Independence of Spanish America*. Cambridge: Cambridge University Press, 1998.

Vazquez, Francisco H. *Latino/a Thought: Culture, Politics, and Society*. 2nd edition. Lanham, MD: Rowman and Littlefield, 2009.

Villoro, Luis. "The Ideological Currents of the Epoch of Independence." In *Major Trends in Mexican Philosophy*, translated by A. Robert Caponigri, 184–219. Notre Dame and London: University of Notre Dame Press, 1966.

4   Nation-Building through Education

Positivism and Its Transformations in Mexico

Alexander V. Stehn

In the first half of the 19th century, as most Latin American countries achieved political independence from Spain or Portugal, a new generation sought further intellectual and cultural emancipation from their colonial past and its accompanying philosophical framework of scholasticism. In the second half of the 19th century, many Latin American intellectuals came to identify with the philosophy of positivism, which originated in Europe with the French philosopher Auguste Comte (1798–1859). Positivism made an especially powerful and lasting impact on Mexico and Brazil. Brazil's flag continues to bear Comte's motto *Ordem e Progresso* ("Order and Progress"). But philosophers across Latin America adapted positivism to address the pressing problems of nation-building and respond to the demands of their own social and political contexts, making positivism the second most influential tradition in the history of Latin American philosophy, after scholasticism.[1]

Since a comprehensive survey of positivism's role across Latin American and Latinx philosophy would require multiple books, we will narrow our scope to the history of positivism and its transformations in Mexican and Chicanx philosophies, proceeding chronologically and focusing on these representative thinkers: Auguste Comte (1798–1857), Gabino Barreda (1818–1881), Justo Sierra (1848–1912), José Vasconcelos (1882–1959), Antonio Caso (1883–1946), and Gloria Anzaldúa (1942–2004). We will pay special attention to how positivism was used to build the Mexican nation and reconstruct Mexican identity through education, creating philosophical debates about the relationships among science, religion, morality, education, race, economic progress, and national development. These debates continue to resonate as we think critically about the respective roles of scientific education—then called "positive" education, now "STEM" education—and moral education in the curricula used to educate a country's youth while reconstructing their ethnoracial and national identities.

Auguste Comte: The French Founder of Positivism

Auguste Comte's *Course on Positive Philosophy*, published in six volumes from 1830 to 1842, provided a philosophical treatment of both the natural sciences and the social sciences, which were in their infancy. Comte's goal was to coordinate all scientific knowledge and establish sociology as the final science that would provide knowledge of social phenomena, which were previously considered to be so complex that there could be no science of them. Comte's philosophy of science also went hand in hand with a sweeping philosophy of history and a grand narrative of human progress, reflected in Comte's most famous idea, the law of the three stages: "Each of our leading conceptions,—each branch of our knowledge,—passes successively through three different theoretical conditions: the Theological, or fictitious; the Metaphysical, or abstract; and the Scientific, or positive."[2] In the theological stage, humans searched for the first and final causes of phenomena and explained anomalies as the work of supernatural agents. The metaphysical stage replaced supernatural agents with abstract entities or elements as causes. In the scientific or positive stage humans limit themselves to studying the laws governing natural phenomena, i.e., "their invariable relations of succession and resemblance" (*PPAC*, 1:2).

It is a considerable historical and geographical leap to the 21st century United States, but in Comte's desire to make all knowledge "positive" or "scientific" we find early roots of the recent push towards STEM (Science, Technology, Engineering, and Mathematics) fields in education. However, Comte believed that philosophy and the social sciences were more universal and ought to reign supreme because only they could achieve a genuinely human (i.e., social) view and direct the knowledge provided by STEM fields to achieve morally or politically progressive ends. This brings us to a crucial question explored by all the philosophers discussed in this chapter: what is education for? For the early Comte, education ought to promote the orderly progress of both the individual and society by advancing the whole of knowledge, which makes the study of philosophy and the social sciences necessary because "the last biological degree, the intellectual and moral life, [borders so closely] upon the social" (*PPAC*, 2:545).

Comte advocated for a universal education (compulsory education was not established in France until 1881) that would attend to both the intellectual and moral development of children by introducing them to the natural and social sciences while developing their personal, familial, and social morality. Comte believed that theological philosophy had subordinated real life to an imaginary life, and metaphysical philosophy had sanctioned egoism, whereas positivism's scientific philosophy "connects each of us with the whole of human existence, in all times and places" (*PPAC*, 2:555). Comte defined morality in terms of "altruism" (a term he coined) and "the purely disinterested affections" while conceiving of education as a "special and permanent exercise" to develop the moral sense so that individual happiness would come to depend upon altruistic actions, social progress, and sympathetic feelings toward the whole human race (*PPAC*, 2:555).

Gabino Barreda's Positivism and the Mexican Education System

Gabino Barreda (1818–1881), a Mexican physician and philosopher, was most responsible for spreading positivism in Mexico. He encountered positivism while studying medicine in Paris and attending Comte's lectures from 1847 to 1851. After more than a decade of teaching in Mexico's National School of Medicine, Barreda's 1867 "Oración cívica" ("Civic Oration") caught the attention of President Benito Juárez. Barreda delivered his speech on Mexican Independence Day, just three months after Mexico had successfully defeated the French military and executed Emperor Maximilian I, whose three-year monarchy had interrupted Juárez's presidency (1858–1864; 1867–1872). Against the backdrop of this political chaos, Barreda aimed "to extract, according to the counsel of Comte, *the great social lessons offered by all these painful collisions that anarchy,* which currently reigns over our spirits and ideas, *provokes all around us.*"[3]

Barreda adapted Comte's positivism to Mexico by using Comte's law of the three stages to provide an interpretation of the "incoherence and frenzy in our national history" and to articulate his generation's sense of duty. Barreda rolled three and a half centuries of Mexican history into a grand narrative of Mexico's emancipation, first from Spain "after three centuries of quiet domination under a system that perfectly combined education, religious beliefs, politics, and administration in order to endlessly prolong a situation of domination and continuous exploitation" (OC, 83). After national emancipation came "mental emancipation" from the foreign tutelage represented by Emperor Maximilian I. Now the time was finally ripe for a "triple emancipation"—simultaneously scientific, religious, and political—whereby Mexico would escape its history of political crisis by rebuilding the nation upon a solid positivist foundation: "Let our motto be Liberty, Order, and Progress; Liberty as a means; Order as a base, and Progress as an end" (OC, 105). Barreda envisioned a bright future whereby the Mexican revolution would finally be over, and the Mexican nation would "walk forever along the florid path of progress and civilization" (OC, 105).

Amidst the recent social and political chaos, President Juárez was especially receptive to three aspects of Barreda's speech: 1) his diagnosis: "anarchy reigning in the spirit and ideas of our age"; 2) his suggested cure: "to gather all wisdom and intelligence into a common synthesis"; and 3) his overarching positivist vision: "progress and civilization" as the key to Mexico's future (OC, 82). Juárez therefore appointed Barreda to undertake a major project of national educational reform. Like Comte, Barreda understood social disorder to be a direct consequence of intellectual and spiritual disorder, but he showed little interest in the later Comte's desire to inculcate altruism via the religion of humanity, in part because Catholicism was so thoroughly entrenched in Mexico. Instead, Barreda sought to achieve the same end through educational reform. He envisioned an educational system founded upon positivist principles that would cultivate a new elite to guide Mexico both scientifically and morally in the positive era.

The resulting *Ley Orgánica de Instrucción Pública* (Organic Law of Public Instruction) sought to reorganize Mexico's educational system in its entirety, unite the nation, and restructure Mexican society by bringing education under a single secular authority while making it both free and compulsory at the primary level. Like Comte, Barreda believed that an encyclopedic unification of all the various fields of knowledge could, if implemented as part of a national education system, provide a foundation for order and progress. And as the idea of grounding the country's well-being in childhood education grew, so too did the idea of Mexican nationhood and a vigorous pride in *mexicanidad* (Mexcianness). Indeed, many of the questions of Mexican identity that came to preoccupy Mexican and Chicanx philosophers over the next century grew out of Barreda's positivist project of national education. According to the Organic Law of Public Instruction, "Enlightening the people is the most reliable and effective method of raising the standards of morality and establishing liberty as well as respect for the Constitution and the laws." In other words, philosophers following in the footsteps of Barreda came to answer the question "What is education for?" with "To make good Mexicans."

Mexican positivism is often caricatured as a form of scientism, but as Barreda's essay "De la educación moral" ("On Moral Education") makes clear, positivism initially sought to place all education in the service of moral, social, and even spiritual progress. Barreda's system of public education replaced the Catholic catechism (the foundation of colonial education) with the subject of "morals":

> Morality is generally confused with religious dogmas, so much so that for many they are not only inseparable but even amount to the same thing. But when we reflect upon the immense variety of religions in contrast to the uniformity of moral rules [...] we cannot help but recognize their independence. Religions continue changing across the distinct phases of humanity [...] but the fundamentals of morals remain the same even though their practical consequences march towards perfection with the progress of civilization. This unequal and independent progress of morals and religions prove that they are not the same thing. Moreover, the fact that a multitude of atheists across history have left us, as Littré says, "indisputable testimonies of a profound morality" proves beyond a shadow of a doubt their thorough and complete separation.[4]

Like Comte, Barreda believed that we could discover the origins of morality in human nature rather than in religious dogma and the supernatural. Psychology could scientifically study human morality in naturalistic terms and sociology could place altruism and the common good on a "scientific foundation that was nobler and simultaneously more magnificent, efficient, and secure in its results than the paltry individual interest whose egotistical tendencies the religions have always resolved to exploit in favor of the common good" (*EM*, 110).

Echoing Comte's criticism of theological and metaphysical explanations of morality, Barreda wrote: "What the Apostle Paul placed outside of us—i.e., the benevolent inclinations of love, veneration, kindness, and humility—*science*, after eighteen centuries of laborious ascension, has come to find in our own being" (*EM*, 114). By taking these moral phenomena as given in our experience, moral philosophy should aim to give a rational, scientific explanation of morals. The question of moral education then becomes eminently practical: how can we further develop the moral conscience of the individual, and even the human species as a whole?

Barreda's answer was that we should allow our immoral tendencies to atrophy while actively exercising our altruistic tendencies:

> It is an uncontested and uncontestable axiom of the science of biology that all organs develop with exercise and atrophy with inaction [...] If we now apply these same principles to the intellectual and affective organs, the same result will undeniably obtain using the same means. And if we direct education in such a way that sympathetic acts (or *altruistic* acts, as Comte called them) are frequently repeated while also avoiding destructive and egotistical acts as far as possible, we cannot doubt that after a certain period of these *moral gymnastics* [...] the good instincts will predominate over the bad. (*EM*, 111–112)

Like Aristotle who viewed ethics as an art of living, Barreda continued:

> Here is the final and positive object of the moral art that will be achieved with the practice of good actions and the incessant repression of bad ones [...] And with the examples of morality and true virtue that will be presented artfully in the schools, exciting in the pupils the desire to imitate them, we are doing nothing more than allowing the spontaneous and imperceptible birth of moral desires. (*EM*, 112)

While Barreda believed that the minds of students should be prepared through the study of science, their moral education should not ultimately rest upon intellectual precepts or fear of punishment but rather the gradual cultivation of sympathetic instincts until "love becomes the irresistible guide of all our actions" (*EM*, 113). Barreda's overarching educational objective was thus identical to that of the later Comte who sought "the essential purpose of true philosophy, to systematize human life as a whole on the principle of the subordination of the intellect to the heart."[5]

Admittedly, there were differences between Barreda's positivism and Comte's. For example, Barreda interpreted Mexican liberalism as an expression of the positive spirit, whereas European liberalism represented a negative spirit for Comte. More dramatically, Barreda seemed to reject the religion of humanity, at least in its cultic form. Barreda's educational reforms attempted to shift responsibility for moral instruction from the priesthood to the educational agencies of the State. In terms of political expediency, Barreda understood that de-catholicizing Mexico was virtually impossible, so he emphasized religious freedom of conscience while seeking to mold the moral conscience of the people into something more uniform using positivism, altering Comte's motto to read: "Liberty as the means; order as the base; progress as the end." By changing the first part of Comte's formula—"Love as the principle"—Barreda left pupils free to their own private Catholic beliefs while nonetheless insisting that they learn the public lessons of a unifying social ethics by studying the lives of the great moralists. In other words, Barreda did not depart from the general thrust of the religion of humanity: educating people into altruism. And even though he made no room for Comte's secular priesthood, Barreda followed Comte's principle of the wise subordination of the intellect to the heart by treating love as the ultimate end of a positivist education: "The heart, improved and perfected through the cultivation and growth of benevolent inclinations, should command; the mind, fortified by science, should obey."[6]

The Evolving "Positivism" of Justo Sierra and the *Científicos*

Barreda passed positivism on to the next generation through both the National Preparatory School, which he established and directed from 1868 to 1878, and the *Asociación Metodófila Gabino Barreda* ([Scientific] Method-Loving Association of Gabino Barreda) founded in 1877. However, this new generation's positivism differed from Barreda's due in large part to an interest in the British philosopher Herbert Spencer's positivism and the application of Darwinian theory to social problems. Despite Barreda's misgivings, they did not shy away from Social Darwinism. For example, Miguel Macedo published an essay arguing that wealth was a form of social superiority that easily led to moral superiority, and Manuel Ramos linked evolutionary biology to sociology using Spencer's concept of "survival of the fittest." This chapter refers to this second generation as Mexican "positivists" to mark the fact that they abandoned much of Comte's and Barreda's moral idealism, and we reserve the terms *positivist* and *positivism* (without quotation marks) for the philosophies of Comte and Barreda.[7]

The terminology gets muddled because "positivism" gained increasing political traction as it came to function as an ideology for the elite interests supporting the regime of the Mexican President Porfirio Diaz whose rule from 1876 to 1911 is generally considered a dictatorship. His advisors called themselves "positivists" and were referred to pejoratively as *científicos* (scientists) because they claimed that science legitimated their positions. By emphasizing the importance of the positivist *method*, this new generation of "positivists" could set aside substantial elements of Comte's and Barreda's positivist *doctrines*. Not just the religion of humanity, but much of Comte's ethical and political doctrines were ignored, alongside Barreda's dream of educating Mexicans into altruism. The original ethics and politics of positivism, which subordinated the interests of the individual to those of society, simply did not suit the interests of the Mexican bourgeoisie. Whereas Barreda's motto was "Liberty as the means; order as the base; progress as the end," the second generation of "positivists" or *científicos* became so fixated on order that they supported a dictator for decades and reconceived liberty in terms of the *economic* liberty of the wealthy.

Justo Sierra (1848–1912) gave the clearest expression to his generation's attempt to establish order from roughly 1880 to 1910. His most famous work, *Evolución política del pueblo mexicano* (*Political Evolution of the Mexican People*), was published at the turn of the century.[8] While it echoed Barreda's positivist philosophy of Mexican history, Sierra's "positivism" was almost completely recast in terms of Spencer's theory of evolution:

> Society is a living being and consequently grows, develops, and undergoes transformations; these transformations are continuous, and their celerity is in ratio to the internal energy with which the social organism reacts to external elements, assimilating them and utilizing them in the course of its growth. Science, converted into an amazingly complex and efficient tool, has accelerated a hundredfold the evolution of certain peoples. (*PEMP*, 343)

By "scientifically" studying the history of the Mexican people, Sierra and the other *científicos* sought to accelerate their evolution through a kind of social engineering.

Comte's sociology, like Spencer's, had also prescribed an evolutionary course for humanity understood as a social organism, but there was a fundamental difference in how each understood this evolution. Comte, who coined the term *altruism* and claimed that positivist morality could be summarized in the motto "live for others," would never have invoked Spencer's phrase "survival of the fittest." Likewise, Barreda argued that it was necessary to "humanize the rich" through moral education, since "society has put wealth in their hands for the common good and common progress."[9] But the *científicos* twisted free from positivism's supposedly outdated moral injunctions in the name of science and social engineering. Social progress and the advancement of the political state were often reduced to a matter of "economic evolution" understood in terms of the investment of foreign capital, new technological infrastructure like railroads, and a growing export economy.

Like Barreda, Sierra still believed that a free, public, and compulsory educational system was the key to the future of Mexico, but his evolutionary "positivism" was more overtly racist:[10]

> We need to attract immigrants from Europe so as to obtain a cross with the indigenous race, for only European blood can keep the level of

civilization that has produced our nationality from sinking, which would mean regression, not evolution. We need to bring about a complete change in the indigenous mentality through education in the school. [...] To blend [the indigenous] spirit and ours in a unification of language, of aspirations, of loves and hates, of moral and mental criteria, to place before him the ideal of a strong and happy country belonging to all—**to create, in sum, a national soul**—is the goal assigned to the future, the program of our national education. (*PEMP*, 368; bold added)

Sierra's view was nevertheless less racist than many of his contemporaries who held that Indians were *not* educable and had nothing to contribute, since they were deterministically "inferior" (this recalls the "The Indian Problem" discussed in chapters 1, 2, and 9). But in contrast to those who argued for the racial superiority of the *criollos*, Sierra held that the real agents of progress in Mexico were the *mestizos*, whom he also identified with the bourgeoisie.

Sierra and the other *científicos* judged that Porfirio Díaz was needed to secure the order necessary to make progress possible, since he founded "the political religion of peace" amidst Mexico's chaotic history (*PEMP*, 359). As the embodiment of the mestizo middle class, Díaz appeared as the nation's savior in Sierra's narrative. Supported by "the submission of society in all its active elements" to create a "social dictatorship," only Díaz could make Mexico strong enough to avoid being economically dominated by the United States (*PEMP*, 366). Barreda's ordering of terms—"Liberty as the *means*; order as the *base*; progress as the *end*"—was subtly but fundamentally altered as political liberty was deferred until the future, transformed from a means into a utopic end. In short, the economic and political order that Díaz made possible was presented as the next step in the natural, social, and political evolution of Mexico.

Although Díaz's rule conferred material advantages upon the Mexican bourgeoisie, it became increasingly difficult to argue that this constituted progress for the Mexican people as a whole. There was growing criticism of the *científicos'* "positivism," and even Sierra publicly moved towards what has been called *anti-positivism* in a 1908 address in honor of Gabino Barreda. But this term is misleading insofar as Sierra was also following in the positivist footsteps of both Comte and Barreda by questioning the assumption that scientific knowledge was everything. Like his positivist predecessors, Sierra came to believe that science must ultimately be transmuted into positive sentiment because "the good fortune of ideas is and always will be to convert themselves into sentiments, the only means of moving the heart of peoples" (*PEMP*, 359).

An even greater continuity lies in the fact that Comte, Barreda, and Sierra each sought to transform the ethical and political lives of their peoples (and humanity as a whole) by instituting a better system of education, which would include not just scientific or technical instruction but moral instruction. In the words of Sierra:

By perseverance in the efforts of acquiring knowledge, one feeds and develops the faculties, thus organizing the training of the will, the exteriorization of character. By the practice of method, one acquires the notion of the necessity of order, as well as the love of truth, by way of one's scientific initiation. And by loving truth, one is prepared to love the good. (*PEMP*, 394)

This passage shows that it is too simplistic to say that Sierra came to oppose positivism. Rather, he came to realize that its vision stood in opposition specifically to the ideologies of Porfirism and Social Darwinism.

Sierra's speech at the opening ceremony of the National University of Mexico in 1910, delivered just two months before the Mexican Revolution, went even further: "At the bottom of every problem—already social and political, taking these words in their widest senses—is a pedagogical problem, a problem of education."[11] Like both Comte and Barreda, Sierra had come to see the heart of education as moral, arguing directly against those who claimed that the university should be a mere knowledge factory or simple producer of science:

The essential element of a character is in the will; to make the will evolve intensely, by means of physical, intellectual, and moral cultivation from boy to man is the sovereign role of elementary school, of school par excellence. Character is formed when the mysterious magnetism of the good is impressed upon the will. Cultivating wills in order to reap egotisms would bankrupt pedagogy. It is necessary to magnetize character with love, to saturate man with the spirit of sacrifice, to make him feel the immense value of social life, to convert him into a moral person in the full and beautiful sense of the word, to perpetually navigate the course of that ideal, making it more real day by day, minute by minute. This is the divine mission of the teacher. (*IA*, 112)

Eight years earlier in the *Political Evolution of the Mexican People*, Sierra had argued that the higher goal of all education was to produce a Mexican soul. He now added that this required the Mexicanization of knowledge:

I imagine this: a group of students of all ages combined into one—the age of full intellectual ability, forming a real personality by force of solidarity and consciousness of their mission, and drawing upon all sources of culture—breaking out [...] and resolving **to nationalize science, to Mexicanize knowledge**. (*IA*, 113; bold added)

To Mexicanize knowledge was to make knowledge mestizo by:

raising one national language over the dust of all the indigenous strains, thus creating the primordial element of the nation's soul. The school, which systematically prepares the citizen in the child, initiating him into the national religion, into the cult of civic duty; this school forms an integral part of the state. (*IA*, 126)

Comte's religion of humanity had become the religion of Mexican nationalism, which only two months later would explode in the form of the Mexican revolution. But Sierra's intentions were anything but revolutionary. Much like the aims of almost all universities today, they were ostensibly middle-class and gently reformist:

> The university is in charge of the national education at the upper-middle and ideal levels; it is the summit where a crystal-clear fountain emerges to irrigate the homeland's newborn plants and raises the soul of the people to its level. (*IA*, 97)

Less poetically put, the National University of Mexico should house the concrete and practical disciplines that maintain the actual life of the nation through commerce and industry, "all that is necessary to persistently protect in the economic order" (*IA*, 97).

Mexico's Athenaeum of Youth: More Anti-Porfirist than Anti-Positivist

According to most scholars, anti-positivism was well established in Mexico by 1909, when the *Ateneo de la Juventud* (Athenaeum of Youth) was founded by a group of young intellectuals responding to the decadence of the Díaz regime and seeking to re-envision Mexico, Mexican identity, Mexican thought, and the Mexican education system.[12] These *ateneístas* are commonly believed to have revolted against positivism by drawing upon other philosophers like Arthur Schopenhauer, Friedrich Nietzsche, Henri Bergson, William James, and José Enrique Rodó. Given this influx of non-positivist intellectual influences and the unfolding revolutionary political landscape in Mexico, the reign of positivism as a semi-official ideology undoubtedly ended with the *ateneístas*. Nevertheless, there are striking continuities between positivism and their two leading philosophers José Vasconcelos (1882–1959) and Antonio Caso (1883–1946). Both were eager to establish themselves as part of a new and original generation of philosophers, but they also acknowledged their intellectual debt to Barreda and the initial activities of the *Ateneo* were made possible by Sierra. In any case, as the Porfiriato neared its end, positivism was no longer *positively* defined by Comte, Barreda, or even Sierra. Positivism increasingly came to be defined *negatively* by its opposition, not just in Mexico but across most of Latin America.

The *ateneístas* sought to philosophize for themselves, but they could not completely escape their early philosophical training in positivism, nor did they aspire to do so. For example, Antonio Caso's 1909 series of lectures in the National Preparatory School harkened back to the "method-loving" society of Barreda in a way that fit Comte's own description of the positivist method:

> In order to understand the true value and character of the Positive Philosophy, we must take a brief general view of the progressive course of the human mind, regarded as a whole, for *no conception can be understood otherwise than through its history.*[13]

Caso's lectures offered a historical panorama of positivism in order to clarify what could be saved, what should be supplemented, and what ought to be thrown out. This method of criticism demonstrated the legacy of Barreda's positivist philosophy of education, as institutionalized in the National Preparatory School where Caso had studied history under Sierra.

Jose Vasconcelos' 1910 lecture "Gabino Barreda and Contemporary Ideas" also returned to Barreda in order to repudiate the bases of Spencerian evolutionism that the *científicos* had used to justify the dictatorship of Porfirio Díaz as a necessary evil.[14] Vasconcelos interpreted Barreda's attempt to cultivate a national spirit by way of a positivist education as a necessary historical stage that moved Mexico beyond the philosophy of scholasticism. Although he acknowledged that "Barreda and positivism did not give us everything we longed for," Vasconcelos nevertheless claimed that Barreda's Comtean positivism had salutary moral effects upon Mexico and described the "abyss between the ideas of yesterday and today" in terms of the revolt against the Spencerian philosophy of the *científicos*. This more nuanced and specific *anti-positivism* (which we prefer to call *anti-Porfirism* for the sake of clarity) also explains Vasconcelos' remark that it was Spencer (not Comte) who up until very recently "was the official philosopher among us" (*GBIC*, 102). Simply put, Vasconcelos found positivism to have been necessary but not sufficient for his generation's intellectual growth.

Vasconcelos ends his lecture with a method for judging whether a philosophical system should be accepted in terms of three meta-theoretical norms to guide the philosophical quest for truth: 1) "The fundamental intuition of the philosophical system must never be in disagreement with scientific laws"; 2) "The synthesis must never infringe upon the formal laws of logic"; and 3) "The moral consequences of the system are … a confirmation of its vitality" (*GBIC*, 111). Once we recognize that all three of these meta-theoretical norms were shared by Comte, Barreda, and the later Sierra, Vasconcelos' closing reflections—often cited as evidence of his "anti-positivism"—appear in a different light:

> With the prudence suggested by the norms just studied, we have attempted to receive new ideas. The positivism of Comte and of Spencer could never contain our aspirations. Today, since it is in disagreement with the data of science itself, we find it lacking in vitality and reason. (*GBIC*, 112)

To say that positivism could not contain the aspirations of the *ateneístas* is perfectly compatible with their aspirations having been shaped by positivism, especially since they launched an assault on the ideology of Porfirism and the social Darwinism of the crasser *científicos* by claiming that they were "in disagreement with the data of science itself."

Positivism and Jose Vasconcelos' *Raza Cósmica*

Vasconcelos published *La raza cósmica* (*The Cosmic Race*) in 1925 after the armed conflict of the Mexican Revolution was over and while serving a seven-year term as Mexico's first Secretary of Public Education. It was Vasconcelos's most influential work, especially in terms of its impact on the later Chicanx movement in the United States. Vasconcelos reimagined and reinvigorated positivist themes to develop the thesis that "the various races of the earth tend to intermix at a gradually increasing pace, and eventually will give rise to a new human type."[15] As Didier T. Jaén notes:

> "Order and progress," the motto of Positivism, did not cease to be the motto of Mexican society after the Revolution. What the Revolution did was to change the basis of that order and to widen the field of social progress [...] beyond economic welfare: Order and progress were not ends in themselves but the basis for an ideal future development. (*CR*, xv)

The fact that Vasconcelos's vision culminated in a new "Aesthetic Age" challenged the values of the *científicos* by drawing upon non-positivist philosophical vocabularies, but Vasconcelos nevertheless envisioned a refigured humanity governed by love, effectively recapitulating the classical positivist's vision but replacing Comte's chief protagonists—France, Europe, and whites—with Mexico, Latin America, and mestizos:

> [Latin America's] predestination obeys the design of constituting the cradle of a fifth race into which all nations will fuse with each other to replace the four races that have been forging History apart from each other. The dispersion will come to an end on American soil; unity will be consummated there by the triumph of fecund love [...] The so-called Latin peoples, because they have been more faithful to their divine mission in America, are the ones called upon to consummate this mission. (*CR*, 18)

As this passage demonstrates, Vasconcelos' philosophy of history was no less sweeping or utopic than Comte's, Barreda's, or Sierra's. Like Comte, Vasconcelos sought to be a great synthesizer with a cosmopolitan vision; like Barreda, he saw an overarching, transnational purpose flowing through the stages of Mexican history; and like Sierra, he saw the mestizo as the chief protagonist with "the mission of fusing all peoples ethnically and spiritually" (CR, 19).

Vasconcelos claimed that this mission would be accomplished by "the law of the three social stages" (CR, 28). When he explained that the phrase "is not to be taken in the Comtian sense, but much more comprehensively," Vasconcelos was not rejecting Comte so much as rolling him into a larger philosophical vision. Both thinkers imagined the world moving from the material/warlike, to the intellectual/political, to the spiritual/loving. Moreover, Vasconcelos's refigured Humanity, the "cosmic race" that is able "to live joy grounded on love" as it is "ruled by sympathy," could only be reached through a long process of moral education like the one that Comte inspired Barreda to develop. Sierra's blending of philosophy of education with a "scientific" racial logic was also evident:

> Inferior races, upon being educated, would become less prolific, and the better specimens would go on ascending a scale of ethnic improvement, whose maximum type is not precisely the White, but that new race to which the White himself will have to aspire with the object of conquering the synthesis. (CR, 32)

Like Comte's original positivism, Vasconcelos's prophecy culminated not "in the triumph of a single race" but rather in "the redemption of all men" (CR, 35). In contrast, "The official policy and the Positivists' science, which was directly influenced by that policy, said that the law was not love but antagonism, fight, and the triumph of the fittest" (CR, 36).

Clearly, Vasconcelos's criticism of the "Positivists' science" was not directed at Comte's or Barreda's positivism, since they claimed that only love is capable of producing a new Humanity. Vasconcelos directed his criticism against the *cientΓficos* and "the vulgarity of Spencerian Darwinism" by citing new scientific discoveries in mathematics, physics, chemistry, and biology. But like Sierra, Vasconcelos modified Comte's philosophy of history by claiming that Latin America's mestizos would lead the creative evolution of the cosmic race:

> Only the Iberian part of the continent possesses the spiritual factors, the race, and the territory necessary for the great enterprise of initiating the new universal era of Humanity ... We have all the races and the aptitudes. The only thing lacking is for true love to organize and set in march the law of History. (CR, 38–39)

Positivism and Antonio Caso's Reflections on Existence as Charity

Vasconcelos and Caso grew up during the dictatorship of Porfirio Díaz and later witnessed the violence of the Mexican Revolution and two world wars. They were therefore somewhat mystified by the appearance of the generous act, which "in the midst of the meanness of the universe, is the strangest contradiction of the facts" (*GBIC*, 106). In contrast to Vasconcelos, Caso gave up on notions of collective progress and sought to understand progress at the level of the individual. Like his positivist forbearers, Caso believed that altruistic acts were the highest pinnacle of human achievement and worked practically to implement an educational system that would shape moral individuals. He served as director of the National Preparatory School founded by Barreda and as rector of the National University of Mexico.

The crux of Caso's thinking is expressed in *La existencia como economía, como desinterés y como caridad* (*Existence as Economy, as Disinterest, and as Charity*). First published as a brief essay in 1916, Caso expanded it into a book in 1919, and substantially revised it in 1943, noting that the essay had constituted his life's preoccupation.[16] Caso wanted to plumb the depths of the ruthless struggle for existence in which human beings find themselves as biological animals while nevertheless making more visible the aspects of human experience that are disinterested and meditating upon the human capacity for altruism. His 1916 preface to "Existence as Economy and as Charity" explained that he was inspired by "the most important event in the evolution of humanity: the development of evangelical ideas and feelings over time" as expressed not by theologians but rather in "the moral biography of some great Christians" (*EEDC*, 28). Caso's "worship of heroes and the heroic in history" was reminiscent of Comte's system of social worship based on the lives of great historical individuals, with its pedagogical counterpart in Barreda's system of moral education.

Caso began with the powerful forces of biology and economics even though he was ultimately more interested in the aesthetic, moral, and religious values that exist alongside and sometimes despite endless biological strife and economic struggle. The biological and economic processes described by Darwin and Spencer appear where organisms obey the law of life that is characterized by conscious or unconscious egoism aiming to achieve "*maximum gain with minimal effort*" (*EEDC*, 31). This is the "real world" of *existence as economy*, but to claim that this is the *only* aspect of existence, as many of the *científicos* did, is ideology masquerading as science. In contrast, Caso sought to philosophize on the basis of *all* experience, which includes *existence as disinterest* and *existence as charity*. He held to the utilitarian, pragmatic, or positivist principle that knowledge generally serves the will, that "intelligence is the faculty of creating tools, instruments of action" (*EEDC*, 32), but Caso also insisted that our being is not fully expended in being tool-using animals, that "the *surplus* of human energy makes man into a possible instrument of disinterested action and heroism" (*EEDC*, 35).

Like Vasconcelos, Caso outlined three historical stages and placed Comtean positivism in the second stage, holding on to Comte's vision of a humanity transformed by love but giving art a greater role to play in accomplishing this transformation. Drawing upon Arthur Schopenhauer and

Henri Bergson, Caso presented art in terms of disinterest: "Art is an opposition to material life, *an idealism or immaterialism,* a clear attitude that *renounces possessing in order to consecrate oneself to contemplating*" (*EEDC*, 36). Insisting that all human beings engage in at least some art or disinterested contemplation of the universe, Caso wrote: "When compared to the biological imperative of minimum effort, art appears to be a shocking waste, a violent and mysterious antithesis" (*EEDC*, 37). Caso believed that positivism could not understand art or charity because it negated the metaphysical competence of reason. He recognized that Comte did this not to condemn human intelligence to ignorance, but rather "to liberate it forever, obligating it to adhere to scientific, *positive* investigations where it could always achieve success in proportion to its energy" (*SPP*, 3:66). Yet precisely what Comte believed to be *positive,* Caso described as *negative*: "The error of positivism consists in having arbitrarily selected the data of experience. *True positivism, which complies with pure experience, will have to admit [...] the ultimate data of intuition*" (*SPP*, 3:67).

The remainder of Caso's essay meditates on the world as charity, or the fact that "heroic altruism" is possible. He claimed that positivism's scientific orientation could not give a satisfactory philosophical account of the very altruism it recommended. But Caso still agreed with the classical positivists that loving *action*, rather than scientific *knowledge*, constituted the height of human existence:

> Like struggle, charity is *a fact*. It is not demonstrated, it is practiced, *it is made*, like life. It is another way of life. You will never have the intuition of an order that is opposed to biological life, you will not understand existence in its profound richness, you will mutilate it beyond remedy, if you are not charitable. Fundamental intuitions must be lived. (*EEDC*, 41)

Setting aside intricate questions about Caso's doctrine of intuition or his metaphysics, Caso described charity as follows: "It is the fundamental religious and moral experience. It consists in going out of oneself, in giving oneself to others, in offering oneself, in making oneself available and lavishing oneself without fear of exhaustion" (*EEDC*, 39). This fundamental moral intuition lined up with Comte's later attempts to "place the intellect in its proper place; adjusting it in that wise subordination to the heart which forms the condition of all harmonious growth."[17] In turn, Comte would have agreed with Caso's words: "Reader: what you read here is only philosophy, and philosophy is an interest of knowledge. Charity is action. Go and commit acts of charity. Then, more than sage, you will be saint" (*EEDC*, 45).

Of course, Caso understood that charity required more than exhortations, which led him to respond to Barreda's philosophy of education while directing the National Preparatory School: "Educated in positivism, we will honor the memory of our educator [Barreda]. It will always have been good for us to have substituted the Comtean doctrine for scholasticism."[18] However, Caso criticized Barreda's educational system for failing to live up to Comte's aim of "subordinating the intellect to the heart":

> Our "National" Preparatory School, just as Barreda envisioned it, did not form anything but the intellect (and even this imperfectly, because human understanding without metaphysical culture will always be a diminished understanding), never sentiment and the will! (*CW*, 6:299)

Caso believed that the goal of moral education was to steer each individual toward altruism and moral sainthood. Like Barreda, Caso was not disposed to accomplish this via the cultic apparatus of Comte's religion of humanity but sought to integrate its moral aims into a system of education that would recognize that "there is no manner of forming a perfect man with primers and formulas, but there does exist a mode of integrating the spirit by sympathy and by conviction" (*OC*, 4:11). In contrast, "The man educated intellectually, only intellectually, only by pure thinking, is a profound egoist" (*CW*, 4:13).

Caso did not explicitly tie this point to the way that Barreda's National Preparatory School had inadvertently produced the *científicos*, who lent intellectual legitimacy to *porfirismo*, an ideology of "existence as economy." But Caso did insist that education must cultivate the other aspects of human existence, i.e., disinterest and charity:

> If we wish, then, to make men in the schools, let us form individual souls, form good animals, improve the race, forming men who are beautiful and ready for action. But at the same time ... let us make man charitable. Let us make him artistic. ... Then we will then have achieved the ends of education. (*CW*, 4:16–17)

In sum, Caso's educational aims with respect to morality were very close to Comte's and Barreda's, just as his views on scientific education were quite close to Sierra's.

The difference was in their philosophical understandings of freedom. Barreda's attempt to reconcile individual freedom with social necessity unintentionally paved the way for the abuses of Porfirism: "Liberty, far from being irreconcilable with order, consists, in all phenomena, both organic and inorganic, in submitting fully to the laws that determine those phenomena" (*EM*, 113). Caso's metaphysics of freedom turned Barreda's logic on its head: "The artist sacrifices the economy of life to the objectivity of innate intuition, whereas the good man sacrifices egoism to come to the aid of the neighbor, to prevent his pain, and such a sacrifice is free" (*EEDC*, 38). Simply put, the biological and economic laws of animal life command egoism, whereas disinterest and charity constitute the rejection of these laws. But since altruism must be freely chosen, Caso wrote:

> The good is like music that captivates and charms [...] the most inti-
> mate part of the soul. It is the coercion of neither pure reason nor
> external life. It is neither deduced, nor inferred, nor admitted; *it is cre-*
> *ated*. The good is freedom, personality, divinity. It is, to sum up with
> the expression of an illustrious Mexican thinker [Justo Sierra], "the
> supernatural that feels like the most natural thing in the world."
> (*EEDC*, 39)

In Caso's philosophy, we thus return full circle to Comte's summary of the subjective principle of positivism as "the subordination of the intellect to the heart."

Chicanx Identity, the Chicano Movement, and Gloria Anzaldúa's Mestiza Consciousness

The legacy of the Mexican philosophers discussed in this chapter clearly transcends national borders and extends to the history of the Chicano Movement, evolving conceptions of Chicanx identity, and Chicanx educa-tion. From Barreda to Caso, a central aim of Mexican philosophy was to build the Mexican nation or recreate the Mexican people by means of edu-cation. This same concern emerged in the 1960s along with a new way of being Mexican during the Chicano Movement, which was concentrated in the U.S. Southwest, i.e., the lands of Northern Mexico that were annexed by the United States as a result of the Mexican-American War, and which many Chicanxs began referring to as Aztlán, the place of origin of the pre-Columbian Mexican civilization commonly referred to as the Aztecs. The term was popularized by Alberto Baltazar Urista Heredia (1947–), better known by his pen name Alurista. Born in Mexico City, Alurista moved to San Diego, California when he was thirteen. In 1969, he attended the First National Chicano Youth Liberation Conference and read a moving poem that was adopted as the preamble to *El Plan Espiritual de Aztlán*, one of the most famous political manifestos of the Chicano Movement, which Alurista also helped to draft:

> In the spirit of a new people that is conscious not only of its proud
> historical heritage but also of the brutal "gringo" invasion of our terri-
> tories, we, the Chicano inhabitants and civilizers of the northern land of
> Aztlán from whence came our forefathers, reclaiming the land of their
> birth and consecrating the determination of our people of the sun,
> declare that the call of our blood is our power, our responsibility, and
> our inevitable destiny.[19]

El Plan also referred to Chicanos as "a bronze people with a bronze culture" or more simply as La Raza de Bronze, one of the ways that Vasconcelos had named *la raza cósmica*. It boldly declared "the independence of our mestizo nation," and called for "total liberation from oppression, exploitation, and racism" (*PEA*, 27).

Attempting to transcend "all religious, political, class, and economic factions or boundaries," *El Plan* claimed that nationalism "is the common denominator that all members of La Raza can agree upon" (*PEA*, 27). Despite being contentious, especially for many indigenous people reluctant to endorse a sweeping narrative in which their race and culture seem to disappear into a "higher" mestizo identity, it is a claim that Barreda, Sierra, Caso, and Vasconcelos would have endorsed in their own Mexican contexts. Consider these quotes from the "Organizational Goals" section of El Plan alongside some suggested parallels in brackets:

> UNITY in the thinking of our people ... all committed to the liberation of La Raza [*cf. Barreda's claim that the time was finally ripe for a "triple emancipation" of the Mexican people to be achieved by positivism weaving "all the intellects into a common synthesis."*]
>
> EDUCATION must be relative to our people, i.e., history, culture, bilingual education, contributions, etc. [*cf. Sierra's call to "nationalize science, to Mexicanize knowledge."*]
>
> CULTURAL values of our people strengthen our identity and the moral backbone of the movement. Our culture unites and educates the family of La Raza towards liberation with one heart and one mind. We must insure that our writers, poets, musicians, and artists produce literature and art that is appealing to our people and relates to our revolutionary culture. Our cultural values of life, family, and home will serve as a powerful weapon to defeat the gringo dollar value system and encourage the process of love and brotherhood. [*cf. Vasconcelos' claim that la raza cósmica would initiate an Aesthetic age when "unity will be consummated ... by the triumph of fecund love."*] (*PEA*, 28–29)

Like the classical Mexican philosophers, *El Plan's* authors believed these problems could be solved with a new education system. The second of six action items thus read:

> September 16, on the birthdate of Mexican Independence, a national walk-out by all Chicanos of all colleges and schools to be sustained until the complete revision of the educational system: its policy makers, administration, its curriculum, and its personnel to meet the needs of our community. (*PEA*, 29)

To give a rough idea of how badly the educational system was failing Chicanx youth, consider the fact that in 1967, Mexican American students across the Southwest had a 60% high school dropout rate and exceedingly few were able to attend institutes of higher education. Inequalities like this were the focus of the 1968 East Los Angeles Walkouts, which demonstrated the profound ability of *el movimiento* to mobilize youth.

A month after the first National Chicano Youth Liberation Conference drafted *El Plan Espiritual de Aztlán*, more than 100 Chicanx youth gathered at the University of Santa Barbara to flesh out their vision for a completely revised system of higher education.[20] *El Plan de Santa Barbara* served as a blueprint for Chicano/a Studies programs across the United States, and some of its features are clearly related to the legacy of Mexican positivism and its transformations. The first page of the 155-page document visually represented *la causa* (the cause) as a continuation of the Mexican revolution playing out in the struggles of the United Farm Workers, followed by another drawing with two textual areas of focus that read "LIBERACIÓN" and "POR MI RAZA HABLA EL ESPIRITO." We can read the first as a continuation of Barreda's Civic Oration, which called for the "triple emancipation" of Mexicans as people who had suffered "centuries of quiet domination under a system perfectly designed to endlessly prolong a situation of domination and continuous exploitation by way of education, religious beliefs, politics, and administration" (*OC*, 83). The second text was a variation on the motto that Vasconcelos coined for the National Autonomous University of Mexico: "Por mi raza hablará el espíritu" ("Through my race the spirit will speak"), which *El Plan de Santa Barbara* brought into the present as "The spirit is speaking through my race." After the drawings, the "Manifesto" chapter opened with these words:

> For all people, as with individuals, the time comes when they must reckon with their history. For the Chicano the present is a time of renaissance, of renacimiento. Our people and our community, el barrio and la colonia, are expressing a new consciousness and a new resolve. Recognizing the historical tasks confronting our people and fully aware of the cost of human progress, we pledge our will to move. We will move forward toward our destiny as a people. We will move against those forces which have denied us freedom of expression and human dignity. [*cf. Barreda trying to "reckon with history," Sierra trying to "recognize the historical tasks confronting our people," and the Atheneum of Youth "moving against those forces which have denied us freedom."*] (*PSB*, 9)
>
> Chicanismo draws its faith and strength from two main sources: from the just struggle of our people and from an objective analysis of our community's strategic needs. We recognize that without a strategic use of education, an education that places value on what we value, we will not realize our destiny. Chicanos recognize the central importance of institutions of higher learning to modern progress, in this case, to the development of our community. But we go further: we believe that higher

education must contribute to the formation of a complete man who truly values life and freedom. [*cf. classical Mexican philosophers who linked the destiny of the Mexican people to strategic education, built educational institutions to foster modern progress, and developed a vision of complete education.*] (*PSB*, 9–10)

The destiny of our people will be fulfilled. To that end, we pledge our efforts and take as our credo what Jose Vasconcelos once said at a time of crisis and hope: "At this moment we do not come to work for the university, but to demand that the university work for our people." (*PSB*, 11)

The practical substance of the plan consisted of chapters devoted to organizing and instituting Chicano studies programs, designing a curriculum, recruitment and admissions, support programs, political action, campus organizing, and a number of appendices that provide models of Chicano Studies programs at the graduate, bachelor, and associate levels, as well sample syllabi and course outlines, just as daring in scope as the reconstruction of education instituted by Gabino Barreda's Organic Law of Public Instruction. In short, the authors of both the *El Plan Espiritual de Aztlán* and the *El Plan de Santa Barbara* outlined nation-building educational plans for the Chicano nation of Aztlán whose logic and rhetoric bear a substantial resemblance to the nation-building educational plans of Mexicans from Barreda to Vasconcelos.

Of course, the story of Mexican philosophy continued to play out in the United States even after the Chicano Movement waned in the late 1970s. In 1987, the feminist-visionary-spiritual-activist-poet-philosopher Gloria Anzaldúa, who grew up on the U.S. side of the South Texas-Northern Mexico borderlands, published *Borderlands/La Frontera: The New Mestiza* in a mixture of English and Spanish. Dedicated "*a todos mexicanos* on both sides of the border," her book drew upon Aztec philosophy (by way of the Mexican philosopher Miguel Leon-Portilla) and Mexican philosophy (by way of Vasconcelos) to articulate a transformed ideal of "mestiza consciousness." While Anzaldúa's work was continuous with the early Chicano movement in terms of her appeal to Aztlán— Chapter 1 is called "The Homeland, Aztlán / *El otro México*"—her philosophy: 1) widened the sense of *mexicanidad* to include indigenous Mesoamericans and Mexicans on both sides of the U.S.-Mexico border; 2) corrected for Vasconcelos' lack of vision with respect to the gender of the mestizo by calling for a "mestiza consciousness"; 3) broadened Vasconcelos' concepts of *la raza cósmica* and *mestizaje* by simultaneously appealing to indigeneity and allowing for the possibility mestiza consciousness might be developed by people from *any* race or ethnicity; and 4) attempted to transcend nationalist discourse by decoupling the linkage between a people and a nation. Here is the beginning of Chapter 7: "*La conciencia de la mestiza* / Towards a New Consciousness":

Por la mujer de mi raza
hablará el espíritu.

José Vasconcelos, Mexican philosopher, envisaged *una raza mestiza, una mezcla de razas afines, una raza de color—la primera raza síntesis del globo.* He called it a cosmic race, *la raza cósmica,* a fifth race embracing the four major races of the world. Opposite to the theory of the pure Aryan, and to the policy of racial purity that white America practices, his theory is one of inclusivity. [...] From this racial, ideological, cultural and biological cross-pollinization, an "alien" consciousness is presently in the making—a new mestiza consciousness, *una conciencia de mujer.* It is a consciousness of the Borderlands.[21]

A fuller treatment of Anzaldúa's philosophy exceeds this chapter's scope, but these selections illustrate how understanding the legacy of Mexican positivism and its transformations is crucial for understanding subsequent developments in Chicanx philosophy.

Education Today

To bring together the transformations of positivism explored in this chapter—stretching from Barreda's mid-19th century attempt to design a national education system for Mexico to the late-20th century attempts to develop Chicanx Studies and reshape Chicanx identities in the United States—let us consider the current status of moral education that Barreda envisioned as the crown of a positivist education, or what Sierra called "moving the heart of peoples." Whether in Mexico or the United States, we might reasonably complain with Caso that our public schools and universities "[do] not form anything but the intellect." On the positivist model, the Church was supposed to stop providing moral education and leave this project to the State. On this front, we must judge positivism to have been a practical failure, for while it did occasionally recognize and articulate just how incomplete a *merely* scientific or technical education would be, it failed to provide any real substitute for moral reflection and formation, and it was often used as ideological weapon to maintain the rule of the rich and powerful. The philosophical question that the positivists left us—how scientific and moral education are (or ought to be) related—remains alive, important, and unresolved.

Notes

1 The Mexican philosopher Leopoldo Zea (1912–2004), whose work is treated in subsequent chapters, profoundly shaped the last 75 years of scholarship on Latin American positivism. See Zea, *The Latin American Mind* and *Positivism in Mexico.*
2 Comte, *The Positive Philosophy of Auguste Comte,* 1:2. Cited in text with the abbreviation *PPAC,* volume number, and page number.
3 Barreda, "Oración cívica," 82; italics in original. This and all subsequent translations of works cited in Spanish are ours. Cited in text with the abbreviation *OC* and page number.

4 "De la educación moral," 107–108. Cited in text using abbreviation *EM* and page number.
5 Comte, *System of Positive Polity*, 1: xxxv. Cited in text using abbreviation *SPP*, volume number, and page number.
6 Barreda, "Discurso de laudación del artista Juan Cordero," 154.
7 Our choice to reserve the term *positivism* for the philosophies of Comte and Barreda is only stipulative. They are the original positivists in their respective contexts, but our argument does not depend upon the claim that there is something more essentially positivist about their philosophies than the later philosophies of Spencer and Sierra.
8 Sierra, *Political Evolution of the Mexican People*. Cited in text using abbreviation *PEMP* and page number.
9 Barreda, "Informe presentado a la Junta Directiva de Estudios," 127.
10 Comte's positivist doctrine of human progress was also racist. For example, he believed that the religion of humanity would spread from the "white races" of Western Europe to the "less advanced" races across the globe. *System of Positive Polity*, 1:313–317. Comte nevertheless held that the "highest affection for humanity" was "incompatible with any feeling of hatred towards other races" (1:568).
11 Sierra, "Inaugural Address," 112. Cited in text using abbreviation *IA* and page number. Full title: "Discourse at the Inauguration of the National University (September 22, 1910)."
12 See Hurtado, "The Anti-Positivist Movement in Mexico."
13 Comte, *The Positive Philosophy of Auguste Comte*, 1; italics added.
14 Vasconcelos, "Gabino Barreda y las ideas contemporáneas." Cited in text using abbreviation *GBIC* and page number.
15 Vasconcelos, *The Cosmic Race*, 3. Cited in text using abbreviation *CR* and page number.
16 We cite the 1916 essay because it has been fully translated in Sánchez and Sanchez (eds.), *Mexican Philosophy in the 20th Century*. Cited in text using the abbreviation *EEDC* and page number.
17 Comte, *System of Positive Polity*, 1:xxxiv.
18 Caso, *Obras Completas*, 6:298. Cited in text using abbreviation *CW*, volume number, and page number.
19 Alurista, "El Plan Espiritual de Aztlán," 27–30. Cited in text using abbreviation *PEA* and page number.
20 Chicano Coordinating Council on Higher Education, *El Plan de Santa Bárbara: A Chicano Plan for Higher Education*.
21 Anzaldúa, *Borderlands*, 99.

Bibliography

Alurista. "El Plan Espiritual de Aztlán." In *Aztlan: Essays on the Chicano Homeland*, edited by Rudolfo Anaya, Francisco A. Lomelí and Enrique R. Lamadrid. University of New Mexico Press, 2017.
Anzaldúa, Gloria. *Borderlands/La frontera: The New Mestiza*. 2nd edition. San Francisco: Aunt Lute Press, 1987.
Barreda, Gabino. "De la educación moral." In *Opúsculos, discusiones y discursos*, 107–117. México: Imprenta del Comercio de Dublán y Chávez, 1877.
Barreda, Gabino. "Informe presentado a la Junta Directiva de Estudios." In *Opúsculos, discusiones y discursos*, 119–131. México: Imprenta del Comercio de Dublán y Chávez, 1877.

Barreda, Gabino. "Oración cívica." In *Opúsculos, discusiones y discursos*, 81–105. México: Imprenta del Comercio de Dublán y Chávez, 1877.

Barreda, Gabino. "Discurso de laudación del artista Juan Cordero." In *Estudios*, edited by José Fuentes Mares. México: Universidad Nacional Autónoma, 1941.

Caso, Antonio. *Obras Completas*. Edited by RosaKrauze de Kolteniuk. 11 vols. México: Universidad Nacional Autónoma de México, 1971.

Caso, Antonio. "Existence as Economy and as Charity: An Essay on the Essence of Christianity." Translated by Alexander V. Stehn and Jose G. Rodriguez Jr. In *Mexican Philosophy in the 20th Century: Essential Readings*, edited by Carlos Alberto Sánchez and Robert Eli Sanchez, 27–45. New York: Oxford University Press, 2017.

Chicano Coordinating Council on Higher Education. *El Plan de Santa Bárbara: A Chicano Plan for Higher Education*. Oakland, CA: La Causa Publications, 1969.

Comte, Auguste. *The Positive Philosophy of Auguste Comte*. Translated by Harriet Martineau. 2 vols. New York: Cambridge University Press, [1853] 2009.

Comte, Auguste. *System of Positive Polity*. Translated by Richard Congreve. 4 vols. London: Longmans, Green, and Co., 1875–1877.

Hurtado, Guillermo. "The Anti-Positivist Movement in Mexico." In *A Companion to Latin American Philosophy*, edited by Susanna Nuccetelli, Ofelia Schutte and Otávio Bueno. Malden, MA: Wiley-Blackwell, 2009.

Mill, John Stuart. *Auguste Comte and Positivism*. Ann Arbor: University of Michigan Press, [1865] 1961.

Sierra, Justo. *The Political Evolution of the Mexican People*. Translated by Charles Ramsdell. Austin: University of Texas Press, 1969.

Sierra, Justo. *Obras Completas: Discursos*. Edited by Agustín Yáñez. México: Universidad Nacional Autónoma de México, 1991.

Sierra, Justo. "Discourse at the Inauguration of the National University (September 22, 1910)." In *Mexican Philosophy in the 20th Century: Essential Readings*, edited by Carlos Alberto Sánchez and Robert Eli Sanchez, 17–26. New York: Oxford University Press, 2017.

Vasconcelos, José. *The Cosmic Race: A Bilingual Edition*. Translated by Didier Tisdel Jaén. Baltimore, MD: Johns Hopkins University Press, 1997.

Vasconcelos, José. "Gabino Barreda y las ideas contemporáneas." In *Conferencias del Ateneo de la Juventud*, edited by Juan Hernández Luna, 97–113. México: Universidad Nacional Autónoma de México, 1962.

Zea, Leopoldo. *The Latin American Mind*. Translated by James H. Abbott and Lowell Dunham. Norman: University of Oklahoma Press, 1963.

Zea, Leopoldo. *Positivism in Mexico*. Translated by Josephine H. Schulte. Austin: University of Texas Press, 1974.

5 The Philosophy of Mexican Culture

Robert Eli Sanchez, Jr.

One of the dominant themes in 20th century Latin American philosophy is whether it exists, and, if so, whether it is original or substantively different from philosophy elsewhere. In 1925, José Mariátegui (Peru) wrote an article titled "Is There Such a Thing as Hispanic-American Thought?" In 1949, Risieri Frondizi (Argentina) publicly doubted the originality of the philosophy produced in Latin America. And in the late 1960s, the Mexican philosopher Leopoldo Zea debated the Peruvian philosopher Augusto Salazar Bondy over the existence of a *distinctly* Latin American philosophy. Was philosophy in Latin America, as Bondy argued, merely European philosophy passing through Latin America, or was it, as Zea argued, peculiarly Latin American?

At the center of this ongoing conversation are two philosophers whose effort to relate philosophy to culture continues to challenge Latin American and Latinx philosophers. The first is Samuel Ramos (Mexico), whose *Profile of Man and Culture in Mexico* (1934) is widely considered the first text in a tradition now referred to as *la filosofía de lo mexicano* (the philosophy of Mexicanness). Ramos was also the first to establish a course at the National University (*Universidad Nacional Autónoma de México* or UNAM) on the history of philosophy in Mexico, one result of which was his pioneering *History of Philosophy in Mexico* (1943). In this book, Ramos claims that the early philosophy of José Ortega y Gasset (Spain) provided Mexicans with "the epistemological justification for a national philosophy." In particular, Ramos claims that a generation of Mexicans was guided by Ortega's dictum, "I am myself plus my circumstance, and if I do not save my circumstance, I do not save myself."

The primary purpose of this chapter is to provide a brief outline of Ramos's philosophy of *lo mexicano*, paying particular attention to his definition of *authentic* Mexican philosophy. In the second section, we will consider two objections to the meaning and possibility of a national philosophy. In the third section, we will consider Ortega's early thought, which I suggest, in the final section, may provide us with a justification of a distinct philosophy defined by cultural identity.

Authentic Mexicanness

In a provocative essay, *The Hedgehog and the Fox*, Isaiah Berlin claims that some people know many small things (foxes) and some know one big thing (hedgehogs). In philosophy, we might cast this as the difference between those who aim to solve a number of philosophical problems and those who develop one idea over the course of their careers. For our purposes, Ramos was a hedgehog. What was Ramos's big idea? At the end of *Twenty Years of Education in Mexico* (1941), he writes:

> Of one thing I am convinced: we will not make it through our crisis with imported doctrines, with ready-made formulas. There is a difficult, but inevitable, task ahead of us: that of creating our own standards and doctrines. We have to commit ourselves tirelessly to this work, without worrying about whether we are called "revolutionaries" or "reactionaries," since, in the end, those names are just misleading labels, mere political fictions. The important thing is to think about the nation's problems objectively, not on the basis of our interests or personal passions. As long as we live plagiarizing and imitating the foreigner, we are lost. A nation's destiny depends on nothing other than itself, on the potential of its own mind and well-practiced and disciplined will. At this point we should not try to solve our problems with culture and education blindly, because it would be unforgivable to repeat the same mistakes. We will prove our intellectual maturity by honestly recognizing our failures and converting them into standards of what we should not do. On that the salvation of Mexico depends.[1]

In many ways, this captures Ramos's philosophy of culture in a nutshell. Because it is so condensed, however, it will benefit from a little unpacking.

"On that the salvation of Mexico depends"

One central feature of the philosophy of Mexican culture is Ramos's belief that philosophy is *instrumentally valuable*. Throughout his corpus, Ramos speaks of the need to solve "our problems" or "the Mexican crisis" or "the problem of Mexico," and he often claims or suggests that philosophy is fundamentally an applied discipline.[2] So, in one sense, Ramos believed that philosophy could, or at least ought to try to, "save" Mexico from its immediate problems. But he also suggests a broader understanding of "salvation" in the following line: "Philosophy for us Hispano-Americans is not worthwhile only as a conception of the world and human life, but as an instrument to locate our world, life, and position in the more general picture of human understanding.[3] Philosophy, in other words, is not just instrumental in that it helps to solve practical problems; it also provides a sense of one's historical location and cultural identity.

To develop this sense of "salvation" further, Ramos explains why it was important that a philosopher (in particular, José Vasconcelos) be put in charge of education reform in Mexico (see chapter 4):

> But there is no doubt that the aim that inspired reform emerged from a profound understanding of the needs of the Mexican people. In my judgment, Vasconcelos was the first to understand this very simple truth (so simple that nobody had seen it): that what most urgently has to be taught to the Mexican people is how to live. ... There we find our people, who know how to *endure* life, which is not the same as knowing how to *live*, but rather, knowing how to die, which is the negation of all wisdom. (*TYEM*, 56)

The goal of philosophy, then—the foundation of all wisdom—is to find something to live for, a cultural *mission* or *destiny*, as Ramos sometimes puts it.

In the *Profile of Man and Culture in Mexico*, Ramos writes, "Up to now, Mexicans have known only how to die; it is time they learned how to live,"[4] and he asks, forcefully, "What then does the Mexican live for?" (*P*, 65) Until she can answer this question, the Mexican cannot hope to solve Mexico's practical problems.

"As long as we live plagiarizing and imitating the foreigner, we are lost."

In the *Profile*, Ramos writes: "Today very serious problems persist because the schism between the culture inspired in our cathedrals, and the other, which emanates from our ruins" (*P*, 85). That is, on Ramos's account, one explanation of Mexico's problems—social, political, economic, and cultural—is its inability to resolve its racial and ethnic hybridity (*mestizaje* in Spanish). For Ramos, the problem became especially acute after Mexico achieved its independence from Spain in 1821, at which point, he argues, Mexican culture vacillated between what Ramos calls *false Europeanism* and *false Mexicanism*.

By false Europeanism, Ramos is referring to a cultural tendency to reject wholesale the peculiarities of Mexican culture in favor of European ideas, customs, and institutions. It is a kind of cultural conservatism built on a blind imitation of European culture, which, at times, could be comic, as when Mexican elites "adorned their houses with mansard roofs, even though it never snows in Mexico" (*P*, 53). In general, though, it amounts to the belief that the salvation of post-colonial Mexico depends on measuring up to European culture *at the expense* of the reality of Mexican culture:

> The original sin of Mexican Europeanism was its lack of a standard for selecting foreign seeds of culture which in our spiritual earth could have produced the appropriate remedies for particular needs. That standard should have been none other than reality itself, but reality was unknown because all our attention and interest had turned to Europe. (*P*, 101–102)

Immediately after the Mexican Revolution, which corresponds to the height of nationalism in Mexico, the pendulum had swung the other way. Mexicans began to blame Europe for the persistence of their social, political, and economic problems. And they were growing intellectually suspicious of the hallmarks of modern Western culture, such as capitalism, individualism, industrialization, and the universality of Reason. As a result, Mexican artists and intellectuals pursued the roots of Mexican identity in pre-Columbian indigenous culture, and they aimed to celebrate and cultivate their own folk traditions. (For more on *indigenism*, see chapter 9.) For Ramos, however, this newfound Mexicanism was equally false, and for the same reason:

> The Mexican never takes into account the reality of his life, that is, those limitations which history, race, and biological conditions impose on his future. The Mexican plans his life as if he were free to choose any course of action that appealed to his imagination as interesting or valuable. He is unaware that the horizon of possibilities is extremely limited for every man and every people. ... He now proposes to invent a culture, a Mexican way of life, a utopia more extreme than the Europeanized one, because he now thinks he can create something out of nothing. The essential virtue for the Mexican of today is sincerity. Without it he cannot remove the mask with which he disguises his authentic being from himself. (*P*, 73–75)

In both cases, false Mexicanism and false Europeanism, the Mexican fails to realize that she is inescapably both Mexican *and* European, and that authenticity requires confronting the reality of Mexico's cultural hybridity.

For Ramos, authenticity does not require originality. Rather:

> By Mexican culture we mean universal culture made into our own, the kind that can coexist with us and appropriately express our spirit. Curiously enough, the only way available to us—in order to shape our Mexican culture—is to continue learning about European culture. (*P*, 108)

In other words, to forge a distinctly Mexican culture, one that expresses "our most authentic being," does not require inventing Mexican culture from scratch; it requires identifying "a standard for selecting foreign seeds of culture which in our spiritual [land] could have produced the appropriate remedies for particular needs" (*P*, 102).

In short, Mexican culture is not only essentially hybrid but also *derivative*. That is, although it is a mistake to imitate European culture merely *because it is European*, "our capital city should reject all picturesque Mexicanism lacking in universality" (*P*, 112). Further, "we shall never be able to decipher the mysteries of our being unless we can illuminate its depths with a guiding ideal that can come only from Europe" (P, 107). For better or worse, on Ramos's account, all culture has its roots in Europe.

"Creating our own standards and doctrines"

Before we dismiss this last statement as offensive and patently false, we ought to understand why Ramos believes it, or at least clarify what he means. For Ramos, *culture* refers to those products that manifest universal ideals—the true, the beautiful, the just, and the eternal. It is a general term for the various efforts to *transcend* one's immediate experience and biological life. (Compare to Antonio Caso's view of human existence, chapter 2.) Culture, in other words, is the expression of human *dignity* or what distinguishes human beings from the material world.[5]

For Ramos, culture is ultimately cultivated by philosophical inquiry under the light of reason, which he believes was introduced into Western civilization and perfected by "the Mediterranean mind" (i.e., the Greco-Roman origins of Western civilization).[6] But culture is not the product of pure rationality or purely disinterested philosophical reflection. Instead, genuine culture is always "culture in action" (P, 117); it is where universal ideals hit the ground in concrete reality. So, just as it is a mistake to try to cultivate a picturesque Mexicanism lacking in universalism, it is equally mistaken to employ universal ideas only *because they are universal*. Instead, authentic Mexican culture amounts to employing certain universal ideas of Western philosophy *because they are relevant to* Mexican *reality*, that is, to the philosopher's circumstance.

What is *truly* Mexican, then, is not just what originates in Mexico. Authentic Mexican culture need not be original in this sense. But there is another sense of original in which it might be. In *The History of Philosophy in Mexico*, for example, Ramos introduces us to the 19th century Mexican philosopher Benito Díaz de Gamarra, whose corpus "constitutes without any doubt the first *autochthonous* intellectual movement in this region of America" (HPM, 68, my emphasis). He writes:

> What has to be investigated in those philosophical ideas is not the originality of innovative thought, since our history derives from the currents of European idea, but [the originality of] the peculiar form in which these ideas have been reflected in our intellectual life. The truly important thing in our philosophical history is to demonstrate which ideas or doctrines have contributed to the development of the character of our being and of our national culture, and how they have done so: which philosophical ideas have been *assimilated*, becoming vital elements in our existence. (HPM, 64)

In other words, Gamarra's philosophy was original (and autochthonous) not because he developed new ideas but because he applied old ideas *in new ways* or because he *renewed* old ideas in new circumstances.

The key distinction for Ramos is between *imitation* and *assimilation*. When one imitates—or when one *only* imitates—one fails to realize one's own potential and true self. By contrast, when one assimilates, one makes an idea, system, or method one's *own*, suggesting that one can realize one's own potential without having to invent oneself or one's culture from scratch. Again, Gamarra offers an illustration of the difference:

> Gamarra is not an imitator of modern philosophers; he is a mind that has assimilated the content of their philosophy, on his own, after examining and selecting what seemed true in the light of his rational consciousness.
>
> There is another criterion for evaluating Hispanic-American philosophical production, which is to ascertain whether a work, more than being original in the strict sense of the term, has been assimilated to our American existence and influence the organization of our culture. (*HPM*, 67)

Thus, for Ramos, the difference between assimilation and imitation is not just a question of *originality*. If culture is always culture in action, i.e., where universal ideals hit the ground in concrete reality, and if blind imitation is a way of ignoring one's concrete reality, then culture imitated is not culture at all. Conversely, culture assimilated is not only a way of applying universal ideals to local circumstances; it is also a way of engaging those circumstances, in immersing oneself in them, and ultimately developing a clearer sense of who one is, or, in Ramos's case, what it means to be Mexican. For without a clear understanding of one's cultural or national identity, one lacks "a standard for selecting foreign seeds of culture which in our spiritual earth could have produced the appropriate remedies for particular needs" (*P*, 101–102).

A Clearly Defined National Character

In the preface to the third edition of the *Profile*, Ramos describes the text as a *characterology* of the Mexican people (*P*, 4). Like other leading intellectuals of his generation, he wanted to identify and describe *lo mexicano*. What, if anything aside from nationality, makes a Mexican, Mexican? Although Ramos did not initiate the search for *lo mexicano* (Mexicanness), he was perhaps the first to employ psychoanalytic theory to diagnose the Mexican psyche, representing the beginning of what might be dubbed the psychological turn of Mexican nationalism.[7] In a chapter titled "Psychoanalysis of the Mexican," Ramos argues that, at bottom, the Mexican suffers from a collective inferiority complex. To be clear, he is not claiming that Mexicans *are* inferior in any way: "we do not believe in the theory of inferior races" (P, 41). Rather, he believes that the typical Mexican *feels* inferior, particularly to the European and *estadounidense* (someone from the United States), and that he compensates for his perceived inferiority by pretending to be someone other than himself.

In the end, Ramos believes that attributing an inferiority complex to *the* Mexican, that is, the person who represents what it means to be Mexican, helps to make sense of the "mechanism of the Mexican mind." To elucidate how this mechanism works, he offers a character analysis of the *pelado*, who "constitutes the most elemental and clearly defined expression of national character" (P, 58). Although the term *pelado* is nearly impossible to translate—it *roughly* translates as "inner city bum"—it refers to what would have been a familiar character in Mexican society in the 1930s.[8] At a distance, however, we might imagine a destitute figure in the slums with torn clothes, likely drunk, who is easily offended, touchy, and who uses vulgar language and aggressive behavior in order to conceal his deep-seated sense of inferiority and to disempower those who threaten his fragile ego. Like others suffering from an inferiority complex, the *pelado* represents a class of individuals "who manifest an exaggerated preoccupation with affirming their personality; who take a strong interest in all things or situations that signify power, and who have an immoderate eagerness to dominate, to be the first everything" (P, 56).

Although the *pelado* was a minor character in Mexican society whose extreme behavior makes them more of an exception than the rule, Ramos argues that the Mexican's sense of inferiority cuts across class, social position, and education. More basic than how one acts, or whether one tries to affirm one's personality by dominating others, is the extent to which one struggles to conceal their psychological disposition and reality. "The Mexican psyche," Ramos writes, "is the result of reactions that strive to conceal an inferiority complex" (P, 58), which, in "its simplest form ... amounts to superimposing on one's real being the image of what one would like to be, and to interpreting this image as reality" (P, 69–70). Thus, we "can imagine the Mexican as a man who flees from himself to take refuge in a fictitious world" (P, 71). In a word, the clearest indication that one suffers from an inferiority complex are the various ways one tries to conceal one's own sense of inferiority and the reality of one's situation.

At the level of culture in Mexico, this flight from reality takes the form of false Mexicanism and false Europeanism, described above, which are modes of being unwilling to acknowledge the reality of Mexican identity (i.e., its hybridity, *mestizaje*, or what Ramos calls *creole culture*). In the case of false Europeanism, the Mexican imitates European culture in order to measure up to the European, but does so without taking into account the circumstances that distinguish the Mexican from the European. In the case of false Mexicanism, the Mexican disregards or rejects the derivative nature of Mexican identity, leading to false claims of originality (understood as novelty). In both cases, the Mexican distances herself from a conscious awareness of what it means to be Mexican, without which there is no standard for choosing which of the universal ideas apply to Mexican circumstances. She lacks, in other words, an essential condition for the possibility of authentic Mexican culture:

> The task of giving our way of life a characteristic stamp lacked the point of departure it logically should have had: knowledge of the Mexican man. Until his character, his desires, his capabilities, and his historical vocation are defined, all projects for reviving a national sense will be blind attempts doomed to failure. (*P*, 97)

Mexican Humanism

One way of characterizing Ramos's philosophy of culture is to say that he is resisting what he calls "the abandonment of culture in Mexico," a phrase that we now can read two ways. On the one hand, as we have seen, Ramos is critiquing two ways of failing to achieve authentic *Mexican* culture (emphasis on "Mexican"). Neither the imitation of European culture nor the effort to invent an original Mexican culture from scratch adequately appreciates the derivative, hybrid nature of Mexican culture. On the other hand, Ramos is also critiquing an increasingly pervasive worldview, both in Europe and Mexico, "that imagines the world as a machine" (*P*, 99), that is, one devoid of transcendent or objective values that guide us on our path toward living well, not just more comfortably or longer (emphasis on "culture"). As such, the search for Mexican culture should not interest only the Mexican, since the search for Mexican culture is the search for *culture* more broadly, which Ramos believed was in the process of being forgotten in our materialism, enthusiasm for technology, industrialization, and a thoroughly mechanistic view of the world.[9]

At the center of this question of culture, moreover, is the question concerning what it means to be human, for examining the aspiration of culture is a way of asking the following: after we answer all the questions about biological life, and after we achieve maximum comfort and longevity, what is the nature of *human* destiny and the objective values that constitute it? In this way, the search for Mexican culture at the time, insofar as it aims to rescue culture, is a quest for a new form of *humanism*, specifically one that synthesizes Greek and Renaissance humanism. Although Ramos would not systematically develop his new humanism until 1940,[10] he suggests in the *Profile* that the goal of culture is to reconcile a dualistic conception of being human, one that wavers between an emphasis on the objective and spiritual (what he calls Greek humanism) and an emphasis on the subjective or individual and natural (Renaissance humanism). In short, insofar as all culture is "culture in action," the search for Mexican culture in particular amounts

to the same as the quest for a new humanism—namely, an adequate definition of *culture* that does not abandon either the concrete or the universal.

Mexican Philosophy

Yet another way to characterize his project is to say that Ramos aimed to
produce Mexican philosophy, an original contribution whose defining characteristics stand apart from European philosophy. As we have seen, Ramos
is operating with a broad definition of philosophy, which is concerned not
only with abstract problems, the universe, or objective values, but also with
the project of self-knowledge, individual and collective:

> It has always seemed to me that one of the ways of doing Mexican
> philosophy is to reflect on our own philosophical reality, the reality of
> Mexican philosophers and their ideas, to find out if there are dominant
> features that characterize the national mind. (*HPM*, 63–64)

Ramos's effort to reconstruct the history of Mexican philosophy also indicates the path toward Mexican authenticity. He argues that "there is not in
the entire history of our thought a single philosopher who can be considered
original or creative. To this day, we cannot boast of having contributed a
great philosophical view to universal culture" (*HPM*, 66). But it does not
follow that Mexican philosophy is completely unoriginal. Instead, defining
authentic Mexican identity amounts to identifying which of the long list of
objective values are particularly relevant "to the project of knowing their
country and elucidating their national character" (*HPM*, 67).

Finally, the project of studying and producing Mexican philosophy is part
and parcel of the new humanism envisioned by Ramos. By championing the
development of philosophy in Mexico, Ramos believed that he was helping
to cultivate an appreciation for the objective values of culture that would
help Mexicans "avoid the monstrosities that arise from fetishizing the
machine" (*P*, 70). At the same time, by insisting on the value of philosophy
for Mexican life, and on the possibility of a distinctly Mexican philosophy,
Ramos believed that he was helping to demonstrate that all culture is culture
in action. In other words, making the case for a national philosophy, for
Ramos, was one expression of his effort to substantiate a fuller conception
of being human, one that fully appreciates and attempts to synthesize the
spiritual and biological elements of human life.

No Brands of Philosophy

Not surprisingly, Ramos's philosophy of Mexican culture received its share
of critics. Aside from Ramos's unflattering portrait of the Mexican, some
critics object to the idea that Mexican identity has an *essence*. Mexico
covers a wide territory with a diverse population, so any discussion of *the*

Mexican soul, some argue, is motivated by political interests that ultimately exclude more than they include. Others, such as Emilio Uranga, objected to Ramos's use of psychoanalysis to define the Mexican (see chapter 6). And still others continue to object to the Eurocentric assumptions underlying Ramos's philosophy of culture and of *lo mexicano*. For the purposes of introducing the philosophy of José Ortega y Gasset, however, we will focus on two criticisms of national philosophy, which the historian of Mexican philosophy Patrick Romanell summarizes well:

> The reason that the Mexican author hardly goes beyond his program-matic intentions of making a positive case for a national philosophy of Mexico, is that he really cannot, strictly speaking. As the early Ramos initially realized only too well, philosophy as such belongs to "the sphere of the universal" and, if so, philosophy of Mexican culture (or history) cannot be philosophy except by fiat, ex hypothesi. A brand of tequila, for example, can be marked "Made in Mexico," but a brand of philosophy cannot (at least not in the same sense).[11]

Frondizi

The first objection is articulated by Risieri Frondizi in 1949, who argued that Latin Americans had, by and large, failed to produce an original con-tribution to philosophy, in part because they were too concerned with the authenticity or originality of their own philosophy. Every people, Frondizi claimed, possesses a worldview. That is, he agrees that there is a Mexican experience or form of life, just as there was a Hellenistic form of life. However, to count as *philosophy*, a worldview must be subjected to critical self-examination. Further, Frondizi believed, what distinguishes philosophy from ideology is that it ought to be done in a "purely philosophical con-text," that is, independently of non-philosophical interests (personal, reli-gious, political, or economic). Philosophy is a purely *disinterested* discipline, and even though the truths of philosophy might be applied after they are established, utility is not a criterion of philosophical truth.

With these defining features of philosophy, *sensu stricto*, it is not hard to see why Frondizi objects to Ramos's philosophy of Mexican culture or the larger trend in Latin America that it represents. Simply, the effort to culti-vate authenticity through nationalization—to make philosophy authentically Mexican—puts the cart before the horse. While Frondizi does not rule out that philosophy in Mexico or Latin America might eventually exhibit local color, or that it can express a Mexican or Latin American worldview, authenticity is a consequence of its first being genuine philosophy. However, if the primary goal is to be different or authentic—or, more generally, if it has any goal other than truth—a body of work simply is not philosophy.

Frondizi takes aim at the influence of José Ortega y Gasset's philosophy in Latin America, particularly his claim that "I am myself plus my circumstance." What counts as *my* circumstance, Frondizi asks? Is it my circumstance as an individual, a citizen, a Catholic, a human being? For Frondizi, the problem with the phrase is not just that it is vague; it is primarily that it encouraged Latin Americans not to examine the proper object of philosophy (what he refers to as "the 'totality' of being as such"). Instead, by placing the emphasis on "my," Latin Americans became increasingly preoccupied with their idiosyncratic, local, and immediate (i.e., non-philosophical) circumstance. To be clear, Frondizi does not lament that philosophers also have practical concerns, or even that Latin American philosophers are typically more engaged in political life than their North American counterparts (see the introduction to this volume). He is only claiming that a concern for originality or authenticity in philosophy undercuts the potential value of philosophy in Latin America:

> One can be a man in the abstract no more than one can be an Argentinian in the abstract. Each one of us bears upon his shoulders a series of qualities progressively diminishing—like concentric circles—and ending at the point which constitutes our individuality of flesh and blood. We are men, of western culture, of the twentieth century, Ibero-Americans, Argentinians, etc. These characteristics are not incompatible; we do not have to choose one or the other. We are able to unite these different qualities; to look at the world from the various perspectives. They all form part of "my situation" and I ought not, nor am I able, in all strictness, to renounce them. The possible error will consist in trying to view the great through the small. Will it be necessary to repeat that we are not able to see through the keyhole of a narrow nationalism?[12]

Villegas

A second objection was formulated by the Mexican philosopher Abelardo Villegas in *La filosofía de lo mexicano* (1960). In the concluding chapter, "The Problem of Truth," Villegas also takes aim at Ortega's influence on philosophy in Mexico. In particular, he argues that Ortega's claim that truth is a matter of perspective leads to a kind of solipsism, which Villegas calls "historical monadism." If it were true that we can only make sense of the universe from our own perspective or historical location, how can we explain scientific progress, let alone the idea of objective truth?

Villegas agrees with Ortega that philosophy, like life, is historical in the sense that authors and texts exist in time and it originates in the context of concrete historical circumstances. But he does not agree that a genetic account of philosophical truth (i.e. its origin story) entails its *historicity*, as Ortega seems to suggest. In other words, just because a truth is discovered at a particular time or place does not mean that only someone who occupies that particular position can grasp or comprehend that truth. Just the opposite. For Villegas, part of what distinguishes truth from belief is precisely that truth is not particular to one's historical location or perspective.

To develop his critique, Villegas argues that what distinguishes us as human beings, and further as individuals, is that we are *creative*, or more specifically, that we create artifacts of history that have lasting significance and that speak to future generations. In other words, rather than think of history as that which isolates us from others outside our peculiar set of circumstances, we typically think of history as that which connects us and binds us to something that transcends one particular historical location. In this way, the philosopher in search of truth is not unlike the great novelist in the following respect: it is precisely by immersing themselves in their own circumstances, i.e., that which individuates them, that they draw out a transcendent, objective, or universal idea, question, lesson, or truth.

One might point out to Villegas that *calling* truth objective or universal does not rule out that it is subject to individual historical perspective, since how truths are received is always a matter of interpretation. In response, Villegas claims that the historian (of philosophy) is not a "forger of worlds." So, while the truth or significance of same claim may be *open to interpretation*, not all interpretations are created equal, and some are simply false.

> This evidently demonstrates how the historical event, in itself, has a particular constitution, a particular determination or individuality that does not allow every kind of predication; that is, it gives us a margin of error. … Only when we consider man as enclosed in his own life, in his own circumstance, can we say that the past does not speak for itself, which is when we can endow it with every predication imaginable.[13]

We can disagree, for instance, about what best explains why a few hundred men were able to conquer a few hundred thousand people in 1521, but we would not take someone seriously if they said that really it was the British who conquered the Aztecs. And we would not take them seriously because there is a fact of the matter that, even if we can't view it in its naked truth, is independent of interpretation and helps us to evaluate competing interpretations. Indeed, we disagree because we believe that there is something that counts as *the truth*.

So, for Villegas, while there is nothing problematic in itself about the philosopher examining the Mexican circumstance, we should not think of the phrase *la filosofía de lo mexicano* as suggesting that there is anything peculiarly Mexican about Mexican philosophy. That is, the *philosophical* search for *lo mexicano* does not lead to a unique Mexican perspective, privy to its own set of truths, as Ramos's account suggests. Instead, Villegas claims that "to return to the individual, to the most characteristic that we possess, is not to fall once again into narcissism, into a solipsism or a closed nationalism; on the contrary, it is to contribute to *human experience*."[14]

The Theme of Ortega's Time[15]

In his *History of Philosophy in Mexico*, Ramos claims that José Ortega y Gasset had provided a generation of Mexicans with "the epistemological justification to nationalize philosophy." Specifically, in the *Meditations on Quixote* (1914) and *The Modern Theme* (1923), Ortega had developed the doctrine of *vital reason* and demonstrated the *historicity of philosophy*, encouraging Mexican philosophers to aim their sights at their own state of affairs. "I am myself plus my circumstance, and if I do not save my circumstance, I do not save myself," Ortega proclaimed in 1914. But what exactly did he mean?

To make sense of Ortega's claim, it is worth pointing out that it began as a critique of *idealism*, specifically the view that reality is dependent on human thought in some way. For the idealist, the conscious subject is "the fundamental reality" from which the reality of everything else is derived. Now, while Ortega agreed with the idealist that it is meaningless to speak of reality independent of a perceiving subject, he thought it was equally incoherent to speak of a perceiving subject independent of reality. For Ortega, the main epistemological challenge was to define both the self or "I" and reality in such a way that one does not get reduced to the other. So he claimed that fundamental reality is neither the conscious subject nor the independent object, but the "interplay" or "business" (*quehacer*) of the ego and the world. In a word, for Ortega, it is life.

Ortega's critique of idealism was central to what he called "the theme of our time," which "comprises the subjection of reason to vitality, its localization within the biological scheme, and its surrender to spontaneity" (*MT*, 58). Concerning "the problem of truth," Ortega asks, "How can we admit truth, which is complete in itself and invariable, to the society of human vitality, which is essentially mutable and varies from individual to individual, from race to race, and from period to period?" (*MT*, 28) In other words, for Ortega, modern philosophy, which he believed was primarily concerned with the problems of epistemology, could be characterized as a contest between rationalism and relativism, which gave priority to reason or life (vitality), respectively. The challenge for 20th century philosophers, for whom Ortega thought he was speaking, was to reconcile the two positions which, on Ortega's account, were equally extreme.

Consider Descartes, a paradigm rationalist who, in his effort to establish indubitable truths under "the light of reason," renounces customary opinion, the five senses, and his immediate world (basically what Ortega roundly calls life or vitality). Descartes also argued that what is real can be quantified and what cannot be quantified is illusory, i.e., that reality is that which one discovers through mathematical reasoning or *more geometrico*. As Ortega points out, truth for Descartes was a-historical, and life and history amount to a long sequence of human error:

> If it were not for the offenses of the will the first man would long ago
> have discovered all the truths that are accessible to him; in the same
> way there would have been no variations in opinion, law and custom; in
> short, there would have been no history. (*MT*, 31)

By contrast, the relativist swings the pendulum far in the opposite direction.
By starting with the fact of life and history—the constant variation in opinion, law, and custom—the relativist renounces the notion of objective truth
as fiction or a utopian ideal. For Ortega, then, the modern theme aims to
resolve the following dichotomy:

> On the one side stands everything vital and concrete in [man's] being,
> his breathing and historical reality. On the other, that rational nucleus
> which enables us to attain truth, but which nevertheless has no life. It is
> an unreal phantom, gliding immutably through time, alien to the vicis-
> situdes which are a symptom of vitality. (*MT*, 30)

The Double Character of Culture

For Ortega, thought is a vital or biological function, "like digestion, or the
circulation of the blood … [I]t is an instrument for the benefit of my life, an
organ of it, regulated and governed by it" (*MT*, 37–38). However, although
thought is beneficial to life, it remains objective since the "business of thought
is to reflect [or represent] the world of phenomena, to adjust itself to them in
one way or another: in short, to think is to think the truth, just as to digest is to
assimilate victuals" (*MT*, 38). In other words, thought is a vital function, like
digestion, but it only performs its function if it is concerned with objective
truth. To be concerned only with how things appear is not to think at all, and
thus not to benefit from thought or from that species of thought we call reason.

By developing the "double character" of thought and its relation to truth,
which constitutes the basis of his response to both the rationalist and the
relativist, Ortega also provides us with a broad definition of *culture*, which
includes all vital functions that, on the one hand, benefit living organisms,
and that, on the other hand, do so only to the extent that they obey objective laws. Such functions include taking pleasure in beauty, seeking justice,
and believing in God. As an example, Ortega claims that part of what
makes aesthetic appreciation *pleasurable* (a subjective fact) is precisely that
the experience is not subjective. I do not take *aesthetic* pleasure in what I
happen to like, but in *beauty itself*, a unique form of pleasure based in what
it is reasonable for me to expect *everyone* to find beautiful.

On behalf of his generation, Ortega agrees that the values of culture (the
true, the beautiful, the just, the eternal) are valuable only to the extent that
they are experienced in life. They are not abstract objects governed by
objective laws, as Plato thought, but a feature of human life (vitality or
spontaneity) that values objectivity. Conversely, subjective experience does

not undermine the objectivity of all experience. Instead, it serves as a condition of objectivity in the following way:

> When a sieve or a net is placed in a current of liquid it allows certain things to permeate it and keeps others out; it might be said to make a choice, but assuredly not to alter the forms of things. This is the function of the knower, of the living being face to face with the cosmic reality of his environment. ... His function is clearly selective. (*MT*, 88)

To paraphrase, when the relativist says that all truth is relative or subjective ("true *for me*"), she is right in that one only pays attention to those objective truths that are relevant to one's life. But she is wrong to claim that because truth is subject to *relevance* there is no such thing as the kind of objective truth the rationalist puts her stock in.

At points, Ortega seems to be suggesting something stronger than the idea that truth is subject to relevance, as when he writes that

> [e]very life is a point of view directed upon the universe. Strictly speaking, what one life sees no other can. Every individual, whether person, nation or epoch, is an organ, for which there can be no substitute, constructed for the apprehension of truth. (*MT*, 91)

Such statements do suggest that Ortega's perspectivism results in what Villegas calls "historical monadism." However, unlike Nietzsche's perspectivism, Ortega is also making a metaphysical claim about the nature of reality.

> Cosmic reality is such that it can only be seen in a single definite perspective. Perspective is one of the component parts of reality. Far from being a disturbance of its fabric, it is its organizing element. A reality which remained the same from whatever point of view it was observed would be a ridiculous conception. (*MT*, 90)

To say, then, that what one life sees no other can is not to place a limitation on knowledge, but is a way of saying that reality itself is like a prism in that there is no single point of view that captures all of its possibilities at once. As Ortega says, "the sole false perspective is that which claims to be the only one there is" (*MT*, 92). The universe is an infinite set of perspectives, which should not be thought of as limited perspectives *on a single reality*, which God might view in a single glance, but as constituents of reality.

Transforming Philosophy

Like all great systems of philosophy, Ortega's "circumstantialism" places a demand on philosophy itself.[16] For Ortega, modern philosophy had become "primitive" and could be characterized as *self-forgetful*:

The "primitive" painter depicts the world from his point of view, that is, in obedience to ideas, valuations, and sentiments which are peculiar to him; but he believes he paints it as it is. For the same reason he forgets to introduce his own personality into his work; he offers us the work as if it had made itself, without the intervention of any particular agent; it is fixed at a definite position in space and at a definite moment in time. (*MT*, 93)

In similar fashion, concerning the nature of truth, the modern philosopher forgets that although "the most important point about a scientific system is that it should be true ... it must also be understood" (*MQ*, 11). Ortega is not referring to the difficulty of grasping the complexity of a scientific system, as the young student struggles in an advanced physics course. He is referring to the fact that a philosophical or scientific system, true or false, is brought down to earth in a definite set of circumstances, without which it would make no sense. Even if Einstein were right, he could not have convinced Newton at the end of the 17th century. Nor did Einstein happen upon the theory of relativity one fine day. He was a representative of a generation who went in search of it. In short, truth emerges at a particular point in history, not by accident, but because of the intervention of a particular agent making sense of her *own* world.

In the *Meditations on Quixote*, Ortega defines philosophy as "the general science of love" or *amor intellectualis*. To love something, for Ortega, is to make it indispensable to oneself, the way a parent feels that an essential part of himself exists in his child. But to love something is also to bring a previously insignificant object to its full, plenary significance. Love finds *logos* or a rational account in every object, however small, and connects each object to the objects that surround it, and eventually to everything else. Not to love something is to isolate it and grow indifferent to it. As the general science of love, then, the goal of philosophy is the two-fold task of linking everything to everything else *and* uniting everything else to one's self (*MQ*, 33).

We can say, then, that Ortega's circumstantialism consists of two parts, which, for the sake of convenience, can be characterized as the theoretical and the practical. On the one hand, Ortega is at pains to show the interdependence between life and culture and reintroduce the agent into philosophy ("I am myself plus my circumstance"). On the other hand, he claims that the aim of philosophy is salvation ("if I do not save my circumstance, I do not save myself"). For Ortega, to save one's circumstance means to demonstrate the universal significance of the humble objects that surround each one of us, unnoticed. In describing his own meditations as a series of salvations, he writes:

Along with lofty themes, these *Meditations* deal with very frequently with the most insignificant things. Attention is paid to details of the Spanish landscape, of the peasants' way of talking, of the folk dances

and songs, of colors and style in dress and implements, of the peculiarities of the landscape, and in general of the minute manifestations
which reveal the innermost character of a race. ... I consider it urgent
that we also direct our reflective attention, our meditation, to what is
near us. (MQ, 41)[17]

And such salvations are urgent because "the reabsorption of circumstance is
the concrete destiny of man" (MQ, 44).

Conclusion

As a matter of intellectual history, Ortega's influence on Ramos, and by
extension, Latin American philosophy, is questionable. Some intellectual
historians now claim that, as a matter of historical record, Ramos had not
read Ortega as closely as he later claimed to, and that saying that Ortega
provided the epistemological justification of a national philosophy was
merely Ramos's attempt, ex post facto, to place himself at the center of
Mexican philosophy. Whether or not this is true, the parallels between
Ramos and Ortega are nevertheless striking—perhaps even more striking if
Ramos had not read Ortega before 1934—and they continue to inspire
Latinx philosophers to cultivate a philosophy defined by their own circumstance and cultural identity. So, by way of conclusion, and in response to the
above objections, here are a few ways in which Ortega's early philosophy
might help us to justify an ethnic philosophy (see chapters 11 and 12 for an
overview of what counts as an ethnic philosophy).

In response to the worry that there is no such thing as *lo mexicano*, or *lo
Latinx*, we might invoke Ortega's concept of a *generation*, which I left
implicit in the previous section. It seems that the main worry about philosophizing about the *essence* of Mexican or Latinx identity hinges on thinking about essence as Plato, Descartes, or logicians do, i.e., in terms of
necessary and sufficient conditions, since there are no traits that all and only
Mexicans or Latinxs share. However, when Ortega speaks about "the theme
of *our time*," his "generation," "the innermost character of the race," etc.,
he is speaking from the point of view *of history*, not logic, and writes that
the essence of each generation—which he calls "the most important conception in history" (MT, 15)—"is a particular type of sensibility, an organic
capacity for certain deep-rooted directions of thought, [meaning] that each
generation has its special vocation, its historical mission" (MT, 19). So,
although Ortega claims that each generation possesses a peculiar and unique
"physiognomy," something that sounds suspiciously like "essence" in the
logical sense, he describes the essence of a racial, ethnic, national or other
social group in terms of sharing a "sensibility," "direction of thought," or
"historical vocation"—terms that are much less stringent than the identity
criteria of logic and thus, as accurate descriptions of large groups or traditions, much more promising.

In response to Frondizi's worry that a national (or ethnic) philosophy is not philosophy at all if it is guided by non-philosophical interests, we might explore Ortega's definition of philosophy as the general science of love. Again, to save or reabsorb one's circumstance is not to try to rescue or improve it for the sake of a non-philosophical end, such as political recognition. (Ortega would have been offended by the phrase "identity politics.") Instead, the aim of philosophy is to find universal meaning in the silent objects that surround us and connect them to ourselves and to everything else. We might go further and argue that Frondizi's insistence that we philosophize from "a purely philosophical context" is a utopian ideal that affirms the very dichotomy between interested and disinterested inquiry that Ortega rejected.

Frondizi is nevertheless right to lament that Ortega's use of the phrase "*my* circumstance" is vague. But given Ortega's definition of philosophy, its vagueness might be precisely the point. Frondizi argues that students of Ortega who are interested in "a self-interested philosophy" (one interested in the self as much as the not-self)[18] make the philosophically fatal mistake of trying to see the great through the small. However, Ortega would respond that while it is important not to confuse the small for the great—philosophy requires some hierarchies if it is to avoid chaos—it is equally important not to ignore the small in view of the great, since: "For the person for whom small things do not exist, the great is not great" (*MQ*, 45).

Finally, in response to Villegas's claim that Ortega's perspectivism undermines objective truth or our ability to explain scientific progress, we might refer back to Ortega's response to the problem of truth. Recall that truth is grounded in our immediate circumstance partly in that it serves a vital function, but it only performs that function insofar as it (as well as the other values of culture) aspires to universality and objectivity. The epistemological challenge today is not just one of establishing the criteria of truth but of figuring out how to reconcile the circumstantial and the universal without abandoning either. Also, it is worth remembering that Ortega's circumstantialism (ratio-vitalism, the historicity of philosophy, perspectivism) is not only an epistemological thesis about the nature of truth, but also a metaphysical thesis about the nature of reality. We may be stuck with limited access to objective truth, not because we gain access to it from a limited perspective that cannot be shared, but because reality itself is carved up into points of view. If that is right, then the real error would be to abandon one's own point of view, both as an individual and as a member of a social group, the only one we can inhabit, for no view at all.

Notes

1 Ramos, "Twenty Years of Education in Mexico," 61–62. Cited in text using the abbreviation *TYEM* and the page number.
2 After the Mexican Revolution of 1910, Mexican intellectual across a variety of disciplines wrestled with the problems that led to the Revolution, including the

challenges of building a stable political state, integrating Mexico's large indigenous community into Mexican society, and reforming and extending education throughout Mexico. Ramos thought that philosophy was no exception. For a clear introduction to "the crisis of Mexico," see Cosío Villegas, "Mexico's Crisis."

3 Ramos, "The History of Philosophy in Mexico," 67. Cited in text using the abbreviation *HPM* and page number.

4 Ramos, *Profile*, 11. Cited in text using the abbreviation, *P* and the page number.

5 Before moving on, we recommend Googling the phrase "in the world but not of it."

6 Incidentally, at the end of the first chapter of his *History of Philosophy of Mexico*, Ramos rejects the idea that the Aztecs practiced "philosophy," since they failed to achieve a critical reflective distance from their religious and customary beliefs. That is, since they did not seem to employ Reason in the way European philosophers do, following Greek and Christian philosophers. Partially in response to Ramos, when Miguel León-Portilla famously argued, 15 years later, that the Aztecs did in fact practice philosophy, he did not argue that they cultivated a philosophy of their *own*, but rather that they did in fact practice what the Greeks called philosophy.

7 See Salmerón, "Mexican Philosophers," and Villoro, "La cultura mexicana" [Mexican Culture].

8 See also Bartra, "Does It Mean Anything to Be Mexican?"

9 In this respect, Ramos was greatly influenced by the German philosophers Max Scheler, Oswald Spengler, and Ernst Robert Curtius.

10 cf. Ramos, *Hacia un nuevo humanismo* [Toward a New Humanism].

11 Romanell, "Samuel Ramos on the Philosophy of Mexican Culture," 96–97.

12 Frondizi, "Is There an Ibero-American Philosophy," 353.

13 Villegas, "The Problem of Truth," 256.

14 Villegas, "The Problem of Truth," 259. My emphasis.

15 The Spanish title of *The Modern Theme* is *El tema de nuestro tiempo*, which we believe is better translated as *The Theme of Our Time* or even *The Contemporary Theme*. We prefer either of the latter translations in part because Ortega sought to distinguish the theme of *his* time from modern philosophy, which begins roughly with Descartes in the 17th century. So, the to the extent that the popular English translation of the title suggests that Ortega is concerned with the theme of modern philosophy, it is misleading and should be updated.

16 Though Ramos speaks of Ortega's ratio-vitalism and historicism, "circumstantialism" nicely captures the various aspects of his philosophy, including his perspectivism.

17 Compare this characterization of Ortega's philosophy to Armstrong's characterization of Latin American philosophy in the introduction to this volume.

18 For a discussion of "the not-self" and its relation to the value of philosophy, see Russell's *The Problems of Philosophy*, particularly the chapter titled "The Value of Philosophy."

Bibliography

Bartra, Roger. "Does It Mean Anything to Be Mexican?" In *The Mexico Reader: History, Culture, Politics*, edited by Gilbert M. Joseph and Timothy J. Henderson, 33–40. Durham: Duke University Press, 2002.

Berlin, Isaiah. *The Hedgehog and the Fox: An Essay on Tolstoy's View of History*. Chicago: Ivan R. Dee, 1993.

Cosío Villegas, Daniel. "Mexico's Crisis." In *The Mexico Reader: History, Culture, Politics*, edited by Gilbert M. Joseph and Timothy J. Henderson, 470–481. Durham: Duke University Press, 2002.

Frondizi, Risieri. "Is There an Ibero-American Philosophy?" *Philosophy and Phenomenological Research* 9, no. 3 (March, 1949): 345–355.

Mariátegui, José Carlos. "Is There Such a Thing as Hispanic-American Thought?" In *The Heroic and Creative Meaning of Socialism: Selected Essays of José Carlos Mariátegui*, edited and translated by Michael Pearlman, 116–119. Amherst, NY: Humanities Books, 1996.

Ortega y Gasset, José. *Meditations on Quixote*. Translated by Evelyn Rugg and Diego Marín. New York: W. W. Norton & Company, 1961.

Ortega y Gasset, José. *The Modern Theme*. Translated by James Cleugh. New York: Harper & Row, 1961.

Ramos, Samuel. *Hacia un nuevo humanismo*. México: Fondo de Cultura Económica, 1962.

Ramos, Samuel. *Profile of Man and Culture in Mexico*. Translated by Peter G. Earle. Austin: University of Texas Press, 1962.

Ramos, Samuel. "The History of Philosophy in Mexico." In *Mexican Philosophy in the 20th Century: Essential Readings*, edited by Carlos Alberto Sánchez and Robert EliSanchez, Jr., 63–72. New York: Oxford University Press, 2017.

Ramos, Samuel. "Twenty Years of Education in Mexico." In *Mexican Philosophy in the 20th Century: Essential Readings*, edited by Carlos Alberto Sánchez and Robert EliSanchez, Jr., 53–62. New York: Oxford University Press, 2017.

Romanell, Patrick. "Samuel Ramos on the Philosophy of Mexican Culture: Ortega and Unamuno in Mexico." *Latin American Research Review* 10, no. 3 (Autumn, 1975): 81–101.

Russell, Bertrand. *The Problems of Philosophy*. Oxford: Oxford University Press, 1997.

Salazar Bondy, Augusto. "The Meaning and Problem of Hispanic American Thought." In *Latin American Philosophy for the 21st Century*, edited by Jorge J.E. Gracia & Elizabeth Millán-Zaibert, 379–398. Amherst, NY: Prometheus Books, 2004.

Salmerón, Fernando. "Mexican Philosophers of the Twentieth Century." In *Major Trends in Mexican Philosophy*, translated by A. Robert Caponigri, 246–287. Notre Dame: University of Notre Dame Press, 1966.

Villegas, Abelardo. "The Problem of Truth." In *Mexican Philosophy in the 20th Century: Essential Readings*, edited by Carlos Alberto Sánchez and Robert EliSanchez, Jr., 245–259. New York: Oxford University Press, 2017.

Villoro, Luis. "La cultura mexicana de 1910 a 1960." *Historia Mexicana* 10, no. 2 (Oct.–Dec., 1960): 196–219.

Zea, Leopoldo. "The Actual Function of Philosophy in Latin America," In *Latin American Philosophy in the Twentieth Century: Man, Values, and the Search for Philosophical Identity*, edited by Jorge J.E. Gracia and Elizabeth Millán-Zaibert, 357–368. Amherst, NY: Prometheus Books, 2004.

6 Mexican Existentialism

Carlos Alberto Sánchez

The Existentialist Position

According to Robert Solomon, existentialism is a philosophical "position" rather than a tradition or a particular methodology.[1] In its French version, existentialism positions itself as a radical individualism and promotes the view that the self is a product of both the choices one makes and the struggle to deal with the consequences of those choices. It claims that "existence precedes essence," or, less abstractly, that the individual creates herself in the process of existing, rather than living out an existence already made, or predetermined by history, culture, world, or God. The power of self-creation, ultimately, implies that the individual is free, particularly from those powers that would otherwise create him or her—again, history, culture, world, or God.

Existentialists, and here I refer to European existentialists (most of whom, it is worth noting, rejected the "existentialist" label),[2] operate within a large conceptual arsenal that includes, for example, considerations of the notions of freedom, throwness, anxiety, responsibility, death, subjectivity, faith, absurdity, and even boredom.[3]

As a primarily European philosophical position, existentialism can be traced back to the works of St. Augustine, but it finds its first notable expressions in Søren Kierkegaard and Friedrich Nietzsche in the 19th century. In the 20th century, philosophers such as Miguel de Unamuno and Jose Ortega y Gasset (Spain), Martin Heidegger and Karl Jaspers (Germany), and Jean-Paul Sartre, Simone de Beauvoir, Albert Camus, and Gabriel Marcel (France) sought to lend clarity to existentialist themes, grappling with their significance, their usefulness, and their justification. For the most part, these figures took the abstract existentialist principle that "existence precedes essence" as a starting point for their philosophizing, which meant that they were committed to the view that the essence of being human, that primary characteristic that defines the human being as a human being, is not an *a priori* determination of our existence but is something we, as individual subjects, create in the process of living. That is, our own immediate, lived experience shapes and makes us *who we are*. Moreover, because at the moment of our birth we are *thrown* into a world already populated with customs, laws, and expectations, an event about which we have no say, we are ultimately *responsible* for the progress of our own life, for our choices, and for our future. This means that our sense of self, and our individuality, must, if we are to live authentically, take precedence over any other fact that would pretend to determine our becoming—whether that is history, society, or mass culture. Our thrownness and our responsibility to our own self-creation also highlight our own finitude, i.e., the prospect of our own personal death. Thus, our entire existence is marked by an originary anxiety and dread over our own, *eventual* demise. All of this means that, for existentialists, the uniqueness of our own individual experience matters; it means that our lives are lived in the concreteness of time and place, and, thus, that philosophically reflecting on that concreteness will reveal truths that can help us live a more authentic, or at least less superficial, existence.

The Arrival of Existentialism in Mexico

Much has been written on European existentialism, its themes, its history, and its figures. (The reader will find this literature readily available.) The same cannot be said about the appropriation of existentialism elsewhere. Thus, our concern in this chapter has to do with the way in which the existentialist position was appropriated in Mexico by Mexican philosophers in the middle of the 20th century.

European existentialism takes hold of the Mexican philosophical consciousness with the arrival of the Spanish *transterrados*—transplanted exiles from the Spanish civil war—Joaquin Xírau, José Gaos, Juan-David García Baca, Eduardo Nicol, Maria Zambrano, and others.[4] Of monumental importance is José Gaos's readings, lectures, and translation of Heidegger's *Being and Time* in the early 1940s, whereby Heidegger's philosophy is seen as proposing, according to one of Gaos's earliest Mexican students, Edmundo O'Gorman, "a guide for the authentic life,"[5] one representing the origins of a burgeoning Mexican existentialist position. In Heidegger's phenomenological existentialism Mexican philosophers found a means to justify the value of their own historicized and concrete thinking (the beginnings of which we see in the previous chapter). Towards the end of the decade, however, as Emilio Uranga, another of Gaos's early Mexican students recalls,[6] allegiances shift to French existentialism, and, in particular, to the existentialist philosophy of Jean-Paul Sartre, Gabriel Marcel, and Maurice Merleau-Ponty, who perhaps because of their clarity and, in the case of Merleau-Ponty, a willingness to consider the Mexican contributions to existentialism, quickly found philosophical apprentices in Mexico.[7] This allegiance to French existentialism is announced through a series of public lectures given by *el grupo Hiperion* in 1947–1948 that paired the existentialist stance with Hiperion's generational theme, their call to arms, namely, the question as to what it means be Mexican (a project that would come to be known as *the philosophy of lo mexicano*).[8]

The shift from German to French existentialism is illustrated in Emilio Uranga's brief essay, "Two Existentialisms," where Uranga, one of the most important philosophers of the period and a leader of *el grupo Hiperion,*[9] writes that initially (the early 1940s) "existentialism had been amongst us ... a way of talking about Martin Heidegger."[10] The phenomenological existentialism of Heidegger, with its focus on temporality and being-in-the-world, was better suited, Uranga suggests, to serve as an entryway into those problems that preoccupied Mexicans at the time, namely, problems dealing with a cultural and historical identity fractured and traumatized by the events of the Mexican Revolution and its aftermath. However, Uranga laments that the influence of Gaos's readings and introductions of Heidegger had an oppressive and marginalizing effect, as it encouraged a prejudice about the nature of philosophy and the philosophical—if it wasn't "serious" or "technical" then it wasn't philosophy, but, worse, if it wasn't "Heideggerian," then it wasn't existentialism. As Uranga rightly observes, "even in philosophy we find fanaticism" (*DE*, 174). This prohibition motivated members of *el Hiperion* to go beyond Heidegger, to Sartre and Merleau-Ponty, who, at least culturally speaking (according to Uranga, the French and the Mexican were more similar than, for example, the British, especially when it came to the origins of culture, the influence of religion, and their poetic sensibilities), had more in common with Mexicans than Heidegger could ever have. The operative reason for the shift, however, has to do with ethics, or, more specifically, with Heidegger's *lack* of an ethical stance in *Being and Time*. Uranga writes: "For my generation, more concretely, for the 'Hiperion' group, what really matters is to know how Sartre deals with moral themes and not with how Heidegger will identify Being or Nothingness in his work" (*DE*, 175). And this, because, the question of morality—the question dealing with human conduct and the good life—"involves consequences which are of much greater and vital importance than those proposed by Heidegger" (*DE*, 175). In this way, existentialism in its French version was appropriated for the sake of the Mexican community, a means to clarify and address the problematic that kept Mexicans hidden from themselves and unable to *commit* to the project of their own future.

Luis Villoro's "Genesis and Task of Existentialism in Mexico" echoes Uranga's account of existentialism's arrival in Mexico in the 1940s, but tells us in more detail why and how the appropriation of existentialism took place and under what conditions. According to Villoro, the introduction of the existentialist position comes via the popular works of Fyodor Dostoyevski, Miguel de Unamuno, and José Ortega y Gasset at the turn of the 20th century. Its introduction into the academy does not come until 1939, when the Mexican philosopher Antonio Caso offered a course on Søren Kierkegaard and Nicolai Berdiaeff. But a sustained and dedicated study of existentialism as a philosophical position comes with the arrival of the

Spanish exiles. Villoro, like Uranga, places the origins of the Mexican existentialist position with Gaos, with whom "the name Heidegger is announced for the first time in Mexico toward the end of the 1930s,"[11] and "[f]inally, in the winter of 1942, Juan David Garcia Bacca gives a course on existentialism at the Department of Philosophy and Letters" (*GP*, 237). "But," he continues, "it is Jose Gaos who truly introduces Heidegger's philosophy. In the span of five years (1942–47) [Gaos] offers courses on *Being and Time*, courses that until today give a systematic exposition of his philosophy" (*GP*, 237). The value of these courses was (and is) without measure. As Villoro puts it: "[f]ew academic courses had left to that point such a profound imprint in Mexico than those given in the 'Heideggerian' years. Ever since then there has been a surge in interest for existential philosophy" (*GP*, 237).

Villoro recalls that existentialism caused a "sudden, intense ... and spontaneous" reaction upon its arrival (*GP*, 233). But this reaction was not due to the novelty of the position or to its promise, but to the fact that it seemed like a *familiar* way of thinking about human life; that is, the spontaneity of the reaction, its immediacy, pointed to a prior intimacy with it and with what it reveals. In other words, Mexicans had always been existentialists, missing only the philosophical language that would help articulate what had always been understood pre-theoretically. Thus, Villoro says:

> The appearance and acceptance of existentialism amongst us responds to a concrete situation that we can only understand if we take into account its temporal dimensions: its projection toward the future and its overcoming negation of the past ... The yesterday that we encounter will be *our* yesterday. (*GP*, 233)

Once articulated, existentialism offered, as Villoro puts it, "a conscious project of self-knowledge that lends us the basis for a future self-transformation" (*GP*, 241). In this way, existentialism as a philosophy offers a *way* to individual and social transformation and change.

Despite the eventual shift from German to French existentialism, it is in this context and within the limits of these two currents of thought that we may talk about "Mexican existentialism," a philosophical stance that although remaining faithful to basic existentialists tenets regarding existence, freedom, and finitude does not concern itself with exegesis but with application—although exegesis was certainly part of the project.[12] Mario Teodoro Ramirez notes that existentialism in Mexico "was an effort to recover the spirit of that philosophical current and apply some of its concepts and perspectives to the matter at hand: thinking about Mexican reality."[13] The Mexican appropriation was thus more than academic; it was the effort of Mexican existentialists to put philosophy to work for the Mexican circumstance. As Guillermo Hurtado puts it, they were "existentialists who took as their object of study not the abstract person or European man as studied by the European existentialists, but the Mexican person,"[14] a focus that is important because it signals a desire to lend an identity to existentialism itself, or that points to a conscious effort to affirm a particularity and a uniqueness to Mexican philosophy more generally.

Three Existentialist Themes in Uranga, Villoro, and Zea

Given the historical situation of post-Revolutionary Mexico, one defined by a palpable tension between the urge for modernization and the memory of Revolution, together with the social, cultural, historical, and metaphysical fracturing that this brought about, Mexican philosophers sought a philosophical stance that affirmed and justified their own situated existence.[15] That is, they sought to understand what they believed was a common feeling of loss and fragmentation, of anxiety, and historical contingency. Mexicans, in other words, sought a philosophical position that could make sense of their existence as Mexicans.

Mexican identity itself was at stake in the search for a unique philosophical voice. The historical experience of colonization had revealed an essential mestizaje, a cultural or historical mixture, or an essential tie to two different and competing cultures, that made a metaphysical and practical claim to their identity. Thus, Mexican identity and philosophy had to grapple with a permanent and unavoidable duality, with an inability to possess an uncompromised and justified historical being. It had to grapple, more importantly, with ways of community-making, of validating the moral call for social and historical responsibility, but most importantly, with questions of authenticity, that is, with the question of what being properly Mexican truly meant.

They found their voice in existentialism—especially in its French version. Mario Teodoro Ramirez writes that young Mexican philosophers at the time found in French existentialism "a philosophy that had at its center commitment and authenticity before the catastrophe of World War II."[16] Of course, French existentialism didn't *teach* Mexican philosophers the value of commitment or responsibility, nor did French existentialism *introduce* the value of authenticity, freedom, or contingency into the Mexican mind; these values had always been there, although buried and silenced by the mire of history, the memory of trauma, or the fog of revolution. There is always an impetus to be responsible, to be authentic, and to be committed, just like there are always explicit clues into one's duality, contingency, and finitude. However, this impetus and these clues can be hidden by the spectacle of life one way or another. Existentialism was the opportunity to look through and into that spectacle and find what was always operative in Mexican life.

Thus, it was the language of existentialism that appealed to the Mexican philosophers, who adopted and adapted the language and the lessons to their own Mexican circumstance. Emilio Uranga writes:

Definitively, what decides the value of existentialism is its capacity to lend ground to a systematic description of human existence, but not of human existence in the abstract, but of a situated human existence, in a situation, of a human existence located in a determinate geographic *habitat*, in a social and cultural space also determined and with a precise historical legacy.[17]

The value of existentialism *for Mexicans* is thus its ability to justify the concern with the practical, the concrete, and the particular. This is, indeed, what Mexican existentialists such as Uranga, Villoro, and Zea heard in the existentialist mantra that says "existence precedes essence," namely, a justification of the privileging of the concrete over the abstract, the particular over the universal, and the contingent over the permanent. Luis Villoro puts it in the following terms:

> Existential philosophy, which directs itself to being and not merely to becoming, gives us the adequate instruments to validate our task. Over its explicit project of revealing being itself, we place the transformation of being in a sense both individual and social.[18]

The adoption or appropriation was, in this way, transformative, allowing Mexican intellectuals to articulate truths related to their own being in ways that were both penetrating and practical.

Let us consider the manner in which three existentialist ideas were appropriated in Mexico.[19]

"Accidentality" and "Insufficiency"

The idea of *throwness*—of being cast out into a world, shipwrecked on a reality, or abandoned to an existence already made and determined in all of its aspects—is appropriated by Mexican existentialists as the notion of "accidentality." Accidentality is the view that Mexican persons are defined in their being (that is, ontologically) as accidents of European conquest, colonization, and philosophy; the view that Mexicans have been intrinsically and historically determined by their contrast to a European self-conception and worldview that thinks of itself as fully formed, permanent, and substantial; and, it is the view that finiteness and contingency defines Mexican life. That is, before the Spaniard, who presents himself as the very instantiation stability, permanence, and universality, the Mexican is a random attachment, an unnecessary dependent, an *accident*. Uranga defines this being accidental of Mexican existence in the following way:

> The accident is fragility: oscillation between being and nothingness. This means that its "fit" in being, its adhesion to being expressed in the modality of being-in, is not protected by an inalienable right, but rather

whatever may be the form of its inheritance, it is always revocable. The accident is constantly threatened by displacement [*desalojamiento*]. Attached to being, it can always be torn off from its "there," exterminated. Whatever it holds on to, whatever handle it grabs on to, can be removed. It was born to be-in and at the same time to not-be-in.[20]

Accidentality is impermanence, randomness, and insubstantiality. Recognizing oneself as accident is a necessary step in liberating oneself from the false delusion of one's "substantiality" and absolute self-sufficiency; it is to recognize one's "insufficiency" (a term that Uranga proposes as different than the psychologistic notion of "inferiority"). (Compare Uranga's notion of "insufficiency" to Samuel Ramos's notion of "inferiority" in the previous chapter.) In Uranga's existential philosophy, this means that at the root of their being, Mexicans are not *sufficient* in their being, they are not *substantial*. The Spaniard, he argues, historically presented himself as permanence itself, as historically sufficient and ontologically substantial—as lacking nothing. This was a false and misleading self-understanding to be sure, but one rooted in the historical confrontation between colonizers and their subjects. That the Mexican—either indigenous or mestizo—has historically been thought of only as a subject of, or in relation to, a colonizing other makes the Mexican an (historical) accidental property of that other. Thus, what is of interest to the Mexican existentialist project is not that the Mexican is thrown into a world that he did play a role in creating and for which he must now be responsible; what is of interest is that he is thrown into this world *as accident* and insufficiency, a situation from which he must then confront the world he did not play a role in creating and to which he must now be responsibly committed. Uranga puts the matter in the following terms:

> Insufficiency, ontologically speaking, characterizes what is accident in relation to substance. *Every modality of being grounded on accident is partly grounded on an absence*, these modes of being are situated in an inconsistent and fractured base. The accident is a *minus* of being, a being reduced or "fragmented" by its relation to nothingness. (*A*, 40, emphasis in the original)

What this means is that *as accident* the Mexican has no stable foundation for a proper metaphysical identity. In other words, the stable foundation *claimed* by the European is a mystery for the Mexican. For the Mexican, his foundation is always already fragmented, movable, splintered by the trauma of conquest, the violence of colonialism, and the uncertainty and insecurity of independence. In this way, the being that constitutes Mexican being is a reduced being, a negative being, or a "minus" of being, and, so, "[n]egatively conceived, the accident is a privation, an absence, a penury, a lack or defect of substance, an insufficient being" (*A*, 40).

However, to say that the Mexican person is (ontologically) accidental or insufficient is not to condemn the Mexican to a perpetual negative where life has no purpose and death is ultimately preferred. It is not a reason to forgo the call of existence itself and sink into the hopelessness and despair of those famed existentialist anti-heroes one finds in Camus's *The Stranger* or in Samuel Beckett's *Waiting for Godot*. It does not mean that because he is accident the Mexican should forgo all commitment and responsibility. On the contrary, insufficiency and accidentality describe the actual condition of humankind in general, and so, Uranga says confidently, Mexicans, in living and recognizing their accidentality and insufficiency, are closer to the truth of being human than those who fail to do so. The truth is that *all there is* is accidentality and insufficiency, concreteness and particularity, and this because the range of one's vision is restricted to what stands right before one, in one's immediate or familiar experience. In one of his most revealing passages, Uranga writes:

> *we are not very certain of the existence of the human being in general and, secondly, that whatever passes itself off as human being in general, that is, generalized European humanity, does not appear to us to define itself as accidental, but precisely as an arrogant substantiality.* (A, 43, italics in the original)

"Zozobra" and "Nepantla"

According to Mexican existentialism, the "inferiority complex," a psychological condition which Samuel Ramos, in his *Profile of Man and Culture in Mexico* (1934), had diagnosed as constitutive of the Mexican person, was a modality of a much deeper ontological condition: insufficiency. Insufficiency describes the mode of being of the human as an incomplete project. The Mexican, by recognizing his insufficiency, is thus closer to the truth of being human than his European counterpart who thinks of himself as substantial and complete. But Mexicans are closer to this truth because, once again, they know their existence to be fragile, "always revocable," and always "threatened by displacement," that is, accidental.

Related to insufficiency, accidentality refers to an identity that is always fleeing from itself, hesitant, indecisive, contingent, and incapable of that essential synthesis on the basis of which peoples from other cultures have steadfastly affirmed their humanity, or their belonging to the world. This lack of permanence in one's being is manifested in the view that reality is constantly slipping away, that everything is revocable and unhinged, and that the world itself is threatening and overwhelming. But, more specifically, this lack of permanence points to a lack of ground or foundation.

In accordance with the 16th century Dominican friar Diego Durán's observation that the Mexican character is a product of "two laws," the indigenous and the Christian, Uranga refers to the being of the Mexican as perpetually "oscillating and pendular" (A, 93). Reaching further back to the conceptual arsenal of pre-Hispanic culture, Uranga captures the oscillating and pendular movement of Mexican being with the Náhuatl concept of nepantla. *Nepantla* designates a being "in between, in the middle, in the center" (A, 93). The middle, the in-between, or the center is the point to which Mexican being returns as it swings to and fro the different laws that frame its possibilities of existence. In this sense, Mexican identity is dynamic rather than static, a constant migration from extremes to center and from center to peripheries, never settled in "one at the expense of the other" (A, 93). Nepantla thus designates the un-groundedness of Mexican being, leading Uranga to say that *nepantla* is "the cardinal category of our ontology" (A, 93).

If *nepantla* is a fundamental ontological category in Mexican existentialism, then *zozobra* designates its existential correlate. As the name for a modality of a being rooted in rootlessness, whose *urgrund* (i.e. the most real being or fundamental reality) in the no-where between this and that history, this and that culture, or this and that identity, *nepantla* does not capture the sense, or feeling, of this rootlessness or loss of belonging. Appealing to Ramón López Velarde, the famous Mexican poet, Uranga calls this sense of loss *zozobra*. Zozobra names the anxiety of not knowing where one stands at any one time. Uranga defines it as follows: "a not knowing on which [extreme] to depend on, or what is the same, a dependence on the two extremes [of our identity] ... a grasping at both ends of the chain" (A, 94). Zozobra is thus an anxious hesitation and indecision before the demands of precarious, pendular existence.

As the existential correlate of *nepantla*, *zozobra* ultimately provokes a rational decision, namely, the decision to cover over the abyss with a stable, essentialized or essentializable, identity, history, or culture. The anxiety of breakdown, which is *zozobra*, motivates a desire for universality and eternity. Thus, the attraction of European or Indigenous identity, which represent the two options for the Mexican, is that these are static, defined, and unambiguous, giving one the illusion of permanence, ground, and stability. From this desire for permanence and origin emerge those ideologies that aim to essentialize identity, painting a caricature of the Mexican, for example, or of *lo mexicano*, as homogenous in *his* identity and resolute in his resolve. But this homogenous image hides a "mode of being that incessantly oscillates between two possibilities, between two affects, without knowing on which of these to depend, on which of these to cling to for justification" (A, 105). This is *zozobra*, and Uranga points to it as the un-grounded *urgrund* that defines Mexican identity. That is, *zozobra is not* "a fixed and solid ground" [*punto fijo y roqueño*], but is rather like "moving sand on which nothing firm can stand" (A, 105). Regarding this concept, Luis Villoro adds: "The privileged sense of zozobra reveals the accidentality of being itself and of the world. This one appears as insubstantial and fragile; we thus try to flee from our own insubstantiality by seeking substance" (GP, 242).

Zozobra is thus definitive of Mexican existence. But it is also an existential characteristic that defines the human being as accident *in general*. Because Mexicans are more familiar and thus closer to zozobra (and to accidentality and nepantla), Uranga makes the further point that the being that defines the Mexican is also the being that defines the human, so that the human *should* model itself (in attitudes and existential comportment) to the Mexican, an affirmation meant to suggest that Mexican existence should be attended to by all. He writes:

> The originary lived experience [vivencia originaria] of *lo mexicano* should serve us to measure and calibrate what it means *to be Mexican* and to determine the essential thematic nucleus that words, isolated or in context, poetry or prose, have organized, denominated, or expressed.[21]

And elsewhere:

> It is not about constituting Mexicanness, or that which particularizes us, as human, but the opposite, it is about constituting the human in terms of Mexicanness. Mexicanness [*lo mexicano*] is the point of departure for the human; whatever resembles that which is Mexican calibrates itself as human, and whatever is dissimilar or strange to the being of the Mexican loses that calibration. (*A*, 45)

Thus, related to existential accidentality are the twin notions of "zozobra" and "nepantla," which, although not identical, name a phenomenon that emerges or is tied to a situation or a concrete reality, namely, the anxiety of existence brought about by not being set or stable in one's being.

Commitment and Responsibility

Again, being accidental does not absolve Mexicans of their commitments and their responsibility. In fact, the knowledge that accidentality defines me is tied to a greater demand for a committed and responsible engagement with my reality, with my circumstances and my future. In this context, Mexican existentialism treats existential themes such as accidentality, thrownness, and commitment as interconnected. Consider Leopoldo Zea, who writes: "In this sense, every person is a committed agent, that is, inserted, *thrown*, or placed in a world in which one must act and for which one must be responsible."[22] Here, Zea places the emphasis not on our insertion or thrownness but on the necessity to act and be responsible for the world in which we find ourselves. To be thrown (a key concept in European existentialism) is to be situated, to be situated is to be committed, and vice versa. Emilio Uranga likewise emphasizes commitment as the only response to our thrownness:

> There is no world which is pure, neither is there pure consciousness; rather, there is always a consciousness in a situation, or commitment, which means at once a thrownness toward the world and the possibility to return to it so as to acquire a consciousness of the sense and essence of our commitment.[23]

The difference, expressed by Uranga as accidentality and insufficiency before substance, is understood by Zea as demanding a rigorous commitment for the past, present, and future of Mexico. He says:

> We have to take responsibility for a past not of our making: yet at the same time, with our attitude, whatever it might be, we commit and take responsibility for a future that must be made by us. In this way, we are responsible for others in the presence of others. This, in short, is the essence of commitment. (PC, 127)

For the Mexican existentialists the notion of absolute freedom endorsed by European existentialism does not fit the historical demands of their own concrete existence. Certainly, the historical facts of colonialism, independence, revolution, and modern First-World imperialism instilled in Mexican consciousness an unambiguous desire for freedom. However, the desire for unconditional freedom takes the form of an "internal" freedom, a freedom to change one's personality or attitude in regards a world already made (as Uranga says, it is a freedom to "enlighten the world").[24] The freedom sought, that is, is the freedom to commit oneself and be responsible for one's circumstance.

In his own confrontation with Sartre, Leopoldo Zea attends not to the absolute freedom of Sartre's early existentialism, but to a mature version of freedom, what Zea calls "situated, committed freedom" (PC, 135). It would be "irresponsible," according to Zea, to "maintain the idea of freedom in a full and absolute sense" when the whole of humanity is in crisis. What is needed, he says echoing Sartre, is a "[r]esponsible freedom, [one] aware of its limits ... [one] always aware" (PC, 135). In this way, Zea follows Sartre by endorsing a view of a limited freedom, where the restriction imposed is the concept of responsibility. Thus, for Zea, freedom and responsibility are two sides of the same coin; or as he puts it, "[w]here there is no responsibility, there is no freedom" (PC, 135). Zea thus arrives at the insight that responsibility is a paramount value for the Mexican (and, ultimately, the Latin American). Thus, because freedom is at stake, responsibility, or *commitment*, and not freedom, must be the value of values, that upon which our very existence rests.

Luis Villoro takes a more phenomenological position regarding freedom (in other words, he seeks to *describe* what freedom *is like*, rather than simply telling us what freedom is). Angst and vertigo, or my being "before the abyss" into which "I could fall at any moment," reveals me in my freedom "because at any moment I can throw myself into [the abyss] will-ingly."[25] But, my being free finds itself always in a context of significance along with things and others, which "reveals the tightly woven fabric of phenomena that imprisons me" (*SC*, 147). The notion that there is a *prison of phenomena* refers to the fact that those things that stand around me (what Ortega called the *circum-stare*) mesmerize me, hold my attention, and thus limit or restrict my involvement. This is an unavoidable imprisonment, since one is always *in-the-world* and thus cannot escape the things that demand our response. This might be seen as a *loss* of freedom, but for Vil-loro, this restrictive freedom has an emancipatory aspect which appears at the first sight of the *other*. In appearing before me, the other reveals her freedom in her ability to "escape my conceptualizations" (*SC*, 149) and, in revealing her freedom, I find that her freedom is made possible through me, or because of me, or in spite of me. Moreover, I become aware that I am willing to lose my freedom in this dialectic with the other as her "fate becomes mine" (*SC*, 149). Similar to Zea, freedom here is subordinated to responsibility: responsibility for another who escapes my grasp yet whose fate is tied to mine.

Responsibility for our world and ourselves is thus the value of values. It is the supreme value, the one to which all values point. Zea says it best when he affirms the nature of philosophy *as* commitment. He writes: "Committing ourselves to the universal and the eternal, without making a single concrete commitment, does not commit us to anything" (*PC*, 138). This does not mean that the philosopher will not pursue the universal or eternal. Villoro notes that this pursuit is a first movement toward a committed and respon-sible philosophy. Villoro writes: "We must take responsibility of our own situation and our own projects. Pure reflection, which reveals our absolute ethical responsibility, is a first condition for an authentic self-knowledge and makes possible any attempt for a future transformation" (*GP*, 242). But as a "first condition," once the philosopher finds his bearings in the contempla-tion of abstract truth or an ideal universality, she must turn to the world and toward the other. For Zea, this turn is a turn to what is most proximal and most personal to the situated human being:

> For what situation must we be responsible? What commitments must our philosophy responsibly make? After all, if we are to be faithful to [our philosophizing], we have to affirm that our *situation* is not that of Jean-Paul Sartre. Our situation is not that of the European bourgeoisie ... Before making ourselves responsible for the world's commitments, we must be responsible for our own concrete situations. We must be con-scious of our situation to make ourselves responsible for it. (*PC*, 137)

The task of Mexican existentialism is thus for Mexicans to shepherd them-selves to a recognition of their own limitations and the responsibilities and commitments that come with that recognition. But this means facing accidentality, zozobra, nepantla, and the burden of history. The future of the Mexican project depends on this confrontation. After all, as Zea says elsewhere, "existentialism does not wish to elude reality, does not evade it, it confronts it, assuming it with all of its consequences."[26]

Uranga stops short of prescribing being socially committed as a moral necessity. Leopoldo Zea, however, finds that our historical difference, which reflects Uranga's ontological notion of accidentality, demands such commitment. Without a commitment to find our way in a world into which we have been thrown as non-Europeans and non-Amerindian, we will not find a solution to our problems. As radically different in our history, culture, and humanity, the solutions to our human problems will not come from our Indigenous past (given its destruction at the hands of the Europeans) nor will it come from our European past (given our difference). As Zea puts it: "Our situation is not that of the European bourgeoisie. Our philosophy, if it is to be responsible, does not make the same commitment that contemporary European philosophy does" (PC, 137). He makes this declaration so as to motivate the emergence of a philosophical consciousness that will make a commitment to the Latin American difference. Ultimately, a commitment to our philosophy and our history will define those aspects of our subjectivity that make one truly human—for Zea, they will define and clarity what freedom itself will mean. "Our freedom is expressed in the *form* in which we assume the inevitable commitment to our circumstance" (PC, 126).

Conclusion

While European existentialism promoted a radical subjectivism grounded on thrownness and absolute freedom, structured by anxiety or angst, and projected toward an always unknown future, Mexican existentialists understood their thrownness and radical situatedness as a ground for commitment and responsibility toward others and toward Mexico. Ramirez rightly notes that "[t]he vindications of 'subjectivity' on the part of [European] existentialism result somewhat alien to Mexican reality."[27] For Mexican existentialists such as Villoro, Zea, and Uranga, existentialism was a move toward a more engaged existence, not toward a radical isolation in the loneliness of existence *à la* Camus. Luis Villoro, for instance, points to the "solitude" of the modern individual as a symptom, not of his original, existential condition, but as a symptom of modernity itself. For Villoro, this means that non-European, and even pre-modern, cultures have it right: the individual is essentially a communal being, and thus community is the original existential condition of persons. A person is not a "being-for-itself," as Sartre would say, but rather, a "being-for-others." Hence, for Villoro, "community is the form of life which is superior … and [consists only] in a personal life praxis which is interpersonal and ethically motivated."[28]

Mexican philosophers approach existentialism not as a philosophical fad, a charge that some have leveled against post-War French existentialism, or even as a rigorous philosophical method, but as the possibility for a critical philosophical articulation of a familiar reality and as a possibility for a more responsible engagement with the history, culture, and future of Mexico. Existentialism, understood in this way, ultimately allows the articulation of a mode of existence belonging to historically marginal peoples, those who are "accidental" due to history or ontological condition, something which in European existentialism was formulated in terms of contingency and finitude; moreover, existentialism makes possible the confrontation with ontological aspects of the human being as these are given in the being of the Mexican person, namely, "zozobra" and "nepantla"—modes of being that reveal freedom and a fundamental ungroundedness as categories of human life (what the European existentialist called "anxiety" or "angst"). Finally, it shows the existential and historical priority of community over subjectivity, implying an ethics of responsibility and commitment, not only to a community in general, but to Mexico in particular.

But Mexican existentialism is also transcendent, and this in a very specific sense. It goes beyond itself, beyond its space-time limitations, and lends itself today, as European existentialism did for the Mexican philosophers in the mid-20th century, to Latinx philosophers in the 21st century. Like the Mexican experience, ours (the Latinx experience) is one involving marginalization, accidentality, zozobra, and ungroundedness, which makes the search for a critical philosophical articulation of our contemporary reality an urgent matter. We feel a kinship with the Mexican existential narrative (in all of its nuances) for many reasons, one of which is historical, another geographical, and still another political. The significance of recognizing this kinship is existential itself, as it justifies us, it justifies our philosophy, our voice, our confidence in joining and contributing to a conversation that surely concerns us as human beings. It is, in this sense, an alternative vision of the human condition, one that is not Eurocentric. But, most importantly, it also lends us concepts that apply directly to us and which do not seem alien but familiar and known (via historical familial relations) such as accidentality, zozobra, and nepantla. With these concepts we can begin an analysis of our own situated condition, we can reframe our identities as accidental, for instance, and from this refuse the hegemony of the Western intellectual tradition as we endeavor to create our own.

To conclude, Mexican existentialism is a way to talk about what makes Mexican life both unique and genuine, just as a Latinx existentialism will be a way to talk about what makes our life unique and genuine. While existentialism was, for the Mexican philosophers, a method of reading Mexican culture, its allure had to do with the fact that it was seen as the language of Mexican experience itself—that is, of those things that Mexicans were already familiar with in their *being* Mexican. And we can do the same. So the existentialism position here is not merely a position, or a stance, but a *description* of a form of life which is always already being lived; it thus affirms for us both, Mexicans and Latinxs, that we are, and *as a matter of fact*, or genuinely, or authentically, grappling with a radical existence. But perhaps Mexican existentialism's most valuable lesson is that in the revelatory articulations of Mexican existence as accidental, *zozobrante*, and responsible, Mexicans are able to communicate a *universal* presence, that which in its difference affirms their belonging to a human community by communicating in its particularity what is common to all. As Emilio Uranga notes, with existentialism "Mexico will make its own particular turn toward the universal, appropriating the European without apology, feeling in the European spirit something co-natural but simultaneously capable of being overcome."[29]

Notes

1 Solomon, *Continental Philosophy Since 1750*, 173.
2 Ibid.
3 See Kauffman, *Existentialism from Dostoevsky to Sartre*; or Solomon, *Existentialism*. This list is clearly not exhaustive. Many more common characteristics can be found and elaborated upon. John Wild, for instance, makes the case that the "life-world," as the objective ground of action, is common to all existentialists. See Wild, "Existentialism as a Philosophy."
4 See Pereda, *La filosofía en Mexico en el siglo XX*, 278–279 [Philosophy in Mexico in the 20th Century].
5 Quoted in Romanell, *Making of the Mexican Mind*, 181.
6 Uranga, "Dos existencialismos," 173.
7 Maurice Merleau-Ponty visited Mexico City in January of 1949 at the request of the Mexican existentialists. During his visit, he reportedly pledged to dedicate space in *Le temps moderne*, of which he was editor at the time, to post-War Mexican philosophy. See Uranga, "Dialogo con Maurice Merleau-Ponty," 10. See also Luis Villoro, "Genesis y proyecto del existencialismo en Mexico" [The Beginning and Project of Existentialism in Mexico]. Indeed, the event of Merleau-Ponty's visit was front-page news in Mexico City. The picture accompanying Uranga's "Dialogo" depicts a smiling Merleau-Ponty flanked by reporters and dignitaries, among them, Emilio Uranga.
8 See Sánchez, *Contingency and Commitment*, especially chapter 1; Villoro, "Genesis y proyecto del existencialismo en Mexico," 241.
9 See Hurtado, *El Hiperion*, ix–x.
10 Uranga, "Dos existencialismos," 173. Cited in text using the abbreviation *DE* and page number.
11 Villoro, "Genesis y proyecto," 236. Cited in text using the abbreviation *GP* and page number.
12 The work of Ricardo Guerra stands out in this respect. See, for instance, Guerra, "Jean Paul Sartre."
13 Ramirez, "Villoro, el existencialista," 297.
14 Hurtado, *El Hiperión*, xiii.
15 The importance of the Mexican Revolution to the formation of 20th century Mexican identity, the modern Mexican state, and Mexican philosophy itself, cannot be understated. The event of the Revolution represented a moment of rupture, a break between what Mexican had been since the conquest and colonization and what Mexico *had* to become, a place of freedom, opportunity, and equality. But more than that, it was a moment of existential crisis, where

Mexicans came face to face with their own human limitations in the midst of death and the destruction of their own existence.

16 Ramirez, *Luis Villoro*, 171.
17 Uranga, "Merleau-Ponty," 240.
18 Quoted in Uranga, *Análisis del ser del mexicano*, 80fn13.
19 There were more appropriations, of course, but for the sake of brevity, we focus on only three. For instance, freedom was a major theme taken up by Mexican existentialist (see, Guerra, "Jean Paul Sartre").
20 Uranga, *Análisis del ser del mexicano*, 51. Cited in text using the abbreviation *A* and page number.
21 Uranga, "Merleau-Ponty," 234.
22 Zea, "Philosophy as Commitment," 126. Cited in text using the abbreviation *PC* and page number.
23 Uranga, "Merleau-Ponty," 227.
24 As is the case with Jorge Portilla. See Sánchez, *The Suspension of Seriousness*.
25 Villoro, "Solitude and Communion," 146. Cited in text using the abbreviation *SC* and page number.
26 Zea, "El existencialismo como filosofía de la responsabilidad" [Existentialism as a Philosophy of Responsibility].
27 Ramirez, "Villoro," 300.
28 Ibid., 309.
29 Uranga, "Merleau-Ponty," 241.

Bibliography

Guerra, Ricardo. "Jean Paul Sartre, filosofo de la libertad." *Filosofía y Letras* 16, no. 32(1948): 295–307.

Hurtado, Guillermo, ed. *El Hiperion*. Mexico: Universidad Nacional Autonoma de Mexico, 2006.

Kauffman, Walter. *Existentialism from Dostoevsky to Sartre*. New York: Penguin, 1975.

Pereda, Carlos. *La filosofía en Mexico en el siglo XX: Apuntes de un participante*. Mexico: Dirección General de Publicaciones, 2013.

Ramirez, Mario Teodoro. *Luis Villoro: Pensamiento y Vida*. Mexico: Siglo XXI Editores, 2014.

Ramirez, Mario Teodoro. "Villoro, el existencialista," *Eikasia* (July2015): 297–311.

Romanell, Patrick. *Making of the Mexican Mind: A Study in Recent Mexican Thought*. Lincoln, NE: University of Nebraska Press, 1952.

Sánchez, Carlos Alberto. *The Suspension of Seriousness: On the Phenomenology of Jorge Portilla*. Albany: SUNY Press, 2012.

Sánchez, Carlos Alberto. *Contingency and Commitment: Mexican Existentialism and the Place of Philosophy*. Albany: State University of New York Press, 2016.

Solomon, Robert C. *Continental Philosophy Since 1750: The Rise and Fall of the Self*. Oxford: Oxford University Press, 1988.

Solomon, Robert C. *Existentialism*. Oxford: Oxford University Press, 2004.

Uranga, Emilio. "Maurice Merleau-Ponty: Fenomenología y existencialismo." *Filosofía y Letras* 15, no. 30(1948): 219–241.

Uranga, Emilio. "Dialogo con Maurice Merleau-Ponty." *Mexico en la cultura*, March 13, (1949): 3–4.

Uranga, Emilio. *Análisis del ser del mexicano y otros ensayos sobre la filosofía de lo mexicano (1949–1952)*. Edited by Guillermo Hurtado. México, DF: Bonilla Artigas Editores, 2013.

Uranga, Emilio. "Dos existencialismos." In *Análisis del ser del mexicano y otros escrito sobre la filosofía de lo mexicano (1949–1952)*. México: Bonilla Artigas Editores, 2013.

Villoro, Luis. "Genesis y proyecto del existencialismo en Mexico." *Filosofía y letras* 18, no. 36(1949): 233–244.

Villoro, Luis. "Solitude and Communion." In *Mexican Philosophy in the 20th Century: Essential Readings*, edited by Carlos Alberto Sánchez and Robert Eli Sanchez, 141–155. Oxford: Oxford University Press, 2017.

Wild, John. "Existentialism as a Philosophy." *The Journal of Philosophy* 57, no. 2 (1960): 45–62.

Zea, Leopoldo. "El existencialismo como filosofia de la responsabilidad." *El Nacional*, 5 June1949, section 3.

Zea, Leopoldo. "Philosophy as Commitment." In *Mexican Philosophy in the 20th Century: Essential Readings*, edited by Carlos Alberto Sánchez and Robert Eli Sanchez, 125–140. Oxford: Oxford University Press, 2017.

7 Liberation Philosophy

Grant Silva

Liberation philosophy is a well-established current of thought within the range of works that make up Latin American philosophy. In its most general formulation, it is a way of doing philosophy *for the sake of human freedom*. This sense of freedom is not generalizable or abstract, as liberation philosophers emphasize the importance of place and are attentive to their social existence when philosophizing; *where* one thinks matters for liberation philosophy. This tradition therefore stands in solidarity with the words of the Black feminist philosopher and liberatory thinker Angela Davis, who is famous for saying, "We have to talk about liberating minds *as well as* liberating society." With the exception of maybe Comtean positivism (see chapter 4), one is hard-pressed to find a current of thought in Latin American philosophy more determined to put thought into action.

Despite various precursors throughout the history of Latin American thought, the explicit formalization of liberation philosophy occurred in Argentina in the 1960s. Shortly after, due to the dissemination of ideas, as well as the political repression and the displacement of various thinkers within this tradition, liberation philosophy became a widespread critique of the various socioeconomic, political, and philosophical problems afflicting Latin America and the Caribbean.[1] Since most of these problems are rooted in the European colonization of America, the spread of liberation philosophy throughout the Americas can be described as a "decolonial awakening," one that is still underway.[2] This tradition is not so naïve, however, to assume that philosophical criticism alone can alleviate human suffering. Instead, liberation philosophy warns of the hazards of philosophy serving as ideology, that is, philosophy as a set of beliefs justifying a status quo. For this reason, liberation philosophy is often at odds with mainstream academic philosophy insofar as professional philosophers limit their activity to interpreting historical texts, analyzing language or concepts, furthering academic debates, and promoting individualistic conceptions of "enlightenment."

Liberation philosophy is perhaps one of the few philosophical movements autochthonous (i.e., "indigenous" or "native") to the region. This is not to deny that liberation philosophers draw from European philosophy. Like much of Latin American and Caribbean culture, liberation philosophy is an amalgamation of diverse philosophical methodologies and ways of know-ing.[3] Nevertheless, it does not import ideas without considering their rele-vance in Latin America and the Caribbean. If it were not so engaged, liberation philosophy would be subject to the criticism of "using the mas-ter's tools to dismantle the master's house," to cite the phrase made famous by Audre Lorde (the nub of this criticism implies that one is not "dis-mantling" anything by taking up its conceptual apparatuses).[4]

In what follows, I examine the philosophies of Ignacio Ellacuría, Enrique Dussel, and Leopoldo Zea in order to explain what it means to do philoso-phy for the sake of freedom. Specifically, I provide an overview of the cri-tical, decolonial, phenomenological-existential, and historicist motivations for liberation philosophy. Along the way, I consider criticisms of this tradi-tion while also taking note of its influence outside Latin America and the Caribbean. I conclude with a slight provocation, suggesting that "liberation" is a defining characteristic of Latin American philosophy as a whole.

Ideologization and the Social Function of Philosophy

Philosophers of liberation have the tendency of appreciating concepts that convey fluidity and motion. The tradition as a whole seeks to improve human life and not maintain oppressive states of affairs. Essential to the philosophy of liberation, then, is the attempt to call into question those systems of belief, forms of ignorance, and instances of intellectual disengagement that result in what Ignacio Ellacuría, the Jesuit philosopher of liberation, referred to as "ideologization," a process through which a prevailing socioeconomic or political order makes itself into *the* definitive and permanent mode of social organization.[5] Ellacuría refers to this as philosophy's liberating function.

According to Ellacuría, philosophy has always been "about" freedom. He describes this relationship the following way:

> We can say that philosophy has always had to do with freedom, though in different ways. It has been assumed that philosophy is the task of free individuals and free peoples, free at least of the basic needs that can suppress the kind of thinking we call philosophy. We also acknowledge that it has a liberating function for those who philosophize and that as the supreme exercise of reason, it has liberated people from obscurant-ism, ignorance, and falsehood. Throughout the centuries, from the pre-Socratics to the Enlightenment, through all methods of *critical* thinking, we have ascribed a great superiority to reason, and to philosophical reason in particular, as a result of its liberating function.
> [...]
> [T]his matter of *philosophy* and *freedom* gets to the fundamental purpose of philosophical knowledge, which even if it is understood as a search for truth, cannot be reduced to being a search for truth for its own sake. Such classical ideas as the relationship between truth and

freedom (John 8:32), or between interpretation and the transformation of reality (Marx, Thesis 11 on Feuerbach), are an eloquent refutation of that reductionism. (*LFP*, 94)

Ellacuría depicts the interconnectedness of philosophy and freedom in two ways. First, in terms of the material conditions that make possible philosophical inquiry, and second, in terms of the instrumental value of reason and the social function of philosophy. Both are necessary if philosophy is to realize its full liberatory potential. With regard to the first, Ellacuría believes that although any person can ask philosophical questions, professional philosophy demands "freedom from the basic needs that can suppress the kind of thinking we call philosophy." Philosophy, Ellacuría explains, requires the type of freedom that provides philosophers the time to hone the theoretical tools necessary to identify and critique problematic forms of ideology.

"Ideology" refers to a set of beliefs or ideas that are held for reasons other than the satisfaction of pure intellectual curiosity. Ideologies are typically politicized systems of thought that strive to justify a social order or political arrangement even if they pass themselves off as politically neutral. Though ideology is not necessarily bad in itself, Ellacuría focuses on the oppressive function of ideology, specifically the process through which an unjust social structure makes itself out to be *the* definitive mode of human organization (again, "ideologization"). The end result is a "monopolization" of the ways of being human in the world. For instance, since our current political order is one that requires international borders, we assume that they are necessary and unavoidable, which is not the case (for hundreds of thousands of years Homo sapiens resided on this planet without political borders).

For Ellacuría, ideologization refers to repressive forms of ideology that lead people to internalize their suffering (or, coincidentally, their privilege). Individuals and communities start to see their lack of food or water or the exposure to violence and death as somehow ordinary, normal, even necessary. As Ellacuría explains,

> What distinguishes ideologization from ideology is that it unconsciously and unintentionally expresses visions of reality that, rather than manifesting [or revealing] the reality, hide and deform it with the appearance of truth because of interests shaped by classes or social, ethnic, political and/or religious groups. (*LFP* 99)

Ideologization stifles our ability to imagine a different and less destructive world, especially for the dispossessed. The consequence of this is stasis (non-movement) and the denial of the dynamic nature of human life. We start to see the social world in front of us as unchangeable.

If philosophers ignore the social function of philosophy, philosophy runs the risk of becoming ideology. Throughout his dialogues, in addition to illustrating the importance of rational, dialogical inquiry, Plato depicts

Socrates as having a self-imposed duty to assist those stuck in the realm of opinion, dogma, and epistemic hubris, especially as they have a tendency of underwriting corrupt social structures or political institutions. Inspired by the dictum, "know thyself," Socrates views himself as having a philosophical *vocation*, a duty to critically examine his fellow Athenians, especially the self-proclaimed experts who occupy positions of power. This does not mean that he assumed this duty out of idle curiosity or only for his own sake. As the Mexican philosopher Leopoldo Zea writes in "Philosophy as Commitment," Socrates:

> does not seek pure and abstract truth, but the truth of each person, the truth of each citizen, the being of each one of them, that for which each was made, their function, their role, and their place in the community.[6]

Socrates' role as a philosopher, then, was:

> to subject to examination each of his fellow citizens, to find out if they know the art they presume to practice, and to make them aware of their roles. He wants them to find and know themselves. Socrates wants to be the gadfly of his community, its moral conscience. (*PC*, 130)

Socrates had an obligation to *liberate* society from hubris, naked appeals to power, misguided ways of knowing, and falsehood. That was simply what it meant to be a philosopher for him.

In academia today, this view of philosophy can make professional philosophers uncomfortable. Many would rather contemplate philosophical questions that they find interesting or further their academic careers than serve oppressed members of society. I call this philosophizing *from a position of* freedom or philosophy as detachment. Perhaps offended by such a charge, academic philosophers might respond that their work contributes to "the pursuit of truth," which is a rather specialized enterprise (as even Ellacuría admits). Be that as it may, academic philosophy runs the risk of ideologization insofar as it fails to critique prevailing ideology. Philosophy is derelict of its social duty when it hesitates to engage in politics so as not to appear biased or moralizing; when it fetishizes analytical rigor or takes pride in being abstruse; when it concerns itself only with "big questions" that transcend everyday experience. Philosophers become ideologues not by explicitly supporting injustice (although some do), but by pursuing socially unimportant academic endeavors.[7]

Philosophy can do these other things, but not at the expense of its social function. Along these lines, Ellacuría finds value in "foundational" thinkers such as epistemologists or metaphysicians (areas of philosophy that have a tendency to be rather abstract and disengaged). To combat ideology, he writes, "Philosophy must ... be distinctively fundamental, that is, searching for the foundations" (*LFP*, 101). Philosophy ought to reveal the "unfoundedness" of ideologized positions and perspectives, so there is important work for those pursuing truth or trying to discover the conditions that make possible our reality. Nevertheless, he warns: "A position that seeks ultimate and totalizing foundations risk slipping into ideologization, but it also has great possibilities of identifying and combating an imaginary foundation presented as a real foundation" (*LFP*, 101). In short, the philosophical pursuit of truth is necessary, but it can never be reduced to "the search for truth for its own sake," as he states above (*LFP*, 94). This claim levies a responsibility upon philosophers to teach others to love or appreciate reason's liberating function, a point all philosophers purport to appreciate but often fail to put into practice.

Liberation philosophers like Ellacuría, then, strive to restore the social function of philosophy or put it back on the proverbial path of righteousness—to think of it as the vocation personified by Socrates. Dussel summarizes this point in *The Philosophy of Liberation* when he states:

> Philosophy, when it is really philosophy and not sophistry or ideology, does not ponder philosophy. It does not ponder philosophical texts, except as a pedagogical propaedeutic to provide itself with interpretative categories. Philosophy ponders the non-philosophical; the reality. But because it involves reflection on its own reality, it sets out from what already is, from its own world, its own systems, its own space. The philosophy that has emerged from a periphery has always done so in response to a need to situate itself with regard to a center—in total exteriority.[8]

The Persistence of Coloniality

As mentioned above, liberation philosophy stands in solidarity with Angela Davis's statement: "We have to talk about liberating minds *as well as* liberating society." "Liberating society" is not merely a question of establishing formal equality and universal citizenship within a specific political system. Throughout Latin America, the nature and persistence of what is referred to as "coloniality" is such that nation-states are vehicles through which a variety of forms of oppression are reproduced. In fact, the history of the American republics is marred by slavery, serfdom, social stratification, and passive forms of citizenship that accompany national liberation or political independence from European colonial rule. In short, "liberation" is best viewed as a process and not a one-time event.

According to the Mexican philosopher, Luis Villoro, 19th-century national independence movements throughout Latin America were for the most part initiated by and worked in the favor of colonial elites. Comparing the independence movements of Mexico and the United States, he argued that, in both cases, the colonial elite began and ended the movement. "[I]ndependence was at the same time a reformist and a conservative movement," Villoro writes, "It tried to break political and economic dependence while preserving the social structure of the old colony."[9] Nowhere is this more obvious than in Simón Bolívar's *Address to the Angostura Congress* (see chapter 3).

Shortly after the wars for independence from Spanish rule (1819), the Great Liberator convened a legislative congress in the city of Angostura (modern day Ciudad Bolívar) in order to articulate a constitution and system of laws for *Gran Columbia* (what is now Venezuela and Columbia). Inspired by Montesquieu's *Spirit of the Laws*, Bolívar called upon the representatives of the Republic to construct a government and legal system that worked best *for them*, not just import models from foreign governments such as the United States (for more on the risk of blind imitation, see chapter 5). Specifically, Bolívar recommended that they elect a senate that would subsequently assume a hereditary line of succession. This senate would not violate the principle of political equality or constitute a nobility since "the hereditary senate, as part of the people, participates in their interests, in their feelings, and in their spirit." He continues, "For this reason no one should presume that a hereditary senate will be detached from popular interests nor forget it legislative duties."[10]

In a famous passage from this Address, Bolívar praised the racial and ethnic heterogeneity of the Venezuelan people:

> [W]e are not Europeans, we are not Indians, but rather a race midway between the aborigines and the Spanish. Americans by birth and Europeans by rights, we find ourselves in the dilemma of disputing rights of possession with the natives and of sustaining ourselves in the country of our birth against the opposition of the invaders; thus our case is most extraordinary and complex. (*ANG*, 5)

This mix between indigenous and Iberian is the ideal of *mestizaje*, the fusion of multiple races, cultures, and ways of life in the hopes of fostering peace between groups once at odds with one another (note, however, that on account of anti-black racism the African influence is often downplayed in national narratives praising *mestizaje*). In the passage above, Bolívar encourages his audience to think along racial lines, again, pointing out the differences that define them, only then to remind them that "not all hearts are created to love everything beautiful, nor are all eyes capable of bearing the heavenly light of perfection." He goes on:

> My opinion is ... that the fundamental principle of our system depends directly and exclusively on equality as established and practiced in Venezuela. That all men are born with equal rights to society's goods is a notion sanctioned by the majority of learned people, *as also is the notion that not all men are born equally capable of obtaining every social status*—for all should practice virtue and not all practice it; all should be courageous and not all are; all should possess talents and not all poses them. From this derives the most effective difference observed

among individuals of even the most liberally established society. (*ANG*, 9–10. Emphasis added.)

Rather than leave anything to "chance and the luck of elections," a hereditary senate "would be the foundation, the bond, the soul of our republic." He continues, "In political tempest this body would fend off thunderbolts from the government and repulse popular waves" (*ANG*, 12–13). Thus, for Bolívar, the preservation of political independence requires a distinction between active and passive forms of citizenship, a political environment where some rule and others are ruled. Given the racial demographics of his region at the time, it is not hard to imagine how political power was to be distributed and racial hierarchy implemented with Europeans and wealthy *Criollos* (American born Europeans) on top.

The typical defense offered for Bolívar's views is that one cannot reasonably expect former slaves and illiterate people to lead a nation. Nevertheless, as "practical-minded" as he might have been, Bolívar's thoughts demonstrate the ways in which liberation cannot be reduced to the achievement of national independence. His proposal reveals the persistence of "coloniality," a theoretical and philosophical concept central to decolonial thought in Latin America and the Caribbean.

Coloniality does not refer to the rule of an imperial power, like that of Spain over Mexico or Peru. "Coloniality is different from colonialism," writes Nelson Maldonado-Torres:

> Colonialism denotes a political and economic relation in which the sovereignty of a nation or a people rests on the power of another nation, which makes such a nation an empire. Coloniality, instead, refers to long-standing patterns of power that emerged as a result of colonialism, but that define culture, labor, intersubjective relations, and knowledge production well beyond the strict limits of colonial administration. Thus, coloniality survives colonialism. It is maintained alive in books, in the criteria for academic performance, in cultural patterns, in common sense, in the self-image of peoples, in aspirations of self, and so many other aspects of our modern experience. In a way, as modern subjects we breath [sic] coloniality all the time and everyday.[11]

Coloniality leads to the establishment of socially stratified hierarchies of power and domination. It manifests and operates along a variety of "axes" such as race, gender, and sexuality (see chapters 8 and 11). For instance, in colonial America, race was an instrument to control labor.[12] Because of their racial designation, indigenous or African persons were restricted to specific types of service. Both were, as Bolívar gingerly suggests, unfit for political rule. While mixed-race persons fared better—race in Latin America includes an assortment of mixed-racial identities dispersed along a gradient of whiteness—*mestizo/as* or *mulatto/as* occupied the lower rungs of the social ladder. Similarly, biologized and narrow conceptions of gender and sexual difference played a role in the colonial administration of labor, in resource control, and sexual reproduction.[13] Women were "domesticated," not allowed to receive higher education, and treated as a form of property at the service of fathers or husbands. The sexual union between men and women not only solidified men's power over women, but served as an instrument of the state necessary for the promulgation of community—a point that even decolonial and liberatory philosophers were slow to criticize (see chapter 8).

Thus, a "post-colonial" society is not necessarily a society that is *decolonized*, which is why liberation and decolonization is an ongoing "process."[14] While independence from Iberian colonial rule brought political sovereignty, it did little to curb the power dynamic of colonization and the hierarchies of race, gender, and heterosexuality that followed. Instead, the social identities that arose from these categories assisted in the articulation of differentiated levels of citizenship and the restriction of social mobility and "freedom." Much like "ideologization," totalizing forms of social identity have a way of freezing persons in social categories. Frantz Fanon speaks to this when reflecting on how he felt to be called "Dirty nigger!" or referred to by the description, "Look! A Negro!":

> I came into this world anxious to uncover the meaning of things, my soul desirous to be at the origin of the world, and here I am an object among other objects. Locked in this suffocating reification, I appealed to the Other so that his liberating gaze, gliding over my body suddenly smoothed of rough edges, would give me back the lightness of being I thought I had lost, and taking me out of the world put me back in the world. But just as I get to the other slope I stumble, and the Other fixes me with his gaze, his gestures and attitude, the same way you fix a preparation with a dye.[15]

Fanon conveys that sense of being trapped within assigned forms of identity. Using the term "reification," Fanon explains how social categorization works as ideology to reinforce oppressive social and political structures (i.e. because of one's race they are deserving of this form of treatment). It is for this reason that social rather than personal liberation is a more pressing concern within liberation philosophy, as Ofelia Schutte explains.[16]

Personal liberty is a popular theme throughout the history of Latin American philosophy, especially "in sense of self-development for a life of freedom and creativity," as Schutte writes. Nevertheless, such an understanding of liberty misses the critical dimensions of "liberation" and concerns itself with *individual* freedoms, rights, desires, and hopes (*CISL*, 9–10). All of these are important, but if philosophers are exclusively interested in the individualistic dimensions of freedom, philosophy becomes "an affirmation of the autonomy of a thinking subject," as the Caribbean philosopher

Paget Henry puts it. "As the primary instrument of this absolute subject," Henry continues, "philosophy shares in its autonomy and therefore is a discipline that rises above the determinations of history and everyday life."[17] By "rising above the determinations of history and everyday life," philosophy becomes detached and abstract, meaningless some might say, and focused on purely intellectual puzzles devoid of a sense of social responsibility.

Liberation philosophers view philosophy as something more than an affirmation of the autonomy and liberty of individuals. That is philosophical practice *from* the position of freedom rather than *for the sake of* freedom. For liberatory philosophers, the affirmation of autonomy or subjectivity is not as important as the liberation of the *subject-in-struggle*, a struggle for "freedom." This sense of freedom should not be idealized or divorced from social identity. To be liberated from sexism, classism, and racism is not to reinforce the utopian and misguided ideal of a "post-gender" or "colorblind" society (the notion that the problems of racism or sexism would go away if we stopped talking about race and if minorities or women stopped making "a big deal" about being different). Rather than negate difference, human social relations have to work through it, a point that, as I explain below, Zea echoes in terms of history and the development of historical consciousness. Rather than *negating or forgetting* the painful parts of history, the past has to be *liberated*, a move that requires acknowledging and subsuming the past. In terms of social identity, we cannot simply stop seeing race or gender when the social categories connected to these continue to influence the distribution of labor and access to social goods in formerly colonized societies; different and unequal access to healthcare, education, security, likelihood of going to prison, homeownership, freedom from harm, are all affected by the workings of social categories such as race, gender, and sexuality. "Postcolonialism," in this sense, serves the same purpose as "post-race" or "post-gender": they mask oppression. This is why, in the above passage, Maldonado-Torres states that "as modern subjects we breath coloniality all the time and everyday." Or, to quote Davis again, "freedom is a constant struggle."[18]

Latinx peoples in the United States, as well as other racialized groups, have much to gain from this particular intersection of liberatory and decolonial philosophies. In his book *Latinos in America*, while explaining that not all Latinx peoples speak Spanish, eat beans and rice, or dance salsa, Jorge J. E. Gracia writes:

> These examples illustrate the fact that to be Latino does not entail much that is generally associated with the stereotype. But why should this lumping and homogenization generate fear in the Latino population? Why do we find strident voices complaining and warning about this phenomenon? *Because we worry that by being lumped together into one stereotyped group, the reality which we are will be misunderstood—we*

*will be taken as what we are not and this can affect our lives in sig-
nificant ways, some very nefarious to our well being.* Homogenization
becomes particularly dangerous in political contexts because the government often formulates and implements social policy based on
stereotypes.[19]

To this we might add that the problem with stereotypes is that they pre-
define or impose an image of what it means to be affiliated with a particular
group before individuals have a chance to define themselves. In the existentialist language of the early 20th century, it is to have an "essence prior to
existence." Stereotypes delineate how individuals are to be understood, for
example as friend or enemy, and fix people in social structures at the service
of oppression. Rather than eliminating these social categories, human social
existence must be "liberated" from the repressive mechanisms and forms of
prejudice attached to them. "Liberation," in this sense, does not deny difference, but preserves it by thinking of the "self" in relation to others.

Dussel's Analectical Liberatory Philosophy

Liberation philosophy aims for a truly global, as opposed to globalized,
conception of humanity. The former recognizes the multiplicity of cultures,
languages, and ways of knowing and being that constitute humanity; the
latter is a byproduct of a colonizing humanism that sweeps over differences
amongst humans. For liberation philosophy, philosophy is a struggle against
dehumanization. Maldonado-Torres captures this sense of philosophy when
he writes,

> the *telos* [the ultimate aim or goal] of thinking, if there is any, is the
> struggle against dehumanization, understood as the affirmation of soci-
> ality and the negation of its negation. I refer to the negation of sociality
> as coloniality and to its negation and overcoming as decoloniality.[20]

Along similar lines, Dussel's *Philosophy of Liberation* aspires to think *from* a
perspective of oppression, violence, and victimization. It seeks to affirm sociality. In this particular work, Dussel approaches philosophy from "the per-
ipheral colonial world, the sacrificed Indian, the enslaved black, the oppressed
woman, the subjugated child, and the alienated popular culture" (*POL*, 137),
a form of thinking which he calls *analectical* thought. Comprised of the Greek
particles *ano/ana* ("from beyond") and *logos* ("reason" or "rational account
of"), the transliteral meaning of "analectics" or "analogical" is "reason or
rationality from beyond" (*POL*, 158–161). "Analectics" refers to thinking
from beyond the self. The point is not to know the Other, as in having mas-
tery over her or him, but to make possible a way of knowing where the perspective of those inhabiting dominant or hegemonic perspectives is brought
down to earth and rendered "parochial." It is a way of decentering one's own

perspective and therefore making room for others (which does not mean that Others become the center!).

Dussel inherits this sense of Otherness (or "alterity") from the phenomenological ethics of the French Lithuanian Jewish philosopher, Emmanuel Levinas. In *Totality and Infinity*, Levinas launched a critique of Western philosophy that targeted its dependency on psychological egoism and ontology as first philosophy.[21] Levinas's criticism centers on the fact that Western philosophy sets out from the first-person experience of the world ("the self" or the "I"). While this starting point is not unavoidable or intrinsically problematic, it establishes a framework where the rest of existence, the "not-Self," is objectified and made an instrument. From this perspective, dialogue with Others is always "self-centered," and Others are knowable because we see ourselves in them (and thus we do not really see *them*), or, worse, they cannot be understood at all since they represent a radical difference that one cannot empathize with whatsoever (cf. Fausto Reinaga's critique of Indigenism in chapter 9). Other people therefore become a "thing" to be studied cautiously (cf. certain views of undocumented immigrants in chapter 10). All this boils down to the rejection of difference ("they are not like us at all and therefore not human") or the assimilation of difference ("they are human and therefore like us"). Both deny alterity and undermine human sociality.

This ego-centrism reduces the plurality of human ways of being to the perspective of people in positions of power capable of asserting their conception of reality on the world ("ontology"). By contrast, the analectical method is a dialogue between more than one speaker, an exchange that does not reduce the less dominant voice to the perspective of the more dominant. It does not force the Other to think like you. That is the opposite of decentering, what Dussel calls a monologue or "anti-dialogue," which results in involuntary assimilation, "sameness," enclosure, all of which are antithetical to liberation.

Western "modernity" performed this one-sided "exchange" with indigenous peoples during the European colonization of the Americas.[22] In the effort to justify conquest, colonization, and slavery, the modern Western perspective assumed that it represented humanity and knowledge and believed that the Indian "animal" was inferior (see chapter 2). "Uncivilized" and "primitive," indigenous persons were incapable of philosophical thought, one of the supposed hallmarks of Western modernity. The Native American philosopher Vine Deloria Jr. puts it the following way:

> Tribal people have traditionally been understood by Westerners as the last remnants of a hypothetical earlier stage of cultural evolution, and this so-called "primitive stage" of human development is a necessary preamble to any discussion of human beings and the meaning of their lives. Indeed, the stereotype of primitive peoples anchors the whole edifice of Western social thought. We need the primitive so that we can

distinguish Western civilization from it and congratulate ourselves on the progress we have made.[23]

Deloria notes the difficulties facing those who try to convince critics that indigenous peoples practice philosophy, too, since recognizing their rational capacities contradicts the narrative of Western progress and superiority, as well as the supposed "universality" of Western thought, culture, and philosophy.

Much like for Deloria, Dussel ties the disregard for indigenous thought and culture to social and political domination: "Before the *ego cogito*, there is an *ego conquiro*; 'I conquer' is the practical foundation of 'I think'" (*POL*, 3). Combined with what Levinas refers to as "ontology," this egocentric starting point sets philosophy off on an oppressive foot. It makes a vicious form of self-realization (the ego-centrism described above) the end-goal of philosophy and endows the self with the capacity and duty to *nominate* all of existence.

In general terms, ontology is the study of being that provides a rational account of what exists; it is a way of "carving up" the universe into intelligible parts; giving a rational account (*logos*) of things (*ontos*). Much like interpretations of Genesis in which God gives man dominion over the natural world, a gift that subsequently provides the ability to name everything that exists, ontology distinguishes the human subject from the non-human object. The sense of ontology that Dussel has in mind posits "man" as the ultimate subject who can say what exists and how or why, a point that should resonate with Ellacuría's use of ideology above (a set of beliefs meant to support an unjust status quo). However, given that humans do not have direct access to how things *really* are, rival ontologies arise and a "war" over human existence quickly ensues. Thus, in *Philosophy of Liberation*, Dussel claims that *war* is the origin of *everything*, where "everything" here refers to "the order or system that world dominators control by their power and armies" (*POL*, 1). The only way to obviate this warlike atmosphere is to express dominion over others and force your worldview upon them. As he puts it, "The space of a world within the ontological horizon is the space of a world center, of the organic, self-conscious state that brooks no contradictions—because it is an imperialist state" (*POL*, 1).

Besides placing the dyadic relationship between self and Other into the context of colonization, Dussel makes use of the language of "center" and "periphery." The center is Europe, the colonial power which is eventually replaced by the United States and metropoles throughout the Americas; the periphery is the colonial world subject to cultural domination and economic and political control. The center is the place where "Being" unfolds, an ontological realm where the dominant ideology "carves up" the world for its benefit. Dussel writes:

> Critical thought that arises from the periphery—including the social periphery, the oppressed classes, the *lumpen*—always ends by directing

itself toward the center. [This] is its death as critical philosophy; it is its birth as an ontology and ideology. Thought that takes refuge in the center ends by thinking it to be the only reality. Outside its frontiers is nonbeing, nothing, barbarity, non-sense. Being is the very foundation of the system, the totality of the sense of a culture, the macho world of the man of the center. (POL, 3–4)

He continues, "Ontology, the thinking that expresses Being—the Being of the reigning and central system—is the ideology of ideologies, the foundation of the ideologies of the empire, of the center" (POL, 5). "Being" is the known; "non-being" is the unknown. That which is "known" is subject to reason and human rationality. That which is unknown is irrational; it is beyond or outside the scope of human reason and thus incomprehensible.

As an example of carving up the world for one's own benefit, consider the concept of race. While elements of it can be seen in the *limpieza de sangre* ("purity of blood") statutes associated with the Reconquista of Iberian Peninsula and expulsion of the Jews and Moors from Spain in 1492, the *modern* conception of race was invented to justify the appropriation of indigenous land and the enslavement of African Americans during European colonization of the Americas. Providing a "justification" of theft and slavery, "race" carves humanity into natural groupings in a hierarchy. At its core, race is not only a theoretical division of human beings on the basis of phenotypic resemblance, a division that has now been debunked by science. Central to this notion is the subjugation of non-Western peoples to an ideal of progress that places white Europeans on top. This process of racialization erased the local history of colonized and enslaved peoples and supplanted it with a "universal history," a self-serving narrative that recounts the emergence of "modern man" from savagery and barbarity (as Deloria explains above). As Ta-Nehisi Coates writes, "Race is the child of racism, not the father." He continues, "Difference in hue and hair is old. But the belief in the preeminence of hue and hair, the belief that these factors can correctly organize a society and that they signify deeper attributes, which are indelible—this is the new idea."[24]

Race confers a sense of natural superiority and inferiority. It says to the colonized, "No matter how much you adopt the culture, language, or religion of the colonizer, you will always be less on account of racial difference." Racial difference is thus deeper than cultural difference, more "ontologically basic." It is a form of dominating and covering-over; it does a great deal of ideological work. In this context Dussel writes:

Distant thinkers, those who had a perspective of the center from the periphery, those who had to define themselves in the presence of an already established image of the human person and in the presence of uncivilized fellow humans, the newcomers, the ones who hope because they are always outside, these are the ones who a have clear mind for pondering reality. They have nothing to hide. How could they hide domination if they undergo it? How would their philosophy be an ideological ontology if their praxis is one of liberation from the center they are opposing? Philosophical intelligence is never so truthful, clean, and precise as when it starts from oppression and does not have to defend any privileges, because it has none. (*POL*, 4)

Dussel's use of "distant thinkers" is insightful. It signifies the analectical point of departure for liberation philosophy. *Distant* thinkers are those residing "outside" hegemonic circles and totalizing systems, those in colonial peripheries situated in relation to a center (Europe); those for whom their status as rational subjects requires the recognition of spatial connotations or boundaries, that is, terms like "Latin American," "African," "Asian" or, more generally, an aperture or distance from the imposing views of the center; those who must break through images of humanity's past imposed upon through terms like "barbarian, pre-modern, savage, inferior." "New-comers," or those who are free to create, are best suited to ponder reality since they do not have to defend their privilege or ideological perspectives. Dussel's analectical method, then, is a way of maintaining the kind of "distance" that allows for difference (but not so much difference that we lose cross-cultural communication—we are all human after all).

Dussel, of course, has his critics. Schutte, for instance, argues that liberation philosophy was largely the product of white males from Argentina, most of whom were Catholic.[25] To what extent could this class of individuals effectively speak on behalf of the oppressed? Maybe they could speak as "colonized" peoples in the Americas (in a very general sense) or as politically repressed persons, but what do they know about being or thinking as a poor indigenous woman situated within macho culture? Moreover, on Schutte's account, the reliance upon "center" and "periphery" establishes a Manichean framework that ignores the complexity of oppression and liberation. It becomes a story of "good guys" versus "bad guys," an over-simplification of the reality of colonization and coloniality (recall Bolívar's embracement of independence and demand for freedom as a *Criollo* only to reestablish racial hierarchy).

Schutte's larger criticism is that philosophy of liberation is not as practical as it claims to be. Given that it is supposed to convey a sense of "un-masterability," a "non-totalizable" infinity (as Levinas puts it), the idea of alterity or Otherness becomes a stand-in for the divine, chiefly for God. Schutte calls into question the Judeo-Christian foundations of liberation philosophy that she argues doubly oppresses indigenous Americans. Not only is their plight articulated in theological terms, but they continue to be viewed as potential converts, what amounts to a rejection of their alterity.[26]

To develop Schutte's criticism, we might point out that in his early work, Dussel emphasized what he termed "erotics," a relationship essentially defined by the man-woman sexual relationship (*POL*, 78). This early understanding of "erotics" is rooted in Aristotle's "naturalized" account of the state and Catholic doctrine. As a result, we might ask how the philosophy of liberation can describe itself as a pro-feminine, anti-macho philosophy when in such contexts, women, and more to the point, women's bodies, are objectified, or when LGTBQ communities remain alienated from this definition of *eros* and the sense of community apparent in Dussel's early work.

Confronted by this range of criticism, Dussel has not only corrected his views on sexuality and marriage but has also claimed that ethical and political organization are about sustenance of life, a notion that encourages us to think more concretely on behalf of the oppressed. Grounding both his ethics and politics in a material principle, Dussel now begins from the premise that human life is dynamic. Human beings are living entities with an assortment of physical and nonphysical needs. These needs are constantly changing and incapable of complete satisfaction. Resource scarcity is one reason for this incapacity, which is why human beings thrive in communities where networks of trade/barter are established and resources are shared. Unfortunately, human life is also characterized by inequality, oppressive social and political arrangements, and exploitative economic structures. The central targets of Dussel politics of liberation, therefore, are the various forms of oppression, inequality, and injustice which frustrate and diminish human life. His politics of liberation point towards the inevitable breakdown of even just political structures, since, as the attempt to respond to dynamic life, they too are bound to fail.[27]

Zea's Existential-Phenomenological Contribution

Zea's contribution to liberation philosophy develops in terms of "historical consciousness." As a historian of ideas and a philosopher who emphasizes the importance of "place," Zea believes it is an error for Latin Americans to try to erase or ignore their history of colonization. Some philosophers and social theorists have done this as a result of being frustrated by Latin America's past and the inability to overcome what they consider to be their own shortcomings set in motion by colonization (see chapter 5). Others, seeing indigeneity as an impediment to progress, tried to wipe the slate clean, so to speak, by denying the indigenous elements of America in the hopes of "modernizing" Latin American societies (see chapter 4). Instead of negating the past in these ways, Zea strives to *reclaim* it in order to liberate the future. It is similar to the idea that one cannot know where they are going unless they know where they have been.

For Zea, Latin America and the Caribbean are regions that maintain one foot in "West" and one foot in indigenous culture, African culture, or some mixture of these (not to mention an assortment of others). It is difficult to distinguish that which is uniquely "Latin American" without any influence from Western "civilization," a predicament that leads many to a fascination with the idea of originality and the need for authenticity (see chapters 5–6 and 12). However, both authenticity and originality become problematic for Latin Americans insofar as they purport to begin *ex nihilo* (from nothing). The idea that one can be authentic or original without reference to what came before is a fiction that Latin Americans are pushed into accepting because of their history of colonization. For this reason, Zea turns to existential-phenomenology.

An existential-phenomenological analysis begins from the standpoint of human "thrownness" or the "facticity" of human existence (see chapter 6). Human beings, explains Zea, are born into worlds that they do not choose, to parents they do not elect, given specific languages and cultural sensibilities that shape their way of thinking, all of which determine their existence in ways that are beyond our control. When humans become conscious of their existence, that is to say, once a person stops simply existing as a "fact" and becomes aware of their own mortality and finitude, the search for meaning in life is begun. This search for meaning creates the possibility for existential freedom since once profoundly aware of their mortality, one has to *choose* how to live or even whether to continue living (life is no longer something that happened to you but a decision you make). Yet, this freedom of choice has conditions; it is shaped by our historical context. Human beings are, in a sense, forced to use the ideas, mores, and cultural idioms of those that came before them in their search for meaning and in defining themselves, a "cultural world," Zea writes:

> created by others, by our fellow humans, a world with their religion, laws, customs, politics, economy, art and many other forms of expression, but a world in the making of which we have not participated, a world about which no one has been consulted, a world that never has to attend to our needs, desires, and dreams, yet nonetheless, a world that we have to accept as our own. (*PC*, 126)

For Zea, in order to be "authentic," one must assume an attitude towards the present that views it as one's own. Authenticity requires recognizing that we cannot escape the past, since even our innermost thoughts and feelings take place in a language conditioned by those who came before us. Nevertheless, we can take the reins of the present afforded by this past. That means acknowledging our initial state of nonfreedom, as well as embracing our historical context as our own. Such an attitude, as Zea describes it, makes it possible to commit ourselves, which amounts to assuming responsibility for others (those persons in the future) in the presence of others (those persons in the past and present).

Connecting these ideas to social identity, being committed does not mean closing one's eyes to racial or gender difference ("because race and gender are vehicles promoting underserved oppression and privilege, we should stop thinking of ourselves in racialized or gendered terms"). Commitment does not entail a denial of social categorization, but attempts to work through the forms of identity imposed upon us by the past, as difficult and undesirable as they may be. Remember, "to liberate the future by reclaiming the past" means recognizing the artificiality and contrived nature of race or gender, while seeing how these can be important sites for meaning-making (this should recall notions of "liberating" society).

While all of this might make sense to the European or Anglo-American existentialist, achieving historical consciousness is not so easy for Latin Americans (and other colonized peoples) in light of colonization, which, along with coloniality, adds something that is not so easily overcome by committing oneself.

Comparing Latin America to Asia and writing about the "totalizing" force of colonization, Zea writes:

> We do not feel, as Asians do, the heirs of our own autochthonous culture. There was, yes, an indigenous culture—Aztec, Maya, Inca, etc.— but this culture does not represent, for us contemporary Latin Americans, the same thing that ancient Oriental cultures represents for contemporary Asians.[28]

In broad terms, Zea explains that the colonial impositions placed upon "Asia" were primarily technological (a point that an expert on colonialism in the East might take issue with). In the Americas, however, colonization was not limited to material, technological impositions. Instead, one finds a complete and thorough colonization of body, mind, and history. The Martinican writer and thinker Aimé Césaire described it this way:

> *I* am talking about societies drained of their essence, cultures trampled underfoot, institutions undermined, lands confiscated, religions smashed, magnificent artistic creations destroyed, extraordinary *possibilities* wiped out. [...] [M]illions of men torn from their gods, their land, their habits, their life—from life, from dance, from wisdom. *I* am talking about millions of men in whom fear has been cunningly instilled, who have been taught to have an inferiority complex, to tremble, kneel, despair, and behave like flunkeys. [...] *I* am talking about natural *economies* that have been disrupted—harmonious and viable *economies* adapted to the indigenous population—about food crops destroyed, malnutrition permanently introduced, agricultural development oriented solely toward the benefit of the metropolitan countries; about the looting of products, the looting of raw materials.[29]

Domination of this kind not only robs the colonized of their relationship to land and their history, but it also supplants indigenous or "local" ways of thinking with that of the colonizer. The end result is what Rajeev Bhargava terms the epistemic injustice of colonialism, "a form of cultural injustice that occurs when the concepts and categories by which a people understand themselves and their world is replaced or adversely affected by the concepts and categories of colonizers."[30]

In this context, how does one attempt to claim the present as one's own when you neither choose your language or way of thinking and specifically when you are alienated from your original language and conceptual scheme in lieu of one that has been imposed on you? Colonization essentially robs one of the freedom to use anything other than the master's tools. While all human beings are subjugated to the decisions and actions of those who came before them, colonization adds another layer that distances one from choosing how to think for oneself. If this is indeed the intellectual damage caused by colonialism, it is not hard to understand why Latin Americans may have suffered a collective inferiority complex or failed to produce an "authentic" culture in Latin America (see chapter 5). Because of the workings of colonization and the abrupt obliteration of the indigenous past (which, admittedly was not complete—there still persists indigenous influences and ways of being and knowing), Americans were effectively alienated from their past.

Zea describes this alienation as two-fold. Although heirs to Western culture—and by this Zea means that the admixture that created Latin American peoples is a byproduct of the collision between "old" and "new" worlds—the peoples of the Americas are stuck between an "alien" past, on the one hand, and left to be a mere witness to the unfolding of the future, on the other. In "Latin American Philosophy as Philosophy of Liberation," he writes:

> Our problems, the problem of our thought, of our philosophy, have originated in trying to keep in-between two abstractions. The abstraction of a past that we do not consider ours, and the abstraction of a future that we are estranged from. A future already realized by other peoples that, although it has in common with us the fact of having been made by humankind, it is not ours since we did not participate in its realization. We want to jump from one vacuum to another vacuum. The vacuum we deny and the vacuum that we affirm.[31]

Seeking to escape this double-bind, Zea's goal is to reclaim the past but in a way that allows him to embrace of the present authentically and with originality.

As Zea puts it, "Originality is one of the major preoccupations of Latin American culture. Questions about the possibility of a Latin American literature, philosophy or culture are a clear indication of this concern with Latin American originality." Zea then asks: "Originality as against what?" He continues, "Originality with respect to Europe, or Western culture. However, the expression 'with respect to' (*frente*) should rather be interpreted to mean 'in the presence of' (*ante*)."[32] Zea's subtle intervention suggest that "originality" is not the creation of something from nothing; in the Latin American context, it is more akin to the act of "recreating." Taking something that is already there but using it in a "novel" in a way that reflects the particularity of one's existence (cf. notions of originality in chapter 5). This is exactly what the person who wishes to describe the Latin American as derivative or inauthentic tries to do: stop us from being a co-creator of history; limit the Latin American's ability to take "Western" culture and do with it what we find necessary or desire to do.

This sense of recreation requires *acknowledging* the influence and importance of the past, tragic or unbearable though it may be, especially given the history of colonization in the Americas, not *negating* it. Again, it is not unlike the importance of social identities for liberation of philosophers: we do not dismantle racism or sexism by pretending they no longer exist. In the context of colonization, such an attitude empowers Latin Americans to see history as *theirs*, to cultivate a sense of owning the past, that is, of acknowledging the inescapable thrownness of human existence. What colonization does is create a glass wall, so to speak, an alienating and imposing distance, one that limits authentically embracing history. This sense of distance is not the type Dussel appreciates above, for it fixes or freezes a person within a specific past, namely that which European man claims as *his*. Here, the only historical existence afforded to indigenous peoples is one that makes possible the civility of modern man. Moving beyond that historical boundary or "border," like the sense of movement implicit to liberation philosophy as a whole, is therefore exemplified by notions such as Dussel's "*trans*-modernity" or the back and forth, neither-nor, betwixt and between that defines *border* consciousness and the "unmasterability" of *la conciencia mestiza*.[33]

Conclusion: Latin American Philosophy as Liberation Philosophy

Given that he believes the oppression of Latin America derives in part from the dependence on foreign ways of thinking, Zea's liberatory project has important implications for *Latin American philosophy* on a whole. For one thing, Latin American philosophy and liberation philosophy share a couple of normative claims and arise out of a similar set of metaphilosophical commitments, namely the emphasis on philosophizing with a sense of urgency or out of a sense of commitment (i.e., the idea that philosophical thought should respond to pressing social concerns) and the idea that *where* one philosophizes matters philosophically (i.e., the notion that philosophy begins from the particularities of human existence and then aspires towards a *sense* of universality). If this is right, defending the existence and possibility of a distinctive "Latin American philosophy" is an endorsement of a liberatory standpoint (see chapter 12). In opposition to the professionalization of academic philosophy, which has a history of downplaying differences in the name of "universality," claiming that being "Latin American" or "Latinx" is relevant to the practice of philosophy is to embrace the particularity of one's existence whilst philosophizing.[34] It is to say that flesh-and-blood human beings do not begin philosophical reflection from "nowhere" or in an abstract setting (the proverbial chamber of doubt). We begin from where we are, in concrete circumstances with specific histories, as Zea describes.

Given this philosophical starting point, not to mention the pervasiveness of colonization and coloniality throughout all of Latin America and the Caribbean, Latin American philosophy cannot help but be philosophy born of struggle.[35] For a Latin American philosophy to be true to those meta-philosophical commitments articulated above and yet not concern itself in some way with combating the epistemic injustice of colonialism is to negate or ignore the historical context in which this particular philosophy emerges. It is to deny the past (and present), an act that can only be done by ideologues (in the sense of Ellacuría's ideologization) and detached philosophers. As Gloria Anzaldua writes, "In trying to become 'objective,' Western culture made 'objects' of things and people when it distanced itself from them, thereby losing 'touch' with them. This dichotomy is the root of all violence."[36] Why call such a way of doing philosophy *in* Latin America, "Latin American philosophy?"

Of course, not all Latin American or Latinx philosophers share the above commitments, and thus not all philosophers in Latin American do Latin American philosophy, just as not all female philosophers do feminist philosophy. To suggest otherwise would be an injustice and would unfairly discount great philosophy being produced in Latin America or by women. Nevertheless, for those who aspire to work in the tradition of Latin America philosophy, to philosophize means to think in a way that embraces their cultural, ethnic, racial, gendered, or even national difference (all of which are concepts that should not be essentialized, that is, defined by just one characteristic or trait).

This is, of course, a political statement in the context of professionalized academic philosophy, for it says that being Mexican or Mexican-American matters when philosophizing. It is to say that Chicanx or mestiza ways of knowing are valid ways of knowing. Or that one can turn to their Afro-Cubano heritage as a valid source for knowledge. In this sense, perhaps the main task of liberation philosophy remains the liberation of philosophy itself from the purely academic, disengaged activity it has become.

Notes

1 For an overview of the history of liberation philosophy see Cerutti-Guldberg, "Actual Situation and Perspectives of Latin American Philosophy of Liberation"; Mendieta, "Philosophy of Liberation"; Schutte, *Cultural Identity and Social Liberation in Latin American Thought*; Márquez, "Liberation in Theology, Philosophy and Pedagogy"; and Gandolfo, "Liberation Philosophy."
2 See Silva, "The Americas Seek Not Enlightenment but Liberation."
3 One important source for the philosophy of liberation is the work of liberation theologians. "Liberation theology," according to Christopher Rowland, "is a theology which is explored not just in tutorial or seminar but engages the whole

person in the midst of a life of struggle and deprivation. It is theology which, above all, often starts from the insights of those men and women who have found themselves caught up in the midst of that struggle, rather than being evolved and handed down to them by ecclesiastical or theological experts." Liberation theology begins from the experience of those suffering at the hands of economic exploitation and neoliberal imperialism, not to mention those experiences and circumstances afforded by histories of colonialism. Its point of departure is not "detached reflection on Scripture and tradition but the present life of the shanty towns and land struggles, the lack of basic amenities, the carelessness about the welfare of human persons, the death squads and the shattered lives of refugees." Rowland, "Introduction: The Theology of Liberation," 2.

4 See Vargas, "Eurocentrism and The Philosophy of Liberation."

5 Ellacuría, "The Liberating Function of Philosophy," 99. Cited in text using abbreviation *LFP* followed by page number.

6 Zea, "Philosophy as Commitment," 130. Cited in text using abbreviation *PC* followed by page number.

7 Eduardo Mendieta writes, "The philosophy of liberation's philosophical orbit is defined by the axes of critique, commitment, engagement and liberation. As a critique of all forms of philosophical dependency and inauthenticity, it is consciously and avowedly a metaphilosophy. The philosophy of liberation is thus, among other things, a view about what counts as philosophy and how it should be pursued." See Mendieta, "Philosophy of Liberation."

8 Dussel, *Philosophy of Liberation*, 3. Cited in text using abbreviation *POL* and page number.

9 Luis Villoro, "Mexican and North American Independence: Parallels and Divergences," 40.

10 Simón Bolívar, "Address to the Angostura Congress," 12–13. Cited in text using the abbreviation *ANG* and page number.

11 Maldonado-Torres, "Coloniality of Being," 243.

12 See Aníbal Quijano and Immanuel Wallerstein, "Americanity as a Concept, or the Americas in the Modern World-System."

13 See María Lugones, "Heterosexualism and the Colonial/Modern Gender System."

14 One can even view national borders as remnants of colonization and mechanisms perpetuating coloniality, especially when one realizes that informally crossing a border (so-called "illegal" immigration) results in social conditions whereby one's labor is easily exploited and wherein one is racialized in the United States.

15 Fanon, *Black Skin White Masks*, 89.

16 Schutte, *Cultural Identity and Social Liberation*, 9–10. Cited in text using abbreviation *CISL* followed by page number.

17 Henry, "The General Character of Afro-Caribbean Philosophy," 9.

18 Davis, *Freedom is Constant Struggle*. See also Leonard Harris' volume, *Philosophy Born of Struggle*.

19 Gracia, *Latinos in America*, xi–xii [emphasis added].

20 Nelson Maldonado-Torres, "Thinking at the Limits of Philosophy," 261.

21 See Emmanuel Levinas, *Totality and Infinity: An Essay on Exteriority*.

22 "Modernity" refers not only to a time-period that began somewhere between the scholastic era and the Enlightenment, but also to a stage in the unfolding of human progress, one that, according to Dussel and others, is a consequence of the seismic shift in the foundations for knowledge that occurred after Christendom's encounter with "America." While for medieval Christendom the Bible was a pivotal foundation for knowledge about the world, it lacked reference to the Americas and thus stood incomplete in light of this new "discovery." New foundations for knowledge were in need, thus novel ways of knowing came

about as a result of the types of epistemic inquiries performed by René Descartes and other "modern" thinkers.

23 Vine Deloria, Jr. "Philosophy and Tribal Peoples," 3.
24 Ta-Nehisi Coates, *Between the World and Me*, 8.
25 Schutte, "Origins and Tendencies of the Philosophy of Liberation in Latin American Thought," 275–278.
26 See Daniel Castro, *Another Face of Empire*.
27 See Dussel, *Twenty Theses on Politics* and *Politics of Liberation: A Critical World History*.
28 Zea, "The Actual Function of Philosophy in Latin America," 359–360.
29 Césaire, *Discourse on Colonialism*, 43. Emphasis in the original.
30 Bhargava, "The Epistemic Injustice of Colonialism," 414.
31 Zea, "La Filosofía Latinoamericana Como Filosofía de la Liberación," 288. Translation my own.
32 Zea, *The Role of the Americas in History*, 3
33 For more on the idea of "transmodernity" see Dussel, *The Invention of the Americas*, 137–140. For more on mestiza consciousness see Anzaldúa, *Borderlands/La Frontera*, 99–113. Both of these notions convey the sense of movement that undergirds much of liberation philosophy.
34 See Silva, "Writing Philosophy from a Racialized Subjectivity."
35 See Silva, "Why the Struggle Against Coloniality is Paramount to Latin American Philosophy."
36 Anzaldúa, *Borderlands/La Frontera*, 59.

Bibliography

Anzaldúa, Gloria. *Borderlands/La Frontera: The New Mestiza* (3rd Edition). San Francisco: Aunt Lute Books, 2007.

Bhargava, Rajeev. "Overcoming the Epistemic Injustice of Colonialism." *Global Policy* 4, no. 4(2013): 413–417.

Bolívar, Simón. "Address to the Angostura Congress, February 15, 1819, the Day of Its Installation." In *Nineteenth Century Nation-Building and the Latin American Intellectual Tradition*, edited by Janet Burke and Ted Humphrey. Indianapolis: Hackett, 2007.

Castro, Daniel. *Another Face of Empire: Bartolomé de las Casas, Indigenous Rights and Ecclesiastical Imperialism*. Durham: Duke University Press, 2007.

Césaire, Aimé. *Discourse on Colonialism*. Translated by Joan Pinkham. New York: Monthly Review Press, 2000.

Cerutti-Guldberg, Horacio. "Actual Situation and Perspectives of Latin American Philosophy of Liberation." *The Philosophical Forum* XX, no. 1–2(1988–1989): 43–61.

Coates, Ta-Nehisi. *Between the World and Me*. New York: Spiegel & Grau, 2015.

Davis, Angela. *Freedom is a Constant Struggle: Ferguson, Palestine, and the Foundations of a Movement*. Chicago: Haymarket Books, 2016

Deloria, Jr., Vine. "Philosophy and the Tribal Peoples." In *American Indian Thought*, edited by Anne Waters, 3–12. Malden, MA: Blackwell Publishing, 2004.

Dussel, Enrique. *The Invention of the Americas: Eclipse of "the Other" and the Myth of Modernity*. Translated by Michael D. Baber. New York: Continuum, 1995.

Dussel, Enrique. *Twenty Theses on Politics*. Translated by George Ciccariello-Maher. Durham: Duke University Press, 2008.

Dussel, Enrique. *Politics of Liberation: A Critical World History*. Translated by Thia Cooper. London: SCM Press, 2011.

Ellacuría, Ignacio. "The Liberating Function of Philosophy (1985)." In *Essays on History, Liberation and Salvation*, edited by Michael E. Lee. Maryknoll, 94–119. New York: Orbis Books, 2013.

Fanon, Frantz. *Black Skin, White Masks*. Translated by Richard Philcox. New York: Grove Press, 2008.

Gandolfo, David Ignatius. "Liberation Philosophy." In *A Companion to Latin American Philosophy*, edited by Susana Nuccetelli, Ofelia Schutte, and Otávio Bueno, 185–198. Malden: Wiley-Blackwell, 2010.

Gracia, Jorge J. E. *Latinos in America: Philosophy and Social Identity*. Malden, MA: Blackwell Publishers, 2008.

Harris, Leonard. *Philosophy Born of Struggle: Anthology of Afro-American Philosophy from 1917*. Dubuque, IO: Kendall/Hunt Publishing Company, 1983.

Henry, Paget. "The General Character of Afro-Caribbean Philosophy." In *The Paget Henry Reader*, edited by Jane Anna Gordon, Lewis R. Gordon, Aaron Kamugisha, and Neil Roberts, and Paget Henry, 9–26. London: Rowman & Littlefield, 2016.

Levinas, Emmanuel. *Totality and Infinity: An Essay on Exteriority*. Translated by Alphonso Lingis. Pittsburgh: Duquesne University Press, 1969.

Lugones, María. "Heterosexualism and the Colonial/Modern Gender System." *Hypatia* 22, no. 1(2007): 186–209.

Maldonado-Torres, Nelson. "On the Coloniality of Being: Contributions to the Development of a Concept." *Cultural Studies* 21, no. 2(2007):240–270.

Maldonado-Torres, Nelson. "Thinking at the Limits of Philosophy." In *Reframing the Practice of Philosophy: Bodies of Color, Bodies of Knowledge*, edited by George Yancy, 251–270. Albany: SUNY, 2012.

Márquez, Iván. "Liberation in Theology, Philosophy and Pedagogy." In *A Companion to Latin American Philosophy*, edited by Susana Nuccetelli, Ofelia Schutte, and Otávio Bueno, 297–311. Malden: Wiley-Blackwell, 2010.

Mendieta, Eduardo. "Philosophy of Liberation." *The Stanford Encyclopedia of Philosophy* (Spring2016 Edition). Edited by Edward N. Zalta. http://plato.stanford.edu/archives/spr2016/entries/liberation

Quijano, Aníbal and Immanuel Wallerstein. "Americanity as a Concept, or the Americas in the Modern World-System." *International Journal of Social Sciences*, no. 134(1992): 549–557.

Quijano, Aníbal and Immanuel Wallerstein. "Coloniality of Power, Eurocentrism, and Latin America." *Nepantla: Views from the South* 1, no. 3(2000): 533–580.

Rowland, Christopher. "Introduction: The Theology of Liberation." In *The Cambridge Companion to Liberation Theology Second Edition*, edited by Christopher Rowland. Cambridge: Cambridge University Press, 2007.

Schutte, Ofelia. "Origins and Tendencies of the Philosophy of Liberation in Latin American Thought: A Critique of Dussel's Ethics." *The Philosophical Forum* XXII, no. 3(1991): 270–292.

Schutte, Ofelia. *Cultural Identity and Social Liberation in Latin American Thought*. Albany: SUNY Press, 1993.

Silva, Grant. "Why the Struggle Against Coloniality is Paramount to Latin American Philosophy." *American Philosophical Association Newsletter for Hispanic/Latino Issues in Philosophy* 15, no 1(2015): 8–12.

Silva, Grant. "The Americas Seek Not Enlightenment but Liberation: On the Philosophical Significance of Liberation for Philosophy in the Americas." *The Pluralist* 13, no. 2(2018): 1–21.

Silva, Grant. "On the American Philosophical Association Newsletter Difficulties of Writing Philosophy from a Racialized Subjectivity." *Hispanic/Latino Issues in Philosophy* 18, no 1(2018): 2–6

Vargas, Manuel. "Eurocentrism and The Philosophy of Liberation." *APA Newsletter on Hispanic/Latino Issues in Philosophy* 4, no. 2(2005): 8–17.

Villoro, Luis. "Mexican and North American Independence: Parallels and Divergences." In *Liberation in the Americas: Comparative Aspects of Independence Movements in Mexico and the United States*, edited by Robert Detweiler and Ramón Ruiz, 19–42. San Diego: The Campanile Press (San Diego State University), 1978.

Zea, Leopoldo. "La Filosofía Latinoamericano Como Filosofía de la Liberación." In *La Filosofía Como Compromiso de Liberación*, edited by Liliana Weinberg de Magis and Mario Magallón, 287–296. Caracas: Biblioteca Ayacucho, 1991.

Zea, Leopoldo. *The Role of the Americas in History*. Edited by Amy A. Oliver. Savage: Rowman & Littlefield, 1992.

Zea, Leopoldo. "The Actual Function of Philosophy in Latin America." In *Latin American Philosophy for the 21st Century: The Human Condition, Values, and the Search for Identity*, edited by Jorge J. E. Gracia and Elizabeth Millán-Zaibert, 357–368. Amherst, New York: Prometheus Books, 2004.

Zea, Leopoldo. "Philosophy as Commitment." In *Mexican Philosophy in the 20th Century: Essential Readings*, edited by Carlos Alberto Sánchez and Robert Eli Sanchez, Jr., 125–140. New York: Oxford University Press, 2017.

8   Latin American and Latinx Feminisms

Stephanie Rivera Berruz

Introduction

Latin American and Latinx feminisms emerge out of the social and political backdrop of Latin America, the Caribbean, and the United States. Hence, the scope of the field is wide and includes diverse positions. The diversity of ideas represented by Latin American and Latinx feminisms is owed to its wide geographical landscape framed by many diasporic conditions that have generated points of contact and convergence. Nevertheless, the tradition broadly coheres around its desire to contextualize ideas in a way that appreciates the intimate bond between theory and lived experience.

   This chapter has two central aims, one expository and the other argumentative. First, the expository goal is to introduce the tradition of Latin American and Latinx feminisms, and in so doing provide historical context to the ideas and figures therein. It is important to note that what can be presented in a single chapter is not exhaustive. Yet, the task remains urgent and important. The voices of women and gender non-conforming people within Latin American philosophy, specifically in the context of the U.S., are often underrepresented or are omitted from the history of Latin American philosophy. For instance, it is not unusual to see the work of women and gender-non-conforming peoples in the history of Latin American philosophy as a mere topic within Latin American philosophy rather than constituting an independent rich and complex tradition of its own. It is for this reason that Cynthia Paccacerqua has noted that Latin American and Latinx feminisms are specters of the Latin American philosophical tradition.[1] In light of the historiographical omissions within Latin American and Latinx philosophies, tracing the ideas of Latin American and Latinx feminisms proves to be difficult, since the ideas are not necessarily identifiable through their historical impact. In other words, their ideas did not necessarily have social and political impact. However, historiographical absence does not entail lack of existence. Hence, the argumentative goal of this chapter is to give credence to the claim that Latin American and Latinx feminist ideas exist and are worthy of close attention in spite of their historical and philosophical absence. If strong, this argument contests any philosophical histories that do not acknowledge Latin American and Latinx feminist ideas.

To this point, Latin American feminist scholar Francesca Gargallo has argued that Latin American feminist ideas are older than their impact in history.[2] According to Gargallo, many of the feminist ideas that are now central to the Latin American feminist tradition did not have an immediate historical impact *because they belonged to women*. Hence, the impact of ideas can only be appreciated retrospectively, considering the emergence of feminist ideas independent of their contemporary social and epistemic impact. By providing a brief exposition of the vast theoretical landscape of Latin American and U.S. Latinx feminisms, I aim to make the specter of Latin American philosophy visible, heard, and felt. Rather than asking: "Were there Latin American or Latinx feminist scholars?" we ought to be asking: "What were Latin American and Latinx feminist scholars thinking, writing, saying?"

This chapter opens by describing the origins of feminist ideas in pre-20th century Latin America. I consider the importance of women's ideas as part of the resistance to colonialism and its aftermath by introducing the figures of Anacaona and Sor Juana Ines de la Cruz. Then, in the context of the early 20th century, I discuss the ideas of Luisa Capetillo. Capetillo embodies the claim that Latin American feminist ideas emerge in the nexus between theory and praxis, converging with complex social and political commitments. She also serves as a bridge to the U.S. because of her location, Puerto Rico, drawing attention to the ways the U.S. empire was built upon violent interventions in the Caribbean, creating the conditions for diaspora that frame Latinx feminisms. In the second part of the chapter I orient the reader toward Latinx feminisms through discussions of Ch/Xicana writers, specifically Gloria Anzaldúa, who serves as a bridge to contemporary Latinx feminism. Anzaldúa has been widely influential across disciplines, but for the purposes of this chapter I trace her influence on contemporary Latinx feminist philosophy. I also discuss the ideas of Mariana Ortega, whose account of selfhood is deeply influenced by Anzaldúa. The chapter closes by pivoting briefly back to Latin America to consider contemporary topics on translation and translocation.

Foundations of Latin American and Latinx Feminisms

Contemporary intellectual histories of Latin American and Latinx feminism tend to emphasize the social and political moments of the 1960s and 1970s, which frame women's social movements in Latin America, the Caribbean, and the U.S. Yet, the ideas that ground the social and political claims of women's social movements are much older. The foundations of Latin American and Latinx feminist claims are found in feminist reflections on gender and difference in a world reconfigured by the colonial project.[3] Colonialism required the invention of race, gender, and the regulation of sexuality to produce capitalistic modernity.[4] Colonial violence includes the violent dislodging of Native American populations and the introduction of a global schema that constructed the concept of humanity through gendered whiteness framed by religious doctrine (see chapters 2 and 9). Hence, the ideas that emerge in this context are often born out of strategies of resistance and struggle to the colonialism and its aftermaths.

In this context, the ideas of non-white women before the 19th century are seldom considered. Marked by their perceived status as non-human, many were illiterate, and their existence has not been documented in traditional textual form.[5] Nevertheless, they spread ideas about resistance that were transferred orally and which have a legacy that exists today. One example can be found in Anacaona, Taino chief (*cacica*) of Jaragua Hispañola. She was executed during the Spanish occupation of Hispañola in 1503. Prior to her execution she was offered clemency in exchange for her role as a concubine. She refused and was publicly hanged, thus enacting a politics of colonial resistance that continues to be immortalized in the oral histories of Haiti, Dominican Republic, and Puerto Rico. Her ideas about resistance are not represented in a history that privileges the written word, but her historical prominence is felt in songs and national origin stories. For example, Haiti often cites her as a symbolic Indigenous mother of the nation. She is also found in the rhythms of salsa, where the song "Anacaona" by Cheo Feliciano orally conveys her story of embodied resistance. If we were simply to privilege a version of history that is oriented around written word, Anacaona would cease to exist. Hence, her narrative exemplifies the claim that to trace Latin American and Latinx feminism, we must broaden the meaning of the history of philosophy.

One of the oldest documented feminist writers of Latin America is Sor Juana Inés de la Cruz (1651–1695). She was born in San Miguel Nepantla (now referred to as Nepantla de Sor Juana Inés de la Cruz). In 1669 she entered the Order of the Jerónimas, and was able to dedicate herself to studying and writing. She remained part of the convent until her death. Scholars have wondered why Sor Juana entered the convent, but for an intellectually inquisitive woman living in the 17th century there were not many options that supported the flourishing of an intellectual life. The convent afforded her the space, albeit in solitude, to fortify intellectual pursuits. Sor Juana wrote poetry, drama, and philosophy. Her writing closely examined the intellectual life of women. However, as interest in the Baroque style of writing diminished so did attention to her oeuvre. It was not until 1951 that her complete works were published.[6] Amidst the development of feminist social movements in Mexico, she was recovered as a foundational feminist figure whose work warranted not just literary, but philosophical attention.[7]

Sor Juana explored intellectual histories and demanded recognition of women's writing.[8] In so doing, she challenged intellectual histories that have silenced women. This point is most notably reflected in her essay "Response to Sister Filotea," one of her most famous pieces of writing, in which she responds to Sister Filotea de la Cruz about her right not to be silenced. Under the pseudonym of Sister Filotea, the bishop of Puebla had admonished Sor Juana for her vocalizing her ideas. Sor Juana responds by arguing that the silencing of women in the church denies the reality that there have always been wise women and defends the intellectual rights of women by citing extensive historical precedent.

To begin, Sor Juana argues that to be silenced in the 17th century for being a woman directly contradicts a long history of the contributions of wise women. She writes:

> A Julia, a Corinna, a Cornelia; and in sum, the vast throng of women merited titles and earned renown: now as Greeks, again as Muses, and yet again as Pythonesses. For what were they all but learned women, who were considered, celebrated, and indeed venerated as such in Antiquity?[9]

Sor Juana establishes that women *can* make meaningful contributions to the teachings of the Catholic Church by demonstrating that there have been women with intellectual pursuits who were vocal and socially visible.[10] The response is significant not just because of its central claim, but because of the argumentative strategy Sor Juana uses to advance her defense of the intellectual rights of women. She constructs a genealogy of female intellectuals and in doing so gives new meaning to history.[11] Consider the following lines:

> I had no need of exemplars, nevertheless the many books that I have read have not failed to help me, both in sacred as well as secular letters. For there I see a Deborah issuing laws, military as well as political, and governing the people among whom there were so many learned men. I see the exceedingly knowledgeable Queen of Sheba, so learned she dares to test the wisdom of the wisest of all wise men with riddles, without being rebuked for it; indeed, on this account she is to become judge of the unbeliever. I see so many and significant women: some adorned with the gift of prophecy, like an Abigail; others, of persuasion, like Esther; others, of piety, like Rahab; others, of perseverance, like Anna [Hannah] the mother of Samuel; and others infinitely more, with other kinds of qualities and virtues.[12]

In this passage Sor Juana argues that there is no historical precedent for the silencing of women by reminding her audience of the social impact of women's voices. In this passage she supports her argument by constructing a historiography that names the many women who have charted an intellectual path for her own studies and ideas. Thus, she demonstrates the falsity of the claim that women should be silent by drawing attention to the historical existence of wise women and their social impact. As a result, she reconfigures the grounds on which intellectual histories have been drawn. She demands that an accurate historical account necessarily ought to include women's voices.

Sor Juana's methodology in the essay also merits attention. In order to vindicate the intellectual rights of women she insists on the importance of women in education. Put simply, women should be educated in order to further advance the intellectual lives of other women. To this effect she writes:

> Oh, how many abuses would be avoided in our land if the older women were as well instructed as Leta and knew how to teach as is commanded by St. Paul and my father St. Jerome! Instead, for lack of such learning and through the extreme feebleness in which they are determined to maintain our poor women, if any parents then wish to give their daughters more extensible Christian instruction than is usual, necessity and the lack of learned older women oblige them to employ men as instructors to teach reading and writing, numbers, and music, and other skills. This leads to considerable harm, which occurs every day in doleful instances of these unsuitable associations.

This passage demonstrates that Sor Juana saw the harms generated by the exclusion of women from intellectual histories, which are two-fold. On the one hand, the absence of women from intellectual history produces a false perception that women have not led intellectual lives. On the other hand, the absence of women from intellectual histories also reproduces the lack of women in educational roles who can mentor, teach, and support other women in their intellectual pursuits. In order to resist these harms, Sor Juana produces a genealogy of intellectual women that serves to justify their role in education as well as their contributions to philosophical histories more broadly.

Sor Juana remains one of the most cited Latin American feminist figures. However, it is important to appreciate that she sits among other women who have advocated for social change and made possible the richness of Latin American feminist thought.[13] The theoretical foundations of Latin American feminisms are found in the ideas and practices of women well before contemporary feminist movements. Their resistance to colonialism, insights into conditions of alterity, and their advocacy for intellectual rights form part of a rich groundwork that undergirds contemporary feminist thought in Latin America and the Caribbean and continues to flow into the United States. Thus, these intellectual ancestors remind us that the lack of historical visibility does not imply lack of philosophical influence. Furthermore, they demonstrate the important relationship between theory and practice given that their ideas were very much engendered through their practices of resistances.

Latin American Feminist Ideas of the 20th Century

In the 19th and early 20th century, Latin America and the Caribbean is marked by major social and political changes that frame the development of ideas throughout the region. The Latin American wars of independence stretched from 1808 to 1926 in the wake of the Haitian Revolution (1794–1804). With the exception of Cuba and Puerto Rico, Latin America and the Caribbean saw a major shift in power as a result of national wars of independence. However, the story of Latin America and the Caribbean at this juncture cannot be understood outside the context of U.S. interventionism, which undergirds the production of empire initiated by the seizure of Native lands and the project of slavery (see chapter 2). On the heels of independence movements in Latin America, the U.S. issued the Monroe Doctrine (1823) in an effort to establish its influence in the region. The Monroe Doctrine stated that the U.S. would oppose any intervention of European powers in North or South America. In doing so, however, the U.S. ensured that its power and influence in the region would remain undisturbed. In 1848, for instance, Mexico signed the Treaty of Guadalupe Hidalgo which ended the Mexican-American war (1846–1848), created the U.S.-Mexico boundary of the Rio Grande, and relinquished ownership of present day California, Arizona, Nevada, Utah, and part of Wyoming, Colorado, and New Mexico. In 1898, the Spanish-Cuban-U.S.-Philippine War materialized U.S. imperialism through the annexation of Puerto Rico, the Philippines, Guam, and Hawaii. In the years that follow, the U.S. occupied major production centers of tropical goods in the Caribbean and Central America in order to maintain its dominance in the region. Hence, the role of the U.S. in Latin American and Caribbean politics exemplifies the shift of power dynamics from models of colonialism to imperialism, which continues to characterize U.S. involvement in the region to this day.

In the context of shifting political horizons, feminist ideas in the 20th century emerge as part of interventions for broader social transformation impacted by the political shifts just described. Although not understood as feminist in their times, many of the ideas that stem from this historical moment thematically converge with broader claims about labor equality, access to education, and the right to vote. It is important to note here that the acquisition of the right to vote is often signaled as the apex of feminist movements. However, there is a much richer and deeper story in the context of Latin America and the Caribbean given the political complexities that frame the early 20th century. The multiplicitous historical conditions across the region serve as thematic catalysts for the writings of the time.

For example, Luisa Capetillo (1879–1922) born in Arecibo, Puerto Rico was an anarcho-syndicalist writer and activist who worked to cultivate workers' consciousness through the dissemination of her ideas. She took gender and sexual equality to be central features of class emancipatory struggle. Capetillo worked as a "reader" for much of her life, someone who would read aloud to tobacco workers in cigar factories. A reader's pay would come directly from workers' wages, affording them the flexibility to read what workers wanted. As a result, readers served as a platform to build class consciousness, often reflecting on working conditions, extensive work days, and little pay. They read local newspapers, philosophical texts, plays, and their own writings. Capetillo became a reader at a time of radical labor politics in Puerto Rico, which placed her at the nexus of a transnational social movement given that anarchism was transnational as it stretched throughout the Caribbean, Central America, Spain, and some cities in the United States. Most of the agricultural labor force was illiterate. However, the role of readers in tobacco factories ensured that tobacco workers were some of the most radically conscious social groups. In this context, Capetillo's writing was to be heard at a time when the U.S. was occupying Puerto Rico and strengthening its status as an imperial power.

Capetillo authored four books over the course of her lifetime: *Ensayos libertarios* or *Libertary Essays* (1907), *La humanidad en el future* or *Humanitiy in the Future* (1910), *Mi opinión* or *My Opinion* (1911), and *Influencias de las ideas modernas* or *Influence of Modern Ideas* (1916). Her ideas evolved into a radical sexual politics undergirded by anarchist principles, most of which can be found in *Mi opinión* (1911). In this book she maintained that gender and class were co-constitutive and structurally oppressive. As a result, the struggle for liberty and emancipation required the participation of all people, not just women. This point is clearly seen in the following lines:

> We need to expound some new system or doctrine, in order to get out of this labyrinth, in which we lose all noble sentiments and the most altruistic of aspirations. We have the duty to form groups or associations with the expressed purpose of emancipation. To accept things as they are, without proposing new forms of freedom is cowardice.[14]

She continues: "Those capitalists who think that they are exempt from these concerns because they have the means for an easier life. This concerns them too. Listen up! You have children, and these become infected with the diseases caused by poverty" (*NW*, 70).

It is clear then that Capetillo's emancipatory project was one that involved the whole of society. Nevertheless, her concerns were always grounded in the conditions of the working poor of Puerto Rico, whose livelihoods she understood as part of a continuation of slavery. To this effect she writes:

> Peasants! From generation to generation you have seen things pass by without greater abundance in your homes. Your slavery has not disappeared; before your master maintained you, depriving you of your will. Now he has left your will free, but he deprives you of the means of

using that will. It is the same type of slavery with different methods. They oppress you, they humiliate you, tie you down to the land, to the machine, to the humiliating work that annihilates and brutalizes you, thereby stripping you of your status of free men, putting obstacles in the way of universal redemption. And still, you do not worry about anything except politics, which will offer you nothing, nor defend your rights, they use your ignorance to tie you down and wear you down always against your will. (NW, 114)

Capetillo's sexual politics were most explicitly reflected in her ideas about the institution of marriage, which she understood as the prostitution of love. Given that marriage is a contract regulated by the church and state, it is built upon conditions of inherent inequality from the position of women. As such, Capetillo advocated for its abolishment. Furthermore, she argued that love could not be regulated by law and required conditions of freedom to be truly honored. Freedom in love required the lack of duties, rights, and obligations toward partners. As a result, both people always retained the right to exit unworkable relationships without harm (NW, 34). For working, poor Puerto Rican women in the late 19th and early 20th century, this entailed access to an education that would not recreate conditions of dependency. As an anarchist, Capetillo was vehemently opposed to the existence of the state as the means of regulating wealth and power. The state created the conditions under which working people were exploited. This point is most clearly seen when she asks: "Why reproach women a natural life? Why make love an exclusive need of men?" (NW, 32) Making love free through the abolition of marriage was part of a larger emancipatory framework where freedom in love is identified with justice. Speaking to this particular relationship between love, freedom, and justice she states: "Freedom in love for women the same as for men is nothing other than a great act of justice" (NW, 34).

Capetillo's emancipatory project coincides with the suffrage movement of Puerto Rico, which was largely dominated by elite women's voices. The suffrage movement maintained the importance of the right to vote for literate women. In this context, Capetillo rarely articulated claims with respect to the right to vote consistent with her position on the unviability of the state. However, there is record of her stating that if the project of suffrage is to get off the ground at all, it can only do so by including all women, not just those who can read.[15] At this time forty percent of the tobacco work force and eighty percent of the agricultural work force was illiterate.[16] Hence, her critique of literacy requirements speak to the broader class conditions around which her emancipatory politics was framed. Her claims speak more broadly to the way in which Capetillo embodied her own philosophical commitments. Her ideas were very much a way of life, a disposition informed by anarchist thought. However, in the case of Capetillo, embodying resistance took on a new form. She never married even though she had three children and she resisted sartorial gendered norms by dressing in men's clothing. She was often referred to as the "woman in pants." Both choices serve as examples in which Capetillo charted her own ideas about liberty, freedom, and emancipation through her lived experiences, always grounded in larger social projects. The target for Capetillo was never solely women, but rather conditions that would yield more freedom and that transcended nation-building projects that required the production of normative citizen subjects. Capetillo demonstrates the complexities that frame the evolution of what we now call feminist ideas in a geopolitical landscape fraught with colonial histories and imperial legacies. Furthermore, she illuminates the ways in which historical conditions operate as catalysts for the development of thought. In the context of Puerto Rico, the conditions of Spanish colonialism and the U.S. military invasion frame Capetillo's anarchist project and make possible simultaneous claims with regard to anti-colonial and anti-imperial resistance.

A single chapter cannot adequately explain the breadth and depth of Latin American feminist ideas of the 20th century. They are multiple, at times contradictory, and emerge in different geopolitical contexts. It is important to note, however, that the resources we have today are indebted to the historiographical work of many people, particularly women, who expressed themselves in the context of great adversity and sought to recuperate and make accessible the ideas of women lost to the pages of history.[17] Luisa Capetillo stands as an excellent example of this process in that her thought was rescued from the archives of history by feminist projects that sought to locate foundational figures of feminist thought.[18]

U.S. Ch/Xicana and Latina/x Feminisms[19]

Historically, what we call Latina/x feminisms today is rooted in the Ch/Xicana feminist struggles of the 1960s and 1970s, a vast terrain of ideas that emerged in the context of social and political movements that sought to improve the conditions of Mexican descended peoples in the United States (see chapter 4). Influenced by the Black Power movement and the politically charged climate of the times, the Chicano movement aimed to create more equal conditions for Mexican descended peoples while simultaneously articulating a separatist ethnic nationalist resistance.[20] The conditions of the paradox created multiple strands of resistance, which translated into various agendas, leaders, and organizations. Ch/Xicanas, paralleling other women of color movements, coalesced into a struggle to confront sexism and racism as interlocking oppressions. The critiques of sexism were oriented around resisting machismo, which created immediate gender constraints on everyday life. For instance, their writing resists the construction of an ideal womanhood that was shaped by cultural nationalism and which equated cultural survival with traditional gendered norms that understood Ch/Xicanas as the anchor of the family and home. As a result, Ch/Xicanas were often given subordinate positions in the movement and are forgotten in the narratives of resistance. Their critiques of racism engaged contemporary debates with white women feminisms whose racism erased women of color more broadly from the feminist conversation, and they never took for granted the fact that racism permeates everyday life. The vast landscape that is Ch/Xicana feminist thought does not have unifying themes, but is a complex tradition that responds to various interlocutors: women of color, white women, Chicanos, academics, and white heteronormative society, to name a few. If one can speak of any defining feature of Ch/Xicana feminist thought, it is its appreciation of heterogeneity, where theory and practice cannot be separated, and its recognition that the multiple subject positions we occupy are always intermeshed, complex, and at times incommensurable.[21] It is always a theory in the flesh.[22] One of the most widely known figures from the Ch/Xicana feminist tradition is Gloria Anzaldúa (1942–2004). She has been one of the most influential figures in both Ch/Xicana feminisms and Latina/x feminisms. Furthermore, she continues to reflect the way in which histories, place, and space serve as a catalyst for the formation of ideas given that she is writing from a border town in the Rio Grande Valley (see chapters 4 and 11).

Anzaldúa was born in the Rio Grande Valley on the Texas/Mexican border. Her scholarly corpus rejects simplistic accounts of identity and explores myriad dimensions of identity that stem from being a border dweller, growing up in between multiple cultures. She writes across genres, including poetry, prose, children's stories, autobiographical narratives, and theoretical essays. *Borderlands/La Frontera: The New Mestiza* (1987) has been her most influential work, but it sits amidst a broader body of writings. Co-edited with Cherríe Moraga, *This Bridge Called My Back: Writings by Radical Women of Color* (1981) was one of the most influential anthologies in the history of women of color feminisms in the United States. In 1990 she edited *Making Face, Making Soul: Haciendo Caras*, and she co-edited *The Bridge We Call Home* (2002) with AnaLouise Keating. The *Anzaldúa Reader* (2009), edited by AnaLouise Keating, compiles her poetry, prose, and fiction demonstrating her versatility as an author. In 2015, *Light in the Dark/Luz en lo Oscuro: Rewriting Identity, Spirituality, Reality* was published posthumously with the editorial support of AnaLouise Keating. Anzaldúa's work deeply influenced many fields in the humanities. She also stands as one of the most iconic figures of Ch/Xicana feminisms forging a path for Latina/x feminisms. Her work speaks to the lived experiences of many border dwellers and crossers in the U.S. as well as abroad.[23]

Anzaldúa's work explores themes of embodiment, place/space, experience, knowledge, spirituality, language, and identity. *Borderlands* is written in the language of the borderlands, shifting between English and Spanish throughout the text. The borderlands she speaks of are multiple, as noted in the following lines from the preface of the first edition:

The actual physical borderland that I am dealing with in this book is the Texas-U.S. Southwest/Mexican border. The psychological borderlands, the sexual borderlands and the spiritual borderlands are not particular to the Southwest. In fact, the Borderlands are physically present wherever two or more cultures edge each other, where people of different races occupy the same territory, where under, lower, middle, and upper classes touch, where the space between two individuals shrinks with intimacy.[24]

The borderlands are in-between spaces where contradictions emerge and where multiple identities can co-exist. It is a place of anger, trauma, and wounds, as well as a space of new possibilities. Anzaldúa describes the U.S.-Mexico border as an open wound that bleeds as the two cultures grate against each other, and in that process forms a different culture, a border culture, where the *atravesados* or the border traversers dwell. The *atravesados* are "the squint-eyed, the perverse, the queer, the troublesome, the mongrel, the mulatto, the half-breed, the half dead; in short those who cross over, pass over, or go through the confines of the 'normal'" (*B*, 25). Hence, Anzaldúa's project speaks to those who are marginalized and exist at the crossroads of complex social dynamics. From a border space the book explores the myriad dimensions of identity that emerge in the spaces that are outside of the norm: the experiences of cultural tyranny, machismo, violence, and trauma that make possible new experiences of those whose existence has been deemed unthinkable.

The last chapter of the book, one of the most widely cited, "La conciencia de las mestiza: Towards a New Consciousness," provides an account of what Anzaldúa terms "mestiza consciousness," which emerges through the border clash. Building on the idea of mestizaje from the work of José Vasconcelos (see chapter 4), Anzaldúa develops an account of the mestiza that is made possible by the context in which she writes: the U.S./Mexico borderlands. Informed by Aztec thought (see chapter 1), mestiza consciousness engenders a radical appreciation for ambiguity where incompatible frames of reference are always present, and conceptual rigidity is not an option. Mestiza consciousness requires a strategic flexibility and a tolerance for the ambiguous in order to survive.

> The new mestiza copes by developing a tolerance for contradictions, a tolerance for ambiguity. She learns to be an Indian in Mexican culture, to be a Mexican from an Anglo point of view. She learns to juggle cultures. She has a plural personality, she operates in a pluralistic mode— nothing is thrust out, the good, the bad, and the ugly, nothing rejected, nothing abandoned. Not only does she sustain the contradictions, she turns the ambivalence into something else. (*B*, 101)

The mestiza way, as she calls it, is the way of being in the world that is made possible by the in-between produced by the borderlands. By elaborating a theory of the mestiza Anzaldúa also explores themes of "linguistic terrorism," spirituality, identity, sexuality, self-knowledge, violence, and imperialism. These topics are explored in relationship to one another, often weaved together to reveal the ways in which they interact. Consider the fifth chapter of the book titled "How to Tame a Wild Tongue," which explores the relationship between language and identity. Anzaldúa writes:

> For a people who are neither Spanish nor live in a country in which Spanish is the first language; for a people who live in a country in which English is the reigning tongue but who are not Anglo; for a people who cannot entirely identify with either standard (formal, Castilian) Spanish nor standard English, what recourse is left to them but to create their own language? A language which they can connect their identity to, one capable of communicating the realities and values true to themselves—a language with terms that are neither *español ni inglés,* but both. We speak a patois, a forked tongue, a variation of two languages. (B, 77)

Here Anzaldúa demonstrates that language is linked with identity. Language is the mechanism by which we communicate who we are and how we exist: "Ethnic identity is twin skin to linguistic identity—I am my language" (B, 81). Yet, insofar as this is the case, language also succumbs to social forces that marginalize and oppress people. Hence, she uses the term "linguistic terrorism" to track the experience of speaking and being outside of the U.S. norm and aims to reveal the relationship between language, identity, and power.

The themes explored through the corpus of her work have served as points of entry for many Latina/x feminist projects in philosophy and throughout the humanities.[25] However, many have resisted treating Anzaldúa as a philosopher since her ideas are not easily categorizable within dominant philosophical frameworks.[26] Nevertheless, Anzaldúa's impact cannot be measured, only witnessed in the myriad ways in which her ideas permeate across many fields. She helped to transform the fields of American studies, Chicano/a studies, literary studies, and women and gender studies, and continues to be honored in a variety of ways.[27] Furthermore, U.S.-based Latina/x feminisms are deeply indebted to the work of Anzaldúa.[28]

One contemporary example is the scholarship of Mariana Ortega. Her most recent book, *In-Between: Latina Feminist Phenomenology, Multiplicity, and the Self* (2016), draws on Anzaldúa's work to develop an account of the multiplictous self, one that experiences both multiplicity and oneness by virtue of the multiple social identities it occupies.[29] Ortega's work is indebted to Latina/x feminist thought more broadly and bridges diverse lines of thought toward a project that seeks to give a more full and complex account of selfhood. Ortega does so by using Latina/x feminist thought as her theoretical grounding.

In the introduction of *In-Between,* Ortega spells out the defining features of Latina feminist phenomenology: (1) attention to the lived experience of Latinx peoples in the U.S.; (2) emphasis on quotidian embodied experience; (3) attention to the intermeshed dimensions of social identities and oppression; (4) attention to the omissions of Latinx experiences in philosophical discussions that presume a white male norm; (5) appreciation for historical processes that give Latinx identity meaning; (6) the development of experiential knowledge that can re-shape dominant norms of Latinidad (*IB*, 10). Drawing on Latina/x feminist philosophies, primarily those of María Lugones and Gloria Anzaldúa, Ortega develops an account of the self that appreciates its multiplicity while simultaneously attending to the ways the experience of the multiplictous self is revealed through conditions of not-being-at-ease (*IB*, 61). To be multiplictous is to have multiple social identities (e.g. race, class, sexuality, dis/ability, ethnicity, religion) that must be negotiated while being both a part of distinct worlds and in between them (*IB*, 75). However, the multiplictous self still retains existential continuity despite its multiplicity. It is flexible, decentered, and never fully integrated, but also capable of highlighting or shifting different identities in different contexts (*IB*, 76). In Ortega's terms:

> In sum, the multiplictous self should not be understood by way of additive analysis. Rather, this self has experiences shaped by the intersectional intermeshedness of various social identities. I am not the sum of my social identities—member of the middle-class + woman + Latina + professor + other identities. The intermeshedness of these identities continually informs my experiences as I am being-in-worlds and being-between-worlds. Moreover, understanding the multiplictous self as flexible or "mobile" means recognizing this self's decenteredness, or not having an *a priori* central identity. (*IB*, 76)

The multiplictous self is one that continuously travels. As a result, the question of home(s) and belonging are also key in Ortega's analysis. For Ortega, full membership and belonging in worlds is an imaginary space of mythic formation that needs to be reframed. She proposes the concept of "home-tactis," practices that grant new possibilities of belonging as well as senses of being with others without appealing to a fixed location of home that require claims of authenticity (*IB*, 205). To this effect, consider the following lines:

> The home question is particularly difficult for the multiplictous self whose life and context are such that she has to continually world-travel, and thus the home question becomes a question of *homes*. Reflection on such a question paradoxically shatters any illusion of there being a definite place of belonging, while it also shatters the very multiplicity of our selves by way of feeling and a questioning—that feeling of wanting to come home and that question of whether there is a home (or even homes) for me—as if there were a will to belong in the same way that Nietzsche claims there is a will to truth that inspires us to many a venture. (*IB*, 197)

Ortega illuminates the ways in which being a multiplicitous self requires reflection on the notion of home whereby where one feels at home becomes a question about the fluidity of location and relation. As a result, the multiplicitous self develops strategies of place-making. Ortega's *In-Between* is itself an example of one such strategy. Ortega opens the book by noting that the text functions as her hometactic:

> Feeling comfortable in the world of philosophy has not been easy for me. This book is my *hometactic*, my attempt at finding a sense of belonging and ease within a discipline that forgets the contributions of those regarded as "others." (*IB*, 1)

In developing her account of the multiplicitous self, Ortega draws from a large body of work developed by Latina/x peoples who have taken the concept of *experience* as central to their work. Latina/x feminist thought has used the concept of experience as one from which to develop theories of selfhood and identity (*IB*, 7). Ortega's scholarly corpus is a testament to the importance of centering experience in developing accounts of self, but it also connects other authors who have developed philosophically rich conversations about identity. In philosophy, the work of Ofelia Schutte, Linda Martín Alcoff, Jacqueline Martínez, María Lugones, Juanita Ramos, and Paula Moya have been deeply influential as each takes seriously the role of experience in shaping how we think about being Latina/x. Furthermore, Ortega reminds her readers that the centrality of experience to Latina/x feminist thought should not be all that surprising given that experiential accounts of what it means to be Latina/x describe complexities and multiplicities that are often ignored from many social spaces, philosophy chief among them. She writes: "Their appeal to experience is, in my view, a disclosure, a making visible, audible, a making perceptible, those beings in marginalized and nondominant positions whose histories have been previously erased, ignored, or covered up" (*IB*, 7).

The attention that experience has received in philosophy also reminds us of the complexities encompassed by the very term: Latina/x. It should be clear that the term Latinx/a is not monolithic (see chapter 11). Rather, it encapsulates a range of identities framed by conditions of diaspora, migration, immigration, border dwelling-crossing as well as sexuality, spirituality, ethnicity/race, and class. By centering Latina/x experience, U.S. based Latina/x feminist thought has been able to closely and critically examine the complexity of identity, which is often framed in social and political spaces that are unkind and unwelcoming to such multiplicity. Hence, we should not think of one Latina/x feminism, but rather of multiple feminisms whose work bridges ideas of experience, oppression, and identity in ways that extend into other hemispheric terrains and speak to a wide range of audiences.

Translocating Thought: Hemispheric Dialogues Between Latin/a America and Latina/x Feminisms

In closing, I want to highlight the importance of the concepts of translation and translocation found in the work of Latin/a American and Latina/x feminisms. Translation and translocation signal the way in which the landscape of the Latin/a American and Latina/x feminisms pushes readers to consider the importance of context and the migrations of ideas in a globalized world. Specifically, translation and translocation highlights the claim that ideas travel and can re-center the "North" as the producer of thought and marginalize other voices. This theme is directly taken up in *Translocalities/Translocalidades* (2014) through a series of essays that interrogate the travel of discourses within politically embedded terrains across diverse localities, especially between Latin America and the U.S.[30] In doing so the book brings together many voices that develop a politics of translocation attentive to the heterogeneity of Latinidades as well as to the diverse subject positions that shape Latin/a/x American lives across multiple borders.[31]

These texts are extremely important as we consider the future of Latina/x and Latin/a American feminisms and ideas about movement, borders, travel, and geopolitics shaping our epistemic practices. Centering concerns about the complexities of translation, with the legacy of colonialism that permeate all facets of life, Latina/x and Latin/a American thought is pushing the conversation in directions that can better appreciate the complexities of the world that we currently inhabit. For instance, in 2016 the journal *Meridians: Feminism, Race, Transnationalism* published a two-part special issue dedicated to thinking about the relationship between political and cultural translation in the context of black feminist diasporic thought. The editors sought to center Afro-Latinx feminist voices in order to interrupt the tendency to over-emphasize English-speaking Black women as the only voices of black diasporic thought.[32] As such, the volume takes the project of translation as "politically and theoretically indispensable to forging feminist, pro-social justice, antiracist, postcolonial/decolonial, and anti-imperial political alliances and epistemologies."[33] Hemispheric dialogues within Latin/a American and Latin/x feminisms continues to demonstrate that there is much work to be done, but provides a methodological framework that appreciates the many complicated historical braids and strands that make the work both necessary and possible.

Conclusion

I have sought to demonstrate the existence of a rich and diverse philosophical tradition by providing an expository overview of the vast terrain of thought that constitutes Latin American and Latinx feminisms. However, there is much work that remains to be done. Scholars need to look for ideas in spaces and places often regarded as non-philosophical, as the bodies in question were never fully rendered human. We must understand that the quest for wisdom is never pure and is always related to our social and historical context. As Ortega states in the conclusion of *In-Between*:

> [L]et's reconstruct the way we do philosophy; let's drop the false idols and break the imposing statues that are gatekeepers of the profession; and let's ignore the empty promises of justice and neutrality and not allow those who have no disposition for understanding each other's way of life define what really should be a love wisdom, not of exclusion. (*IB*, 220)

Notes

1 Paccacerqua, "Specters in Latin American Philosophy," 18.
2 Gargallo, "La historicidad de las ideas feministas en américa latina," 18.
3 Ibid., 18.
4 For a more in-depth account of this claim see the following series of essays by Lugones: "Heterosexualism and the Colonial / Modern Gender System," "Toward a Decolonial Feminism," and "Coloniality of Gender."
5 Gargallo, "Presentación," 12.
6 Gargallo, "Presentación," 2010, 12.
7 Femenías, "Philosophical Geneologies and Feminism in Sor Juana Inés de la Cruz," 131.
8 Ibid., 153.
9 Sor Juana Inés de la Cruz, "Response to Sister Filotea," 54–55.
10 Femenías, "Philosophical Geneologies and Feminism in Sor Juana Inés de la Cruz," 137.
11 Ibid., 135.
12 Inés de la Cruz, "Response to Sister Filotea," 54.
13 Two notable examples include: Flora Tristán (1803–1844) and Rita Cetina Gutiérrez (1846–1908). Tristán was a French descended woman living in Peru who advocated for women's equality in the context of workers' rights. Gutiérrez was from Mexico and is often cited as Mexico's first feminist because of her activism. She founded La Si011previva in Mérida, which was Mexico's first secular school for poor girls and art college for young women.
14 Capetillo, *Nation of Women*, 70. Cited in text using abbreviation *NW* and page number.
15 Valle Ferrer, *Luisa Capetillo*, 48.
16 Ramos, "Introducción," 14.
17 Some notable figures in this conversation include Francesca Gargallo and Grace Prada-Ortíz. Both have immensely aided in assembling a different archive form which to think about women's ideas. Furthermore, the work of Ofelia Schutte bridges Latin America and the United States. Her career devoted a lot of energy to Latin American feminist dialogues that bridge South-North hemispheres. Her contribution to the anthology *Feminist Philosophy in Latin America and Spain* was one of the first to make the writings of Latin American feminist philosophers accessible in English. Among these is the work of Graciela Hierro, as well as Celia Amorós, and Maria Luisa Femenías, all of whom continue to occupy important nodes in Latin American feminist conversations.
18 Another key example can be found in Vera Yamuni (1917–2003). Regarded as the one who brought feminism to Mexico, Yamuni is an impactful yet understudied figure in the history of Mexican feminisms. She was born in Costa Rica to

Lebanese parents and emigrated to Mexico, where she earned a masters and doctorate in philosophy from the Universidad Autónoma de Mexico (UNAM). She studied under José Gaos, and her merits as a scholar are most reflected in the diversity of her academic strengths. She was not only an expert in humanities and languages, but also went on to study medicine-surgery. As a result, her scholarly interests were expansive: philosophy, languages, medicine, feminism, and Arabic thought.

19 I use the "x" in both Xicana and Latinx throughout the chapter to represent the multiple ways in which these terms are written, articulated, and experienced. In the context of Xicana, the use of the "x" links to the indigenous Nahuatl language and serves as a linguistic memory of Indigenous culture. In the context of Latinx, the use of the "x" serves to intervene on the gendered nature of language and the omissions it produces. I do not adjudicate on what the most appropriate use of term is, but rather honor their uses by its multiple representations.

20 Garcia, "Introduction" to *Chicana Feminist Thought*, 2.

21 Arredondo et al., "Introduction" to *Chicana Feminisms*, 1.

22 The use of the phrase "theory in the flesh" harkens to the canonical publication of *This Bridge Called My Back: Writings of Radical Women of Color*, edited by Cherríe Moraga and Gloria Anzaldúa, which brought together the writings of women of color across many race/ethnic/class struggles. It is the title of the second part of the book which theorized the struggles of women of color from multiple positionalities as they confront white racism. There are many important figures that form the tradition of Ch/Xicana feminist thought. To name a few: Cherríe Moraga, Emma Pérez, Norma Alarcón, Martha P. Cotera, Chela Sandoval, Laura Pérez, and Gloria Anzaldúa.

23 A very many thanks to Rafael Vizcaíno who recently brought to my attention that her work has been used to theorize the border between North and South Korea.

24 Anzaldúa, *Borderlands*, 19. Cited in text using the abbreviation *B* and page number.

25 In philosophy, U.S. based Latina/x feminist scholars have been working with the ideas found in the corpus of Anzaldúa's work. *Hypatia* published a special cluster on Latina feminism (Spring 2016) edited by Mariana Ortega, which brought together diverse lineages of Latina/x feminist thought. Anzaldúa's work permeated a lot of the essays represented in the cluster. For instance: Paccacerqua, "Gloria Anzaldúa's Affective Logic of *Volverse Una*"; Pitts, "Gloria E. Anzaldúa's *Autohistoria-teoría*"; Ruíz, "Linguistic Alterity and the Multiplicitous Self." Each exemplifies the ways Anzaldúa has bridged into philosophy by treating her as a philosophical figure with a rich body of work.

26 The Roundtable on Latina/x Feminisms coordinated by Mariana Ortega is one important locale that has largely contributed to the cultivating rich theoretical conversations with Anzaldúa's scholarly corpus. The Roundtable on Latina feminism has served as a borderspace of theoretical production that brings together diverse lineages of Latina/x feminisms. As such, it has greatly contributed to the dissemination of Latina/x feminist philosophy, which treats the work of Latina/x subjects as philosophical without any hesitation, but also honors the diverse histories that have made Latina/x feminisms possible. "In the Flesh and Word: Latina Feminist Philosophers Collective Labor," co-authored by Cynthia Paccacerqua, Andrea J. Pitts, Natalie Cisneros, Elena Flores Ruíz, and myself speaks to the importance of the Roundtable as a philosophical space of political gathering that bridges worlds and honors complex differences.

27 Two years after her death the Society for the Study of Anzaldúa was founded in order to provide a space for Anzaldúa's vision of resistance in difference and community to be continued. Moreover, her personal papers (correspondence, written works, audio tape interviews, reviews, clippings, photographs, posters,

artwork, and collected materials) can be currently found in the Benson Latin American Collection at the University of Texas at Austin. Her alters are housed in the Special Collection and Archives of the University of California, Santa Cruz, where she was a graduate student in literature and had nearly completed her Ph.D. at the time of her death.

28 One notable example in this genealogy is Maria Lugones, whose work has also been extremely important in Latina/x and Latin/a American philosophy. Lugones' book, *Pilgrimage/Peregrinajes: Theorizing Coalition Against Multiple Oppressions* (2003) takes up challenges and ideas posited by Anzaldúa. Throughout the book Lugones draws on Anzaldúa's reflections of mestiza consciousness, anger, and internalized whiteness to give her own account of ontological pluralism, intermeshed oppressions, and the possibilities of coalitional struggle.

29 Ortega, *In-Between*, 18. Cited in text using the abbreviation *IB* and page number.

30 Alvarez, "Translocal Feminist Politics of Translation," 1.

31 Ibid., 2.

32 Alvarez et al., "Translations Across Black Feminist Diasporas," v-ix.

33 Ibid, v.

Bibliography

Alvarez, Sonia E. "Introduction to the Project/Enacting a Translocal Feminist Politics of Translation." In *Translocalities/Translocalidades*, 1–18. Durham: Duke University Press, 2014.

Alvarez, Sonia E.et al. "Translations Across Black Feminist Diasporas." *Meridians* 14, no. 2(2016): v–ix.

Anzaldúa, Gloria, ed. *Making Face, Making Soul/Haciendo Caras: Creative and Critical Perspectives by Feminists of Color.* San Francisco: Aunte Lute Books, 1990.

Anzaldúa, Gloria. *Borderlands: La Frontera; The New Mestiza.* 3rd ed. San Francisco: Aunte Lute Books, 2007.

Anzaldúa, Gloria. *Light in the Dark/Luz en lo Oscuro: Rewriting Identity Spirituality and Reality.* Edited by AnaLouise Keating. Durham: Duke University Press, 2015.

Anzaldúa, Gloria and AnaLouise Keating, eds. *This Bridge We Call Home: Radical Visions for Transformation.* New York: Routledge, 2002.

Arredondo, Gabriela F.et al. "Introduction." In *Chicana Feminisms: A Critical Reader*, edited by Patricia Zavella*et al.*, 1–18. Durham: Duke University Press, 2003.

Capetillo, Luisa. *Nation of Women: An Early Feminist Speaks Out: Mi opinión: sobre las libertades, derechos y deberes de las mujeres.* Edited by Félix V. Matos Rodriguez. Translated by Alan West-Durán. Houston: Arte Público Press, 2005.

Femenías, María Luisa. "Philosophical Geneologies and Feminism in Sor Juana Inés de la Cruz." In *The Role of History in Latin American Philosophy*, edited by Arleen Salles and Elizabeth Millán-Zaibert, 131–158. Albany: SUNY Press, 2005.

Femenías, María Luisa and Amy A. Oliver, eds. *Feminist Philosophy in Latin America and Spain.* Amsterdam: Rodopi, 2007.

Garcia, Alma M. "Introduction." In *Chicana Feminist Thought: The Basic Historical Writings*, edited by Alma M. García. New York: Routledge, 1997.

Gargallo, Francesca. "La historicidad de las ideas feministas en américa latina." *Archipelago* 13, no. 49(2005):17–20.

Gargallo, Francesca, ed. "Presentación." In *Antología del pensamiento feminista nuestroamericano: tomo 1 del anhelo a la emancipación.* Venezuela: Biblioteca Ayacucho, 2010.

Inés de la Cruz, Sor Juana. "Response to Sister Filotea," In *Latin American Philosophy for the 21st Century*, edited by Jorge J.E. Gracia and Elizabeth Millán-Zaibert. Buffalo: Prometheus Books, 2004.

Keating, AnaLouise. *The Gloria Anzaldúa Reader*. Durham: Duke University Press, 2009.

Lugones, María. *Pilgrimages/Peregrinajes: Theorizing Coalition Against Multiple Oppressions*. Lanham:Rowman & Littlefield, 2003.

Lugones, María. "Heterosexualism and the Colonial / Modern Gender System." *Hypatia* 22, no. 1(Winter, 2007), 186–209.

Lugones, María. "Coloniality of Gender." *Worlds & Knowledges Otherwise* 2 (2008): 1–17.

Lugones, María. "Toward a Decolonial Feminism." *Hypatia* 25, no. 4(Fall, 2010), 742–759.

Méndez, Susan C. "Reading Cristina García's The Agüero Sisters as Latina Feminist Philosophy." *Hypatia* 31, no. 2(Spring2016), 388–403.

Moraga, Cherríe and Gloria Anzaldúa, eds. *This Bridge Called my Back: Writings of Radical Women of Color*. 4th ed. Albany: SUNY Press, 2015.

Ortega, Mariana. *In-Between: Latina Feminist Phenomenology, Multiplicity, and the Self*. Albany: SUNY Press, 2016.

Paccacerqua, Cynthia. "PHIL 3371 Specters in Latin American Philosophy: Chicana and Latina Feminisms." *APA Newsletter on Hispanic/Latino Issues in Philosophy* 11, no. 1(Autumn2011), 18–20.

Paccacerqua, Cynthia. "Gloria Anzaldúa's Affective Logic of Volverse Una." *Hypatia* 31, no. 2(Spring2016), 334–351.

Paccacerqua, Cynthia*et al.*"In the Flesh and Word: Latina Feminist Philosophers' Collective Labor." *Hypatia* 31, no. 2(Spring2016), 437–446.

Pitts, Andrea J. Gloria E. "Anzaldúa's Autohistoria-teoría as an Epistemology of Self-Knowledge/Ignorance." *Hypatia* 31, no. 2(Spring2016), 352–369.

Ramos, Julio. "Introducción." In *Amor y anarquía: Los escritos de Luisa Capetillo*, edited by Julio Ramos, 11–58. Rio Piedras: Ediciones Huracán, 1992.

Roelofs, Monique. "Navigating Frames of Address: María Lugones on Language, Bodies, Things, and Places." *Hypatia* 31, no. 2(Spring2016), 370–387.

Ruíz Flores, Elena. "Linguistic Alterity and the Multiplicitous Self: Critical Phenomenologies in Latina Feminist Thought." *Hypatia* 31, no. 2(Spring2016), 421–436.

Valle Ferrer, Norma. *Luisa Capetillo, Pioneer Puerto Rican Feminist*. New York: Peter Lang Publishing, 2006.

Vernonelli, Gabriela. "A Coalitional Approach to Theorizing Decolonial Communication." *Hypatia* 31, no. 2(Spring2016), 404–420.

9 Indigenism in Peru and Bolivia

Kim Díaz

This chapter explores Indigenism in Peru and Bolivia by focusing on the thought of Manuel González Prada, José Carlos Mariátegui, and Fausto Reinaga. Broadly speaking, Indigenism is the study of and advocacy for Native or Aboriginal peoples primarily by Westerners, the ideologies that support the development of Native/Aboriginal peoples, whether these ideologies are articulated by Westerners or Native/Aboriginal peoples. It also refers to a genre of literature, poetry, and social sciences that focuses on Native or Aboriginal peoples.

Indigenism has a complicated and evolving history. For instance, Bartolome de Las Casas was an Indigenist given that he advocated that American Indians were indeed humans (see chapter 2). Granted, Las Casas took the European male to be the standard of humanity and thereby suggested that American Indians were somehow less than human. But he nevertheless argued that American Indians had souls. Indigenists have advocated that if given the proper training and education, that is, if American Indians were "civilized," they might be as intelligent as Europeans—again, employing European civilization as the standard. Indigenism is thus complicated and oftentimes problematic, largely because the unquestioned standard of civilization and humanity is always either European or mestizo (i.e., a mix of European and Indigenous).

There have been numerous examples of brutal treatment of American Indians by Europeans throughout the Americas by Indigenists. One example is the colonization and forced conversion to Christianity of American Indians by the Spanish and Portuguese, who believed the Indigenist argument that American Indians have souls in need of salvation and should thus be converted to Christianity. Another example was the American and Canadian Indian Boarding School, such as The Carlisle Indian School in the U.S., which also claimed to "help" American Indians. The school administrators and faculty believed in the American Indian's potential to be educated and civilized. Thus, American Indian children were separated from their families and taken into the American and Canadian Indian Boarding Schools where they were stripped of their culture and language, their spiritual beliefs, and their Indian names, all under the pretext of achieving their human potential of becoming civilized. The Carlisle schools' mission was to "kill the Indian and save the man" and the children were often raped and abused in the process. In yet another example José Vasconcelos led a nationwide literacy movement after the Mexican Revolution (see chapter 4). Again, given the Indigenist's belief that American Indians were capable of becoming civilized, thousands of American Indian children were taught Spanish and forced to assimilate into the Mexican national culture, losing their own culture and languages.

As we will see, American Indians have fared somewhat differently in Latin America than in North America (the U.S. and Canada). By and large, American Indians were stripped of their land and placed on reservations throughout the U.S. but there was less assimilation and less miscegenation than there was in Latin America. One could say that the relationship between the colonizers (the Spanish, Portuguese, and British) and the colonized (American Indians) has been more complicated in Latin America than in the U.S., which the ideas of Manuel González Prada, José Carlos Mariátegui, and Fausto Reinaga demonstrate.

Just as the U.S., Latin American countries have engaged in the deliberate genocide of American Indians. For example, in his efforts to "civilize" Argentina, Domingo Faustino Sarmiento, the Argentinian president from 1868 to 1874, openly declared war against the Guaraní Indians of Paraguay in the 1860s, as well as the Araucanian and Pampas Indians in the 1870s and 1880s. Sarmiento meant to rid the Argentinian land of American Indians in order to make it available for European immigrants. After exterminating thousands of American Indians, he carried out the mandate from Article 25 of the 1853 Argentinian Constitution, which was designed to recruit European immigrants to Argentina by providing them with economic benefits to encourage them to live, work, and help civilize the Argentinian people.

Luis Villoro (1922–2014), a Mexican philosopher and Indigenist, was critical of how American Indians have been largely assimilated into the mestizo culture either by force, as was the case during the Spanish colonization, or by persuasion, as was the case mentioned above with José Vasconcelos. Much of Villoro's work on democracy and social political philosophy was influenced by American Indian culture, deriving most of his ideas from American Indian communities, specifically the Tzotzil peoples of Chiapas.[1] Villoro's concern was that due to the homogenization of Mexican society, the significance of the history and values of the Indigenous peoples has been virtually erased.

This chapter explores two Indigenists from Peru, Manuel González Prada and José Carlos Mariátegui, and one "Indianist," Fausto Reinaga, from Bolivia. The main difference between Indigenism and Indianism is that their respective philosophies express what each of them believes has gone wrong and what needs to happen in order for American Indians in Peru and Bolivia *to be free*, and what gaining this freedom entails. For González Prada and Mariátegui, freedom is the ultimate goal, but Reinaga asks what life ought to look like after American Indians are free. In other words, while González Prada and Mariátegui are primarily concerned with securing political freedom for American Indians, neither explores how life might be for American Indians once this freedom is won. By contrast, while Reinaga also seeks political freedom for the American Indian, he envisions a society in which American Indians and mestizos productively live and work together. As we review their philosophies, we consider how each of these three philosophers grapples with (a) Spanish colonization, (b) independence and nation-building, and (c) communist revolution. Despite their differences, however, all three philosophers can be considered *post-colonial thinkers* who developed their ideas after independence from Spain and each writes about the place of the American Indian in the newly established republics.

González Prada

Manuel González Prada (1844–1918) is not an American Indian but a member of the elite class of Peru that emerged after Peru gained its independence from Spain in 1824. He wrote in the late 1800s and his ideas gained popularity after the War of the Pacific between Bolivia and Peru against Chile (1879–1883). Before allying with Bolivia, Peru was confident that it would win the war, given that it had been one of the viceroyalties in the Americas and Peruvians had grown accustomed to being a nucleus of power. Perhaps it was hubris for Peruvians to believe that since power had been concentrated in their country before, it would continue to be so. Peru lost the war, however, and González Prada grew critical of the liberal government.

In his "Discurso en el Politeama" (1888), González Prada claims that one of the reasons Peru lost the War of the Pacific was that it was unclear what it meant to be Peruvian. At the time, being Peruvian entailed being a descendant of the Spanish born in America (*criollo*); Spanish Americans did not consider the American Indians of Peru to be Peruvians.

> The real Peru isn't made up of the groups of American-born Spaniards and foreigners living on the strip of land situated between the Pacific and the Andes; the nation is made up of the masses of Indians living on the eastern slopes of the mountains. For three hundred years the Indian has been relegated to the lowest strata of civilization, a hybrid with all the vices of the savage and none of the virtues of the European ... [W]ith its armies of undisciplined, unfree Indians, Peru will always march to defeat. If we turned the Indian into a slave, what country should he serve? Like the medieval serf, he will fight only for his feudal lord. (*DP*, 47)[2]

Given that Indians in Peru did not consider themselves Peruvians—and were not considered Peruvian by the Spanish-American—they were not willing to fight against Chile, and this weakened any chance of Peruvian victory. Peru's defeat, as well as González Prada's diagnosis of its defeat, served to bring about awareness of the living conditions that American Indians had to endure. Years later, Mariátegui would write in his *Siete Ensayos de Interpretación de la Realidad Peruana* (Seven Interpretive Essays on Peruvian Reality) that González Prada was "the first lucid moment of Peruvian consciousness."[3]

In his essay *Nuestros Indios* (1904), González Prada recounts how the Spanish enslaved and committed genocide against the Indians, a practice continued by Peruvian liberals in the 19th century.

> Few social groups have committed so many atrocities or have such terrible reputations as the Spaniards and half-breed Indians in Peru ... They decimated the Indians with taxation and compulsory labor ... [disregarding] the laws of the Indies ... the evil continued unabated (although there were from time to time exemplary punishments). It had to be that way. The exploitation of the conquered was officially decreed, and those carrying out the exploitation were urged to do so with humanity and justice: the idea was to commit atrocities humanely and perpetrate injustice fairly ... The republic continues the traditions of the viceroyalty ... the dominators approach the Indian to deceive him, oppress him, or corrupt him ... Under the republic, does the Indian suffer less than under Spanish domination? If there are no longer corregidors with their land grants from the king, there is still compulsory labor and recruitment. The suffering we inflict on them ought to bring down on our heads the condemnation of the human race. We keep the Indian in a state of ignorance and servitude, we humiliate him in the barracks, brutalize him with alcohol, send him out to die in civil wars, and on occasion we even organize manhunts and massacres like those in Amantani, Ilave, and Huanta ... It hasn't been written into law, but it is observed as an axiom that the Indian doesn't have rights, only obligations. In his case, any personal complaint is regarded as insubordination, any group demand an uprising ... Our form of government is nothing but a monstrous lie because a state in which 2–3 million individuals live outside the protection of the law does not deserve to be called a democratic republic.[4]

The Laws of the Indies were established by the Spanish Crown to regulate the interactions between the American Indians and the Spanish settlers and *encomenderos*, Spanish men put in charge of the land, Indians, and other resources subject to the Spanish Crown. González Prada points out that during Spanish colonialism, even though the Spanish committed genocide and enslaved the American Indian, at least they had the Laws of the Indies and Las Casas, who advocated for the well-being of the Indians. Neither was the case under the new republic of Peru; even as a liberal state, Peru did not have laws intended to protect the Indians or an advocate like Las

Casas.[5] Instead of improving, the living conditions of the Indians actually worsened after Peruvian independence.

Given the problematic context that perpetuated the enslavement of Indians, González Prada proposes two possible solutions. Either Spanish Americans have a change of heart and begin treating Indians with the dignity they deserve, or Indians claim their freedom by force.

While González Prada believed American Indians could be educated, he had mixed feelings about education and ultimately did not believe that education would bring about freedom for American Indians.

> Some pessimists… mark the Indian's forehead with a shameful stigma: they say he resists civilization …
>
> What do we mean by civilization? … The ultimate morality, for individuals as well as societies, consists in transforming the war of the human being against human being into lifelong mutual harmony. Where there's no justice, no mercy, no benevolence, there's no civilization … Societies where doing good is no longer an obligation but a habit, where generosity has become an instinctive act—those are the truly civilized societies. The rulers of Peru—have they attained that level of moral excellence? Do they have the right to regard the Indian as a creature unfit for civilization? … If the subjects of Huayna-Capac accepted civilization, we see no reason why the Indian of the republic would reject it, unless the entire race had suffered some irremediable physiological decline. Morally speaking, the indigenous population of the republic is inferior to those discovered by the conquistadors; but moral depression caused by political servitude is not the same as an absolute incapacity for civilization due to organic constitution. Even if it were, who would be to blame?
>
> The facts bely the pessimists. Whenever the Indian has access to instruction or learns through simple contact with civilized persons, he acquires the same level of morality and culture as the descendant of the Spaniard.[6]

For González Prada, to be "civilized" means to be someone who sees the humanity in others and works to cultivate the human spirit. Although he believes in the potential of Indians to be "civilized" through instruction, he does not believe education alone will eliminate all of the problems for American Indians.

> The Indian problem, more than pedagogical, is economic and social … The condition of the native can be improved in two ways: either the heart of the oppressors must be moved to recognize the rights of the oppressed, or the spirit of the oppressed must acquire sufficient virility to punish the oppressors … We shouldn't be preaching humility and resignation to the Indian but pride and rebellion … The fewer authorities he tolerates, the freer he'll be from harm. There's one revealing

fact: the villages farthest from the great haciendas are the ones that enjoy greatest prosperity; the villages least visited by authorities are the most peaceful, the most orderly ... In short: the Indian will be saved by his own efforts, not by the humanization of his oppressors.[7]

Unlike most of the intellectuals and leaders of the new republics who adopted liberalism and positivism wholesale to replace the medieval system of the Spanish (see chapters 3 and 4), González Prada was not a liberal. He did adopt positivism and did argue for individual rights, but he did this not as a liberal but as an anarchist for whom the freedom of each individual comes first, not the authority that is supposed to guarantee freedom.

> The anarchist ideal could be summed up in two lines: unlimited free-dom and the greatest possible good for the individual, with the aboli-tion of the state and private property. If the anarchist is to be condemned for anything, let it be for his optimism and his trust in the inborn goodness of man [...] He rejects laws, religions, and national-ities, acknowledging one single power: the individual [...] Authority implies abuse and obedience manifests abjectness of spirit because the truly emancipated man does not aspire to dominion over his equals nor does he accept any other authority than that of a person over himself.[8]

González Prada was not a liberal or a socialist and he makes this very clear:

> Anarchists or not, workers pursuing a noble end must of necessity avail themselves of a savings means: distrust all politicians. Distrust them all, especially those clowns who cloak themselves in the rags of liberalism and shake the rattles of electoral reform, universal suffrage, civil rights and federalism ... Anarchists should remember that socialism, in any of its multiple forms, is oppressive and rule-bound, quite unlike anarchy, which is utterly free and rejects all rules or any subjection of the indi-vidual to the laws of the majority.[9]

As we'll see in the last section, González Prada's criticism of both liberals and socialists is relevant to appreciating the work of Fausto Reinaga, who agrees with much of González Prada's thought, namely, that neither liberals nor socialists genuinely care for the freedom of American Indians.[10]

Mariátegui

Of the three philosophers explored in this chapter, José Carlos Mariátegui (1894–1930) has been the most influential. Mariátegui came from a middle-class family and was not an American Indian. He is best known for his *Siete Ensayos de Interpretación de la Realidad Peruana* (Seven Interpretive Essays on Peruvian Reality, 1928) in which he provides a historical materialist analysis of Peruvian history.

Mariátegui worked as a journalist and wrote against the government of Augusto B. Leguía who ousted Mariátegui from Peru in 1920 due to Mariátegui's criticisms of the Leguía administration. Exiled in Europe, Mariátegui became intimately acquainted with various socialist theories and when he returned to Peru in 1923, he became convinced of the promise of socialism as a remedy for liberal policies, the same policies that González Prada criticized.

According to Mariátegui's excellent and detailed analysis of the Peruvian economy in the 1920s, a form of communism already existed in the form of the Indian *ayllu*, a community of people who share land and work for the common good. One characteristic of the ayllu is that there is no private property for people to invest in or exploit. With the Spanish conquest, feudalism (or *gamonalismo*) was superimposed on the original organic economy of the ayllu.

Mariátegui explains how the interests and freedom of American Indians never figured into Peru's efforts to gain independence from Spain. Leading up to Peru's independence, upper-class liberal Spanish-Peruvian mestizos, the bourgeoisie, no longer wanted to surrender their resources to Spain and instead allied themselves with England in trade. The Peruvian bourgeoisie entered into economic agreements that made it possible for Peru to trade with England in exchange for guano (fertilizer) and saltpeter. England and the United States invested in the development of railroads in Peru and machinery to continue exploiting local mines and the industrialization of the cities on the coast. As Peru won its independence from Spain and entered the world market as a sovereign nation, capitalism was superimposed on the previous feudal and ayllu economies. Mariátegui writes that early in the Republic "the elements and characteristics of a slave society were mixed into those of a feudal society" (*SE*, 15). With its freedom from Spain, the Peruvian bourgeoisie now had absolute power to continue exploiting the Indians.

> The Peruvian Independence did not constitute, as we know, an indigenous movement. The Creoles and even the Spaniards of the colonies promoted and supported it, and it did take advantage of the support of the indigenous masses. Additionally, some enlightened Indians such as Pumacahua played an important part in the gestation of the Peruvian Independence. Of course the liberal program of the Revolution included the redemption of the Indian, an automatic consequence of the application of its egalitarian postulates. Thus among the first acts of the Republic, several laws and decrees favorable to the Indians were put in place. The redistribution of the land was ordered, the abolition of unpaid labor, etc.; but the revolution in Peru did not represent the arrival of a new ruling class, all these policies were only written. Unwilling governors never enacted them. The landed aristocracy of the

Spanish colony, the sole possessor of power, preserved its feudal rights intact over the land, and consequently, over the Indian. (*SE*, 46)

After independence, feudalism in Peru continued as an economic institution, along with a feudal lord, or *gamonal*, who had absolute power over the land and people who lived on it. In addition to working the land, Indians were forced to fulfill other necessary tasks in the master's house or in the mines:

> Mining is almost entirely in the hands of two large North American companies. In the mines wage-earners dominate, but the pay is negligible, workers' rights are almost null, and policies against work accidents mocked. The system of "enganche," which by means of false advances enslaves the worker, places the Indians at the mercy of these capitalist companies. The misery of agrarian feudalism is so overwhelming that many Indians prefer the luck that the mines offer them. (*SE*, 48)

Mariátegui extends González Prada's proposal that to improve the condition of the Peruvian Indians, either the ruling class would have to have a change of heart or the Indians would have to take their freedom by force. Like González Prada, Mariátegui likewise believed that education was not the solution: "the question of the Indian, more than pedagogical, is economic, it is social" (*SE*, 38). Mariátegui believed that returning the land to the Indians would ultimately solve *el problema del indio* (the Indian problem) because "democratic and liberal institutions are not capable of functioning over a semi-feudal economy" (*SE*, 53). Thus Mariátegui believed that communism would find fertile ground in Peru given that the ayllu was the original economy of Peru and given that Indians made up the majority of the population.

Communists at the 1924 International meeting thought that the best way to establish communism in Latin America would be by first classifying Latin America by language and race.[11] Mariátegui disagreed because he did not believe that race or language were at the center of the Indian problem in Peru. He was convinced the feudal land system was the problem. Also, Mariátegui wished to see Peru end its economic dependence on England and the U.S., and for Indians to be incorporated into the national culture of Peru. He believed that the best way to achieve these goals would be by establishing communism through revolution based on land reform, nation-building, and fighting imperialism. Given the existence and deep roots of the ayllus, Mariátegui believed Peru was primed for communism. In 1929, during the first Latin American Communist Conference in Buenos Aires, the International decided to censor Mariátegui's ideas for being unorthodox.[12] This did not deter Mariátegui, however, and he continued to believe that if Indians joined the revolution, they would be able to bring about communism, and that once in place, Peruvian Indians would have their land and freedom back.

After gaining their independence from Spain, many intellectuals in the new American republics adopted French Positivism. With its emphasis on science, Positivism became a way to break free from the Spanish medieval stronghold on knowledge based on authority. However, Mariátegui believed the power of a revolutionary did not come from his ability to wield scientific knowledge. For Mariátegui, the power of the revolutionary came from his faith, passion, and commitment. In this, Mariátegui was deeply aligned with the French anarcho-syndicalist Georges Sorel and thus Mariátegui broke with the Marxist historical determinism and instead proposed a new approach to bring about the proletarian revolution.

In *Reflections on Violence* (1906), Georges Sorel rejects reform movements to suggest instead the possibilities that exist in the revolutionary unionism. Sorel writes:

> Those who live in the world of myths are free from any kind of rebuttal and cannot be discouraged. It is therefore by means of myths that we understand the activity, the feelings and the ideas of the public when they prepare to enter into a decisive struggle.[13]

Likewise for Mariátegui, the revolutionary was a person who embodied a type of religious, mystical, or spiritual force. Mariátegui also believed the proletarian class should not be mere peaceful spectators but agents of change.

In his 1925 essay "The Man and the Myth," Mariátegui proposes that it would be better for people to develop faith in a revolutionary myth similar to religious faith.[14] He argued that humans fundamentally need to believe in some sort of greater-than-life myth in order to exist and to give purpose to one's actions.

> [A]s announced by Sorel, the historical experience of recent decades has proven that the current revolutionary or social myths can occupy the deep consciousness of men with the same fullness as the old religious myths ... Today we know ... that a revolution is always religious. The word religion has a new value, a new meaning. It serves for something more than to designate a rite or a church. It matters little that the Soviets write on their propaganda posters that "religion is the opiate of the people." Communism is essentially religious. (*SE*, 193 and 264)

Mariátegui proposed developing a revolutionary myth to change the economic situation of Indians in Peru because belief in a myth could be a powerful motivation. Once united by belief in a common revolutionary myth, it would be easy for the agricultural-proletariat base to take the power away from the liberal, positivist bourgeoisie whose politics was founded on the truth of science, which is, at best, temporary.

Fausto Reinaga

Fausto Reinaga (1906–1994) is the third and last philosopher whose work we examine in this chapter. Unlike González Prada and Mariátegui, Fausto Reinaga was an Aymara and Aymara-speaker from Bolivia. Reinaga is extremely critical of Indigenism because according to him, Indigenism is a movement by white people for white people, or *cholaje*, as he calls them (i.e., the white-mixed cholaje class who adopted the European customs and ideology). In Bolivia, there still exists a racially defined system of classification: there are *criollos* (Spaniards born in America), *mestizos* and *cholos* (Americans of Spanish and Indigenous descent), and so on. Although mestizos and cholos are the most common in Bolivia, Reinaga is very critical of cholos because they have assimilated and adopted the European lifestyle and oppress the Indians with their newfound "social capital." There isn't really an exclusively white European class that is purely Spanish or criollo. Rather, the remnants of Whiteness are now carried out by the cholaje whom Reinaga criticizes.

Indigenism, according to Reinaga, is essentially White people trying to make sense of American Indians by studying them, prescribing policies, writing literature and poetry about them, but always from the perspective of White people. Instead of indigenism, Reinaga proposes the term *indianism*, which refers to the development and promotion of Indians *by Indians*, of the empowerment of Indians by Indians.

> Indigenism was a movement of the white-mestizo cholaje; whereas indianism is an Indian movement, a revolutionary Indian movement, which does not wish to assimilate itself to anyone. Indianism proposes freedom. In short, indigenism is assimilation, integration in white-mestizo society; unlike this, indianism is the Indian and his Revolution … Only the Indian will solve the problem of the Indian.[15]

Reinaga comes to this conclusion in *La Revolución India* in which he gives a detailed account of the countless times that the Spanish and their cholaje descendants have used, abused, and betrayed Indians from the Spanish conquest to the 1960s when Reinaga was writing.

Reinaga writes in detail about the stories of the Indian leaders who resisted the Spanish, beginning with Atawallpa (1502–1533), the last Inca emperor murdered by Francisco Pizarro, and Tupac Amaru (1545–1572) and his beheading by the Spanish. Reinaga also tells us of the uprising led by Tupac Amaru II (1738–1781), and how Amaru, his wife, and their children were quartered by horses and their body parts spread throughout Peru as warnings to other Indian insurgents, as well as the uprisings led by Tomas Katari (1740–1781), and Pablo Zárate Willka (?–1905). In every instance, as Reinaga points out, the brutal treatment of these Indian leaders by the Spanish and their descendants becomes more evident. After offering an account of the Bolivian Civil War (1898–1899) and Willka's role in it,

Reinaga describes why and how the Bolivian communists betrayed Che Guevara. Reinaga's criticism is that Bolivian communists were not authentically interested in promoting communist values. Communism happened to be the new political movement through which the cholaje, the old ruling class, could maintain its power and influence. According to Reinaga, the Bolivian communists betrayed Che Guevara and collaborated with the U.S. to ambush him and get Guevara out of their way so they could continue running the country as they had previously done.

Reinaga is very critical of both liberals and communists because both liberals and communists are White people vying for power. Neither liberals nor communists have ever been genuinely concerned with helping Indians regain their freedom.

> The Bolivian population is 95% Indian. Bolivia is shaped and made up by the Indian. The "White" (White cholo or Indian mestizo) does not exceed 5%. This "little handful of Whites" is mounted on the nape of four million Indians; Why? Because the "handful of Whites" is Western and employs Western culture. In other words, religion (Christianity) and the philosophy (of Europe), the school and the university, the government and the parliament, the judiciary and the police, hunger and the shrapnel are all in their hands; and all this concentrated in that "wonderful instrument," called Power. (*RI*, 172)

Although Indians make up the majority of the Bolivian population, they have been ruled by the cholaje who constitute the minority. The Spanish colonists, liberal republicans, and communists have all been members of the Bolivian cholaje. Reinaga's criticism is that while each of these groups has voiced its intention to help the Indian, ultimately none of them ever has.

The Bolivian Civil War (1898–1899) between the conservative and liberal Bolivians is a case in point. The liberal leader, José Manuel Pando, asked the Indian Pablo Zárate Willka to join him in battle against the conservative Severo Fernández Alonso. The alliance between Pando and Willka meant that Bolivian Indians were trained for war and fought alongside the liberals. With Willka as their Indian leader, an unprecedented armed Indian uprising took place. Indians demanded the freedom liberals had promised but instead Pando and the other liberals would not relinquish their power and they executed Willka.

> Liberalism commands: suppress slavery; but in Bolivia the slavery of the Indian is sustained and defended; Liberalism does not approve of the *latifundio* (plantations), because it is a feudal relic; but in this country, the latifundistas are precisely the liberals; therefore, blood and gun fire preserve the latifundio ... Such that under the liberal regime, Bolivia has become a country of European mines worked by Bolivian Indians, mines that enrich the gringos and pile up mountains of Indian corpses. (*RI*, 177)

Reinaga explains how Liberalism (see chapter 3), with all of its promises of freedom and equality, has proved to be empty promises for the Bolivian Indians. It is interesting to note, however, that regardless of their ideological differences, González Prada, Mariátegui, and Reinaga all agree that the ideals of liberalism only helped the Spanish-Americans and their descendants by further oppressing and exploiting the Indians.

In 1953, Bolivia underwent a national land reform, which was designed to abolish the feudalism that defined Bolivia since colonialism. Reinaga is critical of this version of land reform because it proves to be yet another way the Bolivian cholaje exploit Bolivan Indians:

> The Bolivian Agrarian Reform is a trick, a trap to destroy the Indian race. The agrarian reform carried out by the white-mestizo cholaje is a malign, perverse plan; it does not liberate the Indian; it destroys him ...
>
> 1-The Spanish when implementing the feudal-latifundio, served themselves of the ayllu values and emphasis on the "community." Free collective work for the master, and *tupu* (small land) for the subsistence of the slave-servant, constituted the cornerstone of the socio-economic system of the Viceroyalty.
>
> 2-The republic does not alter this regime at all. The cholaje inherits from the Spanish: the latifundio and the servant-pongo. The Indians continued to collectively cultivate the land for the master; who gives them individual use of a *sayaña* (small land parcel), so that the beasts of burden can survive.
>
> 3-The Agrarian Reform suppresses the gamonal master, and hands over the sayaña without a master to the Indian who is really no more than an ex-serf.
>
> 4-The sayaña becomes the individual private property; a private property *sui generis*, because legally the Indian neither owns "his" sayaña nor has the capacity to transfer or bequeath it.
>
> 5-The Indian in this situation is and is not the owner of "his" sayaña. (*RI*, 173)

Reinaga explains how Bolivian Indians did not benefit from the land reform of 1953. His criticism is that the land reform essentially amounted to the Bolivian cholaje selling the land they had stolen from the Indians back to the Indians. Besides this obvious injustice, Reinaga is critical of the details regarding how land reform was instituted since Indians were not allowed to transfer, sell, or gift "their" property as inheritance.

Reinaga is as critical of communism as he is of liberalism. For Reinaga, communists are the same as liberals: Bolivian cholaje vie for power and manipulate Indians to fight their wars and adhere by their policies.

> The Indian, supported by the hard experience of history, supported by concrete facts in the past and present, real, visible and tangible facts of

daily life, does not believe; he must not believe in the "Marxism" or "communism" of the Bolivian cholaje ... The communist parties, working together with the gamonal parties, practice a ruthless racist discrimination with the Indian. When it comes to the fulfillment of the "tasks," where there is danger, mortal risk, it is only and always the Indian "comrades"; full-blooded Indians. It is always the "peasant comrades," always the Indians who must face the shrapnel of the police of the ruling regiment.

But when it comes to international or national congresses, when there are luxury trips and abundant dollars, it is always the "communists" of the white-mestizo cholaje, the white elite of the "Marxism without revolution." (*RI*, 60)

After the Russian Revolution of 1917, socialism arrived in Bolivia. And the white-mestizo cholaje, delirious and fanatical, disguises itself and plunges into the socialist current. Just as the latifundistas of the beginning of the century became liberals, in the same way this time, the latifundistas themselves became socialists and communists. (*RI*, 177)

Fifty years of socialism (which has spread throughout Europe, Asia and Indoamerica), and not a single word for the Indian about his freedom. Just as liberalism, like the Liberal Party and its derivatives, communism wants to assimilate the Indian, hand him over to the white cholaje class ... Communism, like liberalism, does not intend to liberate the Indian; it only wants to assimilate him to the communist society. Communism wants to exterminate the Indian by making of him a different person. Communism wants the alienation of the Indian; it does not want the freedom of the Indian. The communist wants to convert the Indian into a "peasant class" and use the Indian as an element for his own benefit; and, of course, not for the benefit of the Indian Revolution; but for his utopian revolution, the communist revolution ... The Indian who arrives at the ranks of the Communist Parties suffers a brutal racial discrimination. The chiefs of all classes are always white-skinned, they are always members of the white cholaje; therefore, they are the ones in control. They order the Indian around and the "Indian comrade" is the one who faces all the dangers. It is always the "communist" Indian who is the one indicated and designated for the tasks of greatest risk. (*RI*, 181)

Reinaga believes that as long as the racism of the White Bolivian cholaje is not addressed head-on, it makes no difference whether the White Bolivian cholaje are liberal or communist. Beneath the superficial differences between liberals and communists lies a common racism that continues to treat Bolivan Indians as second-class citizens.

Reinaga disagrees with communists who believe the Indian problem is one of class. He is also very critical of communists who try to make the Bolivian Indian into a *campesino* (peasant farmer) so as to categorize them as a class that fits into the communist paradigm. Again, for Reinaga, the underlying problem is race and racism, not class. In his *La Revolución India*, Reinaga writes "we are a race before we are a social class," and he draws from the thought of Franz Fanon, Malcolm X, Charles V. Hamilton, and Stokely Carmichael (*RI*, 63). Reinaga echoes Fanon's idea that people of color must leave Europe behind and focus instead on their own liberation and empowerment. Reinaga is therefore no longer willing to tolerate ideological manipulation by members of the White Bolivian cholaje. Regarding "the Indian problem," there is much speculation concerning its nature and solution. However, Reinaga makes clear that whatever has been said regarding the Indian problem has been articulated by either Spaniards or mestizos, and never once by Indian themselves. It became clear for Reinaga that the Indian problem is not a matter of rights, or a matter of access to private property, or a matter of the proletariat class gaining power.

At bottom, it is a problem of race and racism, whose solution must come from the Indian (hence, Indianism).

> There is no such territorial or rural bourgeoisie in Bolivia; the Indian is not an employee; he does not live on salary. The Indian is not a social class. Then what is he? The Indian is a race, a people, an oppressed nation. The Indian problem is not the "peasant" problem. The authentic peasant fights for fair wages. His goal is social justice. The Indian does not fight for fair wages, which he has never known; nor does he fight for social justice, which he cannot even imagine. The Indian fights for racial justice, for the freedom of his race; a race enslaved since the West put its filthy hands on the lands of Tawantinsuyu. The problem of the Indian is not a matter of assimilation or integration to the "white, civilized" society; the problem of the Indian is a problem of LIBERATION. The Indian cannot, does not have to be a "peasant" of the "white" society; the Indian has to be a free man, in "his" own free society. (*RI*, 29)

Given that historically both liberals and communists have had their own agenda as they sought power, Reinaga recommends that Indians develop their own political party. Also, once Indians are empowered they should re-establish *original* Indian socialist values. Ultimately, Reinaga is not only pursuing freedom for Indians but also trying to cultivate the material conditions in which they might flourish alongside other Bolivians:

> Indianism is not a nebulous metaphysical ideology like *Hispanidad*. It is not an ossified ideology in the "Royal Academies of Language and History," which give off nauseating smells of cemeteries. It is not that. Indianism, more than a living ideology, is an Ideal. The IDEAL of a people, of a Continent on its way towards the conquest of its LIBERATION. (*RI*, 40)
>
> First, the Indian Revolution is the conquest of power by the Indian. For what? For the reinstatement of Indian socialism … The Indians

want to organize a socialist regime; but not with socialism or imported communism, conceived, propagated and programmed by the "communists" of Bolivia and Indoamerica ... United we will be free; and we will come to Power. Separated, we will continue as slaves. Indian unity will give us Power. Separation will make us disappear from the earth. United we will gain Power, and Bolivia and America will be ours; separated, we will become extinct. There will be nothing left of our life. There will be no shadow or dust left over from us. (*RI*, 223)

Reinaga believes Indianism will right the wrongs in Bolivia and the rest of the American continent so that the Bolivian Indians, who constitute the majority, are finally *empowered*. According to Reinaga, Indianism will bring about the kind of State in which *everybody* does well. Although Reinaga does not go into detail about the actual structures and type of state Indianism will bring, he does tell us:

When the Indian liberates himself, he liberates his nation and the antagonist oppressor. By liberating his nation he liberates the mestizo nation from the cholaje. The Indian Revolution will overcome the juxtaposition of the mestizo nation over the Indian nation, united in flesh and soul, organically and psychologically, and for both nations a single nation; of the two Bolivias, one Bolivia. (*RI*, 186)

Conclusion

We have seen how from the mid-19th century to the late 20th century, González Prada, José Carlos Mariátegui, and Fausto Reinaga assess and diagnose the Indian problem and propose a solution that will bring about the freedom and dignity of Indians. González Prada advocated anarchism against liberalism. Mariátegui was likewise critical of liberalism and advocated a revolutionary myth to help bring about communism and the subsequent liberation of Indians. Given Reinaga's historical perspective and experiences, he argued against liberalism and communism and instead proposed Indianism, the empowerment of Indians by Indians.

As mentioned earlier, in spite of their differences, all three philosophers agree that liberalism does not serve the interests of the American Indian. Liberalism was the political philosophy of the criollos and the new republics, but in spite of its popularity among the ruling class, González Prada, Mariátegui and Reinaga did not see how liberals could authentically help American Indians. Among our philosophers, we find a kind of progress: González Prada argues against liberalism and proposes anarchism; Mariátegui proposes communism; and Reinaga argues that, not only is communism inadequate to the task, but also it is essentially the same as communism (i.e., it is simply another way for White people, the ruling race, to maintain their power).

The ideas and criticisms of these philosophers continue to be relevant because they offer a historical and philosophical explanation of why so few American Indians have achieved political power in their respective countries. By reflecting on the ideas of González Prada, Mariátegui, and Reinaga we can see how American Indians in Bolivia and Peru were never truly considered Bolivan or Peruvian citizens, but rather Indians first and foremost. Given this political backdrop, what is the likelihood that American Indians can achieve some level of political power and influence? Before we can answer this question, we must first acknowledge that today many believe that the Indian is all but extinct, having either been exterminated, removed, or thoroughly mixed and assimilated. However, as González Prada, Mariátegui, and Reinaga make clear, we tend to believe this even though it simply isn't true. American Indians continue to constitute large segments of our populations and three American Indians have become president of their respective countries, including Benito Juárez (1806–1872), Zapotec and the first American Indian to become president of any country in the Americas (Mexico), Alejandro Toledo (1946–), Quechua and the first American Indian to become president in Peru, and Evo Morales (1959–), Aymara and president of Bolivia. Morales is, like Reinaga, Ayamara, and openly claims to have been influenced by Reinaga's thinking concerning Indianism. While Juárez, Toledo, and Morales served as presidents of Latin American countries, there has yet to be an American Indian to serve as president in North America. (Charles Curtis (1860–1936), whose mother was Kaw and Osage, did serve as Vice President during Herbert Hoover's administration.) So, now we can ask, what continues to determine the political fate of Indians across the Americas?

The second issue is a *cautionary* lesson that we learn from Reinaga: namely that only those who are intimately familiar with the details of their own situation can (and should) prescribe solutions to their unique problems. Many idealistic and well-intentioned people in the U.S. and other developed countries pretend to take up the plight of another and make it their own. However, as we also see in chapters 1–2, it's possible to make the problem one is trying to solve worse, however well intentioned one might be, e.g., Christian, Liberal, and Communist efforts to solve "the Indian problem." Time and again, people overlook or justify oppressive and exploitive practices in the name of saving, freeing, or otherwise "helping." Perhaps, then, the overarching lesson is to listen to those whom we want to help instead of *imposing* what we think is the right solution *from our own point of view*. In other words, perhaps the lesson is about the value of humility.[16]

Notes

1 See Villoro, "The Major Moments of Indigenism in Mexico."
2 González Prada, "Speech at the Politeama Theater," 47. Cited in text using the abbreviation *DP* to capture the original Spanish title, followed by the page

number. All references to the work of González Prada are drawn from the anthology *Free Pages and Hard Times*.

3 Mariátegui, *Siete Ensayos*, 255. Cited in text using the abbreviation *SE* and page number.

4 González Prada, "Our Indians," 186.

5 The meaning of the word "liberal" has changed over time. These days, we tend to associate a liberal with a member of the Democratic Party (as opposed to a Republican). This hasn't always been the case, in fact, during the time of González Prada and before it, to be a liberal mean to argue in behalf of individual rights against the political power of the King. Liberals wanted to have the right to own, sell, invest, and trade their property without having to give a portion of their profit to the Crown. Since liberals have traditionally supported the rights of the individual against oppressive regimes González Prada expected for American Indians to fare better during the newly established republics which were liberal governments.

6 González Prada, *Free Pages*, 191.

7 Ibid., 194.

8 González Prada, "Anarchy," 224.

9 González Prada, "Socialism and Anarchy," 249.

10 Reinaga wrote about González Prada in his book *El indio y los escritores de América*. Reinaga ultimately disagreed with González Prada due to González Prada's eurocentrism.

11 Becker, *Mariátegui and Latin American Marxist Theory*, 10.

12 Ibid., 49.

13 Sorel, *Reflections on Violence*.

14 Mariátegui, *El Alma Matinal y otras Estaciones del Hombre de Hoy*.

15 Reinaga, *Revolución India*, 70. Cited in text using the abbreviation *RI* and page number.

16 I would like to thank Robert Sanchez for his insightful and helpful suggestions to my chapter as well as his commitment to this project, James Maffie and Alejandro Santana for their encouragement, and Jules Simon and Ivy Santana for sharing their life with me.

Bibliography

Bakewell, Peter. *A History of Latin America: Empires and Sequels 1450–1930*. Malden, MA: Blackwell Publishers, 1997.

Becker, Marc. *Mariátegui and Latin American Marxist Theory*. EUA: Ohio University Center for International Studies, 1993.

Carnero Checa, Genaro. *La Acción Escrita: José Carlos Mariátegui Periodista*. Lima: Biblioteca Amauta, 1980.

Cordova, Viola F., Kathleen Dean Moore, Kurt Peters, Ted Jojola, and Amber Lacy, eds. *How It Is: The Native American Philosophy of V. F. Cordova*. Tucson: University of Arizona Press, 2007.

Cusicanqui, Silvia Rivera. "Ch'ixinakax utxiwa: A Reflection on the Practices and Discourses of Decolonization." *The South Atlantic Quarterly* 111(2012): 95–109.

Deloria, Jr., Vine and Daniel Wildcat. *Power and Place: Indian Education in America*. Golden, CO: Fulcrum, 2001.

González Prada, Manuel. *Free Pages and Hard Times: Anarchist Musings*. Translated by Frederick H. Fornoff. Edited by David Sobrevilla. Oxford: Oxford University Press, 2003.

Mariátegui, José Carlos. *Siete Ensayos de Interpretación de la Realidad Peruana*. Lima: Biblioteca Amauta, 1928.

Mariátegui, José Carlos. *El Alma Matinal y Otras Estaciones del Hombre de Hoy*. Lima: Biblioteca Amauta, 1964.

Mariátegui, José Carlos. *Temas de educación*. Perú: Biblioteca Amauta, 1970.

Reinaga, Fausto. *El indio y los escritores de América*. La Paz, Bolivia: Ediciones PIB (Partido Indio de Bolivia), 1968.

Reinaga, Fausto. *Revolución India*. La Paz, Bolivia: Minka, 1970.

Sorel, Georges. *Reflections on Violence*. Cambridge: Cambridge University Press, 1999.

Turner, Dale. "Oral Traditions and The Politics of (Mis)recognition." In *American Indian Thought*, edited by Anne Waters. Malden, MA: Blackwell Publishers, 2004.

Villoro, Luis. *Estado Plural, Pluralidad De Culturas*. México: Paidós, 1998

Villoro, Luis. "The Major Moments of Indigenism in Mexico." In *Mexican Philosophy in the 20th Century: Essential Readings*, edited by Carlos Alberto Sánchez and Robert EliSanchez, Jr., 156–164. Oxford: Oxford University Press, 2017.

Young, Joseph. "An Indian's View of Indian Affairs." *The North American Review* 254, no. 1(Spring, 1969): 56–64.

Zea, Leopoldo. *El positivismo en México: Nacimiento, apogeo y decadencia*. Mexico: Fondo de Cultura Economica, 1968.

10 Latinx Philosophy and the Ethics of Migration

José Jorge Mendoza

It is hard to disagree with the claim that migration has been an essential, if not defining, characteristic of the human species. Philosophers however have only recently begun to debate questions concerning migration justice. One reason for this is that, even though humans have always moved throughout the world, restrictions on migration (especially immigration restrictions) are themselves relatively new. The kinds of immigration restrictions we now take for granted only came into existence toward the end of the 19th century. Another reason is that before the 1970s most moral and political philosophy (at least in the Western world) was concerned primarily with questions of domestic, rather than global or international, justice. Even the most revered political philosopher of our time, John Rawls, found it necessary to begin his much celebrated *Theory of Justice* under the assumption that his ideal society would be a closed society, one that people entered into by birth and exited only by death. This assumption therefore bracketed important questions about political membership as either self-evident or not important enough to develop a theory of justice.

By the early 1980s things had dramatically changed. Interest in global justice and multiculturalism was emerging among philosophers and at the same time restrictions on migration—both from exiting the "second" world (e.g., U.S.S.R.) and entering into the "first" world—were not only increasing but also being enforced in morally problematic ways. It is therefore not surprising that philosophers became interested in migration justice and that they framed this interest as a question about open-borders: in other words, as a question about whether political communities ever have a right to exclude foreigners seeking admission.

The open-borders debate is intriguing both because it shows how philosophy is relevant to the real world and because it exposes an inherent tension within the dominant political ideologies of our time. Today, most political theorists assume that a state is "legitimate" or "just" to the extent that it is both democratically self-determined (a traditionally communitarian commitment)[1] and adheres to universal human rights norms (a traditionally liberal commitment).[2] The issue of immigration, or at least the question of open-borders, seems to upset this delicate truce between communitarianism and liberalism. Those who tend to give priority to democratic self-determination tend to conclude that states have an unconditional right to exclude non-members, while those who give greater priority to human rights norms tend to believe that states do not have such unrestricted power because that would potentially undermine the equal moral worth of persons or an individual's right to freedom of movement.

In this chapter my aim is not to offer a new defense or objection to the open-borders position, but to outline some key contributions Latinx philosophers have made to the ethics of migration. The first section summarizes some important and original—although often neglected—contributions of Latinx philosophers to the standard open-borders debate. Among the highlights of this section are Jorge M. Valadez's "conditional legitimacy of states" argument; José-Antonio Orosco's communitarian-based argument for a more liberalized admissions policy; Javier S. Hidalgo's claim that people have a moral right (and often an obligation) to disobey immigration laws; J. Angelo Corlett's defense of immigration restrictions on grounds that such restrictions serve to protect Indigenous people's sovereignty and rightful claims to territory; and Amy Reed-Sandoval's freedom of movement argument based on the collective right of trans-border communities.

The second section outlines four ways Latinx philosophers have pushed discussions within the ethics of migration beyond the standard open-borders debate. First, Latinx philosophers have made persuasive arguments about why we ought to reject, or at least be suspicious of, approaches to migration justice that begin by assuming the legitimacy of states. Second, they argue that the issue of enforcement has been overlooked in standard open-borders debates and that questions about how immigration restrictions get enforced has serious ethical implications that must be factored into any satisfactory account of migration justice. Third, they argue that philosophers must not avoid dealing with the social (as opposed to merely juridical) implications of labeling people "illegal" or "anchor babies." Fourth, Latinx philosophers largely believe that the current theoretical resources from which much of the ethics of migration draws from is too Euro- or Anglo-centric. They therefore have begun to incorporate theoretical resources and insights from non-European and non-Anglo philosophers in dealing with questions of migration justice. This chapter will therefore strongly suggest that Latinx philosophers are not only already providing important and original contributions to standard open-borders debates, but also changing the very nature of the ethics of migration.

Latinx Contributions to the Open-Borders Debate

Perhaps the first Latinx philosopher to make a strong contribution to the open-borders debate is Jorge M. Valadez. Valadez is among the first to articulate the tension between a commitment to democratic self-determination and human rights norms and offer a viable resolution. On Valadez's account, states should not have complete control over immigration, but he does not believe that this entails that borders be fully open. Valadez instead proposes an intermediate position that he calls "regulated openness" and defends this position by adopting what he calls a "holistic normative approach." Today, it is commonplace to come across different versions of Valadez's arguments, but rarely is he given the credit he deserves for having developed them. I will therefore summarize some of Valadez's key arguments, both for their own sake and to help familiarize ourselves with the contours of the open-borders debate.

According to Valadez there are two principal arguments that philosophers have offered in defense of open-borders (or the view that freedom to move across borders is a human right). The first is the "moral equality argument." This argument claims that restrictions on immigration turn citizenship into a modern-day feudal privilege and therefore ought to be abolished.[3] The reasoning for this is as follows: citizenship in a developed country comes with unearned privileges, while citizenship in a less-developed country brings severe disadvantages. Given that citizenship is obtained most commonly at or by birth, these citizenship-based inequalities appear to run afoul of a more general commitment to human equality. To put it another way, whatever reasons one might offer for rejecting inequalities based on feudal, racial, or sex differences would seem equally applicable to inequalities based on citizenship. Furthermore, it seems that the only way to end citizenship-based inequalities would be to remove barriers to special privileges currently enjoyed by only a few and help ameliorate disadvantages currently suffered by many. To do this, the fairest, simplest, and most efficient way would seem to be to open borders between nation-states and extend opportunities equally among all human beings.

Valadez offers two original objections to the *moral equality argument.* First, he believes that open-borders would not actually undermine global inequality, and could exacerbate it in some cases. This is because a world of open-borders could increase "brain drain" (i.e., the exodus of skilled and wealthy individuals from poor countries to rich countries) which would be to the detriment of the world's already least well-off countries. Even in a world of open-borders, the world's least well-off are, in most cases, unlikely to have the necessary resources to migrate to other places and thereby take advantage of the new opportunities. On the other hand, wealthy and skilled individuals from underdeveloped countries do and their exodus would make these already poor countries even less well off. Valadez therefore suggests that states ought to have a hand in regulating immigration, but they should regulate it in ways that will "maximize the positive benefits of migration while minimizing its negative effects for the vulnerable people left behind in countries of origin."[4]

Valadez's second objection deals with the difference between ideal equality and equality in non-ideal circumstances. According to Valadez, appreciating this difference shows us why open-borders, even if ideal, are inconsistent with a commitment to equality in non-ideal circumstances. For example, in a world like ours there are many more people from poor countries wishing to immigrate to affluent countries than can be taken in. Given this feasibility constraint, it seems that the most we can ask of affluent countries is that they give priority to those who are in most dire need or are the least well off (e.g., those fleeing extreme poverty or totalitarian regimes). If immigration is akin to a human right, this would mean such prioritizing schemes—which most of us intuitively would find consistent with a commitment to equality—would in fact violate the human rights of those who get denied entry because their situation is not deemed grave enough to merit admission.

A second argument that philosophers often deploy in defense of open-borders is the "freedom of movement" argument. This argument is concerned less with equality and more focused on protecting individual liberty. It points out that immigration restrictions limit an individual's freedom of movement and therefore ought to be rejected as unjust infringements on an individual's liberty.[5] Valadez however observes that there are already various limits on an individual's mobility (e.g., laws against trespassing and traffic laws) and in most cases we do not consider these restrictions infringements on an individual's liberty. Instead, we think they help maximize and promote the liberties of all individuals. So while freedom of movement is consistent with open-borders, it is not enough to show that immigration is itself an inherent human right.

After establishing that immigration is not itself an inherent human right, Valadez considers the possibility that open-borders might still be defended on non-ideal grounds. For example, it could be argued that states in a world like ours are less-than-legitimate and therefore lack the moral authority to regulate immigration. Valadez here provides another original (and under-appreciated) response to this argument for open-borders, which he dubs the "conditional legitimacy of states" argument. Valadez begins by conceding that contemporary nation-states have largely obtained jurisdictional power over their territories through unjust means (e.g., as the result of usurpation, conquest, or colonialism). He suggests, however, that even if nation-states have a less-than-ideal origin story, they can nonetheless be considered "conditionally legitimate" as long as they are performing the necessary administrative functions of governing and do so in ways that respect other political communities and peoples and allow them to flourish. So, despite their checkered past, most nation-states in our world are (or could easily become) *conditionally legitimate*, which would mean that "[a]dvocating [for] open borders as a response to the moral illegitimacy of the territorial powers of nation-states is not acceptable [because] open borders would ... undermine [self-governing political communities'] administrative capacity."[6] This argument does not entail that nation-states therefore have a freehand with respect to immigration. The territorial powers of nation-states are always contingent upon nation-states meeting various conditions, which limit the kinds of immigration policies they may justly adopt. Whatever immigration policy a nation-state adopts, it must be best for everyone that policy affects, not just the members of the receiving state. This would, on Valadez's *regulated openness* account, lead to a world with much more (but never fully) open borders.

Valadez's views on immigration are not discussed much in the literature on the ethics of migration. One exception is the work of José-Antonio Orosco, whose principle criticism is aimed at his *conditional legitimacy of states* argument. According to Orosco, this argument understands nation-states only as administrators of goods and resources and thereby does not account for the fact that nation-states have historically functioned as "a means to preserve and protect a nation, that is, a coherent group of people united by cultural traditions, language, ethnicity, and history."[7] On this more communitarian-based view of states, immigrants are considered a threat not because they might undermine the administrative functions of government, but because they are fundamentally different (i.e., not of the nation) and potentially bring with them new ideas and different ways of being that could challenge or undermine the supremacy of the dominant culture (cf. "the Latino threat narrative" in chapter 3).

Orosco's objection therefore raises two interrelated problems for Valadez's account. First, it shows that it is possible for a nation-state to meet the criteria for *conditional legitimacy* while nonetheless exercising its territorial powers in problematic ways (e.g., implementing racist immigration policies). Second, even if Valadez's account can address this first worry, his response to this worry would only be persuasive to those who already subscribe to liberalism or give priority to liberal principles or values. His account, however, would not have much currency among those who take a more communitarian approach.

This is where Orosco's work provides a valuable contribution to the open-borders debate. Orosco recognizes that communitarians have traditionally viewed increased immigration as a threat and either have opposed immigration in general or argued in favor of strong assimilationist policies. In his book, *Toppling the Melting Pot*, Orosco provides an alternative position that can better achieve the goals of communitarianism, while at the same time arguing for more liberal immigration policies. In this work, Orosco points out that while immigrants bring new customs, traditions, and forms of knowledge, those contributions have historically enriched and enlivened (rather than undermined) host communities and there is no reason to think that future immigration will be any different. Orosco therefore suggests that, instead of rejecting immigration outright or forcing immigrants to assimilate to the dominant culture, values of democracy and solidarity would be better served if immigration, and specifically naturalization, policies allowed immigrants to "retain their distinctive traditions and ways of life … [in a way that will] foster respect and openness to those differences, rather than mere toleration of them."[8] In this way, Orosco comes to a conclusion that is very similar to Valadez's *regulated openness*, but gets to it by appealing to values and principles that traditionally have been more closely aligned with communitarianism.[9]

Another Latinx philosopher who has made important and original contributions to the open-borders debate is Javier S. Hidalgo. Hidalgo is one of the leading proponents of the *freedom of movement* argument. His philosophical strategy has been to highlight the inconsistencies and problematic conclusions inherent in liberal justifications of immigration exclusions. In this way he forces proponents of immigration restrictions into the uncomfortable position of having to choose either their commitments to liberalism or their support for immigration restrictions.[10] While many of the arguments Hidalgo deploys follow standard *freedom of movement* justifications for open-borders, his principle contribution to this debate is his rejection of the idea that individuals have a moral duty to obey immigration laws or assist government officials in their efforts to enforce immigration restrictions.

In this regard, Hidalgo notes that many states currently employ internal immigration enforcement laws that in essence conscript citizens into helping with immigration enforcement efforts. For example, in many states it is illegal for employers to hire undocumented immigrants and in order to be in compliance with this law, employers are asked by government officials to verify the immigration status of their employees. There are similar laws with respect to checking the status of persons seeking housing (e.g., laws prohibiting citizens from harboring undocumented immigrants) and other essential services (e.g., banking and transportation). States also have laws that ask their citizens (e.g., employers or university officials) to report any potential incidents of immigration fraud (e.g., sham marriages). If we begin by assuming that the open-borders position is morally correct, then Hidalgo believes that these laws are not only unjust, but that anyone who complies with them is implicated in violating the rights of migrants. For this reason, Hidalgo believes that citizens not only can, but also have a moral obligation to, disobey these laws, even if disobedience sometimes comes at a cost to them personally (e.g., fines).[11]

Hidalgo argues further that if immigration restrictions are unjust, then migrants who evade, deceive, or even violently resist border agents are not doing anything ethically wrong. In making this case, Hidalgo considers various prominent theories of political obligation and shows how none of these morally require immigrants to obey unjust immigration restrictions and actually permit them to resist these restrictions. An interesting implication of Hidalgo's view is that something many believe to be inherently wrong, clandestinely smuggling people across international borders, turns out not to be because:

> [If] it is permissible for migrants to resist state employees who enforce unjust immigration laws, then it is permissible for smugglers to resist these laws in the same way in order to defend migrants who are unjustly excluded from a state's territory.[12]

One might get the impression at this point that all Latinx philosophers are in favor of (fairly) open borders. This, however, is not the case. One notable exception is J. Angelo Corlett, who subscribes to many of the reasons often given for opposing immigration in general and provides an original objection to open-borders based on a concern for Indigenous peoples, especially those who historically have been victimized by conquest and colonialization. As Corlett writes:

> [T]here is absolutely no question given the history of the Americas, especially North America, that immigration has proven to have one of the most deleterious effects on indigenous populations. And it is precisely the U.S.'s mitigated open door policy of immigration that has wrought considerable damage on indigenous nations ... [an] open borders policy ensures their final destruction even more rapidly.[13]

In other words, even if it is the case that immigration restrictions are inconsistent with liberal principles and that they get enforced in morally problematic ways, immigration restrictions are nonetheless the lesser of two evils. According to Corlett, the more pressing moral concern is the preservation of Indigenous peoples and respect for their moral claim to territory. This will not be possible if the immigration of non-indigenous peoples is not curtailed.[14]

One possible rejoinder to Corlett's view can be found in the work of Amy Reed-Sandoval. Reed-Sandoval uses the Oaxacan trans-border community as an example of Indigenous communities that are currently being torn apart by immigration restrictions and for whom justice can only be served if admissions policies are liberalized. Borrowing terminology from Will Kymlicka, one can think of Corlett as making a hard-and-fast distinction between "national minorities" (e.g., Indigenous peoples) and "voluntary migrants" (e.g., the Pilgrims). On Corlett's view, priority should be given to the interests of "national minorities" because they already have been irreparably harmed by the actions of "voluntary migrants." Therefore, the actions of latter (i.e., immigration) must cease and desist, even when doing so would come at a great cost to them (e.g., death at the border). Reed-Sandoval argues, however, that trans-border communities such as the Oaxacan Indigenous community do not fall clearly on either side of this distinction. Furthermore, the existence of trans-border communities depends on their members being able to routinely cross international borders.[15] Therefore, the same reasons Corlett offers in support of immigration restrictions (i.e., protecting Indigenous communities) seem to speak in favor of free movement across international borders when the case in point is transborder communities.

As we can see from the accounts summarized above, the open-borders debate challenges contemporary moral and political philosophy in important ways. It nonetheless misses a lot of what makes the issue of immigration so morally and politically contentious, namely the excessive enforcement of immigration policies and the experience of being an undocumented immigrant. Concerning these issues, Latinx philosophers have made invaluable contributions that, as we will see in the next section, are beginning to change how philosophers think about the ethics of migration.

Latinx Approaches to Immigration Justice

In this section we will look at four ways Latinx philosophers have pushed the ethics of migration beyond the open-borders debate. First, they have challenged the idea of assuming legitimate states as the natural starting point for discussions about migration justice. This assumption has not only failed to provide substantive normative guidance, but has also obscured many of the reasons migrants should be admitted into existing states. Second, Latinx philosophers have brought to bear concerns with excessive enforcement on the ethics of migration. In doing so they have developed indirect arguments for a more expansive set of immigrant rights and for (more) open borders. Third, Latinx philosophers have extended insights from critical race theory and feminist theory to the ethics of migration by showing how an "illegal" or "anchor baby" identity is more than a legal status; it is a pernicious social identity that has deleterious effects on those it captures. Fourth, Latinx philosophers have contributed to the larger project of decolonizing philosophy by employing the frameworks and critical tools of non-Anglo and non-European philosophers in thinking through migration justice. Below I provide a brief sketch of each of these four and highlight the key contributions of Latinx philosophers.

Less-Than-Legitimate States

In the open-borders debate, the *conventional view* assumes that a state has the right to control immigration so long as it is sufficiently legitimate and it excludes only migrants to whom it has no relationship or connection. In a series of articles, Ernesto Rosen Velásquez has argued that while assuming the *conventional view* is a fine place to begin the theoretical debate over presumptive rights, it is less clear what the practical applications will be for any conclusion drawn from this assumption. This is because most existing states do not meet the strict standard of legitimacy and in most cases immigrants do have strong prior relationships and connections to the countries they seek to join. The *conventional view* therefore provides limited normative guidance for what existing states ought to do and has the further drawback of obscuring or overlooking important historical events and international relations that have played a pivotal role in the construction of contemporary migration patterns. This suggests that philosophers should discard the *conventional view* and examine migration from a more context informed starting position.[16]

Velásquez takes the U.S. as an example, in part because the U.S. is often held up as a model existing state. Nonetheless, the U.S. did not acquire its wealth, territory, power, or even prestige through reputable means. It did so by unjustly dispossessing Native Americans of their land, exploiting the labor of African slaves, and invading sovereign nations (e.g., Mexico and Spain) and taking much of their territory by force. The U.S. continues to recruit (both through formal and informal channels) Mexican labor and has continued to exploit that labor. It has made trade agreements with countries (e.g., NAFTA) that have shifted jobs away from those countries and moved them to the U.S. Finally, it continues to instigate and contribute to unjust armed conflicts throughout the world, but most especially throughout Latin America, which has displaced people and forced them to migrate.[17]

This rendering of U.S. history entails two things. First, the U.S. is not a legitimate state, which according to the *conventional view* would mean that it does not have a right to exclude. Second, even if the U.S. has some right to exclude, this right could not be justly exercised against Latin American (or more specifically Mexican) immigrants because these migrants have a historical and continuing relationship to the U.S. that merits admission. This conclusion puts proponents of a state's right to exclude in a difficult position. They must either accept that a highly regarded existing state, such as the U.S., lacks the right to exclude or they must provide a different (and perhaps less liberal) account to justify a state's right to exclude than the *conventional view*.

One possibility could be to adopt less stringent notion of legitimacy, such as Valadez's *conditional legitimacy*, which only requires a state to perform the necessary administrative functions of governing and do so in ways that respect and allow other political communities and peoples to flourish. Such a view has been tested by Kim Díaz, who responds by pointing out that in establishing free trade agreements and involving itself in armed conflicts throughout the region, the U.S. continues to prosper at the expense of Latin American communities' ability to flourish.[18] So even on Valadez's less stringent account of legitimacy, a country like the U.S. still comes up short. This means that while neither Velásquez nor Díaz necessarily provides a positive argument for open-borders, their arguments nonetheless challenge opponents of open-borders to provide a better (and perhaps more realistic) account of which, if any, existing states have a right to exclude and why.

Immigration Enforcement

As we've seen, philosophers tend to focus on questions concerning admission and exclusion, and rarely look into *how* or to *what extent* these policies may be justly enforced. This omission might be understandable if the "immigration problem" were merely a theoretical exercise or a hypothetical thought experiment, but the "immigration problem" is morally disconcerting to many, not because states (including less-than-legitimate states) have a right to exclude, but because this right to exclude is enforced in morally problematic ways. Questions about enforcement should therefore be regarded as central to an ethics of migration.

This point has not been lost in the work of Latinx philosophers, who regularly make the issue of enforcement the focal point of their work, arguing in one of three distinct ways that the threat of excessive enforcement can only be ameliorated if a state's right to exclude is curtailed or completely eliminated. The first way accepts the *conventional view*, but argues that there are nonetheless limits to the methods and strategies a legitimate state may employ to enforce its immigration restrictions. These limits might at first seem innocuous, but if faithfully adhered to, as legitimate states are morally obligated to do, they provide an indirect justification for (fairly) open-borders. The second rejects the *conventional view* for reasons already alluded to above (in the section on *Less-Than-Legitimate States*) and argues that existing states lack the necessary moral legitimacy to exercise control over their borders and so rely on excessive coercive force to assert this authority. The third argues that even if states can be shown, in Valadez's terms, to be *conditionally legitimate*, they ought not to exercise this authority for nefarious reasons (e.g., a white supremacist social agenda), which seem to be the actual reason immigration restrictions get enforced.

The work of José Jorge Mendoza exemplifies this first approach. Citing examples mostly from the U.S. context, Mendoza shows how most forms of immigration enforcement violate the *principle of proportionality*.[19] These examples include, but are not limited to, enforcement strategies that foreseeably lead to the deaths of thousands of migrants at the border (e.g., "prevention through deterrence")[20] and warrantless searches and seizures inside the country that violate due process and equal protection (e.g., "attrition through enforcement").[21] States typically justify excessive forms of immigration enforcement by suggesting there is no other way of implementing their desired immigration policy. This kind of justification might be open to less-than-legitimate states, but not to legitimate states. Recall that legitimate states are bound by liberal principles to respect the lives and liberties of all persons, including migrants who are unlawfully present or illicitly trying to enter the state. If a legitimate state adheres strictly to its moral and political commitments, it cannot justly engage in excessive forms of immigration enforcement. Instead it would have to deal with the problem of illicit migration by tailoring its immigration policy to more closely reflect the demand for admission, at least up to the point where excessive enforcement will no longer be necessary to implement it. This is the only option open to legitimate states in order for them to remain consistent with the *principle of proportionately* and thereby maintain their legitimacy, even as this constrains its right to exclude. While this is not a direct argument for open-borders, it would mean that existing states, like the U.S., must accept most of the immigrants they currently exclude.

Eduardo Mendieta and Natalie Cisneros take a different approach. Rather than starting with the *conventional view*, they employ genealogical accounts of existing borders. These genealogical accounts bring the reader to a similar conclusion as those arrived at in the section on *Less-Than-Legitimate States*, i.e., that most existing states are less-than-legitimate and so their moral authority to exercise border control is at best questionable. Most existing states, however, do not consider the moral ambiguity of border control as a sufficient reason not to exercise coercion at the border. Instead, this ambiguity is interpreted as a reason for treating border zones and the people who reside in them as morally exceptionable—as dangerous places filled with sub-persons. Border enforcement is therefore given all the benefits normally reserved for combat soldiers and police officers (e.g., the right to kill and to detain), while not being burdened by any of the same limitations (e.g., duties to defend the lives and constitutional protections of all civilians). According to Mendieta this is why it is better to think of "the border not simply [as] a neutral arbiter and sign of sovereignty but a 'genocidal' machine."[22] Cisneros similarly argues that it is due to the moral exceptionalism of borders that harms, like indefinite detainment, can go largely unrecognized when committed against immigrants.[23]

One rejoinder to accounts like those provided above is to suggest that excessive enforcement is an unfortunate but necessary means for governments to ensure the safety of their citizens. In other words, even if governments do not meet the *ideal* standards of legitimacy they can be *conditionally legitimate*, as we have seen above in Valadez's account, and so retain some moral authority to coercively enforce immigration restrictions. In this regard, the work of Grant J. Silva is instructive. Silva has suggested that the perceived threats to national security, which border enforcement and the detainment of immigrants is meant to guard against, are not the kinds of existential threats we normally believe justify exceptional means. The perceived threats that undergird calls for increased border enforcement are really fears of a country losing its white identity and the privileges that come with it. As Silva notes:

> While borders are supposed to demarcate territorial boundaries, when militarized, they often stand in as divides for racial, ethnic, or linguistic differences between peoples. Borders are thereby supported or bolstered by such things as racial, ethnic, or religious difference, even when such differences are the product of national imaginaries. When borders assume these contexts, they become more than just lines in the sand; they become "color lines."[24]

So while this sense of fear is not imagined by large segments of the population, it is both misplaced and not of the right kind—even under *conditionally legitimate* circumstances—to justify the moral exceptions that excessive immigration enforcement requires.

"Illegal" Social Identities

Another lacuna in the open-borders debate is the issue of *undocumented* immigration. Few philosophers discuss this issue and those who do consciously avoid what they consider loaded terms (e.g., "illegal" or "anchor baby") in favor of neutral language such as "irregular" or "unauthorized" migrants. They also continue to employ the *conventional view* and work under the assumption that any "migrants who deliberately enter or stay in a territory without authorization are (at least prima facie) committing a wrong against the state."[25] From this sanitized starting point, most philosophers do come to the conclusion that undocumented immigrants have a right to stay and their status regularized because either they have established sufficient roots in the community or have lived in the country for a sufficient number of years.

For proponents of immigrant rights, there is much to like about this strategy. First and foremost, whatever rights for undocumented immigrants are obtained from such a starting point will undoubtedly be on very strong footing. This is a strategy that begins with commonly held intuitions about fairness and ends with some fairly radical conclusions (e.g., amnesty for nearly all undocumented immigrants). There is then nothing inherently wrong about adopting this strategy for certain purposes, but as Latinx philosophers have correctly pointed out, the issue of undocumented immigration is not exhausted by the question of regularization. There are also social dimensions of designating people "illegal" or "anchor babies" that are concealed by using neutral terms in their place. For Latinx philosophers it is therefore important to analyze these terms and show how labels, which on the surface make reference only to laws or policies, convey an animus toward certain minorities with serious consequences (e.g., discrimination and exploitation). So, regardless of any reason there might be for regularizing the status of undocumented immigrants, philosophers need to investigate the motivations and implications of labeling people "illegal" and "anchor babies."

In the United States, Latinx philosophers—especially those who work in the areas of critical race and feminist theory—have been particularly attuned to the social dimension of undocumented immigration. This is in large part because a Latinx identity has been intricately connected, at least in the minds of many Americans, to being undocumented. As a result, Latinx philosophers tend to be more concerned with the extrajudicial implications and consequences of being socially identified as "illegal" or an "anchor baby," and less concerned with philosophical justifications for regularizing the status of undocumented immigrants (although most do support and believe their views entail amnesty for undocumented immigrants).

Latinx philosophers often begin a discussion about being identified as "illegal" or as an "anchor baby" with the following passage in Gloria Anzaldúa's *Borderlands*:

In the fields, la migra. My aunt saying, "No corran, don't run. They'll think you're del otro lao." In the confusion, Pedro ran, terrified of being caught. He couldn't speak English, couldn't tell them he was a fifth generation American. Sin papeles—he did not carry his birth certificate to work in the fields. La migra took him away while we watched. Se lo llevaron. He tried to smile when he looked back at us, to raise his fist. But I saw the shame pushing his head down, I saw the terrible weight of shame hunch his shoulders. They deported him to Guadalajara by plane. The furthest he'd ever been to Mexico was Reynosa, a small border town opposite Hidalgo, Texas, not far from McAllen. Pedro walked all the way to the Valley. Se lo llevaron sin un centavo al pobre. Se vino andando desde Guadalajara.[26]

In the story recounted by Anzaldúa, we see that the injustices suffered by Pedro would not have been remedied simply by "regularizing" his immigration status. Pedro was already a U.S. citizen, but he lived (and many Latinx still live) under social conditions under which being poor, nonwhite, and of Latin American descent are sufficient to presume one is "illegal." Pedro was therefore guilty of being undocumented until he could prove otherwise. Latinx philosophers have taken Pedro's and other similar stories and argued that such treatment is wrong for three distinct reasons: it violates liberal principles or values, generates serious ontological harms, or works in the service of white supremacy and patriarchy.

From a liberal perspective, José Jorge Mendoza has argued that the treatment of Pedro, and other citizens perceived to be "illegal," is wrong because it demeans their civic standing. This is both a violation of liberalism's commitment to political equality[27] and an undermining of a community's social trust.[28] Going further, Amy Reed-Sandoval has argued that such treatment is more than a violation of political equality. It is also a violation of moral equality. In other words, this kind of treatment is wrong not just in its unequal treatment of *citizens*, but in its violation of human dignity more generally. Pace Mendoza, Sandoval suggests that how Pedro was treated would have been morally wrong even if he had not been a citizen.[29]

While the liberal framework provides a moral and political vocabulary to condemn the injustice of Pedro's treatment, it does not seem to go far enough in expressing the deeper and more experiential harms that come with being labeled "illegal." In an effort to shore up this deficiency, Carlos Alberto Sánchez has put forth a phenomenological account of immigrant identity that outlines two sorts of ontological harms that come with treating people as "illegal." First, Sánchez argues that "papeles" or having proper documentation that prove one's lawful presence (e.g., a green card) is not just a marker of one's legal status, but ought to grant one recognition as a member in good standing within the larger community. This recognition, he argues, is an essential component of one's subjectivity. The treatment that people like Pedro receive undermines the confidence immigrants are entitled to have in their *papeles* and thereby is not just a clerical error, but an undermining of their "effective sense of self and identity."[30]

Second, being "illegal" extends beyond official documentation and is read off the bodies of immigrants. This process, according to Sánchez, "*thingify* and push the undocumented immigrant outside the space of the human."[31] Ernesto Rosen Velásquez has helpfully labeled this space "the zone of non-being" and it complements Mendieta's zone of exception encountered above in the section on *Immigration Enforcement*. Velásquez correctly points out that, according to standard liberal accounts, legitimate states ought never to make lawbreakers (e.g., undocumented immigrants) into outlaws (i.e., those who are completely outside of the law's protection). But reality is far from this liberal ideal. When people are labeled "illegal" they are made vulnerable to much more than say economic exploitation. They become dehumanized in ways that, according to Velásquez, render them rapeable, torturable, and even killable. Velásquez chillingly dubs this process the "third world factory to grave pipeline."[32]

The phenomenological account therefore allows us to describe the experience of being illegal and to articulate the harms that come with it, but this account is also not exhaustive. José Jorge Mendoza and Grant J. Silva have, from a critical race perspective, argued that an "illegal" identity can also function as a proxy or stand-in for a nonwhite identity. Silva has done this by arguing that racism should be understood as inseparably connected to Western colonialism and that current immigration restrictions (and especially the way they are enforced) should be seen as an outgrowth of colonialism. This not only helps to explain how an "illegal" identity comes to be a stand-in for a nonwhite identity, but also how racist immigration policies can be perpetuated even without relying on overtly racialized discourses (e. g., using dog whistle politics).[33]

Mendoza similarly has argued that an "illegal" identity can and does work in the service of white supremacy. This is because xenophobia, while distinct from racism, nonetheless functions in similar ways. Mendoza therefore suggests that we think of a white identity, at least in places like the U.S., as analogous to a braid of race, ethnicity, and nationality. This account, he believes, can do a better job of explaining the ways that seemingly race-neutral terms (e.g., "illegal" or "anchor baby") nonetheless function to promote a white supremacist agenda through an ardent display of nationalism (e.g., "America first" policies).[34]

Along similar lines, Natalie Cisneros and Amy Reed-Sandoval have used criticisms grounded in feminist theory to interrogate terms such as "anchor baby." For them, the deployment of this term is more than a shorthand criticism of family reunification policies. It highlights and helps to resolve a tension within the racist and sexist discourse of contemporary conservatism. On a conservative account, women's contributions to the nation are circumscribed by their ability to produce future citizens. In this way, a woman's civic identity gets reduced to her body and her body is of national importance only to the degree that it performs its essential maternal function. Anything inhibiting this function (e.g., abortion or homosexuality) is considered both deviant and a threat to the nation (e.g., abortion kills future citizens).[35]

On this view what comes to matter most is the health and well-being of the fetus (i.e., the future citizen). This hyper-attention to the fetus has the consequence of obscuring the needs and interest of the pregnant woman, if those needs and interests are not directly related to the fetus (e.g., no abortion even when the life of the mother is at risk). Yet this strong pro-life stance seems to be put on its head when the pregnant woman in question is of an undesirable race, ethnicity, or nationality. In these cases, the racist aspect of conservative discourse tends to foreground the pregnant woman and especially her status (e.g., undocumented immigrant) and in light of this deems the fetus contaminated and therefore a potential threat to the nation (e.g., "anchor baby"). The pregnancy and the fetus are therefore no longer afforded a kind of sacredness. This kind of move allows conservatives to reconcile their sexist pro-life stance with racist efforts to discourage, and even prevent, women of color from seeking basic nutritional and medical support during their pregnancies[36] or protection when they are the victims of sexual and domestic abuse.[37] On this account, it is therefore not difficult to make the connection between the deployment of terms like "anchor baby" and the U.S.'s long and sordid history of racist forced sterilization and eugenics projects.[38]

Decolonizing Immigration Justice

Academic philosophy in the U.S. tends to be divided along "analytic" and "continental" lines. This division runs so deep that on many issues philosophers on either side do not share any of the same literature. The ethics of migration is no exception. Analytic philosophers working on the ethics of migration tend to take the work of John Rawls, Robert Nozick, or of utilitarianism in general as their primary point of departure and their ultimate point of return. Similarly, those who approach the topic of migration from a continental perspective tend to rely almost exclusively on the theories of philosophers such as Giorgio Agamben, Alain Badiou, or Michel Foucault. The gulf between these two sets of migration literature is immense and perhaps unbridgeable.

Despite the depth of this divide there is one thing they share. They rarely, if ever, consult the work of non-Anglo or non-European philosophers. In other words, no matter how fundamentally different they are in their approaches to migration justice, they are nonetheless Euro- and Anglo-centric. This is a problem because (as we have seen in chapters 7, 8, 9, and 11) the absence of non-Anglo and non-European voices only helps reproduce the colonial divide. It gives one the mistaken impression that no idea has validity or can be considered theoretically sophisticated unless it first gives credit to or can be found in the work of an already established white male Anglo or European theorist. In these cases, non-Anglo and non-Europeans are regarded as providing only the matter (i.e., the raw material) on which Anglo or European masters provide the intellectual form (i.e., the finished product).

Increasingly we are beginning to see Latinx philosophers forgo the frameworks of established Anglo and European philosophers and instead adopt the critical frameworks of Latin American theorists. This is especially true in regard to how Latinx philosophers have approached the ethics of migration. In what follows, I outline some of the most prominent examples, but also caution the reader that this is far from an exhaustive list. This is meant mostly as a small sample of what decolonizing a particular area of philosophy might begin to look like.

The first example is Natalie Cisneros and Edwina Barvosa's use of Gloria Anzaldúa. Anzaldúa's *Borderlands/La Frontera* is now a staple in Latin American and Latinx philosophy and, given the subject matter of the book, one would have expected that philosophers grappling with issues of traversing national borders would have consulted her work. Sadly, this has not been the case. Cisneros, Barvosa, and other Latinx philosophers are, however, diligently working to change this. Cisneros in her own work incorporates the insights of Anzaldúa by initially putting them in conversation with Foucault's notion of biopower. Biopower for Foucault is a normalizing regime that deems those who fall outside or resist the norms of society as threatening and perverse. While Foucault uses this concept to explain how various groups within society are wrongfully marginalized, he rarely considers the role biopower plays in the formation and deformation of an "illegal" identity.

According to Cisneros, Anzaldúa's autobiographical and genealogical account of how "illegal" identities "are constituted as perverse, abnormal, and threatening [and] thus made vulnerable to physical violence and economic exploitation"[39] provides us with a helpful supplement (if not alternative) to Foucault's notion of biopower. Furthermore, Anzaldúa offers us a counter-discourse, via her notion of Mestiza consciousness (see chapters 4, 8, and 11), that, unlike Foucault's notion of biopower, allows us, according to Barvosa, to derive a positive and productive notion of subjectivity even and especially in its fragmented form.[40]

A second example is José-Antonio Orosco's use of Cesar Chavez's social and political thought. Throughout his work on immigration, Orosco relies heavily on Chavez's definition of social membership to argue that most undocumented immigrants ought to already be considered formal members of the polity given their participation in the community and the density of the relationships they have come to form. This use of Chavez not only provides social and political philosophers with a new and original lens through which to think about the nature of citizenship, but also helps to highlight the depth, richness, and underutilization of Chavez's thought.[41]

A third example is José Jorge Mendoza's use of Enrique Dussel. One of the principle tenets of Dussel's philosophy of liberation is that in order to understand or pinpoint the ethical or political failure of a system or institution one must first locate its victims. Once these victims are identified, we have an obligation to address this failure from the victim's perspective (see chapter 7). Mendoza adopts this Dusselian starting point in his work on immigration both to problematize the *conventional view*, but also to give an account of the ethics of migration from the underside of philosophy. Mendoza therefore begins by asking what migration justice would look like if we started with the assumption that undocumented immigrants are the real victims (not the victimizers) of current immigration policies. What would normative intuitions be then? And would this kind of starting point not make better sense of the world in which we currently live? If so, would we not have to radically rethink the starting point of the ethics of migration?[42]

A fourth example is Amy Reed-Sandoval's use of Carlos Pereda's notion of "exile." In *Lessons in Exile*, Pereda uses this term to describe the experience of upper class migrants from Latin America who have been forcibly displaced because they are fleeing brutal, often U.S. backed, military regimes.[43] According to Reed-Sandoval, however, Pereda's notion of *exile* could be fruitfully applied to the case of all Latin American immigrants and their descendants. This is because they too have experienced their lives in the U.S. through a sense of loss, sadness, and eventual philosophical inspiration that Pereda's notion describes. Reed-Sandoval therefore suggests a new broader term, "Desplazada/o," which is inspired by Pereda's work, but that extends his insights to the entire Latinx experience.[44]

A fifth example is Daniel G. Campos's use of Maria Lugones and Octavio Paz. In *Loving Immigrants in America* Campos employees Lugones's concepts of "playfulness," "world-travelling," and "loving perception" to help make sense of his attempts to make a home for himself in the U.S. South as a Latin American immigrant. Campos's account also highlights the fact that part of the immigrant experience includes a severing of the people and places they have cherished. When this happens, a sense of solitude, as described by Paz in *Labyrinth of Solitude*, begins to seep into one's life. Campos, however, provides a more optimistic reading of Paz, by suggesting practices of communion that can help one dance out of the labyrinth.[45]

Conclusion

One of the difficulties in writing a chapter like this is that most of the relevant literature is not found in mainstream publications of moral and political philosophy. Instead it is scattered throughout lesser known (and often obscure) journals and edited volumes. As this chapter has tried to show, this is not because of the quality of the ideas or a lack of interest in the subject. It is due to two related factors. The first is that the ethics of migration, as a philosophical issue, has been too rigidly defined by mainstream philosophers. The second is that this rigidity discourages, and sometimes prohibits, creative and original contributions to migration justice. As a result, regardless of the quality of their work, Latinx philosophers have had a disproportionately difficult time finding a home for their work.

My hope is that this chapter, as well as the work that it represents, encourages philosophers to expand the conversation on an ethics of migration and, to the extent that the immigration is a defining issue for Latinx philosophy, to explore an underappreciated body of philosophical literature. One way or another, Latinx philosophers are often directly affected by the social implications of immigration policy, and thus have a vested interest in exploring the often overlooked dimensions of this multifaceted topic, such as being a foreigner in your own country, and the legacy of colonialism and imperialism on immigration policy. As a result, we have every reason to expect that the pursuit of migration justice will continue to be a defining issue for Latinx philosophy.

Notes

1 "Communitarianism" is any moral or political doctrine that gives priority to the well-being of a community over the interests of an individual. It often sees individuals as always dependent on their community and thereby always indebted to it.
2 "Liberalism" is any social or political doctrine that gives greater importance to the rights of the individual over the interests of the community. It sees totalitarian regimes (e.g., communities that demand complete and unquestioned obedience from its subjects) as perhaps the greatest threat to individual rights and therefore is skeptical that individuals ever have unconditional obligations to communities or that communities ever have unconditional powers over individuals.
3 See Carens, "Aliens and Citizens."
4 Valdez, "Is Immigration a Human Right," 226.
5 See Kukathas, "The Case for Open Immigration."
6 Valadez, "Immigration and the Territorial Powers of Nation-States," 11.
7 Orosco, "Comment on Jorge Valadez's 'Immigration and the Territorial Powers of Nation-States,'" 14.
8 Orosco, *Toppling the Melting Pot*, 36.
9 Orosco and Daniel G. Campos have argued that these principles are best understood as commitments to a pluralistic experiential approach found in American philosophy. I do not necessarily disagree, but I still find that much of what motivates Orosco's account, at least for our purposes, is consistent with the principles and values of communitarianism. See Campos, "Living with Immigrants in a Context of Difference: Exclusion, Assimilation, or Pluralism."
10 See Hidalgo, "Associative Duties and Immigration"; "Freedom, Immigration, and Adequate Options"; and "Self-determination, Immigration Restrictions, and the Problem of Compatriot Deportation."
11 See Hidalgo "The Duty to Disobey Immigration Law."
12 Hidalgo, "Resistance to Unjust Immigration Restrictions," 458.
13 Corlett and Unger, "The Collateral Damage of Opening Floodgates," 312.
14 See Corlett and Unger, "How Not to Argue about Immigration."
15 See Reed-Sandoval, "Oaxacan Transborder Communities and the Political Philosophy of Immigration."

16 See Velásquez, "States of Violence and the Right to Exclude" and "Are Undocumented *Migrantes* Illegal?."
17 See Díaz "U.S. Border Wall"; Gonzalez, *Harvest of Empire.*
18 Díaz "U.S. Border Wall."
19 The "principle of proportionality" is a legal or moral principle that aims to discern the correct balance between harms resulting from performing a prohibited action (e.g., stealing a loaf of bread) and harms that result from attempts to prevent or punish such transgressions (e.g., cutting the hands off thieves). As an example, we might think it proportionate (and therefore not unjust) to threaten to publically display pictures of known bread thieves as both a punishment for and as a means to deter bread stealing. Most of us, however, would probably consider cutting the hands off of known bread thieves as a disproportionate response—even if this were the only way to ensure that no bread was ever stolen—and therefore unjust. The *principle of proportionality* seems to tell us that it would be preferable, even if not ideal, for some bread to be stolen rather than have people violently lose their limbs.
20 See Mendoza, "Enforcement Matters: Reframing the Philosophical Debate Over Immigration," and *The Moral and Political Philosophy of Immigration.*
21 See Mendoza, "Doing Away with Juan Crow: Two Standards for Just Immigration Reform" and "The Contradictions of Crimmigration."
22 Mendieta, "The U.S. Border and the Political Ontology of 'Assassination Nation,'" 85.
23 See Cisneros, "Resisting 'Massive Elimination.'"
24 Silva, "On the Militarization of Borders and The Juridical Right to Exclude," 223.
25 Hosein, "Arguments for Regularization," 160–161.
26 Anzaldúa, *Borderlands/La Frontera*, 4.
27 See Mendoza, "Discrimination and the Presumptive Rights of Immigrants;" and "Illegal: White Supremacy and Immigration Status."
28 See Mendoza, "Latino/a Immigration: A Refutation of the Social Trust Argument."
29 See Reed-Sandoval, "Locating the Injustice of Undocumented Migrant Oppression."
30 Sánchez, "On Documents and Subjectivity, 199."
31 Sánchez, "'Illegal' Immigrants: Law, Fantasy, and Guts," 4.
32 Velásquez, "Criminalization and Undocumented Migrante Laborer Identities in the Zone of Nonbeing," 153.
33 See Silva, "Embodying A 'New' Color Line."
34 See Mendoza, "A 'Nation' of Immigrants;" and "*Illegal*: White Supremacy and Immigration Status."
35 See Cisneros, "'Alien' Sexuality: Race, Maternity, and Citizenship."
36 See Reed-Sandoval, "Crossing U.S. Borders While Pregnant."
37 See Cisneros, "Mestizaje and 'Alien' Identity;" and Reed-Sandoval, "Locating the Injustice of Undocumented Migrant Oppression."
38 See Cisneros, "'Alien' Sexuality: Race, Maternity, and Citizenship."
39 Cisneros, "Mestizaje and 'Alien' Identity," 6.
40 See Barvosa, "Applying Latina Feminist Philosophical Approaches to the Self to Reinterpret Anti-Immigrant Politics in America."
41 See Orosco, *Cesar Chavez and the Common Sense of Nonviolence.*
42 See Mendoza, "The Political Philosophy of Unauthorized Immigration."
43 See Pereda, *Lessons in Exile.*
44 See Reed-Sandoval, "'Immigrant' or 'Exiled'?"
45 See Campos, *Loving Immigrants in America.*

Bibliography

Anzaldúa, Gloria. *Borderlands/La Frontera: The New Mestiza*. San Francisco: Aunt Lute Books, 1999.

Barvosa, Edwina. "Applying Latina Feminist Philosophical Approaches to the Self to Reinterpret Anti-Immigrant Politics in America." *APA Newsletter on Hispanic/Latino Issues in Philosophy* 11, no. 2(2012): 16–21.

Campos, Daniel G. *Loving Immigrants in America: An Experiential Philosophy of Personal Interaction*. Blue Ridge Summit, PA: Lexington Books, 2017.

Campos, Daniel G. "Living with Immigrants in a Context of Difference: Exclusion, Assimilation, or Pluralism." *The Pluralist* 13, no. 2(2018): 109–118.

Carens, Joseph H. "Aliens and Citizens: The Case for Open Borders." *Review of Politics* 49, no. 2(1987): 251–273.

Cisneros, Natalie. "'Alien' Sexuality: Race, Maternity, and Citizenship." *Hypatia* 28, no. 2(2013): 290–306.

Cisneros, Natalie. "Mestizaje and 'Alien' Identity: Gloria Anzaldúa on Immigration." *APA Newsletter on Hispanic/Latino Issues in Philosophy* 12, no. 2 (2013): 3–7.

Cisneros, Natalie. "Resisting 'Massive Elimination': Foucault, Immigration, and the GIP." In *Active Intolerance: Michel Foucault, the Prisons Information Group, and the Future of Abolition*, edited by Perry Zurn and Andrew Dilts, 241–257. New York: Palgrave Macmillan, 2016.

Corlett, J. Angelo, and Kimberly Unger. "The Collateral Damage of Opening Floodgates: Problems with Kevin R. Johnson's Arguments for U.S. Immigration Reform." *Philosophy and Society* 24, no. 4(2013): 299–314.

Corlett, J. Angelo, and Kimberly Unger. "How Not to Argue about Immigration." *Philosophy and Society* 24, no. 2(2013): 277–288.

Diaz, Kim. "U.S. Border Wall: A Poggean Analysis of Illegal Immigration." *Philosophy in the Contemporary World* 17, no. 1(2010): 1–12.

Gonzalez, Juan. *Harvest of Empire: A History of Latinos in America*, revised edition. New York: Penguin Books, 2011.

Hidalgo, Javier S. "Associative Duties and Immigration." *Journal of Moral Philosophy* 10, no. 6(2013): 697–722.

Hidalgo, Javier S. "Freedom, Immigration, and Adequate Options." *Critical Review of International Social and Political Philosophy* 17, no. 2(2014): 212–234.

Hidalgo, Javier S. "Self-determination, Immigration Restrictions, and the Problem of Compatriot Deportation." *Journal of International Political Theory* 10, no. 3 (2014): 261–282.

Hidalgo, Javier S. "Resistance to Unjust Immigration Restrictions." *The Journal of Political Philosophy* 23, no. 4(2015): 450–470.

Hidalgo, Javier S. "The Duty to Disobey Immigration Law." *Moral Philosophy and Politics* 3, no. 2(2016): 1–22.

Hosein, Adam. "Arguments for Regularization." In *The Ethics and Politics of Immigration: Emerging Trends*, edited by Alex Sager, 159–179. London UK: Rowman & Littlefield International, 2016.

Kukathas, Chandran. "The Case for Open Immigration." In *Contemporary Debates in Applied Ethics*, edited by Andrew I. Cohen and Christopher Heath Wellman, 207–220. Malden MA: Blackwell, 2005.

Mendieta, Eduardo. "The Right to Political Membership Democratic Morality and the Rights of Irregular Immigrants." *Radical Philosophy Review* 14, no. 2(2011): 177–185.

Mendieta, Eduardo. "The U.S. Border and the Political Ontology of 'Assassination Nation': Thanatological Dispositifs." *Journal of Speculative Philosophy* 31, no. 1 (2017): 82–100.

Mendoza, José Jorge. "A 'Nation' of Immigrants." *The Pluralist* 5, no.3(2010): 41–48.

Mendoza, José Jorge. "The Political Philosophy of Unauthorized Immigration." *APA Newsletter on Hispanic/Latino Issues in Philosophy* 10, no. 2(2011): 2–6.

Mendoza, José Jorge. "Discrimination and the Presumptive Rights of Immigrants." *Critical Philosophy of Race* 2, no. 1(2014): 68–83.

Mendoza, José Jorge. "Doing Away with Juan Crow: Two Standards for Just Immigration Reform." *APA Newsletter on Hispanic/Latino Issues in Philosophy* 15, no. 2(2015): 14–20.

Mendoza, José Jorge. "Enforcement Matters: Reframing the Philosophical Debate Over Immigration," *Journal of Speculative Philosophy* 29, no. 1(2015): 73–90.

Mendoza, José Jorge. "Latino/a Immigration: A Refutation of the Social Trust Argument." In *Migration Policy and Practice: Interventions and Solutions*, edited by Harald Bauder and Christian Matheis, 37–57. New York: Palgrave Macmillan, 2015.

Mendoza, José Jorge. "Illegal: White Supremacy and Immigration Status." In *The Ethics and Politics of Immigration: Emerging Trends*, edited by Alex Sager, 201–220. London UK: Rowman & Littlefield International, 2016.

Mendoza, José Jorge. *The Moral and Political Philosophy of Immigration: Liberty, Security, and Equality*. Blue Ridge Summit, PA: Lexington Books, 2017.

Mendoza, José Jorge. "The Contradictions of Crimmigration." *APA Newsletter on Hispanic/Latino Issues in Philosophy* 17, no. 2(2018): 6–9.

Orosco, José-Antonio. *Cesar Chavez and the Common Sense of Nonviolence*. Albuquerque: University of New Mexico Press, 2008.

Orosco, José-Antonio. "Comment on Jorge Valadez's 'Immigration and the Territorial Powers of Nation-States.'" *APA Newsletter on Hispanic/Latino Issues in Philosophy* 7, no.2(2008): 13–14.

Orosco, José-Antonio. *Toppling the Melting Pot: Immigration and Multiculturalism in American Pragmatism*. Bloomington, IN: Indiana University Press, 2016.

Pereda, Carlos. *Lessons in Exile*. Translated by Sean Manning. Leiden, Netherlands: Brill, 2019.

Reed-Sandoval, Amy. "'Immigrant' or 'Exiled'? Reconceiving the Desplazada/os of Latin American and Latina/o Philosophy." *APA Newsletter on Hispanic/Latino Issues in Philosophy* 15, no. 2(2016): 11–14.

Reed-Sandoval, Amy. "Locating the Injustice of Undocumented Migrant Oppression." *Journal of Social Philosophy* 47, no. 2(2016): 374–398.

Reed-Sandoval, Amy. "Oaxacan Transborder Communities and the Political Philosophy of Immigration." *International Journal of Applied Philosophy* 30, no. 1 (2016): 91–104.

Reed-Sandoval, Amy. "Crossing U.S. Borders While Pregnant: An Increasingly Complex Reality." *The Hastings Center Report* 48, no. 5(2018): 5–6.

Sánchez, Carlos Alberto. "On Documents and Subjectivity: The Formation and Deformation of the Immigrant Identity." *Radical Philosophy Review* 14, no.2(2011): 197–205.

Sánchez, Carlos Alberto. "'Illegal' Immigrants: Law, Fantasy, and Guts." *Philosophy in the Contemporary World* 21, no. 1(2014): 99–109.

Silva, Grant J. "Embodying A 'New' Color Line: Racism, Anti-Immigrant Sentiment and Racial Identities in the 'Postracial' Era." *Knowledge Cultures* 3, no. 1(2015): 65–90.

Silva, Grant J. "On the Militarization of Borders and The Juridical Right to Exclude." *Public Affairs Quarterly* 29, no. 2(2015): 217–234.

Valadez, Jorge. "Immigration and the Territorial Powers of Nation-States." *APA Newsletter on Hispanic/Latino Issues in Philosophy* 7, no. 2(2008): 6–13.

Valadez, Jorge. "Is Immigration a Human Right?" In *Cosmopolitanism in Context: Perspectives from International Law and Political Theory*, edited by Roland Pierik and Wouter Werner, 221–248. Cambridge: Cambridge University Press, 2010.

Valadez, Jorge. "Immigration, Self-Determination, and Global Justice: Towards a Holistic Normative Theory of Migration." *Journal of International Political Theory* 8, no. 1(2012): 135–146.

Velásquez, Ernesto Rosen. "States of Violence and the Right to Exclude." *Journal of Poverty* 21, no. 4(2016): 310–330.

Velásquez, Ernesto Rosen. "Are Undocumented Migrantes Illegal?" *Peace Review* 29, no.1(2017): 104–111.

Velásquez, Ernesto Rosen. "Criminalization and Undocumented Migrante Laborer Identities in the Zone of Nonbeing." *Critical Philosophy of Race* 7, no.1(2019): 144–159.

11 Latinx Identity

Andrea J. Pitts

Who am I? How should I understand myself in relation to the categories of which I am a member, including my culture, citizenship, race, gender, age, and so on? How do I want others to see me, understand me, and value me? What if I do not neatly fit into the available categories that exist in my society? These questions constitute a series of rich philosophical discussions that have been posed by U.S. Latinx philosophers. While identity, in one way or another, has long held the fascination of Latin American philosophers, Latinx theorists in the United States have attempted to address a subset of identity-related questions over the last several decades, including questions on the metaphysical status of the self (e.g. "Am I one or many?" or "How does existence of the self remain continuous over time?"), on how the identities of U.S. communities descended from differing parts of Latin America bear cultural, familial, and/or nationalist ties to the diverse nations, cultures, and peoples of Latin America, and, finally, questions regarding the relationships between differing identity categories such as race, ethnicity, and gender.

This chapter examines a few contemporary philosophical debates regarding the status of U.S. Latinx identities. There are a number of philosophical facets of identity worth exploring, including a number of themes not addressed in this chapter such as existential approaches to authenticity and alienation, political conceptions of subjecthood/citizenship, and historical/genealogical approaches to the formation of identity.[1] Here, we focus on a small subset of the available philosophical discussions regarding identity. One set of questions within these debates focuses on whether Latinx identities are racial or ethnic identities. A related set of questions concerns how gender functions as a constituting feature or aspect of U.S. Latinx identities. This chapter addresses these two sets of questions in an effort to highlight several possibilities for developing a multidimensional and historically engaged conception of identity. In this vein, the chapter seeks to explore a conception of identity that maintains a pluralistic approach to the varied forms of meaningful group- and self-identifications that comprise U.S. Latinx identity categories. While there are many topics not explored here, it is useful to begin with these few debates to help frame the terms and features that may shape our senses of ourselves, our senses of one another, and our understandings of the social worlds we inhabit.

To address these concerns, the first section of the chapter focuses on the question of whether Latinx identity is a racial or ethnic identity, looking closely at the writings of Jorge J. E. Gracia and Linda Martín Alcoff. These two theorists have been pivotal in addressing questions of race and ethnicity for areas of philosophical analysis including studies of political philosophy, metaphysics, language, structural oppression, and resistance. The second section of the chapter analyzes how gender functions within Latinx identities. Accordingly, this section considers several formative philosophical discussions among Latin American feminist theorists who have debated the use of *el género*/gender as a category of analysis within philosophical projects since the 1990s. Finally, this chapter aims to bring readers into dialogue with several multidimensional and pluralistic understandings of Latinx identity by addressing a recent debate, beginning in the mid-2010s, regarding the use of the term "Latinx." The final section ties together the race/ethnicity debate and the debate regarding *el género*/gender, thus expanding on some ethical and political considerations that are important for researchers to address when engaging in discussions of Latinx identity.

The Race-Ethnicity Debate

First, consider how people identify as members of particular racial or ethnic groups. Many organizations, political movements, educational curricula, music, art, and public discourse honor, draw from, and sometimes criticize how we embody our specific racial or ethnic identities. For example, a young person, the child of Puerto Rican parents, born and raised in New York, might ask themself or be questioned by others regarding how they identify: as Puerto Rican? as Boricua? as Black? as Latinx? as white? as Caribbean? as American? Moreover, a lot might hang on one's answer to such questions. Depending on the answer, this person might be, for example, considered authorized to speak on a given topic, or worthy of recognition for a specific award, or considered particularly attractive, even "exotic," or denied entry into a local social organization, or questioned about their citizenship, or monitored closely while walking through a convenience store. These kinds of everyday experiences for a number of people of color raise philosophical questions regarding whether people of Latin American descent actually share a common identity. On the one hand, some people claim that Latin Americans share cultural, linguistic, and/or political features that demonstrate a more or less unified ethnic identity that they continue to share in the United States. Other people argue that something other than, or more than, ethnicity defines the lived concrete experiences of U.S. Latinxs. For example, some theorists point to perceivable morphological features (e.g. skin color, accent, facial structure, hair color and texture, etc.) as the basis of systemic patterns of discrimination, marginalization, and violence that

Latinxs experience in the United States. According to this view, Latinx identities are more akin to racial identities, wherein morphological characteristics are thought to be the means by which systemic forms of harm operate. Yet, there are objections that one can raise to both positions, and this section of the chapter will examine some of the complexities of Latinx identities in terms of ethnicity and race categories.

One place to begin outlining this debate is the work of Jorge J. E. Gracia (Cuban American) who has been analyzing identity and Latin American philosophy since at least the mid-1970s.[2] Gracia's work, which has been pivotal in developing Latin American philosophy in the Anglophone United States academy, has focused extensively on whether Hispanic identities should be considered racial or ethnic categorizations.[3] In *Hispanic/Latino Identity: A Philosophical Perspective*, Gracia frames the question by asking, "what we should call ourselves?" Gracia explores a number of terms used to describe peoples of Latin American descent. For example, he analyzes the differences between "Hispanic" and "Latino," and initially makes a case against the use of "Hispanic" (although Gracia will eventually accept the use of this term for reasons outlined below). Put briefly, he argues that the term "Hispanic" does not pick out a set of properties that are common to all peoples potentially referred to as "Hispanic." Even a language such as Castilian Spanish cannot usefully demarcate who should properly be considered "Hispanic." For example, consider a monolingual Guatemalan citizen whose native language is K'iche'. Upon migrating to the United States this person may be categorized as "Hispanic" even if they do not speak Spanish. As such, the use of Castilian Spanish across Mexico, Central America, South America, and the Caribbean cannot clearly demarcate persons who may become categorized as people of Latin American descent in the United States.

Gracia is also concerned with the relationship between racial and ethnic identities, and argues that Latinx identity is not a racial identity. If race is meant to pick out members of a group who share specific physical features or a common genealogy, then Latinxs do not neatly fit this category either. He writes in this regard:

> Many of the people who are called Hispanic belong to different races. What would be the characteristics of a Hispanic race? Even the Iberian Peninsula itself, or even within what we know today as Spain, there is no uniformity of looks or physical make-up. There are even physiological differences between some Iberian groups (for example, the blood profile of Basques is different from that of other Iberians in some important respects). The inhabitants of the Iberian Peninsula are perhaps one of the most mixed people in Europe. Apart from the Celts, Iberians, Basques, Greeks, Phoenicians, Carthaginians, Berbers, Romans, Vandels, Suebi, and Visigoths, the peninsula had a large infusion of Moors beginning in the eighth century and of Jews at various points in its history, and descendants of Amerindians have often moved

to it and lived and mixed with other members of the population. Indeed, there are even Africans, Indians (from India), and Asians who have settled (voluntarily or by force) in Iberia at various times, and who have mixed with the population in Spain and Portugal.[4]

Gracia aims to demonstrate that descent from the Iberian Peninsula does not entail a single set of morphological features that might be categorized in racial terms. Accordingly, countries, cultures, and languages in the Americas that descend from the Iberian Peninsula fail to fall into any specific racial categories.

Gracia also points out that genetic lineage is similarly problematic because it leads to a circular argument. He writes: "If I am Hispanic because I can trace my lineage to my grandparents, what makes them Hispanics?" (*HLI*, 13). Unless there is some prior criterion of membership that determines who is or is not properly considered a member of the group, then there remains no good reason to support genetic lineage as a way of conceiving Latinx identity.

More generally, then, Gracia is largely critical of the idea that Latinxs should be considered members of racial groups, and he thereby turns to the question of whether they share an ethnic identity. For Gracia, to qualify as an ethnic identity, at least four conditions could be proposed:

1   There must be a social group (individual persons by themselves are not ethnic unless they belong to an ethnic group).
2   The group must have distinct and identifiable cultural or social traits.
3   The cultural and social traits that distinguish the group must come from outside the country where the group resides.
4   Those traits must be considered alien to those accepted as mainstream in the country of residence. (*HLI*, 41)

According to these criteria, Gracia concludes, however, that Hispanics/ Latinxs in the United States do not constitute an ethnic group. Many Latinxs residing in the U.S. Southwest do not meet conditions (2) and (4) since they are not alien to the territory in which they reside. As the Chicanx saying goes, "we did not cross the border, the border crossed us." Conversely, since all Anglo Americans are immigrants, they would be considered a unified ethnic group. As these conclusions are deeply counterintuitive, Gracia rejects the (2)–(4) of the above account, and argues that a conception of ethnicity need not rely directly on national boundaries. The current political occupations of indigenous territories in what is now North America (i.e., the continued occupation of indigenous territories by Canada, the United States, and Mexico) need not determine what constitutes an ethnic identity. Rather, Gracia seeks a conception of identity that captures the complicated histories of migration, the drawing of political boundaries, and the specific practices of communities to shape the contours of ethnicity.

One danger with using ethnic labels, Gracia argues, is that they may dangerously and inaccurately homogenize groups of diverse peoples (*HLI*, 45). Thus, his proposal for identifying Hispanics as an ethnic group is to pay particular attention to three aspects of identification that avoid pernicious forms of homogenization and inaccuracy:

1   those who do the naming and set the concomitantly required conditions;
2   the positive or negative character of those conditions; and
3   the breadth and rigidity with which the conditions are understood. (*HLI*, 45)

Gracia defends the first consideration because "to adopt a name and define one's identity is both a sign of power and an act of empowerment" (*HLI*, 46). How one is situated vis-à-vis others determines the resources and forms of authority that are necessary for one to name oneself or others. Gracia also claims that adopting a name and defining oneself is "an act of empowerment because it limits the power of others to name and identify us" (*HLI*, 46). Citing the Judeo-Christian conception of the divine, he writes: "Indeed, it is not surprising that Yahweh ('I am who I am') is the name God chose for himself in the Bible" (*HLI*, 46), since Yahweh, conceived as the supremely authoritative being, has the ultimate power to delimit itself. Conversely, if a person requests to be referred to by a particular name and no one respects their wishes, then that person has been marginalized or denied a minimal amount of autonomy or authority.

Additionally, Gracia states that whether a specific name bears harmful or beneficial connotations is important. This is relevant to keep in mind regarding how and whether a particular ethnic group name supports the peoples it intends to categorize. Gracia proposes that, in cases of empowering practices of self-naming, a number of groups can find ways to develop new forms of shared meaning and connection that often exceed the derogatory connotations that previous terms may have. For example, Gracia notes that the term "Jew" previously carried negative connotations for Jewish people, yet due to the intentional use and revaluation of the term by members of the Jewish community, this term now "has become a sign of power and pride" (*HLI*, 46).

Lastly, for Gracia, whether a term is broadly used to refer to a group or whether the meaning of a term is rigidly controlled are also relevant factors regarding how practices of defining ethnicity occur. For example, consider the possibility that "Latinx" refers *only* to persons of Latin American descent who speak Spanish. This criterion would exclude a number of non-Spanish speaking persons of Latin American descent, and additionally, one might ask *how* one would have to speak Spanish in order to be considered "Latinx" on this account. If the criterion is rigidly enforced, then many people who have never received a formal education in Castilian Spanish would be excluded. Along similar lines, forms of exclusionary and rigid linguistic categorizations prompted Chicanx essayist and poet Gloria E. Anzaldúa to explore identity through the use of hybrid, non-standard languages. Drawing from her experiences growing up on the Texas-Mexico border, she writes:

> For a people who are neither Spanish nor live in a country in which Spanish is the first language; for a people who live in a country in which English is the reigning tongue but who are not Anglo; for a people who cannot entirely identify with either standard (formal, Castilian) Spanish nor standard English, what recourse is left to them but to create their own language? A language which they can connect their identity to, one capable of communicating the realities and values true to themselves—a language with terms that are neither *español ni inglés*, but both. We speak a patois, a forked tongue, a variation of two languages.[5]

Anzaldúa's emphasis and revaluation of hybrid, patois languages such as *Pachuco*, Tex-Mex, and other variations of Spanish and English demonstrates her rejection of rigid forms of linguistic identification for Chicanxs.[6] She writes that because Chicanxs are "a complex and heterogeneous people, we speak many languages" (*B*, 77). In this vein, Anzaldúa's work expands Gracia's third point regarding the potential breadth and rigidity of a given condition for inclusion within an ethnic identity category, including, for example, as linguistic conditions for inclusion. Namely, if the conditions are too narrow, people may bear the brunt of exclusion and denigration. Gracia's own work thereby attempts to preserve the breadth and heterogeneity of Hispanic identities by drawing from the varied and rich histories of persons of Latin American descent.

Gracia's central argument for the use of "Hispanic" represents a "familial-historical" approach (*HLI*, 50). Drawing, in part, from the work of Austrian philosopher Ludwig Wittgenstein, Gracia argues that terms like "Hispanic" must name some common underlying property of members of a group. However, rather than assuming that some property unifies or subsists among members of a given group, a family-resemblance model draws from the historical relationships between members of a given group. He writes:

> [M]y thesis is that the concept of Hispanic should be understood historically, that is, as a concept that involves historical relations. Hispanics are the group of people comprised of the inhabitants of the countries of the Iberian Peninsula after 1492 and what were to become the colonies of those countries after the encounter between Iberia and America took place, and by descendants of these people who live in other countries (e.g. the United States) but preserve some link to those people. (*HLI*, 28)

Moreover, the historical relations to which he refers do not require members of the group to identify themselves as "Hispanic." He states:

> Some of them may in fact consider themselves Hispanic and even have a consciousness of their identity as a group, but it is not necessary that all of them do. Knowledge does not determine being. What ties them together, and separates them from others, is history and the particular events of that history rather than the consciousness of that history; a unique web of changing historical relations supplies their unity. (*HLI*, 49)

The family resemblance model, then, serves to capture those "changing historical relations." Like a family, Hispanic identity is formed by historically situated relationships among members, including legal relationships, genetic relationships, financial relationships, relationships whereby members share living arrangements, and so on. On this view, no one feature unites all and only members of a family or Hispanic identity, and their borders are often shifting and flexible. That is, while there may be genetic, legal, financial, and geographic relationships, no one of these features unifies all members who may be considered Hispanic.

Instead, Gracia claims that 1492, the beginning of the conquest of the Americas by Iberian colonizers (*HLI*, 50–51), is the starting point for the formation of "Hispanics" as a group. Accordingly, the historical events that follow are those that unite persons by their relationship to this event. He writes:

> [M]y proposal is to adopt 'Hispanic' to refer to us: the people of Iberia, Latin America, and some segments of the population in the United States, after 1492, and to the descendants of these peoples anywhere in the world as long as they preserve close ties to them. (*HLI*, 52)

Thus, Gracia might consider Latinxs an ethnic group that is best characterized by their relationships to the history of the Iberian Peninsula and the conquest of the Americas, and, moreover, to the social, genetic, and cultural ties that relate persons living in Latin America, the United States, and elsewhere in the world who retain relationships to those historical events. As such, Gracia provides an account of identity for Latin American descended peoples that attempts to preserve the complexity, heterogeneity, and diversity of the group. Moreover, his account attempts to track the metaphysical question regarding what is said to be "true" or "false" regarding this complex group identity.

Despite the many virtues of Gracia's account, other facets of his account might give us pause. Notably, the stakes of what it feels like to be identified in one way rather than another seem to slip out of view. Moreover, Gracia's approach does not appear to engage directly with how structural oppressions might shape or impact forms of self- and other- identification. For an account that takes up these concerns specifically, let us now turn to the work of Linda Martín Alcoff (Panamanian American).

In her paper "Is Latina/o Identity a Racial Identity?" Alcoff considers whether Latino identity is a racial identity. She frames her concern specifically with the "experience, ideology, and meaning" of identity rather than whether the category of analysis under question bears a strict logical relation to truth/falsity.[7] Recall that Gracia wants to resist homogenization and conceptual inaccuracy, and he argues that one is Hispanic whether or not one identifies as such. While Alcoff also wants to resist homogenization, she attends particularly to the lived experience of Latinxs, the way identity is socially constructed, and she remains committed to analyzing the material consequences that result from how we identify and are identified.

With respect to race and Latinx identity, in particular, she claims "we simply don't fit." Agreeing with Gracia, she argues that race in the United States has long been thought to refer to groups that share relatively homogeneous, visible identifying features that result from biological inheritance (*LRI*, 24). Given that persons who descend from various parts of Latin America do not share any such racialized, biological features, this description of race will not work for this group. That is, Latinxs can have a number of racialized identities that include Black, white, Asian, Indigenous, or any mixture of these racial categories. Even within a given national boundary there is no racial unity that picks out one specific racialized set of features that distinguishes the dominant race in one country from that of another. For example, both Cuban Americans and Puerto Ricans share a wide variety of racialized features.

Alcoff also points out that racial identities often change based on where one is. While anti-Black and anti-Indigenous racisms persist in different forms across the Americas, there are differences in how people are categorized racially across the Caribbean, and North, Central, and South America. For example, official documents may ask about race or not, people may use different terms for different racial categories, and the histories of legal framings of race often differ significantly. She writes:

> [T]hese differences are why many of us find our identity as well as our social status changing when we step off the plane or cross the river: race suddenly becomes an all-important aspect of our identity, and sometimes our racial identity dramatically changes in ways over which it feels as if we have no control. (*LRI*, 24)

The argument that Alcoff eventually proposes suggests that we think of Latinx identity as an ethnic identity. However, as we will see, given what she describes as the "racial realities" of people living in the United States, she also claims that ethnicity is not sufficient to capture the experience of Latinxs in the U.S. Namely, given the persistent forms of racial oppression that mark the lives of people of color, including, for example, state surveillance and policing, patterned employment, interpersonal, and housing discrimination, and forms of epistemic injustice (i.e. denials of credibility or

knowledge based on assumptions about one's competence or reliability),
Alcoff argues that ethnicity is not able to clearly show how these forms of
harm operate. Before directly discussing race, however, let's explore her
defense of a conception of ethnicity.

The first argument in favor of ethnicity is that it points to the shared *cultural* features of Latinx identity, such as language, political histories, religious
traditions, institutional structures, etc., which have given rise to unique forms
of ethnic identities across Latin America, and which cannot be subsumed
under any one racial paradigm. For example, Afro-Cubans, English-speaking
West Indians, and Afro-Brazilians are all considered "Black" in the United
States, but this racial designation overlooks the significant cultural differences
that separate these groups of people, including most obviously, that they do
not share a primary language. In order to capture the plurality of peoples of
Latin America and the Caribbean, some might prefer ethnic designations over
racial ones. Secondly, another argument in favor of the ethnicity paradigm
draws from the function of the term "African American" as an ethnic label,
rather than a racial one. For example, Jesse Jackson's campaign to use the
term "African American" rather than "Black" may set a useful precedent for
Latinxs. The hope here is that ethnic labels can bring more specificity to the
shared practices and historical circumstances of a given group. Third, Alcoff
examines whether identifying as an ethnic group may reduce the harmful
patterns of discrimination and systemic disadvantage caused by racism. The
goal here is to promote the positive cultural and historical contributions and
historical ties of ethnic groups, such as African Americans, by referring to
their significant cultural contributions and avoiding the negative stigmas
associated with racial categories. Finally, with regard to the metaphysics of
group identity, echoing Gracia, Alcoff claims that "ethnicity more accurately
identifies what really holds groups together and how they self-identify, and
ethnicity is simply closer to the truth of Latina/o identity, given its racial
heterogeneity" (*LRI*, 36).

Yet, despite these compelling arguments, Alcoff does not conceive of
Latinx identity *solely* as an ethnic identity, since, despite efforts to the contrary, "perceived racial identity often does trump ethnic or cultural identity"
(*LRI*, 37). To elaborate this point, she discusses the history of Cuban
migration to the United States. While a number of Cuban Americans have
enjoyed a measure of economic and political success in the U.S., there are
significant ways in which Afro-Cubans, as opposed to white or light-skinned
Cubans, have fared quite differently:

> [O]ne cannot argue … that Cubans' strong ethnic identification is the
> main reason for their success; most important has been their ability to
> play an ideological (and at times military) role for the United States in the
> cold war. The enormous government assistances provided to the Cubans
> who fled the Cuban Revolution [largely in the 1960s] was simply unpre-
> cedented in U.S. immigration history: they received language training,

educational and business loans, job placement assistance, and housing allocations, and their professional degrees from Cuban institutions were legally recognized to an extent other Third World immigrants still envy ... The Cubans who came in the 1960s were overwhelmingly white or light-skinned. They were generally from the top strata of Cuban society. It is an interesting question whether Haitians would ever have been treated the same way. The Cubans who left Cuba after 1980, known as the Marielitos, were from lower strata of Cuban society, and a large number were Afro-Cubans and mulattos. These Cubans found a decidedly colder welcome. They were left penned in refugee camps for months on end, and those who were not sent back to Cuba were released into U. S. society with little or no assistances, joining the labor ranks at the level of Puerto Ricans and Dominicans. (*LRI*, 36)

Part of what this example illustrates is that race often plays a significant role in the United States, especially in terms of political and economic success. As such, while Afro-Cuban persons might self-identify as Cuban American in the United States, this identification does not change the material obstacles that the Marielitos or other Afro-Latinx communities confront in the United States.[8]

In the end, Alcoff argues that the category "Latina/o often operates as a racialized category" (*LRI*, 27). That is, unlike Irish Americans and Jews, who were able to transition from essentialist and racialized forms of identification to ethnic identities, many ethnic groups continue to confront obstacles to deracializing their identities, including the fact that "race, unlike ethnicity, has historically worked through visible markers on the body that trump dress, speech, and cultural practices" (*LRI*, 38). Thus, even though an Afro-Cuban person speaks Spanish, was largely educated in Cuba, and engages in religious and cultural traditions of Cuba, this person will nevertheless likely be categorized as "Black" in the United States. This form of racial categorization effectively erases ethnic differences among people of African descent, regardless of culture or geographical differences. She proposes that perceptual practices of labeling and categorizing people by race tends to dominate identification practices in the United States. For ethnic groups of Anglo-European descent, this means, however, that while they may be racialized as white, they are often thought to be capable of retaining an ethnic identity. Thus, Jewish Americans and Irish Americans, for example, are now prominent *ethnic* labels for people racialized as white.

Further, there are also political obstacles to shifting from a model of race to a model of ethnicity for many people of color. Alcoff states:

[A]ssertions of group solidarity among African Americans, Native Americans, and Latinas/os in the United States provoke resistance among many whites because they invoke the history of colonialism, slavery, and genocide. Thus, their acceptances as full players within U.S. society comes at much greater cost than the acceptance of previously vilified groups such as the Irish and Jews—groups that suffered terrible discrimination and violence including genocide but whose history is not a thorn in the side of "pilgrim's progress," "manifest destiny," "leader of the free world," and other such mythic narratives that legitimize U.S. world dominance and provide white Americans with a strong sense of pride. (*LRI*, 39)

Dominant U.S. narratives of the state, including the nation's aspirations toward democratic ideals such as freedom and equality, are called into question when we recall the unjust, immoral, and continuous forms of systemic discrimination, violence, and marginalization that Native Americans, African Americans, and Latinxs experience. Notably, the "systemic" nature of these harms stems from the long histories of abuse that these groups have experienced at the hands of peoples of Anglo-European descent. With respect to Latinxs, in particular, patterns of U.S. military, political, and economic interventionism mark the landscapes of Latin America and the Caribbean (see chapter 2). In addition, Latinxs in the U.S. South and Southwest have also suffered a number of forms of racial violence, segregation, and disenfranchisement. Today, many recent Latin American migrants across the country continue to face daily harassment, political vilification, and discrimination.

In response to these negative aspects of racial categories, a number of authors and activists have also proposed positive forms of racial identification by reclaiming, for instance, Blackness as an important social and political reality of persons living in the U.S. Citing the work of Paul Gilroy, Alcoff states:

For Gilroy, there is a "blackness" that transcends and survives the differences of U.K., Caribbean, and U.S. nationalities, a blackness that can be seen in culture and narrative focus. Blackness is a social location, shared history, and a shared perception about the world. (*LRI*, 40)

While this approach, Alcoff proposes, works well for revaluations of Blackness, she doubts whether such an approach could work for Latinxs and notes that Gilroy's work does not address Black Latinx communities, leaving this question unresolved in his own work.

Given the inability to overcome the reality of race, Alcoff suggests instead that a concept introduced by David Theo Goldberg, "ethnorace," may be more productive. She writes:

Ethnorace might have the advantage of bringing into play the elements of both human agency and subjectivity involved in ethnicity—that is, an identity that is the product of self-creation—at the same time that it acknowledges the uncontrolled racializing aspects associated with the visible body. And the term would remind us that there are at least two concepts, rather than one, that are vitally necessary to the understanding of Latina/o identity in the United States: ethnicity and race. (*LRI*, 42)

Accordingly, ethnorace also captures the fact that some Latinxs who appear phenotypically white will likely not experience the same degrees of racialized violence and marginalization as those appearing more indigenous, Black, Arab, Asian, or mixed. While ethnicity by itself does not capture the historical and everyday forms of visible identifications that are used to systemically advantage or disadvantage particular groups, race by itself homogenizes Latinxs and suggests that visible features such as hair color and texture, skin color, and face shape somehow tell us something about a person or group's culture, which they do not. As such, ethnorace seems particularly helpful in our effort to capture the complexity of self- and other-given forms of identification that impact group identities.

We will return to the race/ethnicity debate at the close of this chapter. For now, let's focus on related philosophical aspect of Latinx identity, namely, the multiplicitous nature of identity, which includes race, ethnicity, gender, sexuality, class, religion, age, ability/disability, and so on.

The Debate Regarding "*el género*-gender"

For many, our lives are often intertwined with confusing, painful, complicated, and sometimes enlivening experiences regarding the facets of our bodies and selves that seem to cut across dominant differences. Perhaps, as María Lugones describes, you are one of the "green-eyed Blacks, never-been-taught-my-culture Asian Americans, émigrés, immigrants and migrants, mixed-bloods and mixed-cultures, solid core, community bred, folk of color" who are her audience for her analysis of self-perception and structural racism/colonialism.[9] Or perhaps you are what Gloria Anzaldúa describes as "una de las otras" (*one of the others*) one who is "a mestiza queer person [who has and lives] in a lot of worlds, some of which overlap."[10] Lugones and Anzaldúa, along with a number of other U.S. Latinx and Chicanx feminist theorists such as Norma Alarcón, Jacqueline Martínez, Cherríe Moraga, Paula Moya, Emma Pérez, Laura Pérez, Mariana Ortega, and Ofelia Schutte, are among the U.S. Latina authors in the 1980s, 1990s, and 2000s who have engaged in a series of rich discussions regarding the plurality of identity and the overlapping forms of social and political power that shape our lives. Notably, these theorists, often drawing from their own socio-political circumstances, articulate the tense, conflicting, and yet sometimes productive relationships in their own embodied identities. For example, Ofelia Schutte (Cuban American) notes in *Cultural Identity and Social Liberation in Latin American Thought* that while her analysis is not focused on Cuba, her interests in cultural identity stem from her reflections on her own identity as Cuban and the political history of Cuba.[11] Likewise,

Mariana Ortega writes in *In-Between: Latina Feminist Phenomenology, Multiplicity, and the Self* that the Nicaraguan revolution of 1979 significantly impacted her life and philosophical interests. In this vein, analyses of lived experience are common across much U.S. Latinx and Chicanx feminist theory.

Building on the previous discussion regarding Latinx identity as a racial/ethnic identity, a number of authors have examined the relationship between race, ethnicity, and gender, in particular. As such, this section of the chapter examines a few arguments regarding gender as a facet of identity. Notably, a number of authors in the United States have adopted a conception of gender to articulate their positionality (one's social location) as bearing significant political, cultural, and embodied content. For instance, Chicana author Gloria Anzaldúa writes of the forms of sexual and intimate partner violence that many women of color experience (*B*, 34–35), and links this violence to the patterns of gender-based violence that women have experienced due to colonial conquest and imperial expansion (*B*, 44). As early as 1981, Anzaldúa used the category of gender to analyze the power relations that shaped her experiences as a Chicana.

However, as Schutte and María Luisa Femenías have argued, the use of "gender" within the context of Latin America is significantly different from how it has been used among U.S. feminist movements, and they describe why some Latin Americans have resisted using gender as a category of analysis.[12] For instance, they state that many Latin American feminist social movements in the 1960s used terms like "patriarchy" (*patriarcado*) and "capitalist patriarchy" (*patriarcado capitalista*) to name the "socioeconomic and ideological conditions legitimating the power of men and of male-dominant institutions over women."[13] The use of these specific terms, they argue, named power and economic relations that the more general term "gender" overlooks or renders invisible.

In fact, it was not until the 1990s that the term *género*, as in *los estudios de género* (gender studies) and *el enfoque de género* (gender focus) came to prominence. But even here feminist critics pointed out that it was being euphemistically. That is, by using gender as a category of analysis, theorists and policy analysts risked losing the more radical connotations associated with a term like capitalist patriarchy, which referred to systemic harms. In this vein, Francesca Gargallo (Italian-Mexican) writes:

> At the beginning of the nineties, they [feminists in Latin America] launched the transition from feminism of social activism to feminism of public policy within the realm of national and international institutions: fighting for quotas in the parties, women's councils, participation in the activities of the United Nations, obtaining offices for women's affairs in the majority of Latin American nations.[14]

The concept of gender, Gargallo argues, served significant purposes during this period of transition. Gargallo traces the work of Latin American feminists such as Eli Bartra (Mexico), Norma Mogrovejo (Peru), Margarita Pisano (Chile), Amalia Fischer (Brazil), and Urania Ungo (Panama) to chart the criticism and political stakes of using a term such as *género*, rather than naming women, women's specific contributions, or the systems of hierarchical power that violate and marginalize women in the Global South.

Another concern raised by feminist critics of this period was that the Spanish term *género* did not carry the same connotations in Spanish as it did in English. The term *"género"* in Spanish, Femenías and Schutte write, "usually meant 'species' or 'kind' (as in *'el género humano,'* humankind), or, if referring to masculine/feminine differences, its domain was grammar (gendered nouns, pronouns, and adjectives)."[15] In this sense, gender as a category of analysis may be considered an imposition and a tactic from Anglo-dominant spaces to depoliticize the efforts of feminist critics in Latin America. (As I suggest in the third section, we find interesting parallels between this debate and those of contemporary critics of the term "Latinx.") Since the use of gender is meant to be more neutral and universal, it has the potential of erasing the specificity of the positionalities of women, the constructive work undertaken by women, and of dislocating the concreteness of feminist engagement.

Lastly, regarding critical discourses of gender, the work of María Lugones (Argentine) has been groundbreaking in this vein. Her 2007 article "Heterosexualism and the Colonial/Modern Gender System," has sparked a series of conversations in Anglophone and Hispanophone feminist communities regarding the desire to universalize the notion of gender. Drawing specifically from Nigerian feminist scholar Oyèrónké Oyèwùmí, Laguna Pueblo feminist scholar Paula Gunn Allen, and Peruvian Marxist sociologist Aníbal Quijano, Lugones argues that the binary gender system of man-woman is a product of modern/colonial Eurocentrism. By examining the structures of pre-conquest indigenous social and kinship relations, she argues that a binary gender system, including the reproductive labor associated with women, is a facet of colonial violence. Within this organizing structure, she states:

> Beginning with the colonization of the Americas and the Caribbean, a hierarchical, dichotomous distinction between human and non-human was imposed on the colonized in the service of Western man. It was accompanied by other dichotomous hierarchical distinctions, among them that between men and women. This distinction became a mark of the human and a mark of civilization. Only the civilized are men or women. Indigenous peoples of the Americas and enslaved Africans were classified as not human in species—as animals, uncontrollably sexual and wild. The European, bourgeois, colonial, modern man became a subject/agent, fit for rule, for public life and ruling, a being of civilization, heterosexual, Christian, a being of mind and reason. The European bourgeois woman was not understood as his complement, but as someone who reproduced race and capital through her sexual purity,

passivity, and being home-bound in the service of the white, European, bourgeois man. The imposition of these dichotomous hierarchies became woven into the historicity of relations, including intimate relations.[16]

Lugones traces the Eurocentric conception of being a "modern" and "civilized" human being as importantly connected to relations of power between colonized peoples and colonizing nation-states. Namely, colonizers were invested in marking and utilizing gender categories such as "man" and "woman" as an exercise of colonial power. One facet of the "civilizing mission," she argues, is to replace and transform the desires, embodiments, labor roles, and societal structures of colonized and enslaved peoples to reproduce the gender norms of the Western world. To combat this, Lugones turns to the work of Aymaran, Yoruban, and Cherokee cosmologies, which cannot be reduced to the Eurocentric binary of man-woman. Moreover, her call to future scholarship on the modern/colonial gender system is to continue to find those points of rupture and inadequacy among colonized and enslaved peoples who have challenged the impositions of a binary Eurocentric framing. Such a move, she proposes, highlights the "historicity of the oppressing ⟵⟶ resisting relation and thus [emphasizes] concrete, lived resistances to the coloniality of gender."[17] As such, European forms of domination, including gender domination, can be considered neither totalizing nor complete.[18]

Accordingly, Lugones's work, as well as that of Schutte, Femenías, Gargallo, and a number of other feminist scholars, indicates the limitations of the use of gender as a category of analysis. In the following section, we conclude by turning to a recent debate regarding further categories of analysis impacting Latinxs that raise philosophical questions regarding identity.

The Debate Regarding "Latinx-Latino/a"

The term "Latinx" began being used on social media, academic publications, and in popular online newspapers in the mid-2010s. The term has circulated across queer, transgender, and non-binary communities to offer a gender-neutral term for people of Latin American descent. While a number of people advocating for the term see the shift away from binary-gendered terms like "Latina" or "Latino" as a positive step toward recognizing and affirming the identities of transgender, non-binary, and genderqueer Latinxs, critics of the term consider its use an imposition and a problematic shift away from common orthographic features of the Castilian Spanish language. Regarding this debate, Catalina M. de Onís conducted interviews with five Latina/o/x scholars. Throughout the interview, we see several proponents of the term stating that:

[T]he use of the "x" goes beyond the issue of gender because it attempts to be inclusive of all those who identify as part of the super diverse

Latinx population and to embrace our uniqueness within the Latinx community. This includes gender, sexual preferences, and transnationality, among many others.[19]

In addition, another proponent states that "Latinx" can be a kind of "reclamation of all kinds of erasure. By using the 'x' we expose erasure and refuse it at the same time" (X, 86). Accordingly, one unifying thread among these views is the opening of linguistic and interpretive space within Latin American-descended communities through the use of the term.

Other proponents of the term point to the importance of the use and pronunciation of terms with the letter "x" in Nahautl, an indigenous language of Mesoamerica. The "x" in words like "Xicana" (pronounced CHEE- or SHEE-cana) have been defended along similar lines. For example, Cherríe Moraga writes, "Throughout this text, I spell Xicana and Xicano (Chicana and Chicano) with an X (the Nahuatl spelling of the 'ch' sound) to indicate a re-emerging política, especially among young people, grounded in Indigenous American belief systems and identities."[20] For Moraga and others, the linguistic shift to integrate Nahuatl sounds and graphemes represents an attempt to practice and emphasize the communicative pluralism that many peoples descended from various geopolitical contexts of the Americas experience. Moreover, her emphasis on indigeneity becomes a "política," a politics, that seeks to reject Eurocentric and Anglocentric linguistic norms, including naming practices for oneself and others.

Yet, critics of "Xicana/o" or "Xicanx" point out that Nahuatl was an alphabetic language imposed on Mexica (often called "Aztec") peoples during conquest. Notably, Nahuatl became used to represent, in a linear and phonetic fashion, the complex pictographs that constituted pre-conquest forms of story-telling, record-keeping, and the writing of history. One critic, Dominick Ortiz writes that terms like "Xicanx" simply refer back to a colonially imposed alphabetic language, and, thus, do not honor indigenous roots.[21]

Other critics argue that terms like "Latinx" impose constraints on Spanish-dominant audiences, and thus serve as a further layer of imperial expansion that should be resisted by Latin American communities. In this vein, one interviewee, Eric César Morales, writes:

Using "x" and "lxs" in Spanish is extensively difficult, for while they seem manageable when written, in pronunciation they read more as "ex" and "lexes." Try saying the phrase, "Mis amigexes en Indiana son lexes Latinexes." The use of "x" interrupts one of the beautiful things about language—that its speakers give it a natural flow. This might sound like a minor issue to bilingual individuals established in the United States, but when Spanish is the only language a person speaks and they're already operating on the margins of society in this country, it's clear that "Latinx" was not meant to be inclusive of their spoken realities ... The "x" termination is not about inclusivity but about making a public and political statement, which comes at the cost of further marginalizing recent immigrants who are increasingly vulnerable in this country. (X, 84–86)

As such, Morales offers another reason to reject the claim that the use of terms like "Latinx" actually further support efforts to critique Euro- and Anglocentrism.

In response to some of these concerns, people defending the use of "Latinx" and "Xicanx" reject forms of linguistic purity that seek to find modes of engagement that are "untouched" by colonial and imperial history and continuing domination. Rather, echoing Roy Pérez, "Language offers ... fluidity and we should take advantage of it" by seeking ways to honor the multiplicity, plurality, and lived experiences of Latin Americans and Latin American-descended peoples today, including our ongoing struggles with imperialism, assimilation, and the harms of colonialism (X, 11).

Pilar Melero, defending the term, also states that the term "Latinx" is not meant to serve as an imposition on others. Rather, she writes regarding Morales' claims:

> This [view] assumes all recent immigrants reject the use of the term, and it even implies that they are all heteronormative. On the contrary, I believe new immigrants, like other people, will make their own decisions on the use of the term, depending on their own socio-cultural background and identity needs. However, I think the option of having a gender-neutral pronoun liberates those immigrants who belong to non-gender conforming communities and feel the need to identify as gender-queer. I think the point is not should we use the x or not, but let it be an option. *El uso o desuso de la palabra va a dictar su futuro* [Whether or not the word is used will determine its future]. (X, 87, italics added)

Melero's point is that "Latinx" may serve as a form of play or a way to augment linguistic practices among Latin American-descended communities in Anglo-dominant spaces. As such, the benefits for creating conceptual space for gender non-conforming, trans, and non-binary people of Latin American descent should remain a significant concern, and if the term "Latinx" is able to help support such efforts, then it ought to remain among the available options for naming and theorizing about the diverse groups of peoples that comprise the geopolitical sites of Latin America. Moreover, as several of the other interviewees state, within Hispanophone contexts, the ending -e may also serve as a useful practice that affirms and includes transgender, non-binary, and gender nonconforming peoples. For example, "Elle está cansade" can be used instead of "Ella está cansada/Él está cansado."[22]

From this charged set of concerns, we can glean that there are notable parallels between the cautions by 1990s feminists in Latin America about forms of political dominance that may stem from the use of the term *género*. Notably, the interviewee above who challenges the use of "Latinx" appears to be concerned that the term "Latinx" is a political move among English-dominant speakers to control and regulate the aesthetic and political features of how the Spanish language is spoken, read, and used.

Yet, if we examine the history of the term *género* across differing sites in Latin America, rather than serving as merely a severe form of depoliticization or censure, as Schutte notes, we actually see a much broader set of responses from within feminist social organizing and academic writing in Latin America. Schutte states that there are roughly four senses of género:

1   *género* as a strictly logical category marking the distinction between women and men as conventionally accepted by various societies ...

2   *género* as a collective term useful for speaking about women of about issues concerning women ...

3   *género* as a designator of elements of group identities or kindred relations among women, useful for speaking about women or women's issues from an involved standpoint ...

4   *género* as a power-laden concept used to regulate the sexual identities of women and men.[23]

In this vein, Schutte's work on the *género*-gender debate indicates explicit ways in which the term has traveled across different sites of analysis and critique, and has created a variety of interpretative lenses for feminist theory in Latin America. Along similar lines, Sandra L. Soto-Santiago, another interviewee in the M. de Onís piece states:

> Communication and how we engage in it is an everyday practice and that cannot be predetermined by any group because it is an organic process that is ongoing. I also believe that the untranslatability of the term ["Latinx"] is what makes it more empowering. It does not seek to create a new rule but rather to dismantle what exists and invites us to re-think how individuals with different ideologies, perspectives, and identities are included or rejected from different spaces or communities through language. (X, 91)

The point here echoes the multiplicity of ways in which a term of identification, critique, or analysis becomes part of our ongoing processes of contestation and meaning-making. Thus, the political or moral value of a given term cannot be delineated in advance.

Claudia de Lima Costa (Brazilian) also proposes that the uses and abuses of terms like "*género*" and "gender" must remain open to analysis and critique, despite their multiplicity. Sharing in a critical vein of scholarship against the universalizing tendency to frame gender as a primary tool of analysis, Lima Costa notes that identities are never fixed, and that we must theorize them as "physical and discursive spaces structured by the operations of power."[24] Within Latina feminism, conceptions of the continued nature of struggle, the plurality of the experiential lives of Latin American-descended peoples, and the ongoing interpretive processes that allow us to make sense of our worlds are all hallmarks of U.S. Latinx philosophy.

We can thus find a core trajectory among the theorists we have explored in this chapter. Namely, Latinx identities are neither stable nor uncontested sites of philosophical investigation. Because they strike at the core of our lived experiences, often serving as the places from which we speak, think, write, and act, identities are a crucial site of Latinx and Latin American philosophy. While we have only reviewed a few questions in this chapter, our hope is that these discussions encourage further study, analysis, and exploration into what our identities are, what they ought to be, and why they continue to matter to us.

Notes

1 For important work on these themes, see these sources from Latin American and U.S. Latinx philosophy: Barvosa, *Wealth of Selves*; Blackwell, Boj Lopez, and Urrieta, "Critical Latinx Indigeneities"; Cisneros "'Alien' Sexuality"; Martí, *José Martí Reader*; Martinez, *Phenomenology of Chicana Experience and Identity*; Méndez, "Notes Toward a Decolonial Feminist Methodology"; Mendoza, *The Moral and Political Philosophy of Immigration*; Ortega, *In-Between*; Paccacerqua, "Gloria Anzaldúa's Affective Logic of Volverse Una"; Pérez, *The Decolonial Imaginary*; Rivera Berruz, "Extending into Space"; Rodó, *Ariel*; Ruíz, "Linguistic Alterity and the Multiplicitous Self"; Velásquez, "States of Violence and the Right to Exclude"; Zea, *The Latin-American Mind*.

2 See, for example, Gracia, "Frondizi's Theory of the Self as a Dynamic Gestalt."

3 Note that I will be using the terms "Hispanic," "Latina/o," and "Latinx" somewhat interchangeably in this section. While there are a number of debates regarding the origins and differences between these terms, some of which I address in the chapter, for now I will simply use them to stand in for another. In some places, I do so to preserve an author's specific language (e.g. Gracia explicitly chooses to use the term "Hispanic"), in other places, I refer to the general category of "Latinxs" to refer to Latin American descended peoples.

4 Gracia, *Hispanic/Latino Identity*, 11–12. Cited in text using the abbreviation *HLI* and page number.

5 Anzaldúa, *Borderlands*, 77. Cited in text using the abbreviation *B* and page number.

6 Given that the term had not become popularized during her lifetime, Anzaldúa did not use the term "Chicanx" in her writings.

7 Alcoff, "Is Latina/o a Racial Identity," 23. Cited in text using abbreviation *LRI* and page number.

8 "The Marielitos" is a term given to the roughly 125,000 migrants traveling by boat from the Mariel harbor in Cuba to the United States in 1980.

9 Lugones, *Pilgrimages*, 151.

10 Anzaldúa, *Gloria Anzaldúa Reader*, 141.

11 Schutte, *Cultural Identity and Social Liberation*, 1.

12 Schutte and Fermenías, "Feminist Philosophy," 403.
13 Ibid., 403.
14 Gargallo, "Multiple Feminisms," 83.
15 Schutte and Fermenías, "Feminist Philosophy," 404.
16 Lugones, "Toward a Decolonial Feminism," 743.
17 Ibid., 748.
18 The oppressing ←—→ resisting relation in Lugones's work refers to her conception of subjectivity. Namely, rather than assuming that persons or groups are either wholly resistant subjects or wholly complicit subject to forms of domination, the oppressing ←—→ resisting relationship marks the tensions within individuals and collectivities between structures of subjugation and patterns of liberatory responses to structural harms. Moreover, resistance and oppression are processes, not properties or features that someone or some group holds/maintains.
19 De Onís, "What's in an 'x'?", 85. Cited in text using abbreviation *X* and page number.
20 Moraga, *Xicana Codex of Changing Consciousness*, xxi.
21 Ortiz, "Why You Might Want to Stop Using the Terms 'Xicana'."
22 For more on this discussion, see Diz Pico, "Le últime jedi y otros usos del neutro"; Alvarez Melledo, "Todas, tod@s, todxs, todes."
23 Schutte, "Latin America," 91.
24 Lima Costa, "Unthinking Gender," 182.

Bibliography

Alcoff, Linda Martín. "Is Latina/o a Racial Identity?" In *Hispanics/Latinos in the United States: Ethnicity, Race, and Rights*, edited by Jorge J.E. Gracia and Pablo de Greiff. New York: Routledge, 2000.

Alvarez Melledo, Elena. "Todas, tod@s, todxs, todes: historia de la disidencia gramatical." *El Diario* (June 27, 2017). Accessed April 25, 2018. https://www.eldiario.es/zonacritica/Todas-todes-historia-disidencia-gramatical_6_659044117.html

Anzaldúa, Gloria. "La Prieta." In *This Bridge Called My Back: Writings by Radical Women of Color*, edited by Cherríe Moraga and Gloria Anzaldúa. New York: Kitchen Table Press, 1983 [1981].

Anzaldúa, Gloria. *Borderlands/La frontera: The New Mestiza*. 2nd edition. San Francisco: Aunt Lute Press, 1987.

Anzaldúa, Gloria. *The Gloria Anzaldúa Reader*. Edited by AnaLouise Keating. Durham: Duke University Press, 2009.

Barvosa, Edwina. *Wealth of Selves: Multiple Identities, Mestiza Consciousness, and the Subject of Politics*. College Station: Texas A&M Press, 2008.

Blackwell, Maylei, Floridalma Boj Lopez, and LuisUrrietaJr. "Special Issue: Critical Latinx Indigeneities." *Latino Studies* 15, no. 2(2017): 126–137.

Bolívar, Simón. *El Libertador: Writings of Simón Bolívar*. Translated by Frederick H. Fornoff. Edited by David Bushnell. New York: Oxford University Press, 2003.

Cisneros, Natalie. "'Alien' Sexuality: Race, Maternity, and Citizenship." *Hypatia* 28, no. 2(2013): 290–306.

De Onís, Catalina (Kathleen) M. "What's in an 'x'?: An Exchange about the Politics of 'Latinx.'" *Chiricú Journal: Latina/o Literatures, Arts, and Cultures*, 1, no. 2 (2017), 78–91.

Diz Pico, Jorge. 2017. "Le últime jedi y otros usos del neutro." *Medium.com* (June 26, 2017). Accessed April 25, 2018. https://medium.com/el-rat%C3%B3n-ciego/le-%C3%BAltime-jedi-y-otros-usos-del-neutro-ae0b491c68bc

Gargallo, Francesca. "Multiple Feminisms: Feminist Ideas and Practices in Latin America." In *Feminist Philosophy in Latin America and Spain*, edited by María Luisa Femenías and Amy Oliver. New York: Rodopi, 2007.

Gracia, Jorge J.E. "Frondizi's Theory of the Self as a Dynamic Gestalt." *The Personalist* 57 (1976): 64–71.

Gracia, Jorge J.E. *Hispanic/Latino Identity: A Philosophical Perspective*. Malden. MA: Blackwell, 2000.

Lima Costa, Claudia de. "Unthinking Gender: The Traffic in Theory of the Americas." In *Feminist Philosophy in Latin America and Spain*, edited by María Luisa Femenías and Amy A. Oliver. New York: Rodopi, 2007.

Lugones, María. *Pilgrimages/Peregrinajes: Theorizing Coalition Against Multiple Oppressions*. Albany: SUNY Press, 2003.

Lugones, María. "Heterosexualism and the Colonial/Modern Gender System." *Hypatia: A Journal of Feminist Philosophy* 22, no. 1(2007): 186–219.

Lugones, María. "Toward a Decolonial Feminism." *Hypatia: A Journal of Feminist Philosophy* 25, no. 4(2010): 742–759.

Martí, José. *José Martí Reader: Writings on the Americas*. Edited by Deborah Scnookal and Mirta Muñiz. Melbourne: Ocean Press, 2007.

Martinez, Jacqueline M. *Phenomenology of Chicana Experience and Identity: Communication and Transformation in Praxis*. Lanham: Rowman & Littlefield, 2000.

Méndez, Xhercis. "Notes Toward a Decolonial Feminist Methodology: Revisiting the Race/Gender Matrix." *Trans-Scripts* 5(2015): 41–59.

Mendoza, José Jorge. *The Moral and Political Philosophy of Immigration: Liberty, Security, and Equality*. Lanham: Lexington Books, 2016.

Moraga, Cherríe. *A Xicana Codex of Changing Consciousness: Writings 2000–2010*. Durham: Duke University Press, 2011.

Paccacerqua, Cynthia. "Gloria Anzaldúa's Affective Logic of Volverse Una." *Hypatia* 31, no.2(2016): 334–351.

Pérez, Emma. *The Decolonial Imaginary: Writing Chicanas into History*. Bloomington: Indiana University Press, 1999.

Ortega, Mariana. *In-Between: Latina Feminist Phenomenology, Multiplicity, and the Self*. Albany: SUNY Press, 2016.

Ortiz, Dominick. "Why You Might Want to Stop Using the Terms 'Xicana,' 'Xicano' and 'Xicanx.'" *LatinoRebels.com* (February 9, 2018). Accessed July 25, 2018: http://www.latinorebels.com/2018/02/09/why-you-might-want-to-stop-using-the-terms-xicana-xicano-and-xicanx-opinion/

Rivera Berruz, Stephanie. "Extending into Space: The Materiality of Language and the Arrival of the Latina/o Bodies." *Inter-American Journal of Philosophy* 5, no. 1 (2014): 24–43.

Rodó, José Enrique. *Ariel*. Translated by Margaret Sayers Peden. Austin: University of Texas Press, 1988.

Ruíz, Elena. "Linguistic Alterity and the Multiplicitous Self: Critical Phenomenologies in Latina Feminist Thought." *Hypatia* 31, no.2(2016): 421–436.

Schutte, Ofelia. *Cultural Identity and Social Liberation in Latin American Thought*. Albany: SUNY Press, 1993.

Schutte, Ofelia. "Latin America." In *Companion to Feminist Philosophy*, edited by Alison M. Jaggar and Iris Marion Young. Malden: Wiley-Blackwell, 1998.

Schutte, Ofelia, and María Luisa Femenías. "Feminist Philosophy." In *A Companion to Latin American Philosophy*, edited by S. Nuccetelli, O. Schutte, and O. Bueno. Oxford, UK: Wiley-Blackwell, 2009.

Vallega, Alejandro Arturo. *Latin American Philosophy from Identity to Radical Exteriority*. Bloomington: Indiana University Press, 2014.

Velásquez, Ernesto Rosen. "States of Violence and the Right to Exclude." *Journal of Poverty* 21, no. 4(2017): 310–330.

Zea, Leopoldo. *The Latin-American Mind*. Translated by James H. Abbott and Lowell Dunham. Norman: University of Oklahoma Press, 1963.

12 Metaphilosophy

Defining Latin American and Latinx Philosophy

Lori Gallegos de Castillo and Francisco Gallegos

Introduction

Some of the central questions that have been explored by Latin American and Latinx philosophers are questions of *metaphilosophy*. "Metaphilosophy" refers to philosophical reflections on the nature of philosophy itself. For example, we might ask: What is the purpose of doing philosophy? How does philosophy compare and contrast with other disciplines, such as science, theology, or literature? And what is the best way of categorizing the different kinds and traditions of philosophy? These are philosophical questions about philosophy as an activity and as a discipline.

In this chapter, we discuss some ways that Latin American and Latinx philosophers have addressed these and other metaphilosophical issues. Our focus will be on the following questions: *What are the defining characteristics of "Latin American philosophy" and "Latinx philosophy"? Do they constitute distinctive traditions of philosophy, and if so, what is especially valuable about these traditions?* In the first section, we begin by examining the views of philosophers who are skeptical of Latin American philosophy. Many of these writers argue that the philosophy that has been produced in Latin America is not original or authentic enough to constitute a distinctive philosophical tradition that can stand alongside other, more established traditions of philosophy, such as ancient Greek philosophy and European philosophy. In the second section, we examine the opposing views of those who defend Latin American philosophy as an original, authentic, and distinctively valuable tradition of thought. In the final section, we turn to similar questions that have been raised about the nature of Latinx philosophy.

As we will see, metaphilosophical writings on the nature of Latin American and Latinx philosophy shed light on a number of other issues, such as Latin American and Latinx identity and the legacy of colonialism. And the inquiry is not over: Latin American and Latinx philosophy are alive today and continue to evolve, even as we speak of them. Thus, this chapter does not aim to provide any definitive answers to these questions. Instead, we hope that this chapter will help to orient, challenge, and inspire philosophers to reflect on—and even participate in shaping—the future of Latin American and Latinx philosophy.

The Questions of Originality and Authenticity

Let us begin with a metaphilosophical examination of Latin American philosophy. Our central question here is: *What are the defining characteristics of Latin American philosophy?* One way that Latin American philosophers have addressed this question is to examine the philosophy that has been produced by Latin American thinkers and try to identify common characteristics of this philosophy that are *original* and *authentic*. In other words, they have broken this question down into two more specific questions:

- *The Question of Originality*—When we look at the philosophy produced in Latin America, what, if anything, can be identified that is significantly different from what can be found in other philosophical traditions?
- *The Question of Authenticity*—When we look at the philosophy produced in Latin America, what, if anything, can be identified that is distinctively Latin American—i.e., an organic expression of the unique life-experiences, concerns, styles, and perspectives of the people of Latin America?

The Questions of Originality and Authenticity are usually framed by comparing the philosophy produced in Latin America to the philosophy produced in Europe and, more recently, the U.S. In this way, these questions reflect a worry that some Latin American philosophers have shared: Is the philosophy that has been produced in Latin America merely an imitation of European or Anglo-American philosophy?

The Skeptics

A Provocative Challenge for Latin American Philosophers

Writing in the 1920s, a century after the Peruvian War of Independence from Spain, the Peruvian philosopher José Carlos Mariátegui hoped that Latin American philosophy would develop into a world-renowned philosophical tradition.[1] However, Mariátegui worried that excessive optimism about the challenges faced by Latin America would make Latin Americans complacent. In order to inspire his fellow Latin American philosophers to work hard to live up to their potential, Mariátegui articulated the Questions of Originality and Authenticity in a deliberately provocative and challenging way. He asked: Does a Latin American tradition of philosophy *even exist*?

In his 1924 essay "Is There Such a Thing as Hispanic-American Thought?" Mariátegui warns that it would be premature to claim that a distinctive tradition of thought had developed in Latin America. The reason, he argues, is that in spite of the political independence from Europe that had been achieved in Latin America and elsewhere, Europe still had a pervasive and profound influence on Latin American philosophy. He explains:

> The existence in Western culture of French thought, of German thought, seems evident to me. The existence of Hispanic-American thought in the same sense does not seem equally evident. All the thinkers of our America have been educated in European schools. The spirit of the race is not felt in their work. The continent's intellectual production lacks its own characteristics. It does not have an original profile. Hispanic-American thought is generally only a rhapsody composed from the motifs and elements of European thought.[2]

Over forty years later, a similarly skeptical view of Latin American philosophy was deployed by fellow Peruvian philosopher Augusto Salazar Bondy. In his essay "The Meaning and Problem of Hispanic American Thought" (1969), Salazar Bondy chronicles European influence over the course of Latin America's intellectual history:

> [W]hat we find in all our countries is a succession of imported doctrines, a procession of systems which follows European, or, in general, foreign unrest. It is almost a succession of intellectual fashions without roots in our spiritual life and, for this very reason, lacking the virtue of fertility ... For this reason these systems were abandoned as quickly and easily as they were embraced, having been chosen by the upper class and the intellectual sectors of Hispanic Americans according to their immediate preferences and momentary affinities. To review the process of Hispanic American philosophy is to relate the passing of Western philosophy *through* our countries, or to narrate European philosophy *in* Hispanic America. It is not to tell the history of a natural philosophy *of* Hispanic America. In our historical process there are Cartesians, Krausists, Spencerians, Bergsonians, and other European "*isms.*" But this is all; there are no creative figures to found and nurture their own peculiar tradition, nor native philosophic "*isms.*" We search for the original contributions of our countries in answer to the Western challenge—or to that of other cultures—and we do not find it.[3]

Salazar Bondy concludes that in the philosophy that has been produced in Latin America, there is an absence of an original and authentic *style* of philosophical inquiry—or as he puts it, an "[a]*bsence of a characteristic, definitive tendency*, and of an ideological, conceptual proclivity capable of founding a tradition of thought" (*MP*, 388).

The lack of originality and authenticity that characterizes Latin American philosophy, Salazar Bondy argues, is a result of the fact that Latin American philosophers have been alienated from the rest of their communities.

There has existed permanently in Hispanic America a great distance between those who practice philosophy and the whole of the community. There is no way to consider our philosophies of national thought, with a differential seal, as one speaks of a German, French, English, or Greek philosophy. It is almost impossible for the community to recognize itself in these philosophies, precisely because we are dealing with transplanted thought, the spiritual products of other men and other cultures, which a refined minority makes an effort to understand and to share. (*MP*, 389)

From his perspective, philosophical works must represent the communities out of which they emerge if they are to be authentic. People should recognize themselves—their own history, struggles, and concerns—when they read these works. Instead, Salazar Bondy finds that there is a gulf between the philosophy that is being produced by a small number of elites in Latin America and the vast majority of people who live there. In his words:

The distance between those who practice philosophy and the community at large is in this case—unlike the normal relationship between the specialist and the public—the abyss between the enlightened elite who live according to a foreign model, and the illiterate, poverty-stricken masses, trapped in the framework of remote and sclerotic traditions. (*MP*, 396)

Thus, according to Salazar Bondy, philosophy throughout the history of Latin America has not emerged from the lived experience of Latin American people but, rather, has been transplanted from another culture. As he puts it, "It has been a plagiarized novel and not the truthful chronicle of our human adventure" (*MP*, 392).

Deeper Connections between Philosophy, Culture, and Colonization

If this skeptical view of Latin American philosophy is correct, we might wonder: Why would philosophers in Latin America have drawn from European philosophy so heavily, rather than seeking inspiration in the perspectives and insights within their own communities?

In answer to this question, Mariátegui argues that although Latin American countries had achieved political independence from European colonizers, Latin American people were still culturally subordinate to Europe and had yet to achieve an independent sense of identity. In his view, the blending of races—European and indigenous—that occurred in the Americas during the process of colonization had not succeeded in creating a people with a "new soul."[4] Instead, Mariátegui argues that, in most Latin American countries, the elite have sought to adopt European ways of thinking and living, while the people and elements of culture that are more closely associated with indigeneity have been denied the highest levels of political and cultural expression. Thus, in his assessment, "The elements of our nation-ality in formation have not yet been fused or welded."[5] In order for there to be a characteristically Latin American tradition of philosophy, he argues, there needs to be distinctive Latin American peoples, and such a people has not yet emerged.

Like Mariátegui before him, Salazar Bondy contends that the reason that Latin American philosophy has not authentically reflected Latin American culture is that, in fact, there is no authentic Latin American culture. He writes:

> A defective and illusory philosophic conscience causes one to suspect the existence of a defective and unauthentic social being, the lack of a cul-ture in the strong and proper sense of the term ... This is the case in Hispanic America. (*MP*, 394–395)

Salazar Bondy adds that, in his view, the reason that Latin America does not have an authentic culture is that colonialism and economic dependence have inhibited its proper development. He explains, "As dependents of Spain, England, or the United States, we have been and continue to be under-developed—if I may use the expression—*under* these powers, and, conse-quently, countries with a *culture of domination*" (*MP* 395).

In spite of these findings, both Mariátegui and Salazar Bondy held out hope that philosophy in Latin America would become original and authentic in the future. According to Salazar Bondy, however, this will only be possi-ble if Latin American philosophers focus on their distinctive circumstances:

> Philosophy in Hispanic America has a possibility of being authentic in the midst of the unauthenticity that surrounds and consumes it, and to convert itself into the lucid awareness of this condition and into the thought capable of unleashing the process to overcome it. It must be a meditation *about* our anthropological status and *from* our own negative status, with a view to its cancellation. (*MP* 397)

In other words, Salazar Bondy argues that in order to be authentic, Latin American philosophy will need to consist of reflections about the unique social, historical, and political circumstances in Latin America, with the aim of elim-inating the negative conditions that have kept Latin American people from achieving an authentic existence. In fact, he says, philosophy could actually be a site in which the people of Latin America transcend their condition of sub-ordination and begin to imagine new ways of living. As he puts it:

> Being the focus of man's total awareness, [philosophy] could, better than other spiritual creations, be that part of humanity that rises above itself, and overcomes the negativity of the present as it moves toward new and superior forms of reality. (*MP*, 397)

In this way, Salazar Bondy hopes that the formation of an authentic Latin American philosophical tradition—together with greater economic independence in the region—could provide an essential impetus for the emergence of an authentic Latin American culture.

Two Related Metaphilosophical Questions

As we have seen, it would be a mistake to assume that those who are skeptical of the originality and authenticity of Latin American philosophy are merely naysayers seeking to diminish the accomplishments of others. Instead, skeptics like Mariátegui and Salazar Bondy are motivated by a sincere belief in the greater potential of Latin American philosophy and culture, and in the course of presenting their provocative analyses they develop some creative and thought-provoking views of their own on topics such as the connections between philosophy, culture, and colonization.

Let us highlight two other areas in which those who raise doubts about Latin American philosophy have made significant philosophical contributions. The first area concerns the question of how philosophy itself should be defined. This issue was addressed by the Argentine philosopher Risieri Frondizi in his 1949 essay, "Is There an Ibero-American Philosophy?" Frondizi begins this essay by putting forward a skeptical view of Latin American philosophy, saying, "Up to the present, Ibero-American philosophy is simply the rethinking of the European problems that have reached our shores."[6] This view should be familiar to us by now (for a related discussion of Frondizi's essay, see chapter 5). But in the course of supporting his conclusion, Frondizi takes a different route, and he encounters a fascinating and difficult question of metaphilosophy, which we can call the Question of Form and Purpose.

• *The Question of Form and Purpose*—Is the purpose of philosophical writing different from the purpose of other kinds of writing, such as poetry and literature? If so, should philosophical writing take on a distinctive form that is suited to its distinctive purpose?

The way we answer the Question of Form and Purpose will influence how we answer the Questions of Originality and Authenticity. After all, Latin American *literature* is widely admired as being both original and authentic, and at least some of this literature addresses philosophical issues in insightful ways. For example, the Argentine author Jorge Luis Borges (1899–1986) wrote short stories and poems that take up positions held by well-known philosophers throughout history and suggest novel approaches to traditional philosophical questions about topics such as the nature of time, infinity, memory, writing, and religion. The same could be said of many other Latin Americans whose writings are philosophical but do not fit the traditional Western philosophical mold. Thus, if this sort of writing counts as genuine philosophy, then this gives us reason to conclude that an original and authentic tradition of Latin American philosophy already exists.

Frondizi argues, however, that we ought to make a sharp distinction between philosophy and poetry, literature, political speeches, and other non-philosophical forms. Genuine philosophy, he says, is presented in a way that prioritizes philosophical concerns. Thus, philosophy aims for clarity of argumentation and analysis, while, in contrast, the writings of poets, novelists, and statesmen are shaped by other concerns and goals, such as creating beauty, telling a good story, or nation-building. As Frondizi puts it:

> It is undeniable that the works of [the Latin American authors] Sarmiento, Bello, or Martí—to mention three great examples—contain philosophical ideas. But such ideas appear as a result of literary or political concerns to which they remain subordinated. In none of them does philosophy have an independent status; none of them set forth philosophical problems motivated by philosophical interests. We are, of course, not reproaching them for this; their work fills us with satisfaction and admiration … We only wish to point out what seems an undeniable fact: that philosophy has been subordinated to non-philosophical interests.[7]

After making this sharp distinction between philosophy and non-philosophy—and thus setting aside the work of any Latin American writer who does not write in a traditional philosophical form, regardless of how creative or insightful it may be—Frondizi concludes that Latin American philosophy lacks both originality and authenticity.

Frondizi's answer to the Question of Form and Purpose may not persuade everyone; indeed, we will examine some opposing views shortly. But by clearly articulating this question and showing its connection to the larger questions about the defining characteristics of Latin American philosophy, Frondizi's article makes an important contribution to the ongoing conversation about the relationship of philosophy to other disciplines of thought.

Another, related area in which skeptics of Latin American philosophy have made positive philosophical contributions concerns a question about how to understand what sort of activity philosophizing is supposed to be and what philosophy can hope to achieve. We can call this the Question of Universality.

• *The Question of Universality* — Is philosophy best understood as the search for absolute truths which are valid for all people at all times? If so, then what sense does it make to talk about the philosophy of a cultural group, e.g. the philosophy of Latin America?

The Question of Universality has been of interest to philosophers for centuries in both Latin America and Europe. One scholar to pose this question as it relates to Latin American philosophy is U.S. philosopher Vicente Medina. In his 1992 article, "The Possibility of an Indigenous Philosophy: A Latin American Perspective," Medina defends a *universalist* view of philosophy, arguing that philosophy seeks to discover universal truths. He thus rejects the *historicist* view that philosophy is best understood as the articulation of the various worldviews of individuals and cultures throughout history. The upshot of Medina's argument in favor of universalism is that the skeptics are correct that there is no such thing as Latin American philosophy. The reason is that, in his view, philosophy is, in all cases, universal, and so philosophizing is not inherently tied in any way to a particular society, culture, or historical situation.

To better understand what is at stake in the debate between the universalist and the historicist, let us compare philosophy to two other activities—mathematics and cooking. According to the historicist, philosophy is like cooking, insofar as both activities tend to reflect the historical and cultural context of practitioners. For example, Mexican cuisine is shaped by the unique foods that are grown in Mexico, as well as the distinctive culinary techniques, styles, and tastes of Mexican culture across time. Likewise, the historicist argues, we should expect Latin American philosophy to reflect the distinctive features of the historical and cultural context of Latin American philosophers.

According to universalists like Medina, however, philosophy is more like mathematics. Mathematics is a universal language that allows those who speak it to transcend their concrete, historical situation. After all, "2+2=4" is equally true in all cultures and all times, and such mathematical truths do not seem to reflect the historical or cultural position of the mathematicians who discover them. From this perspective, there is no such thing as *Latin American mathematics*, because Latin American mathematicians cannot put their own distinctive spin on mathematical truths like "2+2=4." Likewise, Medina argues that philosophy seeks to discover principles—such as the laws of logic—that are transcultural and objective, and which any person can recognize to be true.

According to Medina, when Plato argues for his theory of the state, or Descartes offers his theory of knowledge, these philosophers are seeking to articulate universal truths.[8] Indeed, all genuinely philosophical activity, he says, involves presenting arguments and defending them with reasons that are, in principle, accessible to anyone, and which we can understand and evaluate without knowledge of the philosopher's cultural context. Accordingly, Medina describes his view of philosophy this way:

> One may partly understand by the nature of philosophical inquiry the activity of being critical and thus argumentative. This means that philosophers present arguments and defend them with reasons. These reasons are universally open to inspection to anyone who wants to assess them. Both reasons and arguments may be assessed according to the principles of sound reasoning: coherence, clarity, and the weight of evidence.[9]

On this basis, Medina presses a critique of historicism. He argues that if the historicist believes that philosophy merely aims to discover *relative* (not absolute) *truths*—i.e., basic principles that are valid only within a particular historical and cultural context—then this relativism is self-contradictory: One cannot both advocate for the value of a relativist position in universalist terms while rejecting universalism as the ultimate arbiter of truth. As he puts it, if historicists were to defend their view of philosophy against the universalist view:

> [T]hey would be compelled to appeal at least to some nonarbitrary principle of adjudication in order to establish their point. But if this were to be the case, then they would actually be supporting, instead of undermining, my argument in favor of [universalism] ... Either they abide by the principles of sound reasoning ... and, therefore, provide ammunition for my argument against their ... position. Or they give up the principles of sound reasoning and, therefore, give up the notion of reasonable argumentation altogether.[10]

Again, while Medina's argument may not persuade everyone, it certainly enriches the ongoing discussion about the nature of philosophy—and presents a serious challenge for those who would like to defend the existence of Latin American tradition of philosophical thought.

A Deflated Conception of Latin American Philosophy

In light of the skeptical views we have considered, we may wonder whether it is fruitless to search for characteristics that make the Latin American philosophical tradition different from other traditions and authentic to the unique circumstances of the Latin American community. Perhaps this idea of an original and authentic tradition of Latin American philosophy is "inflated" and overly idealistic. If so, then maybe the best way to define this tradition is simply to say: Latin American philosophy is *the philosophy that has been produced in Latin America.*

This "deflated" view of Latin American philosophy is defended by the U.S. philosopher Jorge J.E. Gracia. According to Gracia, Latin American philosophy is simply the philosophy of the Latin American *ethnos*—that is, the philosophy produced by people of Latin American decent.[11] If Gracia is correct that Latin American philosophy should be defined simply in terms of the ethnic group that produces it, then we should not expect there to be any particular view, perspective, or style that characterizes this tradition. An ethnic group, Gracia says, is like an enormous extended family, and just as with any family, there may not be any particular features that all members share. In a similar way, Gracia argues, we should not expect to find anything more than a relatively vague "family resemblance" that unites the work of

Latin American philosophers (compare to Gracia's view of Hispanic identity, as discussed in the previous chapter).

> My view does not identify what characterizes Latin American philoso-
> phers because Latin American philosophers, just like the members of my
> family, have no property that characterizes all of them at all times and
> places, even if they have all sorts of properties that characterize some of
> them at some times or places. Indeed, consider such examples as Las
> Casas, Sor Juana, Mariátegui, Ingenieros, and Frondizi. Many efforts
> have been undertaken to find such common properties, and so far they
> have failed. In my view, this search should be abandoned because it is
> based on a misunderstanding of the familial-historical character of
> ethne and their cultural products.[12]

Gracia's deflated conception of Latin American philosophy may be appealing to those who are skeptical regarding our ability to identify characteristics of the Latin American philosophical tradition that are original and authentic. Gracia's view highlights the diversity of Latin American philosophers, who, while sharing aspects of a common cultural background, have a wide variety of views and approaches to philosophy. This kind of skepticism about Latin American philosophy is not "negative" or destructive but, rather, is grounded in a celebration of the diversity of Latin American philosophy, which makes it impossible to characterize the work of Latin American philosophers in any simplistic way—as original *or* unoriginal, authentic *or* inauthentic.

The Defenders

In the previous section, we examined the work of philosophers who doubt that the philosophy that has been produced in Latin American constitutes an original and authentic philosophical tradition. We saw that in the course of making their arguments, these skeptics identified several fascinating metaphilosophical questions regarding philosophy's relationship to truth, history, culture, and other disciplines of thought. In this section, we examine some ways that these same questions have been addressed by philosophers who believe that, contrary to what the skeptics claim, there *does* exist a distinctive Latin American tradition of philosophy that is both original and authentic.

As we will see, each of these philosophers are put in a position in which they must reflect critically on why the existence of Latin American philosophy was called into question in the first place. We might even say that these philosophers are forced to engage in "meta-metaphilosophy"—that is, philosophical inquiry about why certain metaphilosophical questions about the nature of philosophy in general, and Latin American philosophy in particular, have appeared to be important or vexing to so many philosophers. In this way, defenders of Latin American philosophy try to reclaim the meta-philosophical debate over the existence of Latin American philosophy as constituting a distinctive line of inquiry that, ironically, actually *contributes* to the originality and authenticity of the Latin American philosophical tradition.

Liberation as the Central Concern of the Tradition

U.S. philosopher Ofelia Schutte argued in 1987 that a distinctively Latin American tradition of philosophy exists, and that this tradition consists of "philosophical studies addressing issues of significance to Latin America's social, cultural, and political history and identity."[13] In particular, she says, Latin American philosophy is characterized by a concern for freedom from oppression, a concern that reflects Latin America's history of struggle with colonial and post-colonial domination.

> [T]here is one primary reality pervading the thought of every Latin American philosopher. This is the issue of dependence and independence. Latin America is not just a different part of the world relative to Europe and North America; it is a dependent part of the world. Moreover, dependence—in terms of power—is translatable into subordination. So while the Latin American philosopher "thinks being" historically in terms of historical being, the structure of the historical situation meeting human reflection is one of vulnerability seeking strength, of dependence striving for freedom from domination. (*LAP*, 25)

Schutte argues that when we look at the work of Latin American philosophers within this framework, it becomes possible "to unite a plurality of perspectives and methods which otherwise might not appear to be interrelated" (*LAP*, 26)—and to see this unity as an authentic expression of the Latin American experience.

In fact, Schutte argues, the failure to perceive the common concern for freedom from oppression that underlies and unites so much of Latin American philosophy reflects a Eurocentric bias and a kind of "colonial reasoning." For example, she says, consider three prominent schools of thought in Latin America: "the theology of liberation, the secular theories of human rights, and the various forms of Marxism found in Latin America today" (*LAP*, 26). If we do not see these schools as unified in their underlying concern for liberation from oppression, they would appear to be "three separate schools of thought, each deriving its philosophical status from its origins outside Latin America" (*LAP*, 26). She continues:

> Liberation theology would be traced back to the theology of Roman Catholicism, human rights theory would be traced to the Enlightenment, and Marxist theories to European, or more recently, Soviet and

Chinese versions of Marxism. In other words, each theory would be judged only as a reflection or copy of something originating outside the continent. But from the standpoint I am ... employing, we can see how these three different and distinct schools of thought, modified by certain historical realities in Latin America, lead to a new unified theory of value according to the common element they all address: namely, the question of the historical and cultural interrelationship of Latin America to the rest of the world, the issue of dependence and independence of Latin America vis-à-vis the rest of the world. (*LAP*, 26)

Schutte adds that many of the most prominent Latin American philosophers address the distinctive ways that conflicts surrounding Latin American identity have shaped the struggle for independence in the region. For example, she says, what we see when we look at the work of the Mexican philosopher Octavio Paz, the Caribbean philosopher Frantz Fanon, or the Argentine philosopher Andrés Roig, is this:

[V]ariations on the theme of how to free oneself from the heritage of inequality and exploitation originating with the Conquest and colonialism. Despite almost five hundred years of assimilation into Western European tradition, many Latin Americans still feel the conflict provoked by the *conquistadores'* subjugation and extermination of millions of Indians who dwelt in the region. The Indians have come to symbolize the ancient, exploited, maternal heritage of the Americas, in contradistinction to the technologically advanced, civilized, foreign conqueror. How to resolve this tension in an unalienated and authentic manner is one of the challenges of Latin American philosophy today. (*LAP*, 27)

From this perspective, even the work of skeptics like Mariátegui and Salazar Bondy—who worry that Latin American philosophy is derivative of European or Anglo-American philosophy—reflect a struggle to achieve independence and an "unalienated" identity, a struggle that Schutte argues is a distinctive feature of Latin American philosophy. If this is correct, then, ironically, the skeptics' worry about the inauthenticity of Latin American culture is itself an authentic expression of the life-experiences, concerns, and perspectives of the Latin American community.

A Defense of Historicism

One of the most notable thinkers to make a case for the existence of an original and authentic Latin American philosophical tradition was the Mexican philosopher Leopoldo Zea. In his 1948 article, "The Actual Function of Philosophy in Latin America," Zea offers an especially insightful analysis of the Question of Universality.

In his article, Zea defends a historicist view of philosophy against the universalist view. In his defense of historicism, Zea acknowledges that philosophy often engages with abstract questions that are universal, in the sense that every person and culture must address them. However, he insists that Latin American philosophers can offer their own distinctive perspective on these universal issues, a perspective grounded in their distinctive life-experiences.

> Among such issues are those of being, knowledge, space, time, God, life, death, etc. A Latin American philosophy can collaborate with Western culture by attempting to resolve the problems posed by the issues that European philosophy has not been able to resolve, or to which it has failed to find a satisfactory solution ... The abstract issues will have to be seen from the Latin American man's own circumstance. Each man will see in such issues what is closest to his own circumstance. He will look at these issues from the standpoint of his own interests, and those interests will be determined by his way of life, his abilities and inabilities, in a word, by his own circumstance. In the case of Latin America, his contribution to the philosophy of such issues will be permeated by the Latin American circumstance. Hence, when we [Latin Americans] address abstract issues, we shall formulate them as issues of our own. Even though being, God, etc., are issues appropriate for every man, the solution to them will be given from a Latin American standpoint. We may not say what these issues mean for every man, but we can say what they mean for us Latin Americans. Being, God, death, etc., would be what these abstractions mean for us.[14]

In this passage, Zea argues that all philosophy represents—consciously or unconsciously—the particular historical circumstances of the philosopher. Thus, in his view, all works of Latin American philosophers will express the their own particular concerns, perspective, and style of thinking: "The Latin American element will be present in spite of our philosophers' attempts at objectivity. It will be present despite our thinkers' attempt to depersonalize it" (*FPLA*, 365).

Zea adds that because Latin American philosophy has been relatively marginalized within the discipline, it contains untapped philosophical resources that could become the source of new life for the discipline, and indeed, for Western culture as a whole. If so, then Latin American philosophers have an opportunity—and perhaps a responsibility—to help shape the future of both philosophy and world history.

> From this we can infer yet another goal for a possible Latin American philosophy. The Western culture of which we are children and heirs needs new values on which to rest. These new values will have to be derived from new human experiences, that is, from the experiences that

result from men being in the new circumstances of today. Because of its particular situation, Latin America can contribute to culture with the novelty of untapped experiences. That is why it is necessary that it tell its truth to the world. But it must be a truth without pretensions, a sincere truth. Latin America should not pretend to be the director of Western culture; what it must aspire to do is to produce culture purely and simply. And that can be accomplished by attempting to resolve the problems that are posed to the Latin American man by his own Latin American perspective. (*FPLA*, 367)

Zea suggests, for example, that Latin American philosophers are well situated to contribute to our philosophical understanding of how to resolve the tension between human individuality and sociality.

Latin American philosophy must begin the task of searching for the values that will provide the basis for a future type of culture. And this task will be carried out with the purpose of safekeeping the human essence: that which makes a man a man. Now, man is essentially an individual who is at the same time engaged in interaction with others, and hence it is necessary to maintain a balance between these two components of his essence. This is the balance that has been upset to the point of leading man to extremes: individualism to the point of anarchy, and social existence to the point of massification. Hence it is imperative to find values that make social interaction possible without detriment to individuality. (*FPLA*, 367–368)

In this article, Zea does not clarify how he envisions Latin American philosophers contributing to this particular philosophical line of inquiry, but taken as a whole, his work suggests that when Latin American philosophers set out to address universal questions, they will start with the challenges posed by the historical legacy of colonization and conquest that characterizes Latin American history, and for this reason, they will be in a unique position to offer original and authentic insights into these universal philosophical questions. For example, when addressing the tension between the individual and society, Latin American philosophers will be in a position to interpret this issue in terms of economic, political, and cultural relations of dependence and independence. In this way, they can offer a distinctive, politically oriented perspective on longstanding philosophical concerns.

Opening the Borders of the Discipline

In her essay "Is 'Latin American Thought' Philosophy?" U.S. philosopher Susana Nuccetelli takes up each of the metaphilosophical questions we have discussed in order to defend the claim that the existing body of works by Latin American philosophers is, indeed, part of a distinctive philosophical tradition. To help to settle the issue, Nuccetelli proposes some basic criteria that she hopes both sides can agree on:

A philosophical work is *characteristically* Latin American if and only if:

1   it offers original philosophical arguments, and
2   it shows that its philosophical topics are in part determined by the relation its proponent bears to social and/or historical factors in Latin America.[15]

Criterion (1) is that of originality, and criterion (2) is what Nuccetelli calls "sensitivity to the environment," or what we might think of as a concern with authenticity. If we accept these criteria, Nuccetelli claims, then we find a robust body of philosophical work—including works by Mariátegui, Martí, and Sarmiento, as well as the 16th century Spanish historian and Dominican friar Bartolomé de Las Casas (chapter 2), self-taught scholar and poet Sor Juana Inés de la Cruz (chapter 8), the Venezuelan political leader Simón Bolívar (chapter 3), and the Uruguayan essayist Enrique Rodó, to name a few—who each score high in both criteria.

However, Nuccetelli does not stop there. In her view, many more authors should be included in the tradition of Latin American philosophy, even though they did not write in standard philosophical prose (for a related discussion, see chapter 8). Nuccetelli thus takes up the Question of Form and Purpose.

Recall Frondizi's argument that many of the great works in Latin America do not count as philosophy because the thought contained within these works is subordinated to non-philosophical interests, such as literary or political concerns. In response, Nuccetelli offers a kind of argument known as a *reductio ad absurdum*—a kind of argument which aims to show that a certain premise leads to an absurd conclusion. She argues that if we accept Frondizi's criterion of form and purpose, then much of what we currently consider to be canonical works of philosophy in the West would be excluded.

> Note that, if applied consistently, it yields startling consequences, for then we should have to exclude from philosophy the works of Thomas Hobbes, Saint-Simon, Jeremy Bentham, John Stuart Mill, Karl Marx, Jean-Paul Sartre, John Rawls and many others! These works, after all, contain philosophical ideas that are clearly subordinated to their authors' social, political, and literary interests—and so would not qualify as philosophy according to [Frondizi's criterion]. On the other hand, Latin American thinkers … who gave hardly any thought to philosophical issues arising locally in the reality of their own societies but devoted themselves instead to alien problems and methods, making no

significant contribution to them, would count as philosophers ... Surely something has gone wrong here. (*LAT*, 533)

Nuccetelli adds that Frondizi's criterion would exclude not only these canonical works of philosophy, but also "most of what is done today in the flourishing areas of applied philosophy" (*LAT*, 533–534).

With this in mind, Nuccetelli concludes that the distinction between "Latin American thought" and "Latin American philosophy" is artificial and ought to be rejected.

The distinction between philosophical thought and strict philosophy, therefore, seems to be an unhelpful contrivance that is better rejected. It doesn't really matter whether Sor Juana's proclamation of women's right to knowledge, Acosta's rebellion against Aristotelian science, Mariátegui's "indigenous question," and so on are classified as either philosophy or philosophical thought, since it is difficult to see how anything of importance could hinge on that distinction. In fact, many of the major figures I have mentioned here are not by any stretch of the imagination philosophers as they are conceived of today. But it is clear that these figures had ideas that are philosophically interesting and were often quite astute in their insights related to these ideas even where they did not argue rigorously, as philosophers are expected to do now. (*LAT*, 534)

Ultimately, Nuccetelli finds that if we expand our conception of philosophy, then it is even more obvious that Latin American Philosophy is an original and authentic tradition of philosophy that can stand proudly alongside other philosophical traditions.

Decolonial Critique and U.S. Academic Philosophy

In the first section of this chapter, we examined the writings of several Latin American scholars who raised the question of whether Latin American philosophy exists. This same question continues to be raised in U.S. today, but in the U.S. context, the meaning of the question is typically quite different.[16] When Mariátegui and Salazar Bondy raised the question, they were concerned with whether philosophical thought in Latin American reflected the people of Latin America in an original and authentic way. They were identifying the lack of a distinctive philosophy as one of the devastating impacts of colonialism and neocolonialism in Latin America, and their skepticism about Latin American philosophy was motivated by a desire to encourage the development of Latin American philosophy and the flourishing of Latin America as a whole.

In the U.S., however, the question of whether there is such a thing as Latin American philosophy often arises from obliviousness about the philosophical work that has been produced in Latin America and incredulity that it could exist. A philosopher raising this question in the U.S. might wonder: If Latin American philosophy existed, would I not have learned about it as an undergraduate student? Would Latin American philosophy not be included in textbooks on the history of philosophy? Would there not be at least one specialist in Latin American philosophy in most philosophy departments? If Latin American philosophy existed, would it not be a part of the philosophical canon in the United States? In other words, when U.S. philosophers ask whether there is Latin American philosophy, the question often has to do with determining whether any Latin American philosophy actually lives up to U.S. standards.

Skepticism about the existence of Latin American philosophy in the U.S. thus takes the form of preemptive dismissiveness of its importance. In response to this dismissiveness, several defenders of Latin American philosophy have answered the skeptical question about its existence by turning the question on its head. Rather than asking whether Latin American philosophy exists, these philosophers ask: Given the amount of original and broadly interesting and impactful philosophical work that has been produced in Latin America, why has it received so little attention and respect in the English-speaking world? What are the conditions in the U.S. that have led academic philosophers to ignore this valuable work?

Rich discussions have developed in response to questions like these. Scholars have proposed a variety of explanations for why Latin American philosophy has been marginalized within the discipline and have analyzed the various ways in which this marginalization takes place.[17] Many of these discussions intersect with the work of feminists and non-Latinx scholars of color who have written extensively on the ways that the discipline of philosophy in the U.S. has tended to exclude certain histories, philosophical projects, and methods, as well as the participation of people of color.

With respect to the marginalization of Latin American philosophy in particular, one thread that runs through many of these discussions is the recognition of a link between the current marginalization of Latin American philosophy in U.S. academia and the long history of Western imperialism and colonization.[18] A central aspect of the legacy of colonialism is the dominant group's assertion of the superiority of their own ways of knowing and a disparagement of the intellectual achievements of colonized peoples. This tendency can take the form of Eurocentric prejudice, or the belief that the highest forms of knowledge (even reason itself!) are a product of Western Europe.

Eurocentric prejudice can be found in the version of the history of philosophy that is taught to many students in the U.S. These students learn that philosophy began in Ancient Greece and reached its culmination in France, Germany, and England, and then in the United States. Meanwhile, African, Native American and indigenous, and Spanish-language philosophical traditions are effectively erased from the story of philosophy, such that many would be surprised to learn that they even exist.[19]

Beyond this historical erasure, the very ways in which philosophy has come to be defined since the mid-20th century has had the effect—intended or not—of shutting many people out of the discipline. Mainstream U.S. philosophers often define philosophy in ways that correspond precisely to the ways in which *they*, Anglo-American philosophers, practice it. They then evaluate Latin American philosophy as deficient when it fails to adhere to the standards entailed by their definition. This creates a double bind for Latin American philosophy. On the one hand, if it is too original—distinct in subject matter or style, for instance—then it risks not being seen as real philosophy. On the other hand, if it successfully complies with the conceptual and methodological norms of Anglo-American philosophy, this leads some to a double down on the criticism that Latin American philosophy is merely imitative.[20] As we will see in the final section, one project of Latinx philosophy has been to generate ways out of this double bind by attending to both the distinctiveness and philosophical richness of Latin American and Latinx philosophy.

Latinx Philosophy

Metaphilosophical questions similar to those we have considered throughout this chapter have emerged in the past several decades surrounding the topic of Latinx philosophy. For example: *What are the defining characteristics of "Latinx philosophy"? Is Latinx philosophy a distinctive tradition of philosophy, and if so, what, if anything, makes it distinctively valuable when compared to other philosophical traditions?*

The emergence of these metaphilosophical questions about Latinx philosophy may reflect some ongoing changes within the discipline of philosophy. While philosophers of Latin American descent have historically faced exclusion and marginalization within the profession, there now appears to be an increasing number of Latinx professional philosophers, many of whom are working on issues related to Latinx and Latin American philosophy. These Latinx philosophers are also becoming more organized, as evidenced by the emergence of conferences, journals, and an American Philosophical Association newsletter dedicated to Latin American and Latinx philosophy. Likewise, there is an increasing number of Latinx students in many colleges and universities, and these students are often eager to learn about Latin American and Latinx philosophy, creating a demand for the creation of a "Latinx philosophy canon" that can be included in syllabi and textbooks (like this one!). At the same time, within the profession as a whole, the concern for inclusiveness has become more prominent, and there is a growing interest among many philosophers to explore alternatives to what has been the traditional, Eurocentric approach to philosophical questions.

In this context, one of the central concerns motivating the desire of some scholars to define "Latinx philosophy" is to highlight the distinctive value of Latinx philosophy, and thereby make it easier for a group that has been historically marginalized to gain recognition and status within the academy. At the same time, these scholars face the challenge of highlighting the value of their contributions to the discipline without inadvertently defining philosophy in a way that results in the problematic exclusion of other marginalized modes of thought, such as indigenous, Afro-Latino, or feminist perspectives. With this in mind, the question that many Latinx philosophers are grappling with today is: How can we define "Latinx philosophy" in a way that highlights its distinctive value—but *without* thereby reproducing the harms of exclusion?

Consider, for example, the following two ways that the term "Latinx philosophy" might be defined.

- *The Ethnic Definition*—"Latinx philosophy" includes any work of philosophy produced by Latinx people.
- *The Substantive Definition*—"Latinx philosophy" includes any work of philosophy that engages with the distinctive concerns of the Latinx community, and/or expresses the distinctive life-experiences, perspectives, and styles of the Latinx community.

Each of these approaches to the definition of "Latinx philosophy" has advantages and disadvantages. For example, the Ethnic Definition has the advantage of not excluding any Latinx philosophers, regardless of what kind of philosophy they work on. On the other hand, one possible disadvantage of this definition is that it would exclude the work of philosophers who are not Latinx, even if their work engages directly with the distinctive concerns of the Latinx community. More generally, this definition suggests that there is nothing philosophically substantive that unifies the work included under the label "Latinx philosophy"—or, indeed, that this term does not function as a description of a distinctive *tradition* of philosophy but, rather, functions as a *merely demographic* category.

Conversely, one advantage of the Substantive Definition is that it would make it easier for proponents to show that Latinx philosophy is a distinctive tradition of thought, and one that offers valuable perspectives on issues that are important to the Latinx community. However, this definition would exclude many works by Latinx philosophers, based on the focus of their work. For example, the work of the prominent Latino epistemologist Ernest Sosa would not be included as part of the tradition of Latinx philosophy under this definition, because Sosa's work does not engage substantively with the distinctive concerns of the Latinx community or express this community's distinctive life-experiences, perspectives, or styles of thought and expression. Another possible disadvantage of the Substantive Definition of "Latinx philosophy" is that it seems to require proponents to specify the

Latinx community's distinctive concerns, life-experiences, perspectives, and styles of expression, in order to determine whether a philosopher's work engages with them. Doing so is quite difficult, however, because the "Latinx community" is extremely diverse. It includes people born all over Latin America, as well as people born in the U.S. who have never been to Latin America and do not speak Spanish; it also includes people from every social class, political and religious persuasion, sexual orientation, and every other dimension of human diversity. With this diversity in mind, we may doubt that it is possible to identify anything close to a single "Latinx perspective" on *any* philosophical question.

The authors of this chapter, Francisco Gallegos and Lori Gallegos de Castillo, have addressed this issue with regard to one segment of the Latinx community. In our article "On the Distinctive Value of Mexican-American Philosophy" (2018), we argue that although the Mexican-American community is extremely diverse, it is possible to identify a common set of concerns shared by this group, including concerns about *immigration, identity, heritage and tradition, language,* and *recognition*, as well as a common set of intuitions shared by this community as a whole, including the intuitions that *colonial histories shape the present;* that *the plight of the immigrant should elicit empathy;* and that *the Mexican-American experience is complex and manifold.* One of our central hesitations with this approach, however, is that it risks misinterpreting or excluding the views of particular people who identify as Mexican-American. The Mexican-American community is extremely diverse, and it feels dangerous or dogmatic to assert which concerns and intuitions are reflective of the Mexican-American community as a whole. This risk is only amplified when we consider the Latinx community, which is much larger and more diverse than the Mexican-American community.

Without the pretense of resolving this issue, then, we conclude here by briefly outlining a handful of the metaphilosophical themes that have been developed by thinkers who identify as Latinx and who have shared their work in self-identifying Latinx philosophical venues in recent years. These themes include:

- Demonstrating to other U.S. philosophers the value of Latin American and Latinx philosophy in its own right and in terms of questions of major interest in Anglo-American and European philosophy;
- Working with Latin American philosophers to think transnationally about philosophical issues of mutual concern;
- Theorizing the nature of the philosophical canon, and pressing for a reconfiguration of the canon to include Latin American and Latinx philosophy;
- Investigating the relationship between disciplinary boundaries and the demographics of practitioners;

- Examining the way in which the discipline of philosophy and academic institutional practices perpetuate colonial oppression, and imagining alternative ways of engaging in scholarly activity that avoid perpetuating coloniality and are responsive to colonial harms;
- Exploring the way in which coloniality has produced the erasure of knowledges emerging out of non-Western frameworks and by non-white thinkers in Latin America; and
- Moving beyond the discipline of philosophy in order to engage with philosophical thought that is not constrained by those disciplinary boundaries.

Given the critical way in which Latinx philosophers have oriented themselves with respect to the discipline of philosophy, it is perhaps unsurprising that Latinx philosophy, Latina feminism, and decolonial philosophy have emerged as frameworks through which some of the richest and most innovative metaphilosophical work is being carried out. Thus, although we leave the question of how to define "Latinx philosophy" unanswered, we can identify a central set of questions to attend to as this conversation continues: Will the concern with liberation from the persistent and oppressive legacies of colonization emerge as the defining characteristic of Latinx philosophy? And will this concern lend to Latinx philosophy an original, authentic, and distinctively valuable perspective on classical philosophical questions, while simultaneously pushing the boundaries of what counts as philosophy?

Notes

1 An important question to ask here is: What were the historical, social, and political conditions that led to this conversation arising in the 20th century? Although many Latin American countries had achieved political independence a century earlier, it seemed that strong national and cultural identities had been slower to coalesce. By the time that Mariátegui was writing, however, a number of scholars were becoming optimistic about the development and trajectory of intellectual life in Latin America. Mariátegui notes that his reflections on Latin American thought developed in response to a growing interest across Latin America in creating an organization of intellectuals across Latin America (See Mariátegui, "Is There Such a Thing as Hispanic-American Thought?", 116–117).

2 Mariátegui, "Is There Such a Thing as Hispanic-American Thought?", 118.

3 Salazar Bondy, "The Meaning and Problem of Hispanic American Thought," 387–388. Cited in text using the abbreviation *MP* and page number. All emphasis is in the original.

4 Mariátegui uses the phrase "new soul" when he quotes the Argentine politician Alfredo Palacios, who claimed that "the intermingling of races has given us a new soul." The phrase refers to the idea that, following the widespread ethnic and racial mixtures that occurred during the period of colonization and the subsequent national independence movements throughout the Americas, distinctive peoples, with their own cultures and destinies, had been created. See Mariátegui, "Is There Such a Thing as Hispanic-American Thought?", 118.

5 Mariátegui, "Is There Such a Thing as Hispanic-American Thought?", 118–119.

6 Frondizi, "Is There an Ibero-American Philosophy?", 350–351.
7 Frondizi, "Is There an Ibero-American Philosophy?", 346.
8 Medina, "The Possibility of an Indigenous Philosophy," 374.
9 Medina, "The Possibility of an Indigenous Philosophy," 374.
10 Medina, "The Possibility of an Indigenous Philosophy," 373.
11 Gracia, *Latinos in America*, 140.
12 Gracia, "Hispanics/Latinos and Philosophy: A Response," 238.
13 Schutte, "Toward an Understanding of Latin American Philosophy," 24. Cited in text using the abbreviation *LAP* and page number.
14 Zea, "The Actual Function of Philosophy in Latin America," 364. Cited in text using the abbreviation *FPLA* and page number.
15 Nuccetelli, "Is 'Latin American Thought' Philosophy?", 529–530. Cited in text using the abbreviation *LAT* and page number.
16 Elena Ruíz examines the shift in the Question of Authenticity across cultural contexts in greater depth in the essay "Latin American Philosophy at a Crossroads."
17 A collection of some of these writings can be found in the volume *Reframing the Practice of Philosophy*, edited by George Yancy.
18 Much of the important theoretical work in describing the ongoing, multifaceted legacy of colonialism beginning with the colonization of the Americas has been developed by a multi-generational and growing group of scholars who are frequently associated with the collective Latin American Modernity/Coloniality/ Decoloniality Research Program (MCD). Some key texts from this group of scholars include: Quijano, "Coloniality and Modernity/Rationality"; Quijano, "Coloniality of Power, Eurocentrism, and Latin America"; Dussel, "World-System and 'Trans'-Modernity"; Dussel, *The Invention of the Americas*; Escobar, "Worlds and Knowledges Otherwise"; Lugones, "Heterosexualism and the Colonial/Modern Gender System"; Mignolo, *Local Histories/Global Designs*; Coronil, "Beyond Occidentalism"; and Maldonado-Torres, "On the Coloniality of Being."
19 See Millán, "Language, Power, and Philosophy." Millán argues that philosophy's "mendacious cultural autobiography," which locates philosophy in this particular set of nations, also bestow on the French, German, and English languages a special status as "philosophical languages."
20 Mignolo describes this double bind in his article "The Geopolitics of Knowledge and the Colonial Difference."

Bibliography

Coronil, Fernando. "Beyond Occidentalism: Toward Nonimperial Geohistorical Categories." *Cultural Anthropology* 11, no. 1(1996): 51–87.

Dussel, Enrique. *The Invention of the Americas: Eclipse of 'the Other' and the Myth of Modernity*. New York: Continuum, 1995.

Dussel, Enrique. "World-System and 'Trans'-Modernity." *Nepantla: Views from South* 3, no. 2(2002): 221–244.

Escobar, Arturo. "Worlds and Knowledges Otherwise." *Cultural Studies* 21, no. 2–3 (2007): 179–210.

Frondizi, Risieri. "Is There an Ibero-American philosophy?" *Philosophy and Phenomenological Research* 9, no. 3(1949): 345–355.

Gallegos, Francisco and Lori Gallegos de Castillo. "On the Distinctive Value of Mexican-American Philosophy." *Inter-American Journal of Philosophy* 9, no 2 (Fall 2018): 22–42.

264 Lori Gallegos de Castillo & Francisco Gallegos

Gracia, Jorge J.E. *Latinos in America: Philosophy and Social Identity*. Malden, MA: John Wiley & Sons, 2008.

Gracia, Jorge J.E. "Hispanics/Latinos and Philosophy: A Response." In *Debating Race, Ethnicity, and Latino Identity: Jorge JE Gracia and His Critics*, edited by Ivan Jaksic, 219–246. New York: Columbia University Press, 2015.

Lugones, María. "Heterosexualism and the Colonial/Modern Gender System." *Hypatia* 22, no. 1(2007): 186–209.

Maldonado-Torres, Nelson (2007). "On the Coloniality of Being." *Cultural Studies* 21, no. 2–3(2007): 240–270.

Mariátegui, José Carlos. "Is There Such a Thing as Hispanic-American Thought?" In *The Heroic and Creative Meaning of Socialism: Selected Essays of José Carlos Mariátegui*, edited and translated by Michael Pearlman, 116–119. Amherst, NY: Humanities Books, 1996.

Medina, Vicente. "The Possibility of an Indigenous Philosophy: A Latin American Perspective." *American Philosophical Quarterly* 29, no. 4(1992): 373–380.

Mignolo, Walter D. *Local Histories/Global Designs: Coloniality, Subaltern Knowledges, and Border Thinking*. Princeton, NJ: Princeton University Press, 2000.

Mignolo, Walter D. "The Geopolitics of Knowledge and the Colonial Difference." *The South Atlantic Quarterly* 101, no. 1 (Winter2002): 57–96.

Millán, Elizabeth. "Language, Power, and Philosophy: Some Comments on the Exclusion of Spanish from the Philosophical Canon." In *Reframing the Practice of Philosophy: Bodies of Color, Bodies of Knowledge*, edited by George Yancy, 327–339. Albany: SUNY Press, 2012.

Nuccetelli, Susana. "Is 'Latin American Thought' Philosophy?" *Metaphilosophy* 34, no. 4(2003): 524–536.

Quijano, Aníbal. "Coloniality of Power, Eurocentrism, and Latin America." *Nepantla: Views from South* 1, no. 3(2000): 533–580.

Quijano, Aníbal. "Coloniality and Modernity/Rationality." *Cultural Studies* 21, no. 2–3(2007): 168–178.

Ruíz, Elena. "Latin American Philosophy at the Crossroads." *Human Studies* 34, no. 3(2010): 309–331.

Salazar Bondy, Augusto. "The Meaning and Problem of Hispanic American Thought." In *Latin American Philosophy for the 21st Century*, edited by Jorge J. E. Gracia & Elizabeth Millán-Zaibert, 379–398. Amherst, New York: Prometheus Books, 2004.

Schutte, Ofelia. "Toward an Understanding of Latin American Philosophy." *Philosophy Today* 31, no. 1(1987): 21–34.

Yancy, George, ed. *Reframing the Practice of Philosophy: Bodies of Color, Bodies of Knowledge*. Albany: SUNY Press, 2012.

Zea, Leopoldo. "The Actual Function of Philosophy in Latin America." In *Latin American Philosophy in the Twentieth Century: Man, Values, and the Search for Philosophical Identity*, edited by Jorge J.E. Gracia & Elizabeth Millán-Zaibert, 357–368. Amherst, New York: Prometheus Books, 2004.

Index

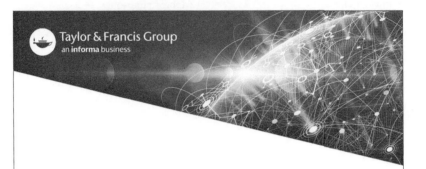